Holiday Portugal

Katharine Wood-de Winne was born in Edinburgh and
was educated there, reading Communications, then
English language and literature at Edinburgh
University. Following a period as a freelance public
relations consultant and journalist she entered the world
of travel journalism. An eighteen-month spell touring
Europe and North Africa resulted in the book *Europe
by Train* (published by Fontana) which is one of the
UK's top-selling guidebooks. As well as working on this
series of Holiday Guides, she is currently involved in
several projects encompassing every aspect of the travel
industry – from backpacking students to round-the-
world first-class tours. She regularly contributes to radio
and TV travel programmes, both in the UK and USA,
and writes articles freelance for numerous publications.
In the course of her work she travels extensively, and
has so far clocked up 48 countries, including Portugal,
which she knows well. She is married and lives in Perth,
Scotland with her husband and young sons, Andrew
and Euan.

George McDonald was born in Dumfries in 1955 and
was educated at Fettes College and Edinburgh
University. Following a spell on the family farm he
toured Europe and North Africa to help research the
guidebook *Europe by Train*. He continues to travel for
a living, researching for the various guidebooks he is
involved in with Katie Wood, and is rarely in one place
for more than three weeks at a time. Home, when he's
there, is Guernsey in the Channel Islands.

Holiday
PORTUGAL

Chief Editor: Katie Wood

Head Researcher: George McDonald

Editorial Assistant: Alastair Dalton

FONTANA/Collins

To Syd, the best of travelling companions

First published in 1988 by Fontana Paperbacks
8 Grafton Street, London W1X 3LA
This revised edition published 1990

Copyright © Katie Wood and George McDonald 1988, 1990

Maps reproduced by kind permission of
the Portuguese Tourist Board, London

Set in Linotron Plantin

Printed and bound in Great Britain
by William Collins Sons & Co. Ltd, Glasgow

The 'Holiday' research team used a Ferguson Videostar
C. Auto Focus CCR in the preparation of this guide, and
an Apple Macintosh Computer to collate all their information.

Contents

Part Two – HOW TO GO

Part Three – WHEN YOU'RE THERE

Part Four – THE COUNTRY

Vocabulary

ACKNOWLEDGEMENTS

Thanks are owed to Mr João Custodio of the Portuguese Tourist Board, and his secretary Gabriella. Also to our Portuguese researchers, and our UK researchers: *Devin Scobie* for the Algarve and Lisbon; *Ishbel Matheson* for the Introduction; *Jenny Dunn* for the Costa Verde, Costa de Prata and Azores chapters, and *Gary Duncan* for the Mountains, Plains and Madeira chapters. This enterprising team produced the research scripts in record time, and much thanks are owed. Special thanks are also due to Joseph, Margaret, Linda and Maria for checking through our manuscript at the eleventh hour. To our team at Fontana thank you for getting the book out on time, and lastly thank you to you, our readers, and please do keep your letters coming about your holidays in Portugal, telling us the good and the bad.

WHAT THIS GUIDE IS ABOUT

For too long now there has been a gulf in the guidebook market. On the one hand there are the 'heavies' – books which, though good in their way, assume the holiday-maker wants a stone-by-stone description of all the ancient remains in the country of their choice and, what's more, assume that their readership is middle-aged, middle-class and predominantly American with a lot of cash to splash about. At the other end of the scale are the back-packing, student-orientated, 'rough it on £15 a day' guides which assume the traveller wants to cover the maximum amount of ground possible and spend the absolute minimum doing so (even if this does mean surviving on one bowl of vegetable rice a day and no baths for two weeks).

But in the middle of these poles lies the vast majority of tourists: normal, fun-loving people who go on holiday to unwind from a year's toil, and who, though not able to throw cash about indiscriminately, are willing to spend enough to enjoy themselves. Predominantly these people fall into the under-forty age group – the 'young ones' keen to see the countries they visit and have a good time in their own way. This guide is written for this sort of person.

It does not wade into pages of history, it just gives you the basics to enable you to make sense of the monuments and places you'll see while on holiday. It does not pretend to be a specialist guide for one group of people (water sports enthusiasts, nature lovers, archaeologists, etc), but it does point you in the direction of where to pursue these types of hobbies once you are in the country. If any one 'hobby' is highlighted more than most it is that of 'sunworshipping' and where best to do it, as time after time surf, sea and sand still come top of most people's priorities for a good holiday.

With Portugal's increasing popularity as a holiday destination we look at options open to would-be travellers and at the pros and cons of all the different packages offered by tour operators. But the guide is not aimed only at package travellers. Independent travellers are remembered, too, and we look in great detail at the crucial decision of whether to opt for a package or independent holiday. All the relevant up-to-the-minute info is in Part One – Before You Go.

Our recommendations for restaurants, night-life, hotels, etc start at the lower end of the market, since we believe the art of using money when on holiday lies in saving it without sacrificing the holiday spirit.

We hope this guide will help you to have a rewarding time in Portugal – a country whose amazing holiday potential in areas north of the Algarve is just beginning to be recognized. Much space is devoted to the Algarve region, for there lies the centre of Portugal's tourist market, but if you feel we have missed anything out, let us know. This is a different type of guide: informal and chatty, not academic and definitive. We are not setting ourselves up as the authority on Portugal. We know a lot and have travelled there extensively, but our knowledge is more on where the best places for different holidays are, than on Portuguese history. If any of our recommendations fails to come up to the mark or if you find a super undiscovered beach which you are willing to share, or a new lively night-spot, write and tell us about it. After all, we all want the same in the end – the memory of at least two glorious, fun-filled weeks to sustain us through the long, dark, winter nights.

NB. Confusingly, the town of Porto also goes by the name of Oporto. For ease of reference, we have called it Oporto.

Part One
BEFORE YOU GO

Key Facts

ENTRY REQUIREMENTS No visas are required for holders of British passports or British Visitors passports, for stays of up to sixty days. Those who wish to extend their stay should apply to the Foreigners' Registration Service, Av. António Augusto de Aguiar, 18, Lisbon (Tel: 55047) or to the regional offices before the expiry date.

POPULATION 10,100,000

CAPITAL Lisbon (pop: 817,600)

CURRENCY Escudo (£1 = 260$00)

POLITICAL SYSTEM Constitutional Democracy

RELIGION Roman Catholic

LANGUAGES Portuguese (some French and English understood)

PUBLIC HOLIDAYS
1 January
Shrove Tuesday
Good Friday
25 April
1 May
10 June
Corpus Christi (mid-June)
15 August
5 October
1 November
1, 8, 25 December

What to Expect

It is the combination of guaranteed sun and affordable prices which accounts for Portugal's increasing popularity among package-tour holiday-makers. Undoubtedly, it is the Algarve in the south which is the premier holiday destination in Portugal. Not surprisingly then, most of the tourist industry is concentrated here. Modern resorts, hotels, villa and apartment complexes, and leisure facilities have sprung up beside the long stretches of sandy beach which are the area's biggest natural attraction.

Although the march of mass tourism has been rapid (all taking place within the last 30 years) its effects have not been entirely random. After the first phase of building, the Portuguese government tried to impose some restrictions on the speed and quality of the development, declaring the southern coast would never become another Costa Del Sol. Efforts have subsequently been made to build new facilities away from existing villages and communities. Nevertheless, despite these finer intentions, you'll have to go far on the Algarve coast to find a traditional fishing village which has not accommodated itself to cope with the influx of tourists in the summer months. In many ways, the Algarve has become a favourite holiday destination for those in search of all the facilities associated with international resorts, but without the hype (or expense) of the jet-set lifestyle. Certainly, in recent years moves have been made to up-market the Algarve image, but as yet the Portuguese equivalent of Marbella has not emerged. Overall then, what Portugal offers to most people, especially families, is a chance to unwind, have a good time and not pay through the nose for it. It is also a 'safe' holiday destination. Unlike Spain, there is little theft or violence and the atmosphere is relaxed, as many people put it, like Britain in the 1950s – but with the sun!

Because the southern coast has become so well established as a traditional holiday destination, one of the biggest challenges to face the Portuguese tourist industry in the past few years has been to persuade people that Portugal *does* exist outside the Algarve. In fact, for such a small country, Portugal has a surprising wealth of natural beauty and historical interest which has been largely overlooked by holiday-makers.

Roughly speaking, the country is usually split up into seven main tourist sections: the interior, which is divided into two regions, the Mountains in the North and the Plains in the South; and the five coastline areas – the Costa Verde (Green Coast), the Costa de Prata (Silver Coast), the Lisbon Coast, Estoril Coast, and the Algarve. In recent years, resorts on the Estoril Coast have become more popular among holiday-makers as a quieter and less crowded alternative to the Algarve and it seems likely that this area, with its good beaches and easy access to the capital Lisbon, is poised for further development in the not-too-distant future. The tourist industry has also recently woken up to the charms (and potential profits) of the Costa Verde and the Costa de Prata. Although temperatures are cooler here due to the more northerly location, there are long stretches of fine beaches and the summer weather is warm and sunny. The scenery in the North, with its green rolling hills and expanses of pine-forests, is some of the best Portugal has to offer and provides a sharp contrast to the semi-arid, Mediterranean-type vistas of the South.

Off the coast of the mainland lie the island of Madeira and the Azores' archipelago, both of which have some quite spectacular scenery. They are of volcanic origin and their landscapes are characterized by craters of extinct volcanoes and an abundance of colourful flora and fauna which flourishes in the semi-tropical climates. The Azores have just begun to nudge their way into tour operators' brochures (no doubt helped by the royal couple Prince Andrew and Sarah Ferguson honeymooning there in '86), but as yet the majority of islands in the archipelago have been left largely untouched by tourism. Madeira, by contrast, has long been established as a traditional winter-holiday destination, especially among the British. The island's mild all-year-round climate has been the main factor in attracting tourists, and in the past few years Madeira has become increasingly prominent as a major summer resort.

For the sightseer, Portugal also has its attractions, although admittedly of fairly modest proportions compared to the compulsive 'been there, seen it' sights of Italy or France. Lisbon is a pleasantly old-fashioned capital city, which is well worth a visit, and most of the historical towns of interest, containing relics of the nation's past glory, are to be found in central Portugal. If it's the 'unspoilt' Portugal you're in search of, turn north to the interior. Here, in the remoter, rural areas especially, the meaning of mass tourism is unknown. The way of life is strongly traditional in character and still centres on the land and religious festivals which abound throughout the year – a complete contrast to the cosmopolitan atmosphere which prevails on the southern coast.

Wherever you go in Portugal, be it the Algarve for a 'sun, surf and sea' holiday, or to Lisbon to explore the cultural delights of the capital city, it will be difficult to escape the single most important influence on the Portuguese history, economy and psyche – the sea. The Portuguese are a nation of seafarers and this is worth remembering when travelling through their country. In fact, for a period of three centuries, beginning with the great sea-discoveries of the 15th century, Portugal ruled one of the biggest empires in the world. This was the nation's Golden Age, when the Portuguese monopolized the main trade routes and prosperity was procured from colonies rich in natural resources. Portugal's subsequent decline has been marked by internal political struggle and the independence of the colonies. The country's fight to establish a stable democratic state was not successful until 25 April 1974, when a military coup overthrew the existing administration and established a multi-party system. Since then, determined efforts have been made by the government to restructure all aspects of Portuguese society in an attempt to raise the country out of its position as one of the poorest nations in Europe.

Today, tourism is one of Portugal's most rapidly growing industries. The package-holiday scene is quite highly developed with almost 200 British tour companies including Portugal in their range of destinations. Although the majority focus on the Algarve, many are now beginning to diversify by offering packages to the Estoril Coast, and also increasingly to resorts on the Costa de Prata and Costa Verde. Specialist holidays, especially golf holidays, are also catered for by tour operators. (For more information, turn to page 110.) The outlook for the independent traveller is good and those going it alone will not find too many insurmountable problems thrown in his or her way. The Portuguese National Tourist Board has offices in the main tourist centres throughout the country, which give out advice and information. Otherwise, finding accommodation on your own is not

really a problem – unless you are planning to go to the Algarve or
Estoril coasts in the peak season. Internal communications (road, rail,
and air) are extensive and of reasonable standard. A general rule of
thumb for those travelling independently is that the further north-east
you go in the country, the fewer facilities (or home comforts!) there
are for the tourist.

When to Go

All over Portugal July and August are the warmest and driest months.
This is also the time when most people take their holidays and head for
the sun, so if you go during these months expect to pay peak season
prices and to find your resort at its busiest. On the other hand, the
advantages of holidaying in mid-summer are that the social scene is at
its liveliest and the maximum facilities available are open to you. April
and May are good months to visit Portugal if you want to see the
country at its best and avoid the crowds. Although temperatures are
generally cooler at this time of the year, sunbathing can still be
actively pursued, especially on the southern coast, and you should
have no problem returning home with an enviable tan. In October,
although the tourist season is officially over, temperatures in the
Algarve are still around the 66°F/19°C mark, and you have the added
bonus of paying off-season prices. By this time, however, the busiest
tourist areas are likely to be worn out by the hectic summer season and
this is a point to bear in mind when you are deciding when to go to
Portugal, as it is often the small things, such as good service and
pleasant staff, that make a holiday worth remembering.

Winter Holidays

If you're thinking about escaping the cold, dreary weather of northern
climes and heading for the sun, then the good news is that the Algarve
and Madeira are well-established as winter holiday destinations.

Winters in both these places are practically non-existent – at least compared to our (freezing) standards! January is the coldest month, when temperatures dip to 54°F/12°C in the Algarve and 61°F/16°C in Madeira. The advantages of holidaying during the winter months are obvious – not only can you bask in sunshine while everyone at home is shivering indoors – but you can take full advantage of off-season tariffs. Going at this time of the year can be almost half the price of a peak-season trip, and in an effort to attract customers, tour operators often throw in extra perks, such as free car-hire, or bigger discounts for children. It works out cheaper to stay longer (sometimes the price difference between staying one week or two is minimal) and for those who wish to avoid winter weather altogether, some tour operators do special packages for stays of up to one or two months. One point to remember is that prices become more expensive again over the festive season (from 4–24 December) so if you're working on a tight budget, arrange your holiday to avoid these times.

The disadvantages of holidaying out of season are that some tourist facilities may be closed down and the social scene is not exactly buzzing. The range of resorts and accommodation offered by tour operators is also reduced in the winter months; not that this is necessarily a bad thing, as there is less chance of you ending up the only bunch of holiday-makers in an otherwise empty hotel!

Outside these areas, the Estoril Coast is featured by some tour companies as a winter holiday destination. The climate here tends to be a bit cooler and you can expect a few rainy or cloudy days. However, if it's not just the sun you're going for, but are also interested in doing some sightseeing, then the resorts on the Estoril Coast provide an excellent base. They have easy access both to Lisbon, the capital, and a number of historical towns in the immediate environs.

The Climate

Coastal Weather

Because of the moderating sea-influence, the coastal areas of Portugal enjoy an extremely mild climate. This is characterized by long, warm summers and short, cool winters. July and August are the hottest months, with temperatures around the 72°F/22°C mark. Good sunbathing weather starts around the beginning of May, when temperatures hot up to a pleasant mid-60s°F. After that things do not really begin to cool down until October when, in the North particularly, you can expect a few overcast or rainy days. The coolest months are December and January, when temperatures dip to around 53°F/12°C.

Average daily temperatures, based on Lisbon:

	JAN	FEB	MAR	APR	MAY	JUNE
°F	53	54	57	60	63	67
°C	12	12	14	16	17	20

	JULY	AUG	SEPT	OCT	NOV	DEC
°F	70	72	69	65	59	54
°C	21	22	21	18	15	12

There is an appreciable climate difference between the North and the South of the country, so if you're in search of 'guaranteed' sun, stick to the southern coast. In the Algarve, temperatures on the coast are easily as hot as those of the Mediterranean countries. A warm wind blowing from North Africa (the Sahara) heats up the sea and, in the summer, water temperatures may be as high as 72°F/22°C. The Algarve's particularly mild climate makes sunbathing possible at practically any time of the year, which is why it has become such a popular winter-holiday destination. By contrast, the northern coasts tend to feel the cooling influences of the Atlantic. In the colder months, relatively high rainfall and strong sea breezes are usually enough to deflect even the hardiest sunbather south to the Algarve.

The islands of Madeira and the Azores enjoy semi-tropical climates which are distinguished by mild, temperate winters. In Madeira, the temperatures reach a maximum of 72°F/22°C in the summer, and a minimum of 61°F/16°C in the winter. In the Azores, hottest temperatures are around the 71°F/22°C mark, and the coolest about 57°F/14°C, although high humidity makes rainfall pretty constant through the summer as well as the winter months.

Inland Weather

The greatest temperature ranges are to be found in the interior of the country. Summers are especially hot as warm winds blow west from the heart of the Iberian peninsula. Without the moderating sea-influence, winters can be very cold, and it is not unusual for snow to be falling in the mountains while the first tourists of the year are cultivating tans in the Algarve.

Average daily temperatures, based on Central Portugal:

	JAN	FEB	MAR	APR	MAY	JUNE
°F	49	51	56	60	62	69
°C	9	11	13	16	17	21

	JULY	AUG	SEPT	OCT	NOV	DEC
°F	73	75	70	63	56	51
°C	22	24	21	17	13	11

Where to Go for What

People often spend weeks deliberating which country to choose for their holiday destination, then leave the final choice of where they stay within the country to either a photo and brief, optimistic write-up in a travel brochure, or to the discretion and persuasive talk of a travel agent (many of whom haven't actually visited the country). This lottery results, not surprisingly, in people having a disappointing holiday simply because they got the facts wrong on this crucial decision. If anything, the decision about which part of the country you base yourself is more important than the choice of country itself, for there is good and bad in every country – Britain, for example, offers the tourist a superb holiday destination, but if the visitor were to opt for two weeks in Sheffield when he really wanted a 'get away from it all' type of break, he would be sadly disappointed. Don't think that the Portuguese equivalents of Sheffield aren't on offer. They are, but unless you're careful you will not know if you've landed one until you've paid hundreds of pounds and arrived at the resort.

In order to match your needs to the most suitable resorts we have divided holiday-makers into certain stereotypes. Doubtless most of you fall into several of the categories, but the idea is to find which resorts crop up under the headings which interest you, and match your needs accordingly.

The following symbols representing the various interests appear throughout this book as an easy guide to the places likely to be of interest:

The Sun Worshipper

The Sightseer

The Socialite

Healthy Holidays

The Nature Lover

The Recluse

PRIVATE. Keep Out

Family Holidays

The Sun Worshipper: *Surf, sea and sand*

Portugal has 525 miles of coastline and much of this is edged by sand. The southern coast by no means has the monopoly on the finest beaches, but it does have the hottest temperatures and widest variety of beach resorts. It is these factors, then, which make the Algarve the first and foremost choice among sun worshippers.

In the west, the Algarve coastline is rugged, interspersed with small, sandy coves and bays, and some really weird rock formations. In the east, the character is completely different and here you can expect to find the *ilhas*, which are really just enormous sandspits, lying offshore. Tourist facilities have developed on the largest of these, and frequent ferry services make them accessible from the mainland.

The biggest resorts are to be found in the west, and practically every little village has been developed (or is in the process of being developed) for the invasion of tourists in the summer months. To the east, development has taken place at a slower pace, which is quite surprising because the beaches here are just as good as, if not better than, the west. However, a couple of years ago, planning permission was granted for a bridge to link the southern coasts of Portugal and Spain, in place of the ferry which currently runs between Vila Real de Santo Antonio and Ayamonte in Spain. As a result of this, the eastern Algarve and its glorious beaches will soon be readily accessible to holiday-makers and day-trippers coming from Spain and further afield in Europe.

Right along the coastline, the main resorts, and many of the smaller ones, offer a range of water sports, such as water-skiing, scuba diving, and windsurfing, which you can occupy yourself with if you get bored with the beach scene. Most resorts are built up around the longest stretches of sand and this means that you don't have to cart your sunbathing gear miles before you reach an appropriate spot. If you do want to escape the crowds, because the coastline is practically one long beach, a smaller, quieter piece of sand is always only a walk, or a short bus-ride, away. Officially, nudist bathing is prohibited throughout Portugal, although staff in the local tourist offices will usually be able to give advice on the most-frequented 'unofficial' nudist beaches, otherwise it's a case of finding a quiet spot and hoping for the best.

Below is detailed a quick résumé of the major beaches and resorts which the dedicated sun worshipper should look out for:

LAGOS is one of the liveliest and most popular resorts on the Algarve coast, and has been a traditional holiday destination with the British (and the Portuguese) for some time now. A number of beaches are within easy reach of the town, the most well-known of which is **Praia Dona Ana**. This sandy stretch is sheltered from winds by a huge outcrop of rock standing in the entrance to the bay.

PRAIA DA ROCHA is a fairly big, modern resort, with the usual concoction of a night-life (discos and a casino) and a wide range of leisure facilities to tempt the tourist. However, the beach is Praia da Rocha's best asset. One of the most famous on the Algarve, this immense swathe of sand is framed by low cliffs, and dominated by huge, unusually-shaped rock formations.

ALBUFEIRA, as all the brochures tell you, is *the* place to be in the Algarve, which means it is also certainly one of the biggest, and busiest during the peak season . . . So why do people return year after year, swearing it is the only place they will go in Portugal? Well, actually, if the truth be told, Albufeira is quite a nice place to stay in. It has an attractive setting, perched on top of red cliffs, overlooking the wide, sandy beach which is sheltered and good for bathing. It has also successfully avoided the impersonality of some large, specially-built tourist complexes; the resort has a good holiday atmosphere, conducive to having a good time on and off the beach.

MONTE GORDO has one of the longest beaches on the Algarve, with mile upon mile of white sands. There are no rocky outcrops surrounding this stretch (unlike the western Algarve) which makes it particulary safe for young children to play on.

Outside the Algarve, the Estoril Coast is the next best option for sun, sand and sea holidays and resorts here are becoming increasingly popular as an alternative to the Algarve.

ESTORIL itself is the main resort. At one time the holiday location for Portuguese kings, it is still a bit of a playground for the rich, boasting the biggest casino in Europe. The long beaches and fine weather have made it also a popular destination among package-tour holiday-makers.

CASCAIS is the second biggest development on the Estoril Coast. Less pretentious than Estoril, it was originally just a fishing hamlet which has metamorphosed into a major tourist resort; good beaches and a young, lively crowd are the town's main attractions.

Further north, on the Costa de Prata and the Costa Verde, there is certainly no shortage of fine beaches. What does tend to be a bit lacking is sun or at least guaranteed sun. Temperatures are cooler, and you can't be assured of cloudfree, rainfree days even in the summer months. However if you are heading north and fancy a few days on the beach, two of the most popular northern resorts are **VIANA DO CASTELO** or **PÓVOA DO VARZIM**.

MADEIRA is one of the best options for the off-season sun worshipper; even in the coldest months the sun is still raising the temperatures to the 62°F/16°C mark. However, the island does have one major obstacle to a 'sun, surf and sand' holiday – it has no beaches. Many hotels have compensated for this problem by installing huge swimming pools for guests to cool off in, but if summer is just not summer without the familiar ritual of staking your pitch on the beach, better stick to the mainland.

 ## The Sightseer: *Sights, historical monuments and archaeological remains*

Unfortunately, the main sights worth seeing in Portugal are concentrated in the centre and north of the country – nowhere near the major tourist resorts. To be fair, however, the Algarve is not the cultural and historical vacuum which most people seem to think it is, although its attractions are fairly modest and largely related to the old quarter of town, which is at the core of most tourist resorts. This means that if you go to the Algarve but also want to do some serious sightseeing, you'll have to make a special point of travelling north. For the independent traveller this isn't too much of a problem as the distances involved aren't immense, but for those going on package holidays it is more difficult. By far the majority of package-tour operators offer one- or two-week deals specifically to the Algarve, or specifically to the Lisbon area, so it is virtually impossible to combine the 'sun and surf' of an Algarve holiday with the cultural pleasures of Lisbon and its environs. Probably the most practical (and cheapest) solution for those interested in combining the two kinds of holiday is to use one of the resorts on the Estoril/Lisbon coasts (**ESTORIL** and **CASCAIS** are the two largest and best-connected) as a base and to make day trips to the major sights.

If you are interested in doing a spot of undiluted sightseeing, then obviously Lisbon is the place to be. Interesting in itself, with the usual cultural and historical attractions of a capital city, it is also a good base to use for making excursions to the old towns in the surrounding area.

In the North, the charm lies chiefly in the beautiful, green, rolling landscape. Historical sights, rarely startling or stunning, are best discovered at a leisurely pace and preferably by car. Most tour operators, offering packages to this part of the country, have recognized this demand and do fly-drive deals from Oporto, the North's main city. The surrounding countryside is dotted with small villages and towns. Most of these have a pleasant, unworldly air and still maintain a visible link with their medieval pasts in their churches and buildings.

For those who do not just want to spectate, but to soak up the history or atmosphere of a place, the Portuguese *pousadas* are worth considering. These state-owned luxury accommodations are usually situated in places of historical or scenic interest throughout the country. The *pousada* buildings themselves are often converted monasteries or castles and those which have been built specially for the purpose have been designed to harmonize with the architecture typical of the area. Similarly, the food which is served for guests' consumption has a special emphasis on the culinary specialities of the region. For more detailed information, turn to the section on *pousada* holidays on page 106.

Below are detailed (from North to South) some of Portugal's main sights which are particularly worth making the effort to see:

DOURO VALLEY – home of the famous port wine vineyards, this is a real 'must' for the sightseer's itinerary. The journey can be made by car or bus-tour (usually starting from Oporto), but by far the best way to do it is by train. This railway line has featured in the *Great Railway Journeys of the World* series and, looking at the scenery, it is not difficult to see why. Going out of Oporto, the river cuts its way through a narrow and dramatic gorge; as you move further inland this opens out and the railway follows the river's path through the vast valley, covered by mile upon mile of port vineyards.

COIMBRA is one of Portugal's most important and best-preserved historical towns and is the home of the country's oldest university. Two cathedrals, an old quarter, and a labyrinth of twisting, narrow streets are the city's other attractions. Although Coimbra is not really within day-tripping distance from Oporto or Lisbon, it is on the main routes south, and it is well worth stopping off here if you are travelling by rail or road. If you are really into ancient ruins, excursions can be made from Coimbra to CONIMBRIGA (ten miles outside the city). This is the site of some pretty impressive Roman remains, dating from the 2nd–4th century AD. The biggest of their kind in Portugal, they are also some of the best to be found in the Iberian peninsula.

LISBON – here, in the capital, are concentrated all Portugal's major museums and art galleries. There is also the ancient Alfama quarter to have a look round, and an abundance of monuments and buildings bearing testament to Portugal's Golden Age of seafaring. Definitely the one place in the country that has enough to occupy even the most avid sightseer for a few days.

From Lisbon can be taken a number of excursions which tour the various historic towns in the vicinity. The places which have the most to offer in the way of sights are MAFRA, QUELUZ, and SINTRA. Sintra, in particular, is worth a day trip in its own right and can also be reached easily from the resorts on the Estoril Coast. The main attraction is its unusual palace which is about half an hour's walk (or a five-minute taxi ride) from the centre of town and is now open to the public, but there are also the beautiful gardens of Monserrate (an hour's walk out of town) and a number of interesting ruins to have a look at.

SAGRES is the one place on the Algarve coast which is worth taking a day trip to see. This wind-swept and desolate place is the most south-western point in Europe and it was here that the first caravels were launched on their voyages of discovery. The School of Navigation, which in its hey-day instructed the likes of Vasco da Gama and Christopher Columbus in the art of seafaring, is situated here, perched high above the Atlantic, and is now open to the public.

Obviously, these suggestions only give the barest idea what there is to see in Portugal, however they are the highlights, the 'musts', which should not be missed. More details on all the sights of the regions are given under the relevant sections.

The Socialite: *Man-watching, night-life, etc*

To be honest, Portugal doesn't have the same attractions for the socialite as, say, the French Riviera or the more up-market resorts on the Italian coast. In the bigger resorts there are a few night-clubs or discos, but these are relatively unsophisticated places and a bit of a disappointment for those who revel in bopping the night away or eyeing up the local talent. Most activity is centred on the bars and restaurants, the most popular of which feature live music or folk singing. In smaller places, the town centre, just as dusk is falling, is a good bet for night-life in the form of man-watching. Park yourself with a drink (preferably a cocktail) on one of the pavement cafés and either watch the world go by, or wait until a suitable member of the opposite sex notices you . . . Promenade or harbour cafés are another possibility, although these are prime day-time rather than night-time spots; it can get a bit too chilly to look glam in shorts and a T-shirt.

Most hotels organize some kind of evening entertainment. This may take the form of piano-playing in the bar and weekly dances or, in the smarter establishments, full-blown night-clubs with all the works. The latter are usually open to non-residents. If this is the kind of thing you're after, concentrate on the larger hotels and travel with a tour operator whose programme is geared towards your needs.

Other more traditional events which liven up Portugal's social scene are the numerous festivals which run throughout the year. These may simply be colourful processions through the centre of town or they may be bigger affairs with fireworks, music, dancing and fairs. The larger festivals which are particularly worth noting are the **Algarve Folk Music and Dance Festival** (three days in September), with representations of various aspects of Portuguese folklore. **Estoril Handicrafts Fair** (from beginning of July to end of August), which has displays of Portuguese craft and regional specialities in food and drink. And on the musical front, there is the **Festas dos Santos Populares**, which begins on 12/13 June, when the heart of Lisbon is decked out in honour of St Antony – bonfires, grilled sardines, singing and dancing; and the **Festas da Senhora da Agonia** at Viano do Castelo on the Costa Verde (mid-August for three days), which is one of Portugal's most colourful festivals, with religious processions, fairs, dancing and music. So each region has its share of local colour, although these suggestions obviously only scrape the surface of the many festivals held throughout the year. For fuller details see the individual sections or apply to the Portuguese Tourist Board in London, for their booklet 'Festivals, Fairs and Folk Pilgrimages'. This gives full lists of dates and locations for all festivals.

The other social event, which as a tourist you will be unable to avoid, is *fado* singing. *Fado* is a musical lament, usually sung by one woman and accompanied by guitars. Unfortunately, at its worst, *fado* singing degenerates to the tacky status of belly dancing in Turkey, or the flamenco in Spain. At the more glossy, Western-style establishments, the entrance fee is ridiculously inflated and the shows are often second-rate, laid on for unsuspecting holiday-makers. For authentic *fado* singing, head out of the touristy areas of town and into the small, backstreet bars. The entertainment usually starts about 8 or 9pm, and carries on until early in the morning.

Bullfighting is another option. The Portuguese version is marginally preferable to the Spanish equivalent. In deference to the audience's sensibilities, the bulls are not killed in public, but in private afterwards. There are thirty-three bullrings throughout Portugal, but the biggest centre is in LISBON and there are fights here throughout the year. On the Algarve, there are rings at VILA REAL DE ST ANTONIO, QUARTEIRA, ALBUFEIRA, PORTIMÃO and LAGOS. Tickets can be purchased on the day of the fight, although in the summer months you'd be advised to get there early – or even better reserve in advance.

For the prime night-life spots then, head to ALBUFEIRA on the Algarve. This resort has long established itself as the best place as regards the social scene on the Algarve, and has the widest (and liveliest) range of pubs and discos. Coming up fast on Albufeira's heels are places like QUARTEIRA and VILAMOURA. Vilamoura, particularly, is one of those up-market developments which are currently in vogue with the tourist industry. This resort boasts, not only the usual array of discos and bars, but also a large casino where you can enjoy your once-a-year spin of the dice.

LISBON is undoubtedly the best place for the socialite in Portugal. Here, you'll find the kind of night-life you want: good bars, restaurants, a choice of discos, live jazz and traditional music. If you are based near or in Lisbon, you will also have the opportunity to indulge in the cultural delights of classical music concerts, ballet or opera.

Away from the Algarve and Lisbon area, you're really struggling for some lively night-life. In the North, concentrate on hotels in resorts. ESPINHO, PÓVOA DO VARZIM, FIGUEIRA DA FOZ are bigger resorts which have casinos in addition to the usual range of attractions.

MADEIRA is altogether a more staid holiday destination where, in some places, dinner-jackets are still the order of the day. The best place to base yourself is the capital FUNCHAL as here you have the choice of bars and restaurants to idle the night away in. As for the AZORES, well, to be quite honest, for all the natural beauty and spectacular scenery, not to mention the fact that Andrew and Sarah chose them for their honeymoon in '86, if you're a socialite at heart, then you'll probably die of boredom on these quiet (oh-too-quiet) islands.

Recording Your Holiday

Video cameras are taking over as the new form of home movies. The trend is set and each year an increasing number of people discover the delights of taking their holiday on film, to be played back on their telly and watched from the comfort of their armchair in the dark winter months. Though a video rig-out is still an expensive business, it's the sort of equipment which once you've had, you feel you can never do without. Photos, slides and cine films just aren't the same after a full colour and sound film, and on holiday where the sky and sea are so blue, and the colours so much more vibrant, a video camera really comes into its own. Those on the market now are well adapted to travelling: lightweight and easy to handle.

If you feel £1200 is a bit too much to splash out, consider hiring. That way you can have the fun of taking a film of your holiday for not much more than the equivalent you'd spend on conventional films and processing. Hiring is widely available in all areas of the UK and is becoming, like the video camera itself, very much a thing of the future.

Healthy Holidays: *The great outdoors/ The sportsman/Spa holidays*

Portugal is a real mecca for sportsmen and healthy types alike. A wide variety of sports are on offer and, in general, the standard of sporting facilities is very high. Among the sports available at resorts are flying, golf, tennis, squash, table tennis, horseriding, athletics, clay-pigeon shooting and a full range of water sports: sailing, water-skiing, pedalos, scuba diving, windsurfing, sea-fishing and, of course, swimming.

The price you pay for sporting activities largely depends on the type of resort you are staying in and what kind of sport you want to play. In recent years, modern tourist complexes with a special emphasis on the provision of high-quality sporting amenities have sprung up along the Portuguese coastline. Holiday-makers based in one of these resorts undoubtedly have the advantage of first-class sporting facilities on their doorstep – but equally they can expect to pay inflated prices for the use of them. Nevertheless, in the majority of resorts, cost is not a prohibitive factor and the popular leisure activities, such as wind-surfing or horseriding, are reasonably priced. Specialist sports, like clay-pigeon shooting, tend to be more costly to participate in and unless you have a lot of money or are a real aficionado you'll probably find it isn't worth the expense.

Many hotels provide something in the way of sports amenities for their guests, such as table tennis, a tennis court, or swimming pool. The more up-market ones have their own squash courts, gymnasiums and saunas. Some of the larger hotels will also organize horseriding, sea-fishing, and sailing trips for guests. Villa and apartment complexes often have a swimming pool located in the vicinity. However, a hefty fee is often charged for the use of these communal pools, so you'd do better to swim in the sea, which is warm, safe – and free!

Facilities are usually geared to suit all aptitudes: from the complete beginner to the experienced sportsman. Tuition can often be arranged at the larger centres for horseriding, tennis, etc, so if you have always wanted to try out a sport but never had the nerve to do it at home, *Holiday Portugal* could be your golden opportunity.

Although the whole coast is well served in terms of the range of sports available, obviously it is the main tourist destination, the Algarve, which has the highest quality and widest variety of sporting facilities. The mild, all-year-round climate of the South means it is possible to indulge in outdoor activities whatever the time of the year. This is not the case on the western-facing Atlantic coasts, especially in the North, where strong winds sweeping in from the sea bring cool weather and rain. However, as the premier tourist region, the Algarve is also the most expensive area in the country and this means you will pay more for sporting pursuits here than in other parts of Portugal.

There are some sports for which Portugal has developed some outstanding facilities, and the foremost of these is **golf**. The Estoril/Lisbon coasts and the Algarve have been called the golfer's paradise, and this is not far wide of the mark. Top-class courses can be found right along the coastline and many of them are world championship standard, designed by famous names such as Frank Pennink, Robert Trent-Jones and Henry Cotton. Resorts for the golf-conscious to consider in the Algarve are **VILAMOURA, QUINTA DO**

LAGO, VALE DO LOBO and on the western edge of the coast, LAGOS, which is near the famous Penina course. On the Estoril/Lisbon coasts, the TRÓIA golf course near Lisbon is considered by many to be the best in Portugal. This course is built on an island/peninsula and can be reached by ferry from the mainland. Otherwise, ESTORIL has very good golfing facilities and CASCAIS is a one-hour drive away from the top-class Quinta da Marinha course on the Estoril Coast. If you are a real enthusiast, it is worth remembering that golf is big business in Portugal and often the green fee rate in peak season can be very high indeed. To overcome this, there are now some tour operators (see 'Who Specializes in What' on page 110) who deal specifically in golf-holidays. These offer special rates on top-class courses, much cheaper than could be obtained if you were playing independently. If you are planning to golf often, it is worth checking these companies out – it could well work out cheaper travelling with a golf-specialist than taking a straightforward package through one of the large tour operators. There are many golf tournaments running throughout the year. Some are for professionals only, but there are plenty for the amateur enthusiast to try his/her luck in. Amateur competitions are held for one week during March at VILAMOURA and QUINTA DO LAGO, and in June and November at VILAMOURA.

Tennis players are also well catered for in Portugal. Many hotels have at least one or two courts, and more sophisticated facilities are available in the South, where special tennis centres (the Roger Taylor Tennis Centre at VALE DO LOBO and the VILAMOURA Tennis Centre) offer professional coaching and unlimited court time. As with golf, tennis has now grown sufficiently in importance for some tour operators to offer special tennis-packages to Portugal. For more details, see 'Who Specializes in What' on page 110.

There are many opportunities for **sea fishing**. Fishing grounds around the Portuguese mainland and the Azores are particularly well stocked and a variety of fish, such as bass, skate, or bream, can be caught. The best time for fishing is between the months of October and mid-January. You can fish off the rocks and headlands around the coast or hire a boat to venture out to sea. Organized trips are available through one of the forty fishing clubs throughout the country, and for the more adventurous there is always the possibility of trying big game hunting, when you can tackle the likes of shark, swordfish or ray.

Centres with good fishing facilities are PORTIMÃO, CARVOEIRO, and VILAMOURA on the Algarve Coast, CASCAIS, LISBON and SESIMBRA on the Estoril/Lisbon coasts, and VIANA DO CASTELO on the Costa Verde.

If it is **sailing** you are interested in, then best stick to the South coast. The largest and most modern marina is at VILAMOURA, but there are many clubs and marinas right along the coastline offering dinghy or yacht hire and a full range of facilities. Sailing can also be pursued on inland lagoons and estuaries at FARO, TAVIRA, PORTIMÃO and VILA REAL DE SANTO ANTONIO. Because of the Algarve's mild climate, it is possible to sail all-year-round off the southern coast, but in the North, inclement weather means the season is restricted to summer and spring.

If **horseriding** is your particular penchant, Portugal offers some excellent possibilities, both for the beginner and experienced rider. In the Algarve, there are facilities in most of the larger resorts and the best-served are PRAIA DA LUZ (close to the Western Algarve Riding Centre, Burgau), QUINTA DO LAGO and VILAMOURA. Both children's ponies and Anglo–Arab mounts are available and, in the South, midnight rides along the beach are a big attraction (available from the Pinetrees Riding Centre, Quinta do Lago). However, perhaps the most spectacular scenery for horseriding is to be found around the resorts on the Costa Verde. Here, horses are available at main tourist centres: VIANA DO CASTELO, OFIR, PÓVOA DO VARZIM, ESPINHO.

Heading inland, away from the coast, the possibilities are much more limited, although wild game **hunting** is an option in the Costa Verde, where shooting of partridge, rabbit, fox, wolf, wild pig and woodcock can be pursued from September through to December. If you are keen to do some hunting while in Portugal, then you need to do a bit of forward-planning as few Portuguese shooting clubs will hire out equipment or allow the use of their facilities.

For those who enjoy the open-air pursuits of **walking** or **rock-climbing**, then the National Park of PENEDA GERÊS in the Mountain region is your best bet. There are nine summits above 1000 feet to be conquered, the highest of which is Nevosa, at 1545 feet. Hiking trails are marked throughout the park and there are also mountain refuges and campsites to accommodate rock-climbers and hikers. Although the park is not within easy reach from the major coastal resorts, it has developed a fairly modest range of leisure facilities (riding, rowing, swimming, fishing) to add variety to your holiday. Accommodation-wise you don't necessarily have to rough it either: there are hotels in Gerês and there is also the possibility of staying in one of the area's *pousadas*.

MADEIRA has also long been a popular haunt with walkers and there are trails to suit all abilities. The more experienced (and well-equipped) can undertake treks through the steep, rough terrain of the island's interior, while for the less energetic there are gentle rambles through some of the island's lovely scenery.

Back at the coast, the best places for **water sports** are concentrated in the western Algarve: QUINTA DO LAGO, VILAMOURA and PRAIA DA LUZ all have windsurf schools for board hire or tuition. Water-slide parks are a recent development in the Algarve. These are designed for families who want to spend a day away from the beach and try out some new type of entertainment. Three such parks are available, Algarve Slide and Splash Water Park, on the road between Portimão and Lagos, Wet and Wild between Almansil and Quarteira, and the Big One, between Alantarilha and Porches. All these offer 'thrills, spills and splashes' and various other watery attractions to occupy kids of all ages. Outside the Algarve, the next best options for water sports are the resorts of ESTORIL and CASCAIS on the Estoril Coast. If you are a keen windsurfer, the small resort of GUINCHO is worth considering, as the good surf of the headland draws enthusiasts from all over the world. Further north, on the Costa Verde, the resorts of PÓVOA DO VARZIM and ESPINHO are the best bets. In Madeira, the capital FUNCHAL or the east coast resort of BAIÁ DE ZARCO have the best-developed sports facilities.

For those with more general sporting interests, the specially-built complexes of VILAMOURA, VALE DO LOBO and AÇOTEIAS on the Algarve, offer some excellent sporting facilities for the young, keen and active. World-class golf courses, tennis and squash courts, an athletics stadium, an international cross-country course, and riding schools are just a few amenities available at these resorts. If you are less of an enthusiast, but still want somewhere which affords good sporting opportunities, consider the larger resorts: ALBUFEIRA, PORTIMÃO and LAGOS are good options on the Algarve Coast, ESTORIL and CASCAIS on the Estoril Coast, and in the North, PÓVOA DO VARZIM and ESPINHO.

For further details concerning the sporting scene in Portugal or for more information about the range of sports listed above, contact the Portuguese National Tourist Office at 1/5 New Bond Street, London W1Y 0NP. Tel: 01-493 3873.

SPA HOLIDAYS

Portugal has a number of mineral and thermal springs where holidays and health cures can be combined. These are concentrated chiefly in the North and centre of the Portuguese mainland, and there are also some to be found on the Azores' archipelago. The northern spas are relatively unsophisticated affairs, offering a cure amid quiet, restful surroundings. Some leisure activities are catered for, although these are nothing ambitious and amount to fishing, boating, excursions, etc. The spas in central Portugal are situated nearer larger population centres, so the recreational amenities here are more diverse and the night-life more lively. In fact, if you choose your spa resort carefully, your 'cure' can easily be incorporated into an otherwise normal holiday.

Among some of the better known spas are GERÊS, VIZELA, and SÃO VINCENTE in the Costa Verde; CURIA, LUSO, CALDAS DA RAINHA and MONTE REAL in the Costa de Prata; CHAVES and SÃO PEDRO DO SUL in the Mountains; MONCHIQUE on the Algarve; FURNAS and VARADOURO in the Azores.

For more detailed information on the location of spas and the types of disorders treated, contact the Portuguese National Tourist Office in London.

 The Nature Lover

Both mainland Portugal and the islands of Madeira and the Azores offer the nature lover ample opportunity to pursue his/her interests. Obviously on the mainland it is the North which should be concentrated on. In the past, this has been one of Portugal's best-kept secrets, as the natural beauty of the area has gone largely undisturbed and unexplored by holiday-makers coming from Northern Europe. This appears to be changing now with the spread of tourist development further up the North Coast. It is now possible to take a package holiday to one of the resorts on the Costa de Prata or Costa Verde (VIANO DO CASTELO, OFIR, PÓVOA DO VARZIM, FIGUEIRA DA FOZ) and, by taking advantage of tour operators' fly-drive deals, trips can be made inland to the surrounding countryside.

One place not readily accessible from the resorts on the coast, but which is a real 'must' for nature lovers, is the national park of PENEDA-GERÊS. This park, in the very north of Portugal (Mountain Region), encompasses some 70,000 hectares. The scenery is quite spectacular, with extensive pine-forests and rugged granite mountains. There is a wide range of flora and fauna, and plenty of opportunity to get in a few fine days' walking. The best base to use for accommodation is the town of GERÊS, lying near the eastern edge of the National Park.

Another place well worth visiting is the BUÇACO forest on the Costa de Prata. This ancient woodland has a bewildering array of trees, lush vegetation and masses of colourful, wild flowers. Paths are laid out throughout the forest, but there are no rules to say that you can't wander off and explore the forest's delights for yourself! If you are intending to spend a few days, the best place to use as a centre is the old spa town of LUSO.

MADEIRA has been called Portugal's 'floating garden' and looking at the scenery, with its amazing wealth of flowers and other vegetation, it is not difficult to see why. Although you may not be interested in making Madeira the subject of botanical research (as many visiting experts are) you should not miss out on a visit to the Botanical Gardens. In these gardens grow a good cross section of the world's botanical delights, which thrive in Madeira's mild, semi-tropical climate. The gardens are situated in the island's capital, FUNCHAL, and this is also the best base to use for seeing the rest of the island, as all the main bus excursions leave from here.

With the AZORES, the injunction to the nature lover is to go now! High finance and prestige tourist developments are poised to move into the archipelago within the next few years, completely changing the face of what is as yet one of most beautiful, remote places in Western Europe. The landscape is volcanic in origin and is characterized by lakes set in the craters of extinct volcanoes, mountains, valleys, hot springs and geysers. The flora and fauna are varied, and of interest to the professional and amateur naturalist alike. In recent years the regional government has shown enough foresight to realize that extensive tourist development could totally destroy the Azores' unique, natural environment and as a result has been setting up nature reserves to protect the landscape . . . However, you only have to look at the Algarve to see that the march of mass tourism is all-embracing and relentless. If you are thinking of going to the archipelago, then the main town, **PONTA DELGADA,** is situated on the biggest island, São Miguel. From São Miguel you can catch connections to the other islands in the archipelago.

PRIVATE Keep Out The Recluse

'Get away from it all'-type holidays are no real problem in Portugal as, apart from the big resorts on the coast, very little of the country has been exploited by tourism. Few tour operators deal with areas beyond the main centres, so there is plenty of opportunity to escape the crowds and head for places where the meaning of mass tourism is unknown.

The inland regions of the Mountains and Plains are the areas for the recluse to concentrate on. In the North, especially, there is beautiful, remote scenery, far distant from the hustle and bustle of the southern resorts. Throughout the interior, there is no shortage of small villages or towns which you can use both as a base and as a haven for peace and quiet. The way of life here is strongly traditional and the sight of an ox and cart trundling along the road will remind you that not only is there no tourist development, but that the industrial and agricultural revolutions have yet to register in this most rural of settings.

By the sea, the northern coastal regions of the Costa Verde and Costa de Prata have gone largely untouched by the tourism. Here, towns like **VILA PRAIA DE ÂNCORA** or **VIANO DO CASTELO** barely qualify as resorts by southern standards, yet have long expanses of fine beaches set amid tranquil, peaceful countryside. Even some of the larger resorts, such as **VILA DO CONDE** or **PÓVOA DO VARZIM**, which verge on becoming busy during the summer, return to their quiet, traditional tenor of life out of season.

However, it is the Azores, more than any other area in Portugal, where you can get the feeling of leaving the world behind and stepping into anonymity. Of the nine islands which comprise the archipelago, only the main one, SÃO MIGUEL, could, by any stretch of the imagination, be called commercialized, so the possibilities here for 'getting away from it all' are limitless.

In true reclusive style, independent travel is really the only way to penetrate these parts of the country. The ideal solution would be to travel by car, but the cost of hiring a suitable car and the price of petrol may make you think twice about extensive motoring. The only other alternative is public transport. The main rail and air-routes are concentrated chiefly in the West, linking up the three main population centres of Oporto, Lisbon and Faro. However, the bus network is extensive and if you don't mind slow, country buses combined with seemingly endless hours of travelling, even the most far-flung destinations in Portugal are accessible.

If you don't want the hassle of organizing your own holiday, at the risk of becoming one of the crowd, the best idea is to take a package holiday to one of the quieter resorts. Again, it is the resorts on the North Coast (FIGUEIRA DA FOZ, ESPINHO, VIANA DO CASTELO, PÓVOA DO VARZIM) which you should concentrate on. From here, it is possible to take trips inland and explore the delights of the northern scenery. Another quiet package-destination is PONTA DELGADA, the capital of the Azores' main island, São Miguel. This is a particularly good option for nature lovers, as there is the opportunity to see a wide range of flora and fauna in their natural, unspoilt settings.

In the off-season, consider the resorts along the Estoril/Lisbon Coast, particularly the smaller ones like TRÓIA or SESIMBRA. This is also the best time for the culture-loving recluse to visit the capital LISBON. Broadly speaking, if you are not too fussy about the weather, and peace and quiet are your main priorities, then the winter months of November through to February represent your best opportunity to come to Portugal and avoid the crowds.

 Family Holidays

More than anything else, Portugal is a holiday destination for the whole family. There really is no problem in choosing your resort, because unlike some of the Mediterranean countries, where the young and trendy gravitate to one place and the older 'afternoon-tea' brigade to another, resorts in Portugal are, by and large, a happy mix of all ages, tastes and pursuits.

The Algarve, with its safe, sandy beaches and suitable hotel facilities, is the best location in Portugal for a family holiday. The plethora of sporting amenities, from clock-golf to windsurfing, means that everyone can do their own thing and there is more than enough to interest even the most energetic of teenagers. Overall, resorts are built up around long stretches of sand and have easy access to the beach. However, watch out for smaller towns on the western Algarve, which are situated on low cliffs above beaches; these are not really suitable for families with toddlers as the descent to the beach is usually steep and more or less necessitates an arm-breaking carry for younger offspring.

Resorts which are particularly good for family holidays are MONTE GORDO on the eastern edge of the coast, which does not have much to offer in the way of glitzy nightclubs, but does have a long safe stretch of sand and is within easy day-tripping distance of Ayamonte and Seville in Spain; ARMAÇÃO DE PÊRA, a few miles away from the much bigger Albufeira, has a number of small, sheltered bays which are particularly good for younger bathers; PRAIA DA ROCHA has a children's playground situated on the beach itself and the big modern development of VILAMOURA also has a long stretch of sandy beach which is suitable for young children.

Many hotels now have a children's playground or playpool. The better establishments offer highchairs, early meals and cots, although you may have to pay a supplement on these. A number of villa and apartment complexes also feature a children's pool and/or play-area. As for mum and dad's night-life, the good news is that baby-sitting services can often be arranged locally in most of the larger resorts.

The best way to suss out the options available is to focus on the holiday brochures which specifically mention what children's facilities are available. It is always a good idea to double-check with your tour operator before you commit yourself, firstly that the facilities advertised do exist and secondly what standard they are maintained to – after all, there is nothing more lethal than a badly-designed, ill-kept children's play area. If in doubt, go for package holidays which say they're specifically recommended for family holidays – that way you have a leg to stand on if the resort does not come up to scratch from the children's facilities point of view.

Most tour operators gear themselves in some way to family holidays. This usually takes the form of child reductions on the basis that he or she shares a room with two full-fare paying passengers. In some cases there is also a reduction if a second child shares the same room. Increasingly, tour companies advertise the 'one child free' option, but if you read the small print, you'll soon realize that free places are limited and allocated on a first-come, first-served basis, so really they are a carrot which the tour operators dangle to get early bookings. Watch out for this seemingly attractive proposition (there may be a good reason why tour operators have to offer this extra concession to fill up a hotel during peak-season), or else you'll find the savings made on one child's place will be eaten up by other 'hidden' expenses.

Away from the Algarve Coast, the resorts on the Estoril Coast (ESTORIL and CASCAIS) are your best options for provision of leisure and hotel facilities. For a smaller resort try SÃO MARTINHO DO PORTO, 60 miles (98km) north of Lisbon. The water of the bay is calm and the gently shelving beach makes it ideal for small children.

Further north on the coast, the sea is not suitable for younger swimmers. The undertow is strong and swimming should not be attempted if a warning flag is shown. GUINCHO, a few miles up the coast from Cascais, is particularly notorious in this respect; strong currents and rough seas mean that at least one person a year is drowned around this headland.

If you want to base yourself inland away from the coast, then, as tour operators do not offer deals to inland destinations, it's more or less potluck as to what hotel facilities are on offer. The range of leisure activities and liveliness of night-life is also severely curtailed. However, if your brood are keen to go it alone, you could try GERÊS (Costa Verde), as a base for the outdoor pursuits available in Gerês National Park. Otherwise, spa towns tend to have better developed facilities (swimming, tennis, cinema, horseriding), because of the steady stream of visitors to their health-giving waters. CHAVES (Mountain Region) and LUSO (Costa de Prata) are the main ones to consider in this respect.

Practicalities

Red Tape

Visitors holding British (or British Visitor's), Canadian, American or Australian passports are allowed to stay in the country for sixty days without a visa (ninety days for Australians). If you are planning on staying more than sixty days, you should apply before the expiry date to Foreigners' Registration Service, Av. Antonio Augusto de Aguiar, 18, Lisbon 1600 (Tel: 55047) or regional branches. Visas may be obtained, before you go, from Portuguese Consulates.

Embassy and Consulate Addresses

Visas can be obtained from the Portuguese Consulate General, 62 Brompton Road, London SW3.

In the *USA* – Embassy of Portugal, 2125 Kalorana, N.W., Washington D.C., 20008.

In *Canada* – Portuguese Consulate, 645 Island Park Drive, Ottawa, K1Y 0B8.

Health Formalities

No vaccinations are required for visitors from the United Kingdom, North America or Continental Europe. An International Certificate of Vaccinations against cholera and smallpox is required for those travelling from countries where these diseases have an epidemic status. Similarly, travellers coming from areas infected by yellow fever must hold the relevant vaccination certificate. This requirement is only applicable to travellers arriving in or going to Madeira or the Azores.

Customs

There are no real problems with customs in Portugal – especially for package tourists. In general, the tedious formalities are got over with as quickly as possible. Here are the allowances to which each adult is entitled.

You may bring unlimited sums of foreign currency (in cash or traveller's cheques) into the country. On leaving Portugal, you cannot take out more money than you brought in, either in Portuguese or foreign currency.

Tourists (over seventeen years of age) may import the following duty-free goods: two bottles of table wine, one bottle of spirits, 200 cigarettes or 250 grams of tobacco, ¼ litre of toilet water, 50 grams of perfume.

Personal effects such as clothes, luggage, small stocks of your favourite tea or coffee, are not questioned providing they are not carried in obviously excessive amounts, but fresh meat is prohibited.

For photographic equipment, the allowance is two cameras and one cine-camera per person, each with ten rolls of film, and one pair of binoculars.

Other more expensive items which you might conceivably be carrying – such as a portable typewriter or sports gear – are allowed although, again, only in quantities suitable for the individual's use. If you are coming for a shooting holiday, you may take a maximum of six guns and 400 cartridges into the country. A ticket will be issued when the weapons have cleared customs, and this will act as your gun-licence while in Portugal. A deposit of Esc.1000$00 is required when entering the country with guns and this charge is refundable on departure.

Money

There is no limit to the amount of foreign currency (in traveller's cheques or cash) which you can take with you. On leaving the country, you cannot take out more currency than you brought in, either in Portuguese or foreign currency. Technically, foreign visitors must take a minimum of Esc.10,000$00, and an additional amount of

Esc.2,000$00 for each day of their intended stay. However, this regulation is intended to deter undesirable itinerants from entering the country and does not really affect the average package tour holiday-maker.

The monetary unit of Portugal is the escudo, which is composed of 100 centavos. The currency symbol is the dollar sign which appears in the middle of a figure, acting as a decimal point separating the escudos from the centavos. Notes and coins are issued in the following denominations:

Coins: 50 centavos; 1, 2.50, 5, 10, 20, 25 escudos
Notes: 50, 500, 1000, 5000 escudos

The Portuguese usually refer to 1000 escudos as a 'conto'.

HOW TO TAKE YOUR MONEY

Although the exchange rate fluctuates, it usually represents best value to wait to buy the majority of your escudos in Portugal, rather than buying before you go. There really is no advantage taking escudo traveller's cheques in preference to sterling or American dollar traveller's cheques, as both are widely accepted throughout the country. However, it is a good idea to take some Portuguese currency with you. This will tide you over the first few days until you have settled into your hotel and sussed out the location of the local banks or exchanges.

Traveller's cheques in your own currency can be exchanged in hotels, banks, tourist offices and some restaurants. The commission fee charged by banks for changing money is low, so it makes sense to have your cheques made out in smaller rather than larger denominations. Always go for a well-known bank or credit card company, i.e. American Express, Thomas Cook, or Bank of England, otherwise you could have difficulties in some of the more rural parts of the country. Remember, also, that you will almost always be required to produce your passport as proof of identity before you can cash your cheques.

All the major *credit cards* (Visa, Diners Club, American Express) are accepted in the larger tourist centres, so if you're planning to holiday in one of the big resorts in the Algarve, this is a safe and convenient way to take your money. Plastic cards won't get you very far, however, in the more remote Portuguese villages and towns, so if you're heading out of the touristy areas, don't rely on this as your main source of money.

Personal cheques with a Eurocheque Card and Eurocheques (available from your bank) are becoming more and more popular among holiday-makers. With these you can cash cheques abroad just as you would with your ordinary cheque book at home. However, the system is not yet fully developed in Portugal and, while you should have no problems in the main tourist centres, the situation is different away from the large coastal resorts. If you are planning to take Eurocheques remember to order them well in advance of your holiday departure, as they may take a few days to come through.

WHERE TO EXCHANGE

Traveller's cheques, foreign currency and personal cheques can all be exchanged at exchange bureaux (*cambios*), which can be found in the centre of most tourist resorts. They are also located in major airports and railway stations, although, if possible, you should avoid changing money here as the commission fee is invariably higher. Tourist offices will also cash cheques, and these have the added advantage of longer opening hours. Hotels and restaurants are another option, but only as a last resort; the commission fees in these places are usually between 5 and 10 per cent. The best place to change money is at a bank, as these charge 200 escudos regardless of the amount exchanged. Most banks are readily accessible in the town centre and as the local exchange rate is fixed there really is not much point shopping around. The independent traveller should not run into too many problems either, as there is usually a bank to be found even in the smallest, northern town. Remember to keep your certificates of exchange. Although it is not strictly necessary to produce these when leaving the country, they are useful to have as proof that you exchanged money and are not trying to take out more money than you brought in. Try to get rid of most of your escudos before you return to this country. Not only will you lose out by changing from Portuguese to British currency, you may have difficulties exchanging some of the larger denomination notes (e.g. 5000$00) in this country.

To summarize then, all these methods have their advantages and disadvantages. Like most holiday-makers, you will probably weigh up the odds and decide that only a combination of the alternatives gives the security and flexibility you require. Some ready cash in escudos and then a choice of traveller's cheques, a credit card or Eurocheques. Overall, traveller's cheques in your own currency are the best way to carry the bulk of your money if you are planning on doing extensive travelling, although Eurocheques or a credit card are equally acceptable in the main tourist centres. If you have a credit card, it's a good idea to take it anyway as a back-up to traveller's cheques. One final point to remember – take some of your own currency with you! It's amazing how many people manage to successfully negotiate the foreign currency maze when abroad and completely forget to take some ready cash with them to pay for buses, taxis, etc on their return to this country.

Banking

Opening hours are 8.30am to 11.45am, and 1pm to 2.45pm, Monday to Friday. During the summer, banks at airports, some of the larger frontier gates and the main tourist centres may have their opening hours extended. In Lisbon, additional opening hours for the main city centre banks are 6pm to 11pm, Monday to Friday.

Insurance

It really is foolhardy to cut back on holiday insurance, yet each year thousands of people make this false economy and live to regret it. Increasingly if you're taking a package holiday you'll have no say in the matter and insurance will be added on to your final bill whether you like it or not. While this at least makes sure you get some sort of cover, remember you are not obliged to take this policy.

Note, then, that you are under no obligation to accept the insurance policy offered by your travel agent. In some instances these are not as detailed as policies bought from large reputable companies, and all too often the package policies mean long delays in the settlement of claims as they are snowed under at the peak of the tourist season. On the plus side, however, the rep at your resort will have been trained in how to handle claims and this will take some of the strain off you. Tour companies also represent a formidable force in the insurance market and their buying power means that they can usually offer a cheaper insurance policy than could be bought on your own. The secret is to read the small print of the insurance policies carefully. Don't assume that because it has the backing of a 'big name' insurance company, that it is necessarily the right policy for you.

If you consider the inclusive package as inadequate for your needs, the best advice is to go to an insurance broker, tell him what you're taking (remember photographic equipment, etc), what you envisage doing (i.e. if you plan spending a lot of time doing water sports) and how long you'll be away. This is a particularly good idea if you're planning on taking some new, expensive equipment with you (many package policies put a limit of around £200 per item on your valuables) or if your chances of requiring medical treatment are higher than average. Also check out the liability clause for delays if it's important that you get home by the date stipulated.

For most people, then, the basic insurance policy offered by tour companies will be sufficient. But for those who are looking elsewhere, Lloyds of London are particularly good and will provide travel insurance for people who normally find it difficult, e.g. disabled people and pregnant ladies. Independent travellers are especially advised to arrange a good insurance policy for themselves as, if anything goes wrong, they have no one (such as ABTA or a travel agent) to argue their case for them.

In terms of medical insurance, most comprehensive travel insurance policies incorporate some kind of coverage for medical costs incurred abroad. The amount which will be reimbursed varies from company to company, but many of the major tour operators offer to cover costs up to £500,000. Reciprocal health agreements exist between Portugal and Britain and, on production of the proper documents (see the Health section below), British citizens are entitled to emergency medical treatment free of charge. However, for more prolonged or serious illnesses, a good insurance policy is essential. If you already have a medical insurance policy in this country, it is worth finding out if this covers you for travel abroad.

North American travellers and those from further afield are strongly advised to procure good travel insurance cover before leaving home.

Having said all this, Portugal as a holiday destination does not represent any more potential problems or threats than any other country popular with holiday-makers. The crime rate is relatively low and standards of health will be acceptable to all but the most fastidious. The odds are that most people will enjoy trouble-free, stress-free holidays in the Portuguese sun, but no one can anticipate the unplanned – like your car breaking down on the way to the airport or the theft of all your luggage. Events like these are disastrous enough in themselves, but if you have a good insurance policy then the disaster won't be compounded by your being left substantially out of pocket with nothing to show for it.

Health

Portugal does not present any major health hazards to the average holiday-maker. If you are travelling from Britain or North America, you are not required to obtain any medical vaccinations (see Health Formalities, page 43), although it is a good idea, as with all the Mediterranean countries, to have a typhoid/polio booster before you go.

Overall, the standards of hygiene in the major population and tourist centres are reasonable and you should have no cause for complaint. Facilities in the more rural areas in North Portugal can be pretty basic and, unless you intend to live as the locals do, it's a good idea to take your own loo paper and soap. Obviously this affects independent travellers more than package-tour holiday-makers, and if you are venturing beyond the main tourist areas, it makes sense to carry your own first-aid kit and to take out some health insurance. Officially, tap water is safe to drink throughout Portugal; however, in the more remote parts especially, you'd do well not to risk any stomach upsets and drink mineral or purified water.

In general, the standard of medicine practised is acceptable, but it does cost – even for the quickest visit to the doctor. If it is something minor that is troubling you, try a *farmácia* first. Portuguese pharmacists are well trained and should be able to guide you around the array of unfamiliar drugs until you get what you want. In larger towns and hospitals there should be no problem finding a doctor that speaks English, but if you require hospital treatment and want the familiarity of home surroundings, then there is a British hospital at 49, Rua Saraiva de Carvalho, Lisbon. Tel: 602020.

British people are entitled to free emergency medical treatment in Portugal. In order to qualify for this treatment go to your local DHSS office, pick up the SA30 leaflet, complete the form CM1 which is attached to it, and then apply for an E111 form. An E111 certificate lasts for two years, and you *must* produce this in order to take advantage of the free medical facilities. This is a useful piece of paper to have anyway – not only does it entitle you to emergency treatment in Portugal, but it also ensures free medical treatment in other EEC countries to the same level as a national of that country would enjoy.

If it is a more serious or prolonged illness which is being treated then you ought to take out a medical insurance policy to cover costs. Often this is integrated into the basic insurance policy offered by tour operators or insurance companies, but if you want to take out a separate medical insurance policy, then check out the AA, RAC and Lloyds, who all offer good deals. The cheapest medical insurance Britons can get, and probably one of the best, is given by Europe Assistance Ltd, 252 High Street, Croydon, Surrey CR0 11NF, 01-680 1234. For a small premium you get a 24-hour advice telephone link with the UK and a guarantee of on-the-spot cash for emergency services. This insurance also covers the expenses that can arise from a car accident, such as hiring another car and flying out spare parts.

Pre-planning and Free Information

The more you know about a country before going, the more you'll get out of your holiday once you're there. Not only can you then locate where the things that interest you are, but you'll be able to plan ahead to make sure you get to see them and don't waste any precious time waiting in tourist information queues. It's amazing how many people still leave on holiday with the picture of their hotel from the travel brochure as their only image of the country they're going to.

Virtually every country imaginable has a National Tourist Office in London and Portugal is no exception. Write to them ahead of your holiday (well ahead as they can take literally weeks to reply) asking for general tourist literature and, if you have any specific hobby or pursuit you're keen to indulge in on holiday, ask them their advice on where best to pursue it and to send you any literature they might have on it (golf, fishing, windsurfing, sailing are some examples). You've nothing to lose as their service is free and if nothing else it'll whet your appetite for what to expect. Request a map if you're considering touring, and accommodation listings if you are travelling independently.

An extremely useful source of information (free and impartial) comes from the travel agent Hogg Robinson. They produce resort reports, which go into detail on what to expect, and give an unbiased report on all the hotels used by the tour operators. These files can be consulted free of charge in any of their agencies.

Thomas Cook produce resort reports, too, and these can be taken away by the public. Much smaller and with no detail on specific hotels, these do, however, contain condensed information on the main resorts, sightseeing, best buys etc, and they give a good idea how expensive drinks and meals will be once you're there. Lunn Poly do a similar kind of thing; their *Guide to Good Hotels* is compiled on the basis of customers' actual experiences and hotels are featured according to their recommendations and comments.

Another source of free information is your local library. This is especially useful if you have a specific interest, such as the country's literature or history. A very good general overview of modern Portugal is also available from the Portuguese Embassy. *Portugal: A Bird's Eye View* reviews every aspect of the country – from the geography and economy, to the historical influences which have shaped the present-day nation.

As far as bought sources go, there are a few other guidebooks worth considering: Collins' *Welcome to Portugal* is a fairly dense, detailed book which is worth considering if you have a specialist interest or if you're planning to do the country in depth; Frommer's *Dollarwise*

Guide to Portugal is a fairly lively account of one man's experiences of Portugal, although you might find the high-flown language a bit hard to take in places; *Fodor's Portugal* (Hodder and Stoughton) is pretty standard stuff, well-researched, comprehensive and informative, but a bit too middle-aged and middle-class to be of much practical use for young(ish) package-tour holiday-makers. Berlitz has three pocket-size guidebooks on the market, featuring the *Algarve, Lisbon* and *Madeira*. These tend to be utopian guides, which means unless you go around with your eyes shut, you'll never see things in the same romantic, poetic light as the Berlitz guide. Never mind, the pictures are nice and if you wade your way through the nostalgia, there is some useful background on major historical monuments and sights. *The Rough Guide to Portugal* (Routledge and Kegan Paul) is another publication worth considering. Although it is really geared towards the student-intellectual types, don't be put off, this guide is well-compiled and especially good for the independent traveller as it gives fairly detailed accounts of the more far-flung places in Portugal.

Budgeting

It used to be that a holiday abroad was only for the well-heeled or a once-in-a-lifetime event. Today, however, lower-price air fares and increased competition among tour operators mean a package holiday to a resort in the Mediterranean could well be cheaper than two weeks touring in Britain. Portugal is a good country for the cost-conscious to visit as over the past four years the value of the escudo has fallen steadily against British and North American currencies. This means holiday-makers going to Portugal now are getting more for their money than ever before.

Tour operators offer a wide variety of deals and there will undoubtedly be one to suit your requirements – and pocket. Major tour companies aim to keep prices down and be competitive, so if you choose carefully a cheap package-holiday need not be at the expense of quality accommodation or service. If you are working with limited resources it is worth considering companies such as Martin Rooks or

Tjaereborg – these specialize in offering budget holidays to those who want to holiday in the sun, but don't have a fortune to spend. Another possibility to 'break away on a budget' is to holiday in the off-season months rather than the July/August period. Out-of-season breaks can often work out at least a third cheaper than the same package taken in mid-summer. Similarly, late bookings advertised in travel agents' windows are a good way to keep costs down. This last option, of course, is only for the flexibly-minded and the quickly organized, as you won't know far in advance whether you are going to land up in a Spanish, Greek or Portuguese resort.

There are various accommodation choices open to the holiday-maker in Portugal. Pensions, self-catering villas, apartments and hotels graded on a one to five star basis are all available through tour operators. Hotel accommodation ranges from bed and breakfast to half- or full-board. Although full-board is undoubtedly the cheapest option, don't be too wary of taking half-board, as eating out in Portugal can be relatively inexpensive and won't knock too big a hole in the holiday budget.

Food, drink and night-time entertainment are all reasonably priced, even in the Algarve, which is the most expensive area in Portugal. A cup of coffee may cost around 60$00, a three course meal from 1500$00 to 2000$00. Wine is inexpensive (under 500$00 a bottle), especially if you drink local varieties, which are frequently very good. Night-life won't break the bank either, although it is worth remembering that away from the glitzy discos, cheaper entertainment can be enjoyed for the price of a few drinks in the small bars which often have live jazz or traditional music shows. You won't have to pay unreasonable fees, either, for the popular leisure activities, such as windsurfing or water-skiing, although use of high-quality facilities, like the world-class golf courses in the Algarve area, are more expensive.

For those who are operating on a tight budget, here are a few tips to bear in mind: packages to lesser-known, smaller resorts on the mainland are invariably cheaper than similar packages to the major tourist centres; if you are in self-catering accommodation, buy local produce – *don't* try to buy your favourite breakfast cereal or jam, as prices for these will be massively inflated; if you are fussy about what your baby eats, take your own supply of baby food as, again, this can be quite expensive to buy; finally, don't drink in the hotel bar – local bars are often much cheaper.

An all-inclusive package-tour holiday is undoubtedly the cheapest way to spend two weeks in the sun. However, if you are keen to go it alone you won't find yourself paying through the nose for accommodation or food. In fact, it is possible to live on £7 or £8 a day if you stay in cheap pensions and buy your own food. For those who don't fancy roughing it, then a single room in a hotel, including a private bathroom and breakfast in the morning, is going to cost you somewhere in the region of 2500$00 to 3500$00 per night.

Undoubtedly the biggest expense involved will be moving around the country, either by car-hire or coach excursions. A week's car-hire of a Fiat Uno/Renault 5 hatchback in the summer months (June to September) will set you back around 30,000 escudos, or around 28,000 in the winter months. It usually works out cheaper to book a car in advance with your tour operator, than to hire through one of the international car-hire firms based in Portugal. Coach excursions organised through tour companies can also be quite costly. Prices may be in the region of 3000$00 to 4500$00 for a full-day excursion to one destination. If you plan on going on a trip taking in several places of interest, expect to pay around the 8000$00 mark. These prices are expensive, given that a lot of people jump on the coach with no idea where they are going or whether the trip suits their special interests. If you prefer to visit quaint, traditional fishing villages, then there is no point in paying for a tour which focuses on the old historic towns of Central Portugal. A far better idea is to check out the places featured on each itinerary (you could do this by referring to the appropriate part of this book) before you commit your money and yourself to a day on a coach.

The cheapest way to get around the country is by train or on the regular bus services. Fares on these are low and it is possible to buy tourist tickets (*Bilhetes Turisticos*) for train travel which are valid for periods of seven, 14 or 21 days. Another saver is a rail cheque (*Cheque Trem*). This gives a reduction of 15 per cent on ordinary fares, is obtainable in five different values, and has no time limit. If you are travelling as a family group and plan on doing fairly extensive train travel, you may consider purchasing a family ticket. This is only valid for distances over 94 miles (151km), and there must be a minimum of three people travelling together on the same train. One adult must pay the full fare, thereafter tickets for those over 12 are half-price, or for those aged four to 12 a quarter of the normal price. Discounts on train travel are also available to senior citizens. Provided proof of age is produced, you may obtain (free of charge) a senior citizen's card (*Cartão Dourado*) which entitles you to a 50 per cent reduction on all trains (except city trains during the rush-hours).

The only other people who qualify for discounts are students. If you can produce your International Student's Identity Card, you are eligible for discounts on entrance fees for museums, exhibitions, etc.

Finally, when working out your budget, remember it's easier to take too much money with you than to have money transferred to your account or sent on. A credit card is the ideal stand-by for emergencies, but an extra £100 or so in your current account or in traveller's cheques does not go amiss. Remember if you do not use all your sterling traveller's cheques in Portugal, you can cash them at face value on return to this country. No commission will be charged if you are exchanging them in a bank/building society where you have an account. When abroad, change money in small amounts, enough to do you for a couple of days. There are two advantages to this: firstly, it is safer as the chances of loss through theft are reduced; secondly, you will be able to keep track of precisely how much money is being spent and budget accordingly. Having small amounts of currency also cuts down the chances of having to change back large quantities of escudos into sterling (at a frequently disadvantageous rate) before you leave the country.

A final tip – don't save your money thinking you'll blow what's left at the Faro Duty Free Shop – Vinho Verde has been spotted at more than twice the price in the supermarket.

Getting Yourself Organized

What to Take with You

Package tour holiday-makers should take the minimum of luggage. Think back to previous years when you returned home with half the clothes unused and remember you'll need to allow a bit of extra room in your luggage for any items you buy over there or for your duty free. Try to travel with hand-luggage. If you're going for a two-week 'sun, sand and sea' holiday there is no reason why you shouldn't be able to pack everything you need into a lightweight bag which can be carried as hand-luggage. Think of the advantages of not having to wait in baggage collection queues wondering if what you checked in will actually reappear.

As for the actual clothes themselves, light casual garments plus a showerproof raincoat and a sweater should be all you require. If you're going on a winter holiday, it's a good idea to pack an extra jumper as temperatures can cool down quite rapidly after night fall. Dress is usually not formal in hotels, so there is no need to pack a suit or evening dress, unless you are staying in a five-star Grand Hotel.

If you're travelling independently, aside from taking the absolute minimum of lightweight kit, you might consider taking a few extra items, such as a travelling alarm clock (for early starts) and an empty water-bottle to fill up with drinking water when you get the chance. For those camping or hostelling, it's advisable to take a money-belt to keep your valuables in and a padlock for youth hostels. A good first-aid kit is a must for independent travellers heading off to remote parts, and a phrase book would not go amiss either.

Although the best advice that can be offered to any holiday-maker is to travel light, taking only the essentials, there are a few items which definitely merit packing:

(1) Take with you all photographic equipment you're likely to need. This includes films for your camera. Buying well-known brand names such as Kodak or Agfa in Portugal can work out very expensive in

comparison with the prices for identical film in this country. The Portuguese version of camera films is often no cheaper and frequently poorer quality. Don't get your film processed when you're out there – Portuguese developing techniques leave a lot to be desired and you're bound to be disappointed by the results.

(2) Any English-language books or magazines you're likely to want for beach reading, again bring from home. Some of the larger resorts do carry a stock of British and American books, but these are generally overpriced and there is no guarantee that what's on offer will be to your taste.

(3) If you are travelling with a young child and prefer certain brands of baby food, it's a good idea to take your own supply with you. It's not impossible to buy British brands in one of the larger Portuguese supermarkets, but the prices for imported food are massively inflated and the chances are the brand you favour won't be available anyway.

(4) Toiletries and medicines should also be brought with you (and this includes suntan preparations, which are more expensive in the resorts than back home). There are few countries which offer cheaper toiletries than Britain, and even if you do find some, the quality could well be questionable. Any prescribed medicines should definitely be brought from home as often the equivalent drug will not be available abroad. Boots do two sorts of medical kits – a Trip Kit at £6.75 and a Holiday Kit at £3.55.

(5) Loo paper and soap are two things not to be overlooked. There really is no substitute for them when you need them, unless you're prepared to resort to some of the more ethnic local habits of the south. Even if you're on a package, it's not a bad idea to pack a roll or packets of tissues as once you're away from the hotels and larger resorts you can't be sure that every bar or restaurant will be equipped.

(6) If you're planning on visiting any of the churches in the country, it's still frowned upon if women don't have a shawl or something to cover their heads and in some cases this is obligatory. Take a light scarf for this purpose and make sure you don't do your sightseeing tours when you're clad in shorts and T-shirt.

Part Two

HOW TO GO

Package v. Independent

One of the great myths which people still believe is that a holiday abroad has to be all or nothing. Either you take a package where everything is organized for you by the tour operator or you go it alone, handling all your own flights, accommodation and internal travel arrangements. This idea of the package v. independent dilemma might once have been true (and still is to a certain extent in those countries where tourism is just developing) but in Portugal where the tour operator scene is well developed, it is possible to reach a compromise between going it alone and having a package tour operator take the sting out of the formalities for you.

A number of tour companies recognize that some holiday-makers like to travel independently in a country, but don't want to fork out large amounts of money for the standard air or train fare out there. Thus an option which is increasingly available to independent travellers is to take a cheap charter flight organized by one of the main tour operators (see Independent Means: By Air on page 118) which gets you there and back, and then to travel independently in the country after that. Another compromise between an all-inclusive package and the freedom to move about independently is to take advantage of the tour operators who offer fly/drive options (see Driving on page 108). This gives you scope to go wherever you want in the country, while releasing you from the additional hassle of organizing flights or hiring cars before you go.

Even if you do opt for a basic beach resort package, many tour operators offer a wide range of self-catering villas or apartments, which give you the freedom to come and go as you please without being tied to fixed meal times. Car hire is also often available at very competitive rates through major tour companies and by taking advantage of this option you can use your resort as a base and take day-trips to places of interest in the surrounding area. This alternative is particularly worthwhile if you are considering staying at a resort on the Lisbon/Estoril Coast, as these places have easy access to a number of historical towns, including the capital, Lisbon, itself.

If money is the only consideration, then without doubt the package-tour holiday-maker comes off best. Not that travelling independently in Portugal is likely to be extortionately expensive – in fact Portugal is one of the cheapest places in Europe in terms of living expenses. However, tour operators are dealing with literally thousands of customers and have a considerable buying power. They can, therefore, afford to offer accommodation to customers at lower prices than could be obtained if you were freelancing. Aside from this price difference, the only other problem facing the independent traveller is moving about the country when you get there. The options are discussed later in the chapter but, in general, you'll find the more you are willing to pay for things like train or coach travel, the better service you'll get. Accommodation prices are reasonable and there is no shortage of small hotels and pensions even in the most far-flung parts of the country.

It is entirely up to the individual's preferences and interests, then, whether you travel independently in Portugal or take a package. If you don't mind sitting back and letting all the arrangements be made for you, then a package is the ideal option. On the other hand, if you are your own boss, and don't want to be one of a crowd, going it alone in Portugal presents no insurmountable problems.

Package Holidays

Tour Operators in Britain Offering Packages to Portugal

There are almost 200 British tour operators who offer holidays in Portugal. Some of these are specialists, others offer only one or two Portuguese destinations as part of their overall package programme.

GENERAL TOUR OPERATORS

With so many tour operators going to Portugal, obviously not all of them are targetted towards certain areas of the customer market, such as golf-packages and *pousada* holidays. Many are general operators, offering standard flight, transfer and hotel arrangements. Of the many on offer we have tested the vast majority and from our personal findings we highlight the following as having something exceptional to offer:

In the lower price bracket, **Martin Rooks**, **Portland** or **Tjaereborg** are well worth looking at. Their 'no frills' approach keeps costs well down, but all are large enough companies to ensure a professional service is given and back-ups in terms of couriers and accommodation are available. This is an important service if you get to your destination only to find you are badly disappointed by the hotel and you find your courier less than helpful. In some small companies no alternative will be available.

In terms of good quality all-rounders **Thomson**, **Enterprise**, and **Intasun** are worth checking out. The market share taken up by these three companies is substantial, but it is clear why: they are all large companies of long standing, who cannot afford to let their standards drop as they have so many repeat customers, year after year. They are middle of the price range, with a wide family appeal. All offer good child discounts and they give genuine value in terms of the standard of their accommodation, professionalism of reps and flight efficiency.

For those who have enjoyed a holiday in Portugal before, but want to see a bit more of the country than the Algarve, **Enterprise** offers tours to a number of resorts right along the Portuguese coastline. In addition to standard packages to the Algarve, the Estoril Coast and Madeira, Enterprise also offers tours to destinations on the Lisbon Coast as well as the Costa Verde. This tour company is also good for the extra options it offers clients, such as fly/drive packages, a coach-tour of Portugal, and a two-centre holiday between Madeira and Porto Santo. Overall, Enterprise manages to cater both for those who just want a conventional beach holiday and for those who want a holiday with a difference, without having to pay through the nose for it.

Thomson offer good deals to resorts on the Estoril Coast. A number of destinations are available and these vary in character and atmosphere from the cosmopolitan Estoril, playground of the idle rich, to the smaller, less formal Cascais and the sleepy, traditional fishing town of Ericeira. Thomson also have a number of well priced holidays to major resorts on the Algarve Coast, and a selection of packages, featuring high-quality hotel accommodation, to Funchal in Madeira.

Intasun offer packages to the major Algarve resorts, which are particularly attractive to families with young children. Child discounts, free holidays for children and kiddies' clubs in specific hotels are a few aspects of Intasun's packages which account for their popularity among cost-conscious parents with limited finances and a couple of energetic kids to keep occupied for a two-week holiday.

Sovereign offer quality in every aspect of their tours. In Portugal's case it means that the wonderful Costa Verde and the mountain regions open up to you, and you can get into the really 'get-away-from-it-all' areas, such as the Peneda-Gerês National Park, staying in the luxury of a 12th-century convent *pousada*, which is the sort of treat generally only available to those who travel independently, with all the hassles that go with this. Sovereign are the only major company to offer tours to all five Portuguese gateways: Faro for the Algarve, Lisbon for the Lisbon and Estoril Coast, Oporto for the Costa Verde, Funchal for Madeira and Ponta Delgada for the Azores.

Olympic is another general tour operator whose brochure is worth obtaining. They are just moving into Portugal, having established themselves in the market as a Greek operator, and they are finding considerable success. They concentrate on the Algarve, offering a wide range of resorts.

There are a few other major tour companies whose brochures are worth scanning for a standard package to the Algarve: **Horizon** offer a number of packages which feature a good range of self-catering apartments or three- to five-star hotel accommodation in the main Algarve resorts, **Cosmos** deal in a mixture of self-catering and hotel deals to a number of Algarve resorts, and at the bottom end of the price-range, **Skytours** offer low-price tours to the major destinations in the Algarve.

On the following pages are the names, addresses, telephone numbers and details of all British tour operators who run holidays to Portugal. Some of these firms are relatively obscure and their brochures will not be widely available but if they specialize in the type of holiday you're after, give them a ring and request a brochure.

Every effort has been made to ensure this list of operators is comprehensive and accurate, but please remember that in the fluctuating world of the travel business, tour companies spring up and go bust with amazing regularity. If you discover any discrepancies, however, please do not hesitate to let me know.

Tour Operators

	Costa Verde	Costa de Prata	Lisbon Coast	Estoril Coast	Plains/Mountains	Algarve	Madeira	Porto Santo	Azores
(1) A Place in the Sun						•			
(2) Abbey Sun						•			
(3) Abreu Travel Agency	•	•	•	•	•	•	•		
(4) Aer Lingus Holidays (Sunbound)						•			
(5) Aer Lingus Holidays			•	•		•			
(6) Air Force	•		•			•	•		
(7) Airlink Holidays						•			
(8) Airsavers			•			•	•		
(9) Airsealand Travel	•	•	•	•		•	•		
(10) Air Tours						•			
(11) Aisling Travel (NI)						•			
(12) Albany Travel			•						
(13) Alcantara Holidays						•			
(14) Algarve Connections						•			
(15) Algarve Sun Villas						•			
(16) Allegro Holidays						•			
(17) American Express Holidays	•		•						
(18) Alblaster and Clarke	•		•		•				
(19) Arrivals							•		
(20) Arrowsmith Holidays							•		
(21) Aspro Holidays							•		
(22) Azore Holidays									•
(23) Baxter Travel		•							
(24) Beach Villas		•		•			•		
(25) Blackheath Wine Trails		•		•				•	
(26) Bladon Lines		•	•	•	•	•	•	•	•

	Costa Verde	Costa de Prata	Lisbon Coast	Estoril Coast	Plains/Mountains	Algarve	Madeira	Porto Santo	Azores
(27) Blue Horizon Holidays			•	•		•			
(28) Blue Skies Holidays			•	•		•			
(29) Bonaventure Holidays			•	•		•			
(30) Bowhills		•							
(31) Bridgeway Travel Services						•			
(32) Brittany Ferries	•	•	•	•	•	•			
(33) Budget Travel						•			
(34) Burstin Travel						•			
(35) C.C. Resorts						•			
(36) Cadogan Travel							•		
(37) Canberra Cruises			•			•	•		
(38) Caravela Tours	•	•	•	•		•	•	•	•
(39) Castaways							•		
(40) Classic Collection Holidays							•		
(41) Club Cantabrica Holidays						•			
(42) Club Méditerranée						•			
(43) Continental Villas						•			
(44) Cosmos Air			•	•		•	•		
(45) Countrywide Holidays							•		•
(46) Cresta Holidays			•	•					
(47) CTC Lines			•				•	•	•
(48) CV Travel						•			
(49) Dan Air Fly-Drive/Flyaway			•						
(50) David Sayers Travel									•
(51) Davies & Newman Travel			•			•			
(52) Designer Holidays	•		•	•		•			

	Costa Verde	Costa de Prata	Lisbon Coast	Estoril Coast	Plains/Mountains	Algarve	Madeira	Porto Santo	Azores
(53) Duggan Holidays						•			
(54) Edwin Doran Sports Travel	•		•	•		•			
(55) Electrolux Hotel Services						•			
(56) Elliot Travel						•			
(57) Enterprise (Redwing Holidays)	•		•	•		•	•	•	•
(58) Euro-Academy (Outbound)			•						
(59) Eurogolf				•		•			
(60) European Villas						•			
(61) Exotic Island Holidays							•		
(62) Explore Worldwide	•								
(63) FD Travel						•			
(64) Falcon Holidays						•			
(65) Flair Fares						•	•		
(66) Fourwinds Holidays							•		
(67) Fred Olsen Travels							•		
(68) Global Air						•			
(69) Global Overland	•								
(70) Hamilton Holidays						•			
(71) Hamilton Travel			•	•					
(72) Harlen Travel	•	•	•	•	•	•			
(73) Hartland Holidays	•	•	•	•	•	•	•		
(74) Hayes & Jarvis	•		•	•		•	•	•	
(75) Holiday Islands							•		
(76) Home and Abroad Services						•			
(77) Horizon Holidays						•			
(78) Hoseasons						•			

		Costa Verde	Costa de Prata	Lisbon Coast	Estoril Coast	Plains/Mountains	Algarve	Madeira	Porto Santo	Azores
(79)	Ibero Travel	•		•			•			
(80)	Independent Coach Travel	•					•			
(81)	Insight International Tours			•		•				
(82)	Intasun Holidays						•			
(83)	J Barter & Sons						•			
(84)	Joe Walsh Tours						•			
(85)	John Hill Travel			•	•		•	•		
(86)	Jonathan Markson						•			
(87)	Just Portugal	•	•	•	•	•	•	•	•	•
(88)	Kestours			•	•					
(89)	Lancaster Holidays						•			
(90)	Lane's Travel Service	•		•			•			
(91)	Lanzaway Holidays						•			
(92)	Latitude 40	•		•			•	•	•	•
(92a)	Leisureline						•			
(93)	Liffey Travel						•			
(94)	London Flight Centre	•		•			•			
(95)	Longmere International	•	•	•	•	•	•			
(96)	Longshot Golf Holidays			•	•		•			
(97)	Maclaine Holidays						•			
(98)	Mancunia Travel		•							
(99)	Martin Rooks Holidays	•			•		•	•		
(100)	Martyn Holidays	•	•	•	•	•	•			
(101)	Meon Villa Holidays						•			
(102)	Merchant Travel Service	•	•	•	•				•	
(103)	Meridian Holidays						•			

	Costa Verde	Costa de Prata	Lisbon Coast	Estoril Coast	Plains/Mountains	Algarve	Madeira	Porto Santo	Azores
(104) Mimosa Travel			•	•		•			
(105) Monarch Air Travel						•			
(106) Montpelier Travel						•			
(107) Multitours						•			
(108) Mundi Color Holidays	•				•				
(109) Ocean Club Watersports						•			
(110) Olympic Holidays						•			
(111) OSL						•			
(112) Osprey Holidays			•						
(113) Owners Abroad	•		•			•			
(114) Page & Moy	•	•	•	•					
(115) Palmer & Parker Holidays						•			
(116) Paloma Holidays						•			
(117) Pearls of Portugal	•	•							
(118) Penta Villas & Apartments						•			
(119) Portland Holidays						•			
(120) Portugal A La Carte	•	•	•	•	•	•	•	•	•
(121) Portugal Connections						•			
(122) Portugala Holidays	•	•	•	•	•	•	•	•	•
(123) Poundstretcher	•		•			•			
(124) Rainbow Holidays				•	•	•			
(125) Ramblers Holidays	•						•		•
(126) Rentavilla						•			
(127) Saga Holidays	•				•		•	•	
(128) Seasun							•		
(129) Select Holidays							•	•	

	Costa Verde	Costa de Prata	Lisbon Coast	Estoril Coast	Plains/Mountains	Algarve	Madeira	Porto Santo	Azores
(130) Skyplane/Skygolf Holidays			●	●		●			
(131) Skytours						●			
(132) Skyworld (Intasun)						●			
(133) Slade Travel	●		●			●			
(134) Small World Sun						●			
(135) Smith Shearings	●	●							
(136) Sol Holidays				●		●			
(137) Soler Touriste						●			
(138) Solo's						●	●		
(139) Something Special Travel						●			
(140) Southfields Travel						●			
(141) Sovereign Holidays	●		●	●		●	●		●
(142) Spes Travel		●							
(143) Stallard Holidays			●						
(144) Starvillas						●			
(145) Sunbound Holidays			●	●		●			
(146) Sunfares						●			
(147) Sunstart (Falcon)						●			
(148) Sunvil Holidays	●	●	●	●	●	●			
(149) Sunward Holidays						●			
(150) Supertravel						●			
(151) Tangney Tours		●	●						
(152) Taylings Abroad		●							
(153) The Algarve Alternative						●			
(154) The Portuguese Property Bureau						●			
(155) The Travel Club of Upminster						●			

	Costa Verde	Costa de Prata	Lisbon Coast	Estoril Coast	Plains/Mountains	Algarve	Madeira	Porto Santo	Azores
(156) The Villa Agency						•			
(157) Thomson Holidays	•		•	•	•	•	•		
(158) 3D Golf Promotion			•	•		•			
(159) Tjaereborg						•			
(160) Top Deck Travel			•			•			
(161) Top Flight Travel	•		•	•		•	•		
(162) Tradjet			•			•			
(163) Transair (Midlands)			•	•		•	•	•	
(164) Traveleads	•		•	•		•			
(165) Travelscene			•						
(166) Travtel Jet Direct						•			
(167) Travelwise						•			
(168) Trips and Travel						•			
(169) Twirltour			•	•		•	•		
(170) Unicorn Holidays	•	•	•	•	•	•	•		
(171) Unijet						•			
(172) Vacations Abroad						•			
(173) Vale do Lobo Villa Holidays						•			
(174) Villa Link Holidays						•			
(175) Villa Plus						•			
(176) Villasun Holidays						•			
(177) Villaventure						•			
(178) Villaworld						•			
(179) Villmar Travel						•			
(180) Vintage Leisure						•			
(181) Wallace Arnold Tours		•		•					

	Costa Verde	Costa de Prata	Lisbon Coast	Estoril Coast	Plains/Mountains	Algarve	Madeira	Porto Santo	Azores
(182) Waymark Holidays							●		●
(183) Windsurf Portugal		●							
(184) Wings Summer Sun						●			
(185) World of Sport							●		
(186) World Wine Tours	●	●	●	●	●		●		
(187) WTT Flights & Leisure						●			
(188) Your Choice			●	●		●			

Type of Holidays Offered:

A LA CARTE: 99, 100, 142.

AIR COACH: 3, 10, 21, 43, 44, 64, 114, 122, 127, 147, 164, 173, 184.

AIRTOURS: (All tour operators except) 36, 47, 67.

APARTMENTS & VILLAS: 1, 2, 3, 7, 9, 11, 13, 14, 16, 20, 21, 24, 26, 27, 28, 29, 30, 31, 33, 34, 35, 38, 41, 43, 44, 48, 52, 55, 56, 57, 60, 66, 68, 70, 72, 73, 76, 77, 82, 83, 84, 87, 89, 91, 92a, 93, 95, 96, 97, 99, 100, 101, 102, 103, 104, 106, 107, 110, 111, 114, 115, 116, 118, 119, 121, 122, 124, 126, 127, 129, 130, 131, 134, 136, 137, 139, 141, 144, 145, 146, 148, 149, 150, 151, 153, 154, 155, 156, 157, 158, 160, 162, 164, 165, 167, 168, 169, 170, 173, 174, 175, 176, 177, 178, 179, 180, 181, 182, 183, 187, 190.

ART CULTURE: 40, 62, 114, 127, 175.

ATHLETICS HOLIDAYS: 24, 136.

BOWLING HOLIDAYS: 104, 130.

CAMPING HOLIDAYS: 41, 128, 161.

CITY HOLIDAYS: 29, 46, 52, 57, 70, 72, 74, 95, 112, 122, 149, 158, 165, 166, 175.

CLAY PIGEON: 31, 38, 104, 156.

COACH TOURS: 3, 69, 80, 81, 122, 135, 161.

CRUISES: 37, 47, 67, 122, 129.

FISHING HOLIDAYS: 38, 40, 66, 122.

FLY-DRIVE HOLIDAYS: 1, 3, 5, 9, 11, 16, 24, 27, 29, 30, 31, 34, 38, 39, 40, 44, 49, 51, 55, 57, 72, 74, 79, 83, 85, 90, 92a, 93, 95, 97, 100, 108, 117, 118, 122, 123, 130, 136, 141, 148, 149, 150, 156, 162, 165, 171, 174, 175, 176, 182.

FOOTBALL TOURS: 9, 24.

GOLF HOLIDAYS: 1, 3, 5, 24, 31, 34, 35, 38, 42, 43, 55, 56, 57, 59, 72, 82, 83, 87, 92a, 93, 95, 96, 104, 107, 122, 130, 136, 148, 156, 158, 159, 162, 165, 174, 176, 178, 181, 188, 189.

HOLIDAYS FOR THE DISABLED: 34, 181.

MANOR HOUSES: 3, 24, 38, 72, 95, 122, 148, 149, 165.

POUSADA HOLIDAYS: 3, 29, 32, 38, 39, 44, 72, 73, 74, 85, 87, 95, 108, 117, 122, 149, 162, 165, 171, 175.

RELIGIOUS TOURS: 3, 98, 122, 127, 142.

RUGBY TOURS: 24, 28, 54, 165.

SAIL DRIVE: 32, 95, 122.

SENIOR CITIZENS' HOLIDAYS: 31, 34, 104, 114, 127, 149, 156.

SQUASH HOLIDAYS: 24, 31, 56, 122, 130, 136, 156, 174, 178.

TENNIS HOLIDAYS: 1, 24, 31, 34, 35, 38, 42, 43, 44, 55, 56, 86, 104, 107, 122, 130, 136, 156, 174, 178, 181.

WALKING HOLIDAYS: 45, 62, 66, 125, 148, 185.

WINDSURFING: 186.

WINE TOURS: 3, 25, 122, 127, 165, 189.

Tour Operators

(1) A PLACE IN THE SUN LIMITED
72 Ledbury Road, London W11 2AH
Tel: 01-221 6969. Telex: 261947.
ALGARVE.
Gatwick/Heathrow/Luton/Birmingham/Manchester/Stansted/Bristol/
Cardiff/East Midlands/Glasgow/Newcastle to Faro.

(2) ABBEY SUN
36/37 Lower Ormond Quay, Dublin 1, Ireland
Tel: 727711. Telex: 32275.
ALGARVE.
Dublin to Faro.

(3) ABREU TRAVEL AGENCY LTD
109 Westbourne Grove, London W2 4UL
Tel: 01-229 9905. Telex: 291566.
COSTA VERDE/COSTA DE PRATA/LISBON & ESTORIL COAST,
ALGARVE, PLAINS/MOUNTAINS, MADEIRA.
Heathrow/Gatwick to Lisbon, Oporto.
Heathrow to Faro, Funchal.

(4) AER LINGUS HOLIDAYS NI LTD (SUNBOUND)
56 High Street, Belfast, Northern Ireland, BT12PU
Tel: (0232) 241110. Telex: 74364.
ALGARVE.
Belfast – Faro.

(5) AER LINGUS HOLIDAYS LTD
Holiday House, 59 Dawson Street, Dublin 2, Ireland
Tel: 795030. Telex: 93776.
ESTORIL, LISBON COAST & ALGARVE.

(6) AIR FORCE (BOB WARREN TRAVEL)
104-112 Marylevone Lane, London W1M 5FU.
Tel: 01-486 0521. Telex: 295435.
COSTA VERDE, LISBON COAST, ALGARVE, MADEIRA.
Flights only.

(7) AIRLINK HOLIDAYS LTD
9 Wilton Road, London SW1V 1LL
Tel: 01-828 7682. Telex: 8814454.
ALGARVE.
Gatwick/Manchester to Faro.

(8) AIRSAVERS (HORIZON)
Broadway, Edgbaston Five Ways, Birmingham B15 1BB
Tel: 021-632 6282. Telex: 335641.
LISBON COAST, ALGARVE, MADEIRA.
Gatwick to Lisbon.
Gatwick, Birmingham, Bristol, East Midlands, Luton, Manchester,
Southend to Faro.
Flights only.

(9) AIRSEALAND TRAVEL LTD
**1 Station Approach, Kingston Road, Tolworth, Surbiton,
Surrey KT5 9NX**
Tel: 01-337 1783. Telex: 934999.
COSTA VERDE/COSTA DE PRATA/LISBON & ESTORIL
COAST/ALGARVE/MADEIRA.
Gatwick, Heathrow, Manchester to Funchal, Lisbon, Faro.
Gatwick, Heathrow to Oporto.

(10) AIRTOURS PLC
Wavell House, Holcombe Road, Helmshore, Haslingden, Rossendale,
Lancashire BB4 4NB
Tel: 0706 260000. Telex: 635126.
ALGARVE – Albufeira, Vilamoura, Praia da Rocha, Cabanas, Lagos,
Alvor.
Stansted/Cardiff/E. Midlands/Newcastle/Birmingham to Faro.

(11) AISLING TRAVEL (NI) LTD
56/58 Berry Street, Belfast BT1 1FJ
Tel: 0232 320442. Telex: 747989.
ALGARVE.
Belfast to Faro.

(12) ALBANY TRAVEL (MANCHESTER) LTD
190 Deansgate, Manchester M3 3WD
Tel: 061-833 0202. Telex: 667174.
LISBON COAST.
Heathrow to Lisbon.

(13) ALCANTARA HOLIDAYS
98/99 Westgate, Grantham, Lincs. NG31 6LE
Tel: 0476 74111. Telex: 377500.
ALGARVE.
Gatwick/East Midlands/Manchester/Glasgow to Faro.

(14) ALGARVE CONNECTIONS (PRESTBURY TRAVEL)
Swanwich House, Prestbury, Cheshire CK10 4DG
Tel: 0625 827746. Telex: 666621.
ALGARVE.

(15) ALGARVE SUN VILLAS
36 Nottingham Road, Gotham, Nottingham NG11 0HG
Tel: 0602 830912. Telex: 377855.
ALGARVE.
Gatwick/Luton/Manchester/E. Midlands/Birmingham/Cardiff/Glasgow/
Newcastle to Faro.

(16) ALLEGRO HOLIDAYS
15a Church Street, Reigate, Surrey RH2 0AA
Tel: 0737 221323. Telex: 919114.
ALGARVE.
Gatwick to Faro.

(17) AMERICAN EXPRESS HOLIDAYS
Portland House, Stag Place, London SW1E 5BZ
Tel: 01-924 2889. Telex: 266162.
COSTA VERDE/LISBON.
Heathrow to Lisbon.
Gatwick to Faro/Lisbon/Oporto.

(18) ALBLASTER & CLARKE
104 Church Road, Steep, Petersfield GU32 2DD
Tel: 0730 66883.
COSTA VERDE/LISBON COAST/PLAINS.
Gatwick to Lisbon.

(19) ARRIVALS
841 High Road, London E11 1HH
Tel: 01-539 5555. Telex: 27576.
ALGARVE.
Gatwick, Manchester to Faro.
Flights only.

(20) ARROWSMITH HOLIDAYS
Royal Buildings, 2 Mosley Street, Manchester, M2 3AB
Tel: 061 236 2361. Telex: 669787.
ALGARVE.

(21) ASPRO HOLIDAYS
42 Bute Street, Cardiff CF1 6AL
Tel: 0222 484151. Telex: 497168.
ALGARVE.
Cardiff/Bristol/Belfast to Faro.

(22) AZORE HOLIDAYS
23 Golden Square, London W1R 3AD
Tel: 01-439 6841. Telex: 296518.
AZORES.

(23) BAXTER TRAVEL
23 Market Place, Holt, Norfolk NR25 6SE
Tel: 0263 712621. Telex: 975222.
COSTA VERDE.

(24) BEACH VILLAS LTD
8 Market Passage, Cambridge CB2 3QR
Tel: 0223 311113. Telex: 817428.
COSTA VERDE/ESTORIL COAST/ALGARVE.
Gatwick, Luton, Manchester, Birmingham, East Midlands, Glasgow,
Stansted, Bristol to Faro.
Gatwick to Oporto.
Glasgow to Lisbon.

(25) BLACKHEATH WINE TRAILS
13 Blackheath Village, London SE3 9LD
Tel: 01-463 0012. Telex: 896131.
COSTA VERDE/ESTORIL COAST/MADEIRA.
Heathrow/Gatwick to Porto, Faro.
Gatwick to Funchal.
Heathrow to Lisbon.

---

(26) BLADON LINES ALTERNATIVES
56/58 Putney High Street, London SW15 1SF
Tel: 01-785 9999. Telex: 295221.
Tailor-made holidays anywhere in Portugal.

---

(27) BLUE HORIZON HOLIDAYS LTD
9 Caledonia Place, St. Helier, Jersey C.I.
Tel: 0534 34117. Telex: 4192330.
LISBON & ESTORIL COASTS/ALGARVE.
Jersey to Faro, Lisbon.

---

(28) BLUE SKIES HOLIDAYS
59 Dawson Street, Dublin 2, Ireland
Tel: 0001 795030. Telex: 93776.
LISBON & ESTORIL COASTS/ALGARVE.
Cardiff, Cork, Dublin to Faro.
Cork, Dublin to Lisbon.

---

(29) BONAVENTURE HOLIDAYS
5 Kensington Church Street, London W8 4LD
Tel: 01-938 3671. Telex: 8813513.
LISBON & ESTORIL COASTS/ALGARVE.
Gatwick to Faro, Lisbon.

---

(30) BOWHILLS LIMITED
Mayhill Lane, Swanmore, Southampton SO3 2QW
Tel: 0489 877627. Telex: 477417.
COSTA DE PRATA.
Gatwick to Lisbon.

---

(31) BRIDGEWAY TRAVEL SERVICES LIMITED
Emerson House, Heyes Lane, Alderley Edge, Cheshire SK9 7LF
Tel: 0625 584531. Telex: 669197.
ALGARVE.
Birmingham, Gatwick, Manchester to Faro.

---

(32) BRITTANY FERRIES
Millbay Docks, Plymouth PL1 3EW
Tel: 0752 221321. Telex: 45380.
COSTA VERDE – LISBON & ESTORIL COAST – ALGARVE –
COSTA DE PRATA – MOUNTAINS – PLAINS.

---

(33) BUDGET TRAVEL
140 Lr. Baggot Street, Dublin 2, Ireland
Tel: 613122. Telex: 30496.
ALGARVE.
Dublin to Faro.

---

(34) BURSTIN TRAVEL
Palace Hotel, Pier Hill, Southend on Sea, Essex SS1 2AJ
Tel: 0702 613011. Telex: 99268.
ALGARVE.
Southend to Faro.

---

(35) C. C. RESORTS LTD
9 Galena Road, London W6 0LT
Tel: 01-748 4446. Telex: 916543.
ALGARVE.

---

(36) CADOGAN TRAVEL LTD
9/10 Portland Street, Southampton SO9 1ZP
Tel: 0703 332551. Telex: 477061.
MADEIRA.
Gatwick/Heathrow to Funchal.

---

(37) CANBERRA CRUISES
77 New Oxford Street, London WC1A 1PP
Tel: 01-831 1331. Telex: 885551.
LISBON/ALGARVE/MADEIRA.

---

(38) CARAVELA TOURS
3rd Floor, Gillingham House, 38/44 Gillingham Street,
London SW1V 1JW
Tel: 01-630 9223. Telex: 918251.
COSTA VERDE/COSTA DE PRATA/LISBON & ESTORIL
COAST/ALGARVE/MADEIRA/AZORES.
Heathrow/Dublin/Manchester to Lisbon.
Heathrow to Oporto/Funchal/Azores.
Heathrow/Gatwick/Dublin/Manchester to Faro.

---

(39) CASTAWAYS
Carew House, Station Approach, Wallington, Surrey SM6 0DG
Tel: 01-773 2616. Telex: 8952244.
MADEIRA.
Gatwick, Heathrow, Manchester to Funchal.

---

(40) CLASSIC COLLECTION HOLIDAYS
9 Liverpool Terrace, Worthing, West Sussex BN11 1TA
Tel: 0903 823088.
MADEIRA.
Gatwick, Heathrow to Funchal.

---

(41) CLUB CANTABRICA HOLIDAYS LTD
146-148 London Road, St. Albans, Herts AL1 1PQ
Tel: 0727 66177. Telex: 8814162.
ALGARVE.
Gatwick/Manchester to Faro.

---

(42) CLUB MEDITERRANEE
106-108 Brompton Road, London SW3 1JJ
Tel: 01-581 1161. Telex: 299221.
ALGARVE.
Gatwick to Faro.

---

(43) CONTINENTAL VILLAS
Eagle House, 58 Blythe Road, London W14 0HA
Tel: 01-371 1313. Telex: 918054.
ALGARVE.

---

(44) COSMOS AIR PLC
17 Homesdale Road, Bromley, Kent BR2 9LX
Tel: 01-464 3400. Telex: 896458.
ALGARVE/LISBON & ESTORIL COASTS/MADEIRA.
Gatwick/Luton/Bristol/Birmingham/Manchester/Glasgow/E. Midlands/
Cardiff/Stansted/Newcastle to Faro.
Gatwick/Heathrow/Manchester to Funchal.
Heathrow/Manchester/Edinburgh to Lisbon.

---

(45) COUNTRYWIDE HOLIDAYS
Birch Heys, Cromwell Range, Manchester M14 6HU
Tel: 061-225 1000. Telex: 667047.
MADEIRA/AZORES.

---

(46) CRESTA HOLIDAYS
32 Victoria Street, Altrincham, Cheshire
Tel: 061-927 7000. Telex: 667171.
LISBON & ESTORIL COASTS.
Heathrow/Manchester to Lisbon.
Gatwick to Oporto.
Glasgow to Lisbon.

(47) CTC LINES
1 Regent Street, London SW1Y 4NN
Tel: 01-930 5833. Telex: 917193.
LISBON, AZORES & MADEIRA CRUISES.

(48) CV TRAVEL
43 Cadogan Street, London SW3 2PR
Tel: 01-581 0851. Telex: 919773.
ALGARVE.
Heathrow to Faro.

(49) DAN AIR FLY-DRIVE & FLYAWAY HOLIDAYS
Norway House, 21 Cockspur Street, London SW1Y 5BN
Tel: 01-930 5881. Telex: 8951292.
LISBON COAST.

(50) DAVID SAYERS TRAVEL
10 Barley Mow Passage, London W4 4PH
Tel: 01-995 3642. Telex: 9419369.
AZORES.

(51) DAVIES & NEWMAN TRAVEL
Norway House, 21 Cockspur Street, London SW1Y 5BN
Tel: 01-930 5881. Telex: 8951292.
LISBON COAST/ALGARVE.
Gatwick to Lisbon and Faro.

(52) DESIGNER HOLIDAYS (BOB WARREN TRAVEL)
104 Marylebone Lane, London W1M 5FU
Tel: 01-486 1315. Telex: 295435.
COSTA VERDE, LISBON & ESTORIL COASTS, ALGARVE.
Gatwick to Porto and Lisbon.
Gatwick and Birmingham to Faro.

(53) DUGGAN HOLIDAYS
20 Mount Pleasant, Liverpool L3 5RY
Tel: 051-709 3111. Telex: 627226.
ALGARVE.
Manchester to Faro.

(54) EDWIN DORAN SPORTS TRAVEL
9 York Street, Twickenham TW1 3JZ
Tel: 01-892 0011. Telex: 8951916.
COSTA VERDE/LISBON & ESTORIL COASTS/ALGARVE.
Gatwick, Heathrow, Luton, Manchester to Lisbon and Faro.

(55) ELECTROLUX HOTEL SERVICES LTD
5-6 Market Place, Wallingford, Oxford OX10 0EG
Tel: 0491 32245. Telex: 848839.
ALGARVE.

(56) ELLIOTT TRAVEL
31 St. George Street, London W1R 9FA
Tel: 01-491 2677. Telex: 264875.
ALGARVE.
Heathrow/Gatwick/Birmingham/Bristol/E. Midlands/Glasgow/Luton/
Manchester/Stansted to Faro.

(57) ENTERPRISE (REDWING HOLIDAYS)
Groundstar House, London Road, Crawley, West Sussex RH10 2TB
Tel: 0293 517866. Telex: 878791.
COSTA VERDE, LISBON AND ESTORIL COASTS, ALGARVE,
MADEIRA, AZORES.
Gatwick and Manchester to Lisbon and Funchal.
Gatwick, Heathrow, Birmingham, Bristol, East Midlands, Glasgow,
Luton, Manchester, Stansted to Faro.

(58) EURO-ACADEMY (OUTBOUND) LTD
77a George Street, Croydon CR0 1LD
Tel: 01-686 2363. Telex: 943604.
LISBON COAST.

(59) EUROGOLF LIMITED
36 London Road, St Albans, Herts AL1 1LA
Tel: 0727 42256. Telex: 927822.
ESTORIL COAST/ALGARVE.

(60) EUROPEAN VILLAS
154 Victoria Road, Cambridge CB4 3DZ
Tel: 0223 314220. Telex: 818166.
ALGARVE.
Gatwick/Manchester to Faro.

(61) EXOTIC ISLAND HOLIDAYS
35 High Street, Tring HP23 4AB
Tel: 044282 8555. Telex: 826170.
MADEIRA.
Gatwick/Manchester to Funchal.

(62) EXPLORE WORLDWIDE LTD
7 High Street, Aldershot, Hants GU11 1BH
Tel: (0252) 319448. Telex: 858954.
COSTA VERDE.

---

(63) F D TRAVEL
5 Barleyfield, Brentwood, Essex, CM15 0BB
Tel: 0277 72339. Telex: 995342.
ALGARVE.

---

(64) FALCON HOLIDAYS
33 Notting Hill Gate, London W11 3JQ
Tel: 01-221 6298. Telex: 883256.
ALGARVE.
Gatwick/Luton/Bristol/East Midlands/Birmingham/Glasgow/Dublin/Cork/
Edinburgh/Manchester/Newcastle/Belfast to Faro.

---

(65) FLAIR FARES
Groundstar House, London Road, Crawley, West Sussex RH10 2TB
Tel: 0293 517866. Telex: 878791.
ALGARVE/MADEIRA.
Gatwick, Heathrow, Newcastle, Manchester to Funchal.
Gatwick, Heathrow to Oporto, Lisbon.
Gatwick, Heathrow, Birmingham, Bristol, East Midlands, Glasgow,
Manchester, Newcastle, Stansted to Faro.
Flights only.

---

(66) FOURWINDS HOLIDAYS
Eastgate Chambers, Market Way, Eastgate Street, Gloucester
GL1 1QQ
Tel: 0452 24151. Telex: 43689.
MADEIRA.
Gatwick to Funchal.

---

(67) FRED OLSEN TRAVEL
Crown House, Crown Street, Ipswich, Suffolk IP1 3HD
Tel: 0473 233022. Telex: 98536.
MADEIRA.

---

(68) GLOBAL AIR
26 Elmfield Road, Bromley BR1 1LR
Tel: 01-464 6666. Telex: 8953010.
ALGARVE.
Heathrow/Gatwick/Belfast/Birmingham/Bristol/Cardiff/Dublin/East
Midlands/Glasgow/Jersey/Luton/Manchester/Newcastle/Stansted to Faro.

(69) GLOBAL OVERLAND
Gelderd Road, Leeds LS12 6DH
Tel: 0532 636456. Telex: 55482.
COSTA VERDE.

(70) HAMILTON HOLIDAYS LTD
23/31 Waring Street, Belfast BT1 2EQ
Tel: 0232 231265. Telex: 747485.
ALGARVE.
Belfast to Faro.

(71) HAMILTON TRAVEL
3 Heddon Street, London W1R 7LE
Tel: 01-437 4627. Telex: 299176.
LISBON & ESTORIL COASTS.
Gatwick and Heathrow to Lisbon.

(72) HARLEN TRAVEL LTD
13 Hurst Lane, East Molesey, Surrey KT8 9EA
Tel: 01-941 3366. Telex: 917407.
COSTA DE PRATA/LISBON & ESTORIL COAST/ALGARVE/COSTA
VERDE/MOUNTAINS/PLAINS.
Gatwick/Heathrow/Edinburgh/Glasgow/Manchester to Lisbon, Faro.
Gatwick/Heathrow to Oporto.

(73) HARTLAND HOLIDAYS
91 Brunswick Crescent, London N11 1EE
Tel: 01-368 4422. Telex: 23596.
COSTA VERDE/COSTA DE PRATA/LISBON & ESTORIL
COASTS/MOUNTAINS/PLAINS/ALGARVE/MADEIRA.
Heathrow/Gatwick/Manchester to Lisbon/Faro.
Heathrow/Gatwick to Oporto.

(74) HAYES & JARVIS LTD.
6 Harriet Street, London SW1X 9JP
Tel: 01-235 3061. Telex: 23759.
COSTA VERDE/LISBON & ESTORIL COAST/ALGARVE/
MADEIRA/PORTO SANTO.
Gatwick/Heathrow to Faro, Lisbon, Oporto, Funchal.

(75) HOLIDAY ISLANDS
10 East Barnet Road, New Barnet, Herts EN4 8RW
Tel: 01-538 5544. Telex: 264681.
MADEIRA.
Gatwick, Heathrow to Funchal.

(76) HOME AND ABROAD SERVICES
7 Wexford Street, Dublin 2, Ireland
Tel: 0001 751177. Telex: 90703.
ALGARVE.

---

(77) HORIZON HOLIDAYS
Broadway, Edgbaston, Five Ways, Birmingham B15 1BB
Tel: 021-643 2727. Telex: 335641.
ALGARVE.
Gatwick, Luton, Stansted, Bristol, Birmingham, East Midlands,
Manchester to Faro.

---

(78) HOSEASONS LTD
Sunway House, Lowestoft, Suffolk MR32 3LT
Tel: 0502 500555. Telex: 975189.
ALGARVE.

---

(79) IBERO TRAVEL LTD
Palladium House, 1/4 Argyll St., London W1V 1AD
Tel: 01-437 6996. Telex: 23410.
COSTA VERDE/LISBON/ALGARVE.
Gatwick to Lisbon/Oporto/Faro.
Manchester to Faro.

---

(80) INDEPENDENT COACH TRAVEL
Blake House, Admirals Way, Waterside, London E14
Tel: 01-538 4627. Telex: 894576.
COSTA VERDE/ALGARVE.

---

(81) INSIGHT INTERNATIONAL TOURS LTD
26 Cockspur Street, London SW1Y 5BY
Tel: 01-839 7060. Telex: 8953901.
LISBON/MOUNTAINS.

---

(82) INTASUN HOLIDAYS
2 Cromwell Avenue, Bromley, Kent BR2 9AQ
Tel: 01-290 0511. Telex: 896089.
ALGARVE.
Gatwick/Luton/Cardiff/Bristol/Manchester/Birmingham/Newcastle/
Glasgow/Belfast/East Midlands/Heathrow/Stansted to Faro.

---

(83) J. BARTER & SONS LTD
92 Patrick Street, Cork, Ireland
Tel: 274261. Telex: 76023.
ALGARVE.
Cork to Faro.

(84) JOE WALSH TOURS
8-11 Lower Baggot Street, Dublin 2
Tel: 789555. Telex: 30537.
ALGARVE.
Dublin/Belfast to Faro.

(85) JOHN HILL TRAVEL (S&L) LTD
Herbel House, 25 High Street, Belfast BT1 2AA
Tel: 0232 232331. Telex: 747336.
LISBON & ESTORIL COAST/ALGARVE/MADEIRA.

(86) JONATHAN MARKSON ALGARVE TENNIS CENTRE
Hertford College, Oxford OX1 3BW
Tel: 01-386 8682. Telex: 915337.
ALGARVE.

(87) JUST PORTUGAL
170 New Bond Street, London W1Y 9PB
Tel: 01-493 8172. Telex: 295228.
COSTA VERDE/COSTA DE PRATA/LISBON/ESTORIL
COAST/ALGARVE/MADEIRA/AZORES/MOUNTAINS/PLAINS.

(88) KESTOURS LTD
Travel House, Elmers End, Beckenham, Kent BR3 3QY
Tel: 01-658 7313. Telex: 896007.
LISBON & ESTORIL COASTS.

(89) LANCASTER HOLIDAYS
26 Elmfield Road, Bromley, Kent BR1 1LR
Tel: 01-290 1322. Telex: 8953010.
ALGARVE.
Heathrow/Stansted/Gatwick/Luton/Cardiff/Bristol/Manchester/
Birmingham/Newcastle/Glasgow/Belfast/East Midlands to Faro.

(90) LANE'S TRAVEL SERVICE LTD
251 Brompton Road, London SW3 2EY
Tel: 01-584 8541. Telex: 918009.
COSTA VERDE/LISBON COAST/ALGARVE.

(91) LANZAWAY HOLIDAYS LTD
The Old Barn, Deane's Close, Stocks Lane, Stevenson, Abingdon,
Oxon OX13 6SY
Tel: 0235 835133. Telex: 9402676.
ALGARVE.
Gatwick, Birmingham, Bristol, East Midlands, Glasgow, Luton,
Manchester to Faro.

(92) LATITUDE 40
13 Beauchamp Place, London SW3 1NQ
Tel: 01-581 1861. Telex: 269482.
COSTA VERDE/LISBON COAST/ALGARVE.
MADEIRA/AZORES.

(92a) LEISURELINE (SUNSET HOLIDAYS)
258 Finney Lane, Herald Green, Stockport SK8 3QD
Tel: 061-499 1991. Telex: 665671.
ALGARVE.
Luton, Manchester to Faro.

(93) LIFFEY TRAVEL
Abbey Mall, 13 Lower Liffey Street, Dublin 1, Ireland
Tel: 0001 734900. Telex: 33573.
ALGARVE.
Dublin to Faro.

(94) LONDON FLIGHT CENTRE
47 Notting Hill Gate, London W11 3JS
Tel: 01-727 4290.
COSTA VERDE, LISBON COAST, ALGARVE.
Flights only.

(95) LONGMERE INTERNATIONAL LIMITED
64 Shirley Road, Croydon CR0 7EP
Tel: 01-656 6545. Telex: 9413257.
COSTA VERDE, COSTA DE PRATA, LISBON & ESTORIL COASTS,
MOUNTAINS, PLAINS, ALGARVE.

(96) LONGSHOT GOLF HOLIDAYS
Meon House, College Street, Petersfield, Hants. GU32 3JN
Tel: 0730 68621. Telex: 86181.
ESTORIL & LISBON COAST/ALGARVE.
Gatwick to Lisbon/Faro.
Birmingham to Faro.

(97) MACLAINE HOLIDAYS LTD
35 Sandford Mill Road, Cheltenham, Glos. GL53 7QH
Tel: 0242 519508. Telex: 43345.
ALGARVE.
Gatwick/Birmingham/Bristol/Manchester/Stansted to Faro.

(98) MANCUNIA TRAVEL LTD
Peter House, 2 Oxford Street, Manchester M1 5AW
Tel: 061-228 2842. Telex: 667630.
COSTA DE PRATA.
Heathrow, Manchester to Faro.

(99) MARTIN ROOKS HOLIDAYS
204 Ebury Street, London SW1W 8UU
Tel: 01-730 0808. Telex: 878791.
ALGARVE – Albufeira, Praia da Rocha, Alvor, Monte Gordo, Carvoeiro.
ESTORIL – Estoril, Cascais. MADEIRA – Funchal. COSTA VERDE –
Esponde, Viano do Castelo.
Gatwick/Manchester to Lisbon, Funchal.
Gatwick/Manchester/Birmingham/Luton/Stansted/East Midlands/Bristol/
Glasgow/Newcastle to Faro.
Gatwick/Manchester to Funchal.
Gatwick to Oporto.

(100) MARTYN HOLIDAYS
Westleigh House, 390 London Road, Isleworth, Middlesex TW7 5AD
Tel: 01-847 5955. Telex: 24669.
COSTA DE PRATA – Sao Martinho do Porto, Figueira da Foz.
LISBON/ESTORIL COAST – Cascais, Ericeira. ALGARVE – Vilamoura,
Olhos d'Agua, Praia de Oura, Albufeira, Castelo, Sao Rafael, Vale da
Parra, Armacao de Pera, Praia da Rocha, Alvor, Lagos, Praia da Luz,
Burgau.
Gatwick/Manchester to Lisbon.
Gatwick/Birmingham/Bristol/Cardiff/East Midlands/Glasgow/Luton/
Manchester/Edinburgh/Stansted/Belfast/Cork/Dublin to Faro.
Gatwick to Porto.

(101) MEON VILLA HOLIDAYS
Meon House, College Street, Petersfield, Hampshire GU32 3JN
Tel: 0730 68411. Telex: 86181.
ALGARVE.
Gatwick/Birmingham/Manchester to Faro.

(102) MERCHANT TRAVEL SERVICE/VILLA CONNECTIONS
104 Marylebone Lane, London W1M 5FU
Tel: 01-486 1577. Telex: 295435.
COSTA VERDE, COSTA DE PRATA, LISBON AND ESTORIL
COASTS, MADEIRA.

(103) MERIDIAN HOLIDAYS
12-16 Dering Street, London W1R 9AE
Tel: 01-493 2777. Telex: 22633.
ALGARVE.
Gatwick/Heathrow/Birmingham/Glasgow to Faro.

---

(104) MIMOSA TRAVEL LTD
21 Cleveleys Road, Accrington, Lancs BB5 5ET
Tel: 0254 35608. Telex: 635562.
LISBON & ESTORIL COASTS, ALGARVE.
Gatwick to Lisbon and Faro.

---

(105) MONARCH AIR TRAVEL
Halcyon House, Percival Way, Luton Airport, LU2 9NU
Tel: 0582 400000. Telex: 827687.
ALGARVE.
Heathrow/Gatwick/Luton/Birmingham/Manchester/Glasgow/Bristol/
Cardiff/East Midlands/Newcastle/Stansted to Faro.

---

(106) MONTPELIER TRAVEL LTD
17 Montpelier Street, London SW7 1HG
Tel: 01-589 3400. Telex: 916087.
ALGARVE.

---

(107) MULTITOURS
21 Sussex Street, London SW1V 4RR
Tel: 01-821 7000. Telex: 917911.
ALGARVE.

---

(108) MUNDI COLOR HOLIDAYS
276 Vauxhall Bridge Road, London SW1V 1BE
Tel: 01-834 3492. Telex: 21168.
COSTA VERDE/MOUNTAINS/PLAINS.

---

(109) OCEAN CLUB WATERSPORTS SCHOOL
204 Amyand Park Road, St Margaret's, Twickenham TW1 3HY
Tel: 01-876 6635.
ALGARVE.

---

(110) OLYMPIC HOLIDAYS LTD
30 Cross Street, Islington, London N1 2BG
Tel: 01-359 3500. Telex: 935628.
ALGARVE.
Gatwick, Birmingham, Glasgow, Luton, Manchester, Newcastle, Stansted
to Faro.

---

(111) OSL
Broadway, Edgbaston Five Ways, Birmingham B15 1BB
Tel: 021-632 6282. Telex: 335641.
ALGARVE – Lagos, Luz Bay, Colinas Verdes, Quinta da Larga Vista,
Armacao de Pera, Albufeira, Guia, Praria d'Oura, Vilamoura, Vale do
Lobo, Garrao, Sao Lourenco, Santa Barbara de Nexe, Quinta da Hollanda,
Quinta das Raposeiras, Loule.
Gatwick, Birmingham, Bristol, East Midlands, Luton, Manchester,
Stansted to Faro.

(112) OSPREY HOLIDAYS LTD
110b St. Stephen Street, Edinburgh EH3 5AQ
Tel: 031 226 2467. Telex: 727285.
LISBON COAST – Lisbon.
Heathrow to Lisbon.

(113) OWNERS ABROAD
Valentine House, Ilford Hill, Ilford, Essex IG1 2DG
Tel: 01-514 4000. Telex: 8954306.
COSTA VERDE, LISBON COAST, ALGARVE.
Flights only.

(114) PAGE AND MOY
136-140 London Road, Leicester LE2 1EN
Tel: 0533 542000. Telex: 34583.
COSTA VERDE/COSTA DE PRATA/LISBON & ESTORIL COAST.
Heathrow to Lisbon/Faro/Oporto.

(115) PALMER & PARKER HOLIDAYS
63 Grosvenor Street, London W1X 0AJ
Tel: 01-493 5125. Telex: 24520.
ALGARVE – Quinta do Lago, Vale do Lobo, Garao, Albufeira, Carvoeiro,
Penina, Lagos, Praia da Luz.
Gatwick/Heathrow/Manchester to Faro.

(116) PALOMA HOLIDAYS LTD
6 Farncombe Road, Worthing, West Sussex BN11 2BE
Tel: 0903 820710. Telex: 878632.
ALGARVE.
Gatwick to Faro.

(117) PEARLS OF PORTUGAL
Riverside Centre, 46 High Street, Kingston, Surrey KT1 1HN
Tel: 01-541 5400. Telex: 933132.
COSTA VERDE, COSTA DE PRATA.

(118) PENTA VILLAS & APARTMENTS
51 Chessington Way, West Wickham, Kent BR4 9NY
Tel: 01-777 2300.
ALGARVE.
Gatwick/Heathrow/Birmingham/Bristol/Cardiff/East Midlands/Glasgow/
Luton/Manchester/Newcastle/Stansted to Faro.

(119) PORTLAND HOLIDAYS
218 Great Portland Street, London W1N 5HG
Tel: 01-388 5111. Telex: 299126.
ALGARVE – Albufeira, Vale do Garrão, Quarteira.
Gatwick/Manchester to Faro.

(120) PORTUGAL A LA CARTE
13 Beauchamp Place, London SW3 1NQ
Tel: 01-581 3104. Telex: 269482.
COSTA VERDE – COSTA DE PRATA – LISBON/ESTORIL COAST –
MADEIRA – AZORES – ALGARVE – PLAINS – MOUNTAINS.

(121) PORTUGAL CONNECTIONS LTD
29 South Street, Chichester, West Sussex PO19 1EL
Tel: 0243 776211. Telex: 869272.
ALGARVE.
Gatwick, Heathrow, Birmingham, Bristol, Cardiff, East Midlands,
Edinburgh, Exeter, Glasgow, Luton, Manchester, Newcastle, Stansted to
Faro.

(122) PORTUGALA HOLIDAYS
290 Muswell Hill Broadway, London N10 2QR
Tel: 01-444 1857/8. Telex: 9419557.
COSTA VERDE/COSTA DE PRATA/LISBON COAST/ESTORIL
COAST/ALGARVE/MADEIRA/AZORES/MOUNTAINS/PLAINS.
Heathrow/Gatwick to Oporto.
Heathrow/Gatwick/Manchester to Lisbon/Faro/Funchal.

(123) POUNDSTRETCHER
Atlantic House, Hazelwick Avenue, Three Bridges, Crawley RH10 1YS
Tel: 0293 518060. Telex: 877455.
COSTA VERDE, LISBON COAST, ALGARVE.
Gatwick to Oporto.
Heathrow to Lisbon.
Gatwick, Heathrow, Birmingham to Faro.

(124) RAINBOW HOLIDAYS – RAINBOW SUNSHINERS
Ryedale Buildings, Piccadilly, York Y01 1PN
Tel: 0904 643355. Telex: 57476.
ALGARVE/LISBON & ESTORIL COASTS.

(125) RAMBLERS HOLIDAYS LIMITED
Box 43, Welwyn Garden City, Herts AL8 6PQ
Tel: 0707 331133. Telex: 24642.
COSTA VERDE/MOUNTAINS/MADEIRA/AZORES.
Gatwick to Faro/Oporto/Funchal.

(126) RENTAVILLA LTD
27 High Street, Chesterton, Cambridge CB4 1ND
Tel: 0223 323414. Telex: 817489.
ALGARVE.
Gatwick, Dublin, Luton, Manchester, Newcastle, Stansted to Faro.

(127) SAGA HOLIDAYS PLC
Saga House, Middelburg Square, Folkestone, Kent CT20 1AZ
Tel: 0303 47000. Telex: 966331.
ALGARVE/ESTORIL COAST/MADEIRA/COSTA VERDE.
Gatwick to Faro/Lisbon/Funchal/Oporto.

(128) SEASUN HOLIDAYS
71 East Hill, Colchester, Essex CO1 2QW
Tel: 0206 869888. Telex: 987726.
ALGARVE.

(129) SELECT HOLIDAYS
Centurion House, Bircherley Street, Hertford, Herts. SG14 1BH
Tel: 0992 554144. Telex: 817848.
ALGARVE/MADEIRA.
Gatwick, Birmingham, Cardiff, Luton, Belfast, Bristol, Glasgow, East
Midlands, Heathrow, Manchester, Newcastle to Faro.
Gatwick, Manchester to Funchal.

(130) SKYPLANE/SKYGOLF HOLIDAYS
327 Lincoln Road, Peterborough PE1 2PF
Tel: 0733 67434. Telex: 32150.
LISBON & ESTORIL COASTS, ALGARVE.
Edinburgh, Luton, Manchester to Lisbon.
Gatwick, Luton, Manchester to Faro.

(131) SKYTOURS
Greater London House, Hampstead Road, London NW1 7SD
Tel: 01-387 9699.
ALGARVE.
Gatwick, Manchester to Faro.

(132) SKYWORLD (INTASUN)
2 Cromwell Avenue, Bromley, Kent BR2 9AQ
Tel: 01-290 6677. Telex: 896089.
ALGARVE.
Gatwick, Luton, Cardiff, Bristol, Birmingham, E. Midlands, Manchester,
Stansted, Newcastle, Glasgow to Faro.

(133) SLADE TRAVEL LTD
15 Vivian Avenue, London NW4 3UT
Tel: 01-202 0111. Telex: 23425.
LISBON COAST/COSTA VERDE/ALGARVE.
Gatwick/Heathrow to Lisbon, Oporto.
Flights only.

(134) SMALL WORLD SUN
2 Mount Lion, Tunbridge Wells, Kent TN1 1VE
Tel: 0892 511733. Telex: 94070357.
ALGARVE.
Gatwick to Faro.

(135) SMITH SHEARINGS/NATIONAL HOLIDAYS
George House, George Street, Wakefield WF1 1LY
Tel: 0924 383838. Telex: 55335.
COSTA VERDE, COSTA DE PRATA.

(136) SOL HOLIDAYS LTD
Churchfield House, 45-51 Woodhouse Road, London N12 9ET
Tel: 01-466 8500. Telex: 929692.
ALGARVE/ESTORIL COAST.
Gatwick, Luton, Manchester, Glasgow, Birmingham, Bristol, East
Midlands, Newcastle, Stansted to Faro.
Gatwick, Heathrow, Manchester to Lisbon.

(137) SOLER TOURISTE
Cox Lane, Chessington, Surrey KT9 1SN
Tel: 01-391 2525. Telex: 928364.
ALGARVE.
Gatwick to Faro.

(138) SOLO'S LTD
41 Watford Way, Hendon, London NW4 3JH
Tel: 01-202 0855. Telex: 923149.
ALGARVE/MADEIRA.
Gatwick to Funchal/Faro.
Glasgow, Manchester to Funchal.

(139) SOMETHING SPECIAL TRAVEL LTD
31 Maidenhead Street, Hertford, Herts SG14 1AN
Tel: 0992 552231. Telex: 818168
ALGARVE.
Gatwick, Heathrow, Birmingham, Bristol, Cardiff, East Midlands, Edinburgh, Exeter, Glasgow, Luton, Manchester, Newcastle, Stansted to Faro.

(140) SOUTHFIELDS TRAVEL LTD
241 Wimbledon Park Road, London SW18 1RJ
Tel: 01-874 9019. Telex: 8954514.
ALGARVE

(141) SOVEREIGN HOLIDAYS (REDWING HOLIDAYS)
Groundstar House, London Road, Crawley, West Sussex RH10 2TB
Tel: 0293 561444. Telex: 878791.
COSTA VERDE, LISBON & ESTORIL COASTS, ALGARVE, MADEIRA, AZORES.
Gatwick, Heathrow, Manchester to Funchal, Lisbon.
Gatwick, Heathrow to Porto.
Gatwick, Heathrow, Birmingham, Bristol, East Midlands, Glasgow, Luton, Manchester to Faro.

(142) SPES TRAVEL
18 Churton Street, London SW1V 2LL
Tel: 01-821 5144. Telex: 266263.
COSTA DE PRATA.
Heathrow to Lisbon.

(143) STALLARD HOLIDAYS
29 Stoke Newington Road, London N16 8BL
Tel: 01-254 6444. Telex: 265010.
LISBON COAST.
Gatwick, Heathrow to Lisbon.

(144) STARVILLAS LTD
25 High Street, Chesterton, Cambridge, CB4 1ND
Tel: 0223 241110. Telex: 74364.
ALGARVE.
Gatwick/Luton/Manchester/Dublin/Stansted to Faro.

(145) SUNBOUND HOLIDAYS
56 High Street, Belfast BT1 2PU
Tel: 0232 241110. Telex: 74364.
59 Dawson Street, Dublin 2, Ireland
Tel: 0001 795030. Telex: 93776.
LISBON & ESTORIL COASTS, ALGARVE.
Belfast, Dublin, Cork, Edinburgh to Lisbon.
Belfast, Cork, Dublin to Faro.

(146) SUNFARES (FALCON LEISURE GROUP)
35 Virginia Street, Glasgow G1 3TX
Tel: 041-552 5382. Telex: 779480.
ALGARVE.
Glasgow to Faro.

(147) SUNSTART (FALCON LEISURE GROUP)
33 Notting Hill Gate, London W11 3JQ
Tel: 01-221 6298. Telex: 883256.
ALGARVE.
Gatwick, Birmingham, Bristol, East Midlands, Edinburgh, Glasgow,
Luton, Manchester, Newcastle to Faro.

(148) SUNVIL HOLIDAYS
Sunvil House, 7-8 Upper Square, Old Isleworth, Middlesex TW7 7BJ
Tel: 01-568 4499. Telex: 8951529.
COSTA VERDE/PLAINS/MOUNTAINS/COSTA DE PRATA/LISBON
& ESTORIL COAST/ALGARVE.
Gatwick to Faro.
Heathrow to Lisbon/Porto/Faro.

(149) SUNWARD HOLIDAYS LTD
Building 3, Exeter Airport, Devon EX5 2AT
Tel: 0392 65128. Telex: 42411.
ALGARVE.
Exeter to Faro.

(150) SUPERTRAVEL LIMITED
22 Hans Place, London SW1X 0EP
Tel: 01-581 2036. Telex: 263725.
ALGARVE.
Gatwick to Faro.

(151) TANGNEY TOURS LTD
73 Crayford High Street, Crayford, Kent DA1 4EJ
Tel: 0322 59511. Telex: 888414.
COSTA DE PRATA/LISBON COAST.
Gatwick to Lisbon, Faro.

(152) TAYLINGS ABROAD (TITHEBARN TAYLINGS LTD)
14 High Street, Godalming, Surrey GU7 1DL
Tel: 04868 28524.
COSTA DE PRATA.
Gatwick to Lisbon.

(153) THE ALGARVE ALTERNATIVE
5 Barley Fields, Brentwood, Essex CM15 0BB
Tel: 0277 74442. Telex: 995342.
ALGARVE.

(154) THE PORTUGUESE PROPERTY BUREAU LIMITED
3-6 The Colannade, Maidenhead, Berkshire SL6 1QL
Tel: 0628 770220. Telex: 94013273.
ALGARVE.
Gatwick, Birmingham, Bristol, Cardiff, East Midlands, Edinburgh,
Glasgow, Luton, Manchester, Newcastle, Stansted to Faro.

(155) THE TRAVEL CLUB OF UPMINSTER
54 Station Road, Upminster, Essex RM14 2TT
Tel: 04022 25000. Telex: 897124.
ALGARVE.
Gatwick/Heathrow/Birmingham/Stansted to Faro.

(156) THE VILLA AGENCY
225 Ebury Street, London SW1V 8UT
Tel: 01-824 8474. Telex: 947093 AGENCY G.
ALGARVE.
Heathrow/Gatwick/Luton/Bristol/Birmingham/E. Midlands/Manchester/
Stansted to Faro.

(157) THOMSON HOLIDAYS
Greater London House, Hampstead Road, London NW1 7SD
Tel: 01-387 9321. Telex: 261123.
COSTA VERDE/MOUNTAINS/LISBON/ESTORIL COAST/
ALGARVE/MADEIRA.
Heathrow/Gatwick/Luton/Manchester to Lisbon.
Heathrow/Gatwick/Luton/Manchester/Bristol/Birmingham/Newcastle/
Stansted/East Midlands/Glasgow/Cardiff to Faro.
Gatwick to Funchal.

(158) 3D GOLF PROMOTION
62 Carcluie Crescent, Ayr, Scotland KA7 4SZ
Tel: 0292 42206. Telex: 776483.
LISBON & ESTORIL COASTS, ALGARVE.

(159) TJAEREBORG LIMITED
194 Campden Hill Road, London W8 7TH
Tel: 01-727 7710. Telex: 298910 TJBORG.
ALGARVE – Albufeira, Valeda Parra, Lagos.
Gatwick/Manchester/Birmingham to Faro.

(160) TOP DECK TRAVEL
131-133 Earls Court Road, London SW5 9RH
Tel: 01-244 8641. Telex: 8955339.
LISBON COAST/ALGARVE.
Heathrow/Gatwick to Faro, Lisbon.

(161) TOP FLIGHT TRAVEL
Golden House, 29 Pulteney Street, London W1R 3DD
Tel: 01-434 2827. Telex: 24559.
COSTA VERDE – Oporto.
LISBON & ESTORIL COAST. ALGARVE. MADEIRA.
Gatwick/Heathrow to Lisbon/Faro/Funchal.
Heathrow to Oporto.

(162) TRADJET (COSMOS)
17 Homedale Road, Bromley, Kent BR2 9LX
Tel: 01-464 3400. Telex: 896458.
LISBON COAST, ALGARVE.
Gatwick, Heathrow, Manchester to Lisbon.
Gatwick, Heathrow, Birmingham, Bristol, Cardiff, East Midlands, Luton,
Manchester, Newcastle, Stansted to Faro.

(163) TRANSAIR (MIDLANDS) LTD
216 Alcester Road, Drakes Cross, Wythall, Birmingham B47 5HQ
Tel: 0564 826264. Telex: 333043.
LISBON & ESTORIL COASTS, ALGARVE, MADEIRA, PORTO SANTO.
Gatwick, Manchester to Funchal.
Gatwick to Lisbon.
Gatwick, Birmingham, Manchester to Faro.

(164) TRAVELEADS LTD
6 New Station Street, Leeds LS1 5DL
Tel: 0532 452022. Telex: 556304.
COSTA VERDE, LISBON & ESTORIL COASTS, ALGARVE.
Manchester to Lisbon and Faro.

(165) TRAVELSCENE LTD
Travelscene House, 11 St Ann's Road, Harrow HA1 1AS
Tel: 01-427 4445. Telex: 264688.
LISBON COAST.
Gatwick, Heathrow, Manchester to Lisbon.

(166) TRAVTEL JET DIRECT
General Buildings, New Street, St Helier, Jersey, Channel Islands
Tel: 0534 76109. Telex: 4192121.
ALGARVE.
Gatwick, Heathrow, Glasgow to Faro.

(167) TRAVELWISE LTD
10 East Barnet Road, New Barnet, Herts EN4 8RW
Tel: 01-441 1111. Telex: 25996.
ALGARVE.
Gatwick to Faro.

(168) TRIPS AND TRAVEL
Park House, 207 The Vale, London W3 7QS
Tel: 01-740 1000. Telex: 914784.
ALGARVE.
Gatwick, Luton, Manchester to Faro.

(169) TWIRLTOUR LTD
65 Halliford Road, Sunbury on Thames TW16 0DF
Tel: 0932 787469. Telex: 919206.
ALGARVE/LISBON & ESTORIL COASTS/MADEIRA.
Gatwick/Heathrow/Luton/Birmingham/Manchester/Glasgow/Stansted/
Bristol/Cardiff/East Midlands/Newcastle/Edinburgh to Faro.
Heathrow to Funchal, Lisbon.

(170) UNICORN HOLIDAYS LTD
Intech House, 34 Cam Centre, Wilbury Way, Hitchin, Herts SG4 0RL
Tel: 0462 422223. Telex: 82453.
COSTA VERDE, COSTA DE PRATA, MOUNTAINS, PLAINS,
LISBON & ESTORIL COAST, ALGARVE, MADEIRA.
Gatwick to Oporto.
Gatwick, Heathrow to Lisbon.
Gatwick, Heathrow, Birmingham to Faro.

(171) UNIJET TRAVEL LTD
'Sandrocks', Rocky Lane, Haywards Heath, West Sussex RH16 3QS
Tel: 0444 458181. Telex: 878255.
ALGARVE.
Gatwick/Luton/Manchester/Birmingham/East Midlands/Bristol/Stansted/
Exeter to Faro.
Flights only.

(172) VACATIONS ABROAD LIMITED
60 Charles Street, Leicester LE1 1FB
Tel: 0533 537323. Telex: 347111.
ALGARVE.
Gatwick/Luton/Manchester/Birmingham/Bristol/East Midlands/Stansted to
Faro.

(173) VALE DO LOBO VILLA HOLIDAYS
31a St George Street, London W1R 9FA
Tel: 01-491 2677. Telex: 264875.
ALGARVE.
Gatwick, Heathrow, Birmingham, Bristol, East Midlands, Glasgow,
Luton, Manchester, Stansted, Southend to Faro.

(174) VILLA LINK HOLIDAYS LTD
Phoenix House, Sandown Road, Coulsdon, Surrey CR3 3HR
Tel: 0737 556636. Telex: 927340.
ALGARVE.
East Midlands to Faro.

(175) VILLA PLUS LTD
18 Verulam Road, St Albans, Herts AL3 4DA
Tel: 0727 36686. Telex: 915131.
ALGARVE.
Gatwick, Heathrow, Birmingham, Bristol, East Midlands, Glasgow,
Luton, Manchester, Newcastle, Stansted to Faro.

(176) VILLASUN HOLIDAYS LTD
9 Portugal Place, Cambridge CB5 8AF
Tel: 0223 350123. Telex: 818396.
ALGARVE.
Heathrow/Gatwick/Manchester/Birmingham to Faro.

(177) VILLAVENTURE LTD
93 Newman Street, London W1P 3LE
Tel: 01-493 3151. Telex: 23487.
ALGARVE.
Newcastle, Stansted to Faro.

(178) VILLAWORLD
19 South End, London W8 5BU
Tel: 01-938 4727. Telex: 296546.
ALGARVE.

(179) VILLMAR TRAVEL LTD
37 Ivor Place, London NW1 6EA
Tel: 01-258 3038. Telex: 268038.
ALGARVE.
Gatwick to Faro.

(180) VINTAGE LEISURE LIMITED
5 Newbold Street, Royal Leamington Spa, Warwickshire CV32 4HN
Tel: 0926 313112. Telex: 31456.
ALGARVE.

(181) WALLACE ARNOLD TOURS LTD
Gelderd Road, Leeds LS12 6DH
Tel: 0532 636456. Telex: 55482.
COSTA DE PRATA/ESTORIL COAST.

(182) WAYMARK HOLIDAYS
295 Lillie Road, London SW6 7LL
Tel: 01-385 5015.
MADEIRA/AZORES.
Heathrow to Funchal, Faro.

(183) WINDSURF PORTUGAL
18 High Street, Kintbury, Berks RG15 0TW
Tel: 0488 58530. Telex: 94011934.
COSTA DE PRATA.

(184) WINGS SUMMER SUN
Broadway, Edgbaston Five Ways, Birmingham B15 1BB
Tel: 021-616 6222. Telex: 335641.
ALGARVE.
Gatwick, Birmingham, Bristol, East Midlands, Stansted, Luton,
Manchester to Faro.

(185) WORLD OF SPORT
8 Market Passage, Cambridge CB2 3QR
Tel: 0223 311113. Telex: 817428.
MADEIRA.

(186) WORLD WINES TOURS LTD
4 Dorchester Road, Drayton, St Leonard, Oxon OX9 8BH
Tel: 0865 891919. Telex: 838998.
COSTA VERDE, COSTA DE PRATA, MOUNTAINS, ESTORIL &
LISBON COAST, MADEIRA.
Gatwick to Funchal.
Heathrow to Oporto.
Heathrow and Gatwick to Faro.

(187) WTT FLIGHTS & LEISURE
Victoria House, 65 Victoria Road, Aldershot, Hants GU11 1SJ
Tel: 0252 344244. Telex: 858755.
ALGARVE.
Gatwick, Birmingham, Bristol, Cardiff, East Midlands, Glasgow, Luton,
Manchester, Newcastle, Stansted to Faro.

(188) YOUR CHOICE (TOUROPA BRITAIN LTD)
Terminal House, 52 Grosvenor Gardens, London SW1W 0NP
Tel: 01-730 8860. Telex: 9413931.
LISBON & ESTORIL COASTS, ALGARVE.

Airlines

Airlines operating direct flights to Portuguese destinations as follows:

(192) TAP-AIR PORTUGAL
19 Lower Regent Street, London SW1.
Reservations:
LONDON 01-828 0262.
MANCHESTER 061-499 2161.

HEATHROW – LISBON – 13.50/16.10 Daily.   } Connections
HEATHROW – LISBON – 19.25/21.45 Thu/Sat.   } for Azores

DUBLIN – MANCHESTER – LISBON – 15.15/16.50/19.30 Mon/Thu
(March-June), Mon/Thu/Sat (June-Oct).

HEATHROW – PORTO – 18.15/20.25 Daily.

HEATHROW – FARO – 11.45/14.25 Thu/Sat/Sun.

HEATHROW – FUNCHAL – 17.15/20.40 Thu/Sun.

(193) BRITISH AIRWAYS

Reservations: 01-897 4000.

HEATHROW – LISBON – 10.25/12.55 Daily.

GATWICK – LISBON – 15.30/18.05 Wed/Thu/Fri/Sat/Sun.

GATWICK – PORTO – 09.00/11.15 Mon/Wed/Fri.

GATWICK – FARO – 11.15/14.00 Tue/Thu/Sat/Sun.

(194) DAN AIR
New City Court, 20 St. Thomas Street, London SE1 9RJ.
Reservations: 0293 820222/0345 100 200

GATWICK – LISBON – 09.10/11.50 Mon/Wed/Fri.
                          14.00/16.40 Sunday.

Who Specializes in What

SELF-CATERING

Self-catering is a popular option with holiday-makers going to Portugal, and especially among those heading to the Algarve. The type of accommodation on offer is usually a choice between apartments or villas, which are often grouped together in specially-built complexes. These developments are designed to be self-contained units, so the chances are that you will find all the leisure and shopping facilities you require in close proximity to your accommodation.

Something Special are specialists in villa and apartment accommodation in the Algarve. They offer a wide range of self-catering facilities to locations right along the coastline, both to the large swinging resorts and the small obscure backwaters in the area. They are a direct-sell company which means you won't find their brochures in travel agents and will have to send off for their literature. **Rainbow Sunshiners** offer a compromise between a package holiday and independent travel. This company offers accommodation-only packages which means you must book your flight separately through a travel agent. The advantage of this is that you are not tied down to the fixed two-week period of a standard package holiday and so can stay as long as you like in your chosen accommodation. **Martyn Holidays** specialize in Algarve holidays and have a range of self-catering apartments at resorts throughout the area, while **Meon Villa** specialize in up-market, high-quality self-catering facilities.

Of the major tour companies, **Enterprise** and **Thomson** offer self-catering packages to a number of different destinations in the Algarve and have a good reputation for high standards and service. Other companies which offer packages to a number of different destinations on the Algarve Coast are **Airtours**, **Hartland Holidays**, and **Travel Club of Upminster**.

Companies which offer packages to resorts other than the Algarve include **Beach Villas** which operates tours to the Estoril Coast as well as the Costa Verde.

COST-CONSCIOUS HOLIDAYS

It pays to shop around for holidays which offer good value for money. Very often, tour companies use the same hotels as their competitors, but prices may vary dramatically from operator to operator for an identical package, depending on the type of customer each firm is trying to attract. Similarly, the cheapest prices may not always represent best value for money. Don't be fooled by the cost – check out precisely what is included in the price of your accommodation and what facilities are available at your hotel. Remember, you more or less get what you pay for and often the extra £30 companies like Thomson or Horizon charge will result in a higher quality hotel.

For a standard two-week beach-based holiday then, it is the major tour operators, such as **Cosmos, Intasun** and **Skytours**, which are the most competitively priced. Aside from the 'big boys', **The Travel Club of Upminster** offers very reasonably priced packages and has a good reputation for high quality accommodation and customer service, and **Flair**, part of British Airways holidays, likewise offers family holidays at competitive prices.

Among the most cost-conscious deals available are the packages based on coach-tours. **ICT** offers a tour from the UK which takes in a stay of several days at a Portuguese beach resort. Other operators offering coach-tours include **Global Overland, Smiths Shearings (National Holidays)** and **Portugala**.

Another way to reduce costs is to holiday out of season and take advantage of the price cuts and freebies which companies offer in a bid to attract customers. Otherwise, costs can be reduced by booking at the last minute, taking potluck on where you land. The Air Travel Advisory Bureau on 01-636 5000 or 061-832 2000 provides information on the best last-minute flight deals, plus villas, apartments and hotels, and their service is free.

Finally, of the direct-sell companies (i.e. you won't find their brochures in a travel agent's, you'll have to phone for them), **Tjaereborg** offer extremely good value for money. Their holidays use very acceptable hotels and their prices are virtually unbeatable.

CAMPING

Club Cantabrica offer holidays to Albufeira, with tents or caravans for sleeping accommodation. The site is well provided for in terms of amenities and leisure facilities and the flights between Portugal and the UK are included in the package price. This tour operator seems to be particularly worth checking out – their facilities are very competitively priced and their clients seem to have a particularly glowing opinion of them as an efficient, value-for-money tour operator.

PRIVATE ACCOMMODATION/SMALL HOTELS

Because of the wide range of hotel and self-catering facilities in the major tourist resorts, there is not much demand for private accommodation among holiday-makers. However, if you want to avoid the impersonal atmosphere of a big hotel or villa/apartment complex, **Enterprise** does offer a few limited deals which feature small pensions and residencias (small hotels) in the major Algarve resorts. Otherwise, **Thomson's Small and Friendly** and **Horizon's Small Hotels** offer a range of packages which are geared towards people who especially want to stay in small, family-run hotels. These represent good value for money and are an excellent compromise for those who want a conventional kind of beach package-holiday without having to be one of a crowd in a large resort hotel.

MANOR HOUSE HOLIDAYS

This is a relatively new option on the package-tour scene, but also one which is growing in popularity, as it represents private accommodation with a difference . . . the chance to indulge in a few days 'lord of the manor' living in some beautiful old rambling manor houses. The establishments featured are usually traditional family homes of the Portuguese aristocracy and are often located in the remoter areas in the North of the country. Such a holiday, then, gives you the opportunity to soak up the atmosphere and character of the 'real' Portugal, a pleasure which has formerly been reserved for the independent traveller. Because these establishments are usually still owned and lived in by families, the number of places in them are limited and there is also a minimum stay of three days. **Abreu, Caravela, Harlen, Portugala** and **Sunvil** are among operators organizing stays in manor houses for customers.

POUSADA HOLIDAYS

A *pousada* holiday offers to the ordinary package-tour holiday-maker the unique opportunity to sample some of the most beautiful areas in

Portugal, with accommodation in magnificent, historical buildings. How about a few days' holiday in an ancient monastery? Or a hill-top castle with a superb view of the surrounding countryside? These are the kinds of delights a *pousada* holiday has in store for you.

Most *pousada* holidays offered by tour companies concentrate on the North of the country, and as stays in *pousadas* are limited to three days in peak-season, packages usually take the form of a car-tour lasting between seven and 14 days. Certain tour operators detail a number of *pousada* tours in their brochures which enable you to make the most of your time, by taking in the main sights and best scenery that the area has to offer. However, these routes are normally only suggestions and companies are usually only too happy to put together a programme which will suit your individual requirements.

Several tour companies now feature *pousada* tours, including **Hartland**, which runs a fairly extensive programme, and **Abreu**, **Caravela**, **Hayes & Jarvis**, **Pearls of Portugal**, and **Sunvil**. If you scan the brochures, you'll soon realize a *pousada* package holiday doesn't come cheap. This is because *pousada* accommodation is usually regarded as equivalent to four- or five-star luxury hotels, not to speak of the extra effort required on the part of the tour companies to offer this highly individual kind of package holiday. However, if money isn't a problem, a *pousada* holiday can take you into the very heart of the most beautiful and unspoilt region in Portugal, not yet overrun by hordes of holiday-makers or prey to the 'carbuncles' of modern tourist developments.

COACH TOURS

Coach tours are undoubtedly one of the cheapest ways to spend a fortnight abroad, but they do tend to have a bit of an OAP image and to a large extent that is deserved – the average age on a coach party is rarely less than 50. Nevertheless, coach holidays are a good way to take a whistle-stop tour of the major sights of a country – something you might not have too much opportunity to do if you took a standard 'sun, surf and sea' package to one of the major Algarve resorts.

Coach tours divide into two broad sections: tours which deal with Portugal only, and tours which visit several countries and take in Portugal *en route*.

Abreu organizes internal coach tours following a flight from Britain. Tours start from Lisbon and concentrate on the northern part of the country, including the Mountain area, which is usually not accessible to the ordinary package-tour holiday-maker.

Those offering coach tours which include Portugal among other countries include **Insight, Global Overland** and **Enterprise**. Insight and Enterprise start the journey by coach after a flight to the continent, while tours with Global Continental originate in Britain and drive by coach to the continent. Reports on Global Continental are above average, and as this company specializes in coach holidays, it's always worth getting their brochure.

ICT offers a variation on this theme, organizing packages which involve a coach journey from Britain to the North of Portugal, where a few days are spent at a beach resort on the Costa Verde, before returning by coach to Britain.

If you're a bit of a wine connoisseur and fancy indulging yourself, the wine tours available in the centre and North of the country are another option open to holiday-makers in Portugal. **Blackheath Winetrails** have a good reputation for interesting and varied itineraries, consisting of a mixture of sightseeing excursions and wine-tastings. **Abreu** features a week-long tour by coach to the main wine-producing areas with flights to and from the country. Other tour operators offering wine tours are **Portugala, Saga, Traveleads** and **World Wine Tours**.

Tour operators specializing in religious tours in Portugal include **Spes Travel**. These consist of either flights to Lisbon, or coach to Fatima. The tours are centred around pilgrimages to Fatima, but also include coach tours to Lisbon and the surrounding area.

DRIVING HOLIDAYS

For those who wish to have the security of taking a package holiday, but don't want to be stuck in one resort for two weeks, then a fly/drive option is worth considering. This combines the advantage of a cheap flight with the freedom of a self-drive car at the other end. **Abreu, Caravela, Enterprise, Sovereign, Sunvil**, and **Suntours**, among many others, all offer this option.

TWO-CENTRE HOLIDAYS

There are few tour operators offering this option in Portugal, partly because of the nature of the country's tourist development. By far the most popular tourist destinations are in the South, whereas the areas of interest to the sightseer are concentrated in the centre and North. In order to make a two-centre holiday attractive to customers, by highlighting the scenic and cultural differences of the country, tour operators would usually have to include the price of an extra flight (i.e. between Lisbon and Faro) in the cost of a two-centre holiday. This would mean that not only would clients have to pay high prices for this 'holiday with a difference', but they would also have to spend another day or so of their valuable holiday time in transit between destinations.

Nevertheless, some tour operators are beginning to experiment with this option and if you have a bit more to spend a two-centre holiday is a good way to see more of what Portugal has to offer. **Enterprise** offers two-centre holidays, which involve a stay on Madeira and a few days on the nearby island of Porto Santo. This is a good deal if you were thinking about going to Madeira, but were put off by the fact there are no beaches on the island, as Porto Santo is basically just a large sandspit with a very beautiful, long golden beach. **Sovereign** also offers two-centre holidays in the North of Portugal. With this package, half your time is spent on the Costa Verde coastline and the remainder in the unspoilt interior, near the centre of the Peneda-Gerês National Park.

ACTIVITY HOLIDAYS

Most major resorts have a wide range of leisure facilities, so if you take a standard package you will be spoilt for choice of sporting amenities, such as windsurfing, golf, swimming, etc. When you are deciding on your resort and tour operator, check out the details given in the brochures to see what sorts of leisure activities are on offer at each resort, and what kind of sporting facilities individual hotels make available for residents.

Alcantara will arrange the facilities for you to play your chosen sport and also organize special competition weeks.

The Travel Club of Upminster issues a useful booklet to customers which deals with activity holidays in the Algarve. This details the locations of the sporting facilities for golf, tennis and squash, riding, deep-sea fishing, windsurfing, etc along the southern coastline. The Travel Club can also arrange a reduced green fee rate for clients intending to golf a lot during their holidays.

GOLF AND TENNIS HOLIDAYS

A few tour operators specialize in offering golf or tennis holidays to customers. If you are an enthusiast, these options are well worth considering – not only will you be able to use top-class facilities, but the price for doing so will be cheaper than could be obtained if you were playing independently.

Several tour operators now offer tennis holidays, including the Jonathan Markson Algarve Tennis Centre; see list on page 75.

Reduced green fees, guaranteed tee-off times and the opportunity to participate in amateur competitions are the special features which most golf-specialist tour operators offer to clients. Tour companies which specialize in golf-holidays are **3D Golf Promotion**, **Eurogolf**, **Skyplane/Skygolf** and **Longshot Holidays**. These firms arrange packages to golf courses on both the Algarve and Lisbon/Estoril Coasts. **The Travel Club of Upminster** can organize reduced rate green fees at certain courses on the Algarve and if customers reserve green fees in advance they can also book starting time and dates at the same time.

WALKING/NATURAL INTEREST HOLIDAYS

Countrywide are acknowledged experts in this field. This company arranges treks through the most scenic and beautiful parts of the islands; painting and rambling tours through the 'floating garden' of

Madeira, and tours exploring the remote, unspoilt landscapes of the Azores. The other attractive feature of Countrywide's packages is that these varied and interesting tours are very reasonably priced, so you won't have to pay through the nose for wanting to take a 'different' kind of holiday. **Ramblers** also arrange walking tours of northern Portugal, while **Waymark** also offer treks to the Azores and Madeira. **David Sayers** arranges natural interest holidays to the Azores.

CRUISES

Unless you're a member of the Royal Family and have your own personalized cruise ship, there are no cruises which deal solely with Portugal and no other country – Portugal is usually just one port of call on a much larger itinerary. **P&O** and **CTC** operate cruises which stop off at Lisbon or Madeira. The brochures to get hold of for details of these are the *Canberra* from P&O and the *Leonid Brezhnev* from CTC. **Fred Olsen** run a cruise with the *Black Prince* which calls in at Madeira. See also **Portugala** and **Select**.

Summing Up

To sum up then, the package holiday scene in Portugal offers good value and a wide range of choice to suit both your interests and your pocket! Undoubtedly, most tour operators have a specific market in mind when they organize their package holidays. If you shop around you will soon find the tour operators which focus on family holidays, be it low-price or exclusive *pousadas*.

Companies like **Thomson** (in their à la Carte range) and **Hayes & Jarvis** all rely on a name for good quality and an 'exclusive' approach rather than the 'bums on seats' image of most major tour companies. Other tour operators concentrate on the young, good-time set, **Thomson's Summer Sun** and **Club Mediterranée** are the main ones to consider in this respect, while **Sovereign** is pitched towards the 'yuppie' market, offering high quality packages with a difference. For the older 50+ age-group, **Saga** and **Intasun** are long established specialists.

The vast majority of tour operators concentrate on the Algarve, though increasingly the Lisbon/Estoril Coasts are becoming more popular; some tour companies, however, specialize in Portugal as a whole, while others aim themselves at a customer who wants a 'different' Portuguese holiday, so they are offering packages to lesser known parts of the country. The main tour companies which offer deals to locations outside the usual tourist destinations are **Abreu**, **Caravela**, **Enterprise**, **Martyn Holidays**, **Portugal à la Carte**, **Sovereign** and **Sunvil**. All these companies deal with resorts on either the Costa de Prata, the Costa Verde or the Azores.

With the decline of Spain and the relative expense of Greece as a holiday destination, it is likely that Portugal's popularity will continue to rise. More and more tour companies are now entering the Portuguese market or are extending their programmes to encompass new areas, such as the Azores or the Costa Verde. These recent developments are good news for the average holiday-maker, as not only will he/she have a wider choice of holiday destinations but the competition for customers among tour companies will ensure that the prices of package holidays are kept down.

As far as the choice of holiday is concerned, you'd be hard pushed to find anywhere better in terms of sporty holidays than Portugal. Because most major resorts have a wide range of sporting facilities, such as sailing, windsurfing, etc, it is not necessary to travel with a specialist company, unless you want non-stop coaching or well above average facilities. If you are a keen golfer or tennis player, it is well worth picking up a few brochures issued by companies who specialize in these types of holiday. Remember, however, that travelling with a specialist company generally tends to be more expensive than the standard two-week package offered by the major tour companies.

The outlook is also bright for those who want to break out of the standard package-holiday mould. The *pousada* and manor house packages are an attractive alternative for those who wish to explore a bit more of the cultural or historic side of Portugal, while the fly/drive option offered by some tour companies combines the freedom of independent travel with the security and inexpense of a package holiday.

Virtually all beach holidays are good value for money, whether they be self-catering or hotel based, although you may find the main

Algarve resorts very busy in peak-season simply because, like you, hundreds of other holiday-makers have been attracted by the prospect of cheap packages and guaranteed sun. When you are choosing your holiday and your tour operator, there are a number of points to bear in mind; what kind of service you want – a tour company catering for family groups or one which focuses on the young, energetic brigade? What you expect from your resort – a quiet, relaxing village or a modern, busy resort with lots of night-life? And finally, how much you want to spend. It really is worth the trouble to shop around and collect as many brochures as you can, as often almost identical packages can vary dramatically in price, simply because tour operators are pitching their sales at different customer markets.

Checklist

As a final reminder to anyone taking a package holiday anywhere, check the following points before booking:

(1) Is your travel agent competent? Unfortunately many are not and all too often it's the large chains of High Street agents who give the worst advice and service. Try to avoid the obvious trainees when you go into the shop and have a list of questions prepared so that you don't end up having to make several trips when one would do.

(2) Is your travel agent a member of ABTA (the Association of British Travel Agents)? If not, think seriously about finding one who is. There are plenty of them who are and membership could make a big difference to you if things start to go wrong.

(3) Having chosen your country of destination, do you really know about all the packages available on the market? Many of the smaller tour operators do not get their brochures into the High Street travel agents but that does not mean their holidays aren't reliable or worth checking out. Check against the list on page 75 and phone for a brochure from any likely looking company.

(4) If the travel agent can't book the holiday you finally selected, don't necessarily accept his/her substitute recommendation. Have your own second and third options sorted out beforehand; or if there really is no substitute, leave the whole idea and consider something completely different. Remember that travel agents are in the business of selling holidays for commissions – unscrupulous agents often don't much care what they sell, but they do like to clinch a sale before you leave the shop.

(5) As for the holiday itself, check the following before paying your deposit:

    (i)   Does the holiday price include all airport or port taxes and security charges (for both the UK and abroad)?

    (ii)   Does it include meals on the journey?

    (iii)   Is it extra for a weekend flight or a day-time departure?

    (iv)   Is transfer between the point of arrival and your hotel included?

    (v)   Be sure you know on what basis you are booked in at your hotel, i.e. full/half-board/B&B.

    (vi)   Are you clear about supplementary charges made for single rooms/balcony/sea view/private bathroom, etc?

    (vii)   Is the insurance sufficient for you? Does it cover pregnant women/disabled people/people going on sports holidays? Is the limit on personal baggage high enough to cover all you are taking? Does it include a clause on delayed departure for your return journey? What provisions does it make for cancellations? Finally, check you're clear about the procedure in case a theft or loss does occur – often these matters have to be reported within a specified time limit and a police report procured.

(6) And finally, before handing over your money, ask:

    (i)   What is the position on cancellations (from both parties' point of view)?

    (ii)   What happens if your holiday needs to be altered significantly – under the ABTA code you must be told and given the choice of accepting either the new hotel/resort/flight, etc, or a full refund. (Alterations caused by bad weather or industrial disputes will only be covered by your insurance.)

(iii) What's the score on overbooking? Is there a 'disturbance' compensation to be paid (there should be under the ABTA code); will the alternative accommodation be of an equally high standard (it must be under the ABTA code).

Once you have gone through all these points you should have a clear understanding of the contract you are signing and your travel agent will undoubtedly be in such awe of your intimate knowledge of the travel industry that you will receive preferential treatment all the way!

If, despite all this good groundwork, you still have cause for complaint, ABTA's address is 55-57 Newman Street, London W1N 4AH. Write to them with full details of your complaint and enclose copies of all your correspondence with the travel agent or tour operator.

Independent Means

The Options

There really isn't too much of a problem finding accommodation in Portugal. In the past ten to 20 years, many modern hotels and villa/apartment complexes have sprung up in major tourist spots, which are usually complete with their own leisure amenities and have easy access to nearby beaches. Hotels are graded from one to five stars on the basis of the facilities and service they offer. Prices for a double room with bathroom attached and breakfast in the morning can range from 2300$00 in a one-star establishment to 19,200$00 in a luxury five-star hotel. The price of the equivalent in an average three-star hotel is about 5000$00.

Other accommodation alternatives are *estalagems*, which are privately-run inns and *pensãoes*, small guest-houses. Pensions are definitely the cheapest place to look for a bed for the night. Some charge as little as £6 for a double room – although the standards of cleanliness and food in these establishments may be nothing to write home about. For an average pension expect to pay around 2400$00 a night for a double, breakfast included.

Bookings for hotels, *estalagems*, and *pensãoes* can be done through the local tourist office or travel agent for a small commission fee. Make clear to the staff you're dealing with what price range you are willing to pay and what type of accommodation you would prefer. Otherwise you may find yourself landing up in a five-star luxury hotel when you would have been quite happy with a bed and floorboards in a small pension. If you get really organized, before you go, apply to the National Tourist Board in London for the small booklets they publish, which give details of hotels in the respective tourist areas. These are not terribly good, as they don't give any idea of prices, and you'll need a detailed map of the town to be able to find any of the places. However, they are useful to have as back-up if you arrive in a town or city late at night when the tourist office is closed, as they can give an idea where to begin looking for suitable accommodation.

A room in private accommodation is another option for the independent traveller. The unofficial way to obtain this type of accommodation is to hang about in a large railway station, look obviously touristy, and wait for someone to come touting for business, offering a room for the night in their house. Obviously there are a few risks associated with this method, but providing a few commonsense precautions are taken, such as seeing the room and negotiating a price before you commit yourself, you should have no problems.

The alternative to this type of private accommodation is residence in Portuguese manor houses. Bookings for these can be made through local tourist offices in each respective area (you must book at least three days in advance) or by obtaining addresses from the National Tourist Board in London and writing off before you go. These manor houses are usually family homes of the Portuguese aristocracy, who have lived there for generations and are now embracing tourism as eagerly as the rest of Portugal. This form of accommodation is particularly good if you are thinking of touring extensively in the interior of the country, as the system is well developed in the Mountains and Plains areas, precisely where the choice of hotels is likely to be limited. (For tour operators who arrange manor house holidays turn to Manor House Holidays on page 106.)

Another alternative to the conventional type of accommodation which is well worth considering is the Portuguese *pousada*. These are government-owned inns, located in areas of historic significance or great scenic beauty. The buildings are often of interest in themselves, as they can range from old castles to ancient monasteries. The *pousadas* which have been purpose-built are designed to harmonize with the architectural style of the area, so you'll never find yourself in a concrete box. Likewise, the food served to guests focuses on the culinary specialities of each individual region. For those freelancing, stays in *pousadas* are limited to three days during high season, but there are no restrictions if you are travelling out of season. Because *pousadas* are an extremely popular form of accommodation, it is more or less necessary to book rooms in advance of going to Portugal. If you're keen on trying out this unusual form of accommodation, contact the *pousada* organization: ENATUR, Avenida Santa Joana Princesa, 10-A, 1700 Lisbon, or write to the National Tourist Board in London for more information. For details of tour operators who specialize in *pousada* holidays, turn to Pousada Holidays on page 106.

If you're keen on going it alone in self-catering, you'd be better to arrange this before you go. Much of the new accommodation development in Portugal has taken the form of holiday apartments or villas and many tour companies feature these self-catering options as part of their general brochures. This, without doubt, represents the cheapest and most secure way to hire this type of accommodation, but if package holidays really are an anathema to you, the alternative is to scour the Sunday newspapers, for details of villas and flats to let by private arrangement. There are more pitfalls if you adopt this course of action, but if you're careful it can be a success: get all the details before you commit yourself, along with a full inventory and recent photograph (to prove it's not a hole in the ground); that way the risks can be minimized.

As for camping, there are numerous sites along the coastline, although the standards and facilities can vary dramatically. The cost of pitching your tent is ridiculously cheap, often only one or two pounds. Away from the coast, the number of official places to camp substantially reduces and more often than not you'll find the best campsites are not the established ones (which are few and far between anyway) but the ones picked on an *ad hoc* basis, in a quiet spot in the middle of a wood – far away from the madding crowd! One proviso – it is illegal to camp on tourist beaches, so if you pitch yourself on a busy stretch of sand near a large resort, you can expect to be moved on. However, a pragmatic approach is usually adopted towards campers and as long as you're not obviously disturbing anyone else's fun, camping rough near the coast should present no problems. For those who like a roof over their heads, then there are 14 youth hostels in Portugal. These cost about 600$00 per night, an IYHA card is required and there is usually an 11 o'clock curfew (midnight in larger towns).

Overall then, the accommodation-scene for the independent traveller is very good. Rooms are competitively priced and places in hotels and pensions can be found throughout the year – although you might feel the squeeze in busy cities and towns during the peak-season months. This is particularly true of the Algarve where many hotels are block-booked by package-tour companies.

So much for the independent accommodation scene. Now let's turn our attentions to the methods of travelling to Portugal.

By Air

There are two main alternatives open to the independent traveller – you can either take a scheduled flight with one of the big airlines or you can book yourself on to a chartered flight through a main tour operator.

British Airways and TAP (Air Portugal) both operate flights to Portugal. There are three main airports on mainland Portugal – Lisbon, Faro (Algarve), Oporto (Costa Verde). Both British Airways and TAP fly to all three mainland locations and TAP also operate direct services to Funchal on Madeira. Connections can be made from Lisbon to Terceira and São Miguel on the Azores and this service runs several times a week during the summer.

Scheduled flights generally work out more expensive than chartered flights, although costs depend on what day of the week you are travelling (mid-week is cheaper than weekends) and what kind of fares you buy. Both TAP and British Airways offer PEX and SUPER-PEX fares to Portugal. A SUPER-PEX fare does not need to be purchased in advance but there is limited availability of seats, so the earlier you book the better chance you have of procuring yourself a

SUPER-PEX fare. This fare entitles you to a maximum stay of one month and there is no guarantee of money back if you cancel. A PEX fare is more expensive, but this allows you a three-month maximum stay and a 50 per cent refund if you have to cancel. The price of a return flight to Lisbon ranges from £170-£210 (mid-week, SUPER-PEX) to £240-£250 (mid-week, PEX).

Charter flights usually represent better value for the holiday-maker, although in fact this depends on your location in the country. Chartered flights leave from most UK airports to Faro. Only a few airports other than Gatwick and Heathrow have charters to Lisbon and Funchal, and you will have to fly from London to get to Oporto. When you start totting up the cost of train journeys, and perhaps overnight accommodation if you're booked on to an early morning flight, you'll soon begin to realize why the fares on scheduled flights aren't as uncompetitive as they might seem. It is also worth remembering that on scheduled flights you can choose your date of departure and what airport you want to fly to in Portugal, rather than having to organize your holiday plans around the limited departure dates and destinations which the chartered flights air companies offer.

However, for the majority of people living near to major airports, chartered flights represent the cheapest and quickest way to get to Portugal. The price of a chartered flight varies, depending on what time of year you are travelling and what company you are travelling with, but even at peak season you should be able to make savings of around £50 per person, compared to the price of scheduled flights. The kinds of operators who offer these kinds of deals are the 'big boys' such as **Horizon**, **Thomson**, **Intasun** or **Flair**, although the smaller tour companies are increasingly offering these facilities too. The best way to suss out who is offering the best deals is to go to two or three travel agents and pick up as many 'flights only' brochures as possible. Usually by mid-January, most of the companies worth considering have their literature in travel agents.

The main drawback with chartered flights is that many of them only fly to destinations where tour operators actually operate package-tours to. The obvious implication of this, then, is that the majority of chartered flights available to Portugal are to Faro, in the Algarve, and some of the bigger companies offer deals to Lisbon. Chartered flights to Oporto, Madeira and the Azores are pretty difficult to find. The reason for this is that tour companies charter aircraft from the airlines and in order to make a profit, and keep prices down, they have to get as many 'bums on seats' as possible. This is good news if you are planning to head to one of the major tourist centres; otherwise you'll have to catch a separate connection to your planned destination. Again, this is another reason why you shouldn't dismiss the price of scheduled flights out of hand, as there is no point making apparent savings on a flight out to Faro in the Algarve, if you really wanted to head towards Oporto in the North.

Chartered flights usually include some form of basic accommodation (i.e. dormitory beds in hostels) to get round the law on the sale of Inclusive Air Holidays to Europe. What this actually means is that on paper included in the price of your flight is some form of very basic accommodation (so the company can legally claim that they are selling you a package holiday consisting of travel and accommodation). It's up to you whether you want to use this accommodation or not, although tour companies do not usually include travel facilities from the airport to your accommodation or even guarantee it will be in the same town the airport is located in!

The only other way to get a cheap flight is to scout around bucket shops, or scan the columns of the Sunday newspapers – but remember to read the small print. You're unlikely to come up with a cheaper way of going than the tour operator charter flight anyway.

Note: on charter flights run by tour operators flight delays are not uncommon and if you're a non-smoker it's advisable to book in early as non-smoker seats are often oversubscribed.

By Rail

After coach travel, travelling by train must be the most harrowing way to get to Portugal. You'll no doubt have a few tales to tell once you stumble off the train (long stretches of train travel give you a good insight into human nature), but you'll probably need a couple of days to recover from the experience. The trains in France aren't too bad – the French TGVs have an excellent reputation for fast, efficient train travel. Once you get into Spain and Portugal, however, it is a different story. Trains are crowded, not too clean in peak season and, above all, infuriatingly slow. Never mind, if you're still under twenty-six you're young enough to stand it and you can buy an Interrail ticket (available from British Rail) or a BIJ ticket (available from Eurotrain) which gets you there for dirt-cheap prices. If you're over twenty-six, then the advice is to forget it – prices for a one-way train journey to Portugal are roughly equivalent to the cost of a return fare on a chartered airline.

However, if you and your family are determined to train it, the direct route from London is a train to one of the channel ports arriving at either Boulogne, Dieppe or Calais, then a connecting service to Paris. In Paris, you change trains and get on the Sud Express which runs through Bordeaux, Dax, Bayonne, Biarritz, Hendaye, crossing into Spain at Irun and on to San Sebastián, Medina Del Campo, Salamanca, Fuenes de Oñoro, into Portugal at Vilar Formoso, then Pampilhosa and arriving Lisbon roughly twenty-five hours after it leaves Paris.

All the hassles of train travel on the continent are somewhat mitigated by the beautiful scenery through which the Sud Express travels. The journey through the Pyrenees in Northern Spain is quite stunning if you get a nice day (it's often quite misty and drizzly if you're travelling out of season) and is well worth abandoning books and card-games for. There are catering facilities through from Paris to Lisbon and, during the summer months, a restaurant car joins the train at Irun and stays on until Lisbon. Second-class couchettes are available from Paris to Lisbon and sleeping cars are available for first-class passengers from Irun onwards.

The other chief route into Portugal is to take a train to Madrid and catch a connecting service to Lisbon. Going this way, you will follow the same track as the Sud Express down to Irun in Spain before branching off to Madrid, where you will have to wait an hour or so before you can catch a service to Lisbon. There's no distinct advantage going the second way, aside from seeing more of Spain. It's a longer route and also slightly more expensive than the Sud Express. First-class sleepers and second-class couchettes can be reserved for the journey between Irun and Madrid. Buffet facilities are available from Paris to Dax and from Madrid to Lisbon.

If you intend to go to destinations in the North of Portugal, then the best idea is to change at Pampilhosa. From here you can catch fairly frequent connections to Aveiro, Vila Nova de Gaia and Oporto in the North, and Coimbra and Fátima on the Costa de Prata. There are a number of daily train services between Lisbon and Oporto, but these take approximately four hours (three if you take an express train), whereas the service between Pampilhosa and Oporto takes around two hours. Connections can be made at Lisbon for Faro in the Algarve. This journey takes approximately five hours and stops at Albufeira, Lagos and Portimão *en route*.

If you're planning to do extensive train travel or if you want to plan your journey in detail before you go, then *Thomas Cook's Continental Timetable* is a good buy. These are issued monthly and contain timetables for train services throughout the continent. Once you've worked out how to read it (it looks complicated but, in fact, is very simple) this is an indispensable guide to have on hand, although you'd still be advised to check the train times in local stations. An excellent guide for those planning extensive train travel in Europe is *Europe by Train*, published by Fontana.

Whichever route you opt for, reservations are strongly advised, as are sleeping arrangements and pre-packed food for the journey.

The approximate cost for a standard-class return to Lisbon is £165 (£230 first class). A supplement of around £6 per person is payable on Express and Talgo trains in France, and the price of a second-class couchette is approximately £7.50 per head.

By Bus

Unless you're motoring and sharing the petrol, going by coach is undoubtedly the cheapest way to get to Portugal . . . it must also rate as one of the most tiring and uncomfortable! To be fair, many long-distance coaches nowadays are equipped with reclining seats, air-conditioning, etc and there are frequent stops throughout the journey. However, this mode of transport is really for the young, back-packing brigade doing Europe on the cheap, and you certainly need the stamina of youth to be able to stand 48 hours of day and night coach travel!

Nevertheless, if you have a masochistic streak, telephone the international service division of National Express Coaches on 01-439 9368, or your nearest major National Express depot. This company runs services to Portugal which stop at Paris (you will have to change here), Coimbra, Lisbon, Faro, and Lagos. The price of a single fare is approximately £70-£75 and returns for £120-£125.

By Car/Campervan

It's a long drive to Portugal – approximately 1,100 miles to Oporto, 1,200 miles to Lisbon, and 1,400 miles to Faro from the channel ports. However this is a relatively cheap way to go if you're travelling in a group and splitting the cost of the petrol.

Obviously what route you take depends on what you want to see before you get to Portugal, but the quickest and most direct way is to take the motorway (you will have to pay tolls on this) from Paris via Tours, Bordeaux, San Sebastián, Bilbao, Burgos. From Burgos you change on to a highway which runs via Valladolid, Salamanca, Guarda, Coimbra and Lisbon.

There is a motorrail service between Paris and Lisbon. Although on the surface this might seem an expensive way to start a driving holiday (approx. £380 second-class return for a car and driver) it is worth weighing up the pros and cons of this scheme. This is especially true if you are travelling in a family group, as the fares for additional passengers represent considerable reductions on the standard Paris/ Lisbon return. The tariff for each additional adult is around £70 return, while a child costs approximately £35 return. In terms of comfort and speed, it could well be that by the time you have paid for motorway tolls and petrol, arranged accommodation and spent a few days getting there, you'd have done better to fork out a little extra on the motorrail service. More details can be obtained from French Railways, 179 Piccadilly, London W1 (Tel: 01-409 3518) or ask for a leaflet at your nearest major British Rail station.

Another alternative is a twice-weekly car ferry from Plymouth to Santander in Northern Spain. The sailing takes twenty-four hours and cuts off approximately 600 miles of motoring. Prices vary according to the type of car you are taking and the time of year you are going, but the approximate cost for a Fiat Uno-type car in high season is £150 return and an extra £100 for each adult travelling. Berths are not included in the price, and cost £10–20, depending on how many people are sharing a berth. For more details apply to Brittany Ferries (Tel: (0752) 221321).

Portuguese frontier posts are usually open from 7am to midnight. In the summer the larger ones, at Tuy/Valença do Minho, Feces de Abajo/Vila Verde da Raia, Fuentes de Oñoro/Vilar Formoso and Caya/Caia are open twenty-four hours. In off-season months, the small frontier posts close at 9pm, and the main posts at 11pm.

The roads in Portugal are of a reasonable standard, although not really suitable for people who fancy themselves as Formula One racing-drivers. There are a few stretches of motorway along the western coast between La Coruña, Oporto and Lisbon and you will have to pay a toll for travelling on these. In the interior, roads are narrow and twisting and you should watch out for animals grazing by the side of the road.

The rule of the road is to drive and give way on the right.

Speed limits are 37 mph (60 km) in built-up areas, 55 mph (90 km) outside town, 26 mph (40 km) minimum and 75 mph (120 km) on motorways.

To drive in Portugal you will need the following documentation and equipment:

A current British or International driving licence
GB stickers
Car registration document
'Green Card' (international insurance certificate)

If you are driving a car which is not registered in your name you must have a letter authorizing its use from the owner and are advised to contact the Portuguese Consulate General before you go to find out how to have this document officially recognized. It is now obligatory for seat-belts to be worn when driving. Cars running on liquid petroleum gas, using either single or dual systems, are forbidden entry into Portugal.

Both petrol (*gasolina*) and oil (*oleo*) can be bought. Petrol stations on country roads, however, are in short supply, so unless you want to be left high and dry, take the opportunity to top up on fuel when you see a garage. There are two grades of petrol: super (equivalent to 4-star) and normal (2-star). These two grades can be mixed to obtain 3-star.

If you are a member of the RAC or AA motoring associations in Britain, they have reciprocal agreements with the Portuguese Automobile Club (ACP), whereby the basic patrol service is available for breakdowns, although your policy will not cover you for garage services. The address for the ACP in Lisbon is 24 Rua Rosa Araújá, (Tel: 563931) and in Oporto, 2 Rua Gonçalo Cristávão (Tel: 29271). Apply to either of these offices for the locations and telephone numbers of outlets throughout the country. Travellers are also strongly advised to have a suitable insurance policy to cover driving abroad. In the case of a serious car accident, phone 115 for the fire, ambulance and police services. On motorways there are special orange-coloured phones which may be used in case of an emergency.

Everyone has their own preference when it comes to a driving holiday, but speaking as someone who has driven on the continent in everything from a Daimler limousine to a battered old Mini, I feel it's worth putting in a word here about what to look for when choosing a car to drive abroad in. Obviously luggage capacity is an important consideration. Fuel economy, spare parts and comfort are the other major considerations. Don't try to squeeze too many people into a car, and remember, you'll return with more than you set out with. When we were researching this section of the guide we used our Vauxhall Carlton 2LGL Saloon, which over any other car we'd tried gave us the best in terms of comfort, room and efficiency. It's worth bearing in mind if you intend doing a lot of holiday motoring or if you're in a position to hire one. A car with a bit of extra power is well worth having on long journeys – and safer.

Hitch-hiking

Generally, it's easier to hitch lifts back from Portugal, rather than the other way around. French drivers do not look favourably on hitch-hikers, so you could spend a lot of time hanging around in France waiting to get a decent lift. Once you get into Spain and Portugal, bus and train travel is very cheap, so it makes sense to travel by public transport rather than take the risks of hitching a ride. The main road south described above in By Car/Campervan (page 123) is the route to concentrate your energies on, although even that can be difficult in peak-season, as most of the traffic is French families heading south for an annual holiday.

By Sea

There's no direct route from the UK to Portugal by sea. If you wish to travel by sea you'll have to consider the cruise options available (see Cruises on page 111). The closest destination which can be reached directly by boat is Santander in Northern Spain. Brittany Ferries run a twice-weekly car ferry here during the summer months (see By Car page 123).

Useful Information

TIME DIFFERENCES

Portugal keeps the same time as the UK, that is, GMT during the winter months, and GMT + 1 during the summer. New York is five hours behind Portuguese time. Clocks change on the last Sunday in March and the last Sunday in September.

ELECTRICITY

The voltage in most places is 220 volt AC. Appliances will require continental two-pin plugs.

WATER

Officially, water is safe to drink anywhere in Portugal, but if you have a delicate stomach you'd do better to drink bottled mineral water, especially if you're travelling into the more rural parts of the country. Probably the best brand of natural mineral water is Luso; it is on sale all round Portugal and can be bought at supermarkets. Sparkling waters include Pechas Salgadas and Água de Carsealhelhas.

Part Three
WHEN YOU'RE THERE

Tourist Information

As part of your holiday preparations it is a good idea to write, before you leave, to the Portuguese National Tourist Board, 1/5 New Bond Street, London W1Y 0NP. This office issues general brochures and maps relating to the individual regions in Portugal. These will give you some idea of the main sights, the leisure and accommodation facilities available, and some background information on the geography and history of the area. If you are keen on a particular sport, make a point of asking for the relevant leaflets to be sent to you. This way, by the time you get to Portugal, you'll not only have some idea of what to expect, but you'll also have a small dossier of useful information at hand for reference even if you end up miles away from the nearest tourist bureau.

In Portugal itself, tourist offices (*Turismo*) can be found in all major towns and resorts. At these bureaux, you will find maps, bus-time-tables and brochures, in English, on what there is to see in the area. Details of bus tours into the surrounding countryside or any special festivals taking place can also be collected from these offices.

The literature available is adequate, although it is region-based and doesn't really tell you much about other areas of the country. If you are doing a lot of travelling and want more general information, go to one of the larger information bureaux, in Oporto, Lisbon, or Faro. The addresses of these are:

Praça Dom Joao I, Oporto (Tel: 317514)
Palacio Fox, Praça dos Restauradores, Lisbon (Tel: 363624)
Rua Ataíde Oliveira 100, Faro (Tel: 24067/26068)

In the Lisbon area, immediate information in English can be obtained by telephoning 369450.

The staff in *turismos* usually speak English and will be able to help with any enquiries you might have to make. They can point out the main areas to look for accommodation or, for a small commission, find you a place for the night in a guest-house or hotel within their area. Opening hours are generally 9am to 6pm, although these are extended in large tourist resorts during the summer months.

Other places to look for useful information are the Portuguese travel and tourist agencies. There are more than 250 different firms throughout the country, but the main ones to look out for are **Star Travel** (American Express reps), **Agência Abreu**, **Viagens Rawes** and **Wagons-Lits Turismo**. Information about accommodation and day-trip excursions are obtainable from these agencies. Bookings and reservations can be made on request.

Sightseeing

There is a surprising wealth of things to see in this country which most people associate with the 'sun, sand and sea' of the Algarve. The best scenery and historical sights are concentrated in the North and centre of the country.

Northern Portugal is ideal for car tours. There are plenty of small historical towns, packed with medieval churches and buildings, and the green, rolling landscapes are quite beautiful. The cooler climate means that, even in mid-summer, temperatures are never too hot to make driving a chore rather than a pleasure.

The centre of the country has many old towns of interest to the sightseer, although the jewel in Portugal's crown has to be the capital city of Lisbon itself, with its relics of the nation's past glories. The major sites of Central Portugal are within day-tripping distance from the large resorts on the Estoril Coast, and can be reached by bus or car. As regards coach excursions, these can often be arranged through your tour operators or through a local travel agent or tourist office. The main coach companies organizing tours are **RN** (Avenida Fontes, Pereira de Melo, Lisbon. Tel: 56 00 15) or **Cityrama** (Avenida Praia da Vitoria, 12-B, Lisbon. Tel. 57 56 41). Most tours are of half-day or full-day duration. Planned excursions can often work out the most comfortable way to do a spot of undiluted sightseeing, although they are not cheap and you should make sure that the sights featured on the tour will be of interest to you. For details of specific sights, see the individual sections or The Sightseer on page 26.

There is a small entrance fee for most museums and galleries. There don't appear to be any hard and fast rules about opening hours, although most places of interest are open 10am to 5pm. The smaller sights may close for lunch (12.30pm–2.30pm). Most galleries and museums are closed on Mondays, except palaces which shut on

Tuesdays. The more popular sights open longer hours during the summer.

Shopping

The Portuguese take an afternoon siesta, so shops close down for two hours at one o'clock. The usual opening hours, then, are 9am to 1pm and 3pm to 7pm, Monday to Friday, and 9am to 1pm on Saturdays. In larger tourist resorts, the main supermarket and department stores do not close for lunch during the week and have longer opening hours at weekends. Major shopping centres usually open between 10am and midnight every day.

There is a wide choice of goods on sale in supermarkets and department stores – the only problem you are likely to run into is finding the Portuguese equivalent of British brand names. Supermarkets do carry a range of imported food from Britain, but prices for these are massively inflated and you'd do much better to buy local produce.

Good buys in Portugal are ceramics, leather, hand-embroidered linen and lace, tiles and copper and there are plenty of souvenir shops or street-sellers in tourist resorts with these items on sale. However, if you have the opportunity, head inland to one of the little towns on market day and do your souvenir shopping there. Local tourist offices usally have small 'What's On' leaflets which will tell you the places and days that markets are held, along with details of any other events or festivals which are taking place in the area. Prices are not fixed in these markets so you will have to barter for your goods. Although, initially, you may feel uncomfortable haggling over a price, remember that this is the way of life in Portugal and, if you don't take it too seriously, you can make a lot of friends this way. If you do accept the starting price the stall-holder quotes, not only will he be most disappointed that you don't enter into the bartering ritual, but you'll be paying a ridiculous price for something that could probably be bought cheaper in a souvenir shop.

Food and Drink

The culinary delights on offer in Portugal for the average holiday-maker are rarely a great voyage of discovery. However, the Portuguese themselves do eat well and you are likely to be served with copious amounts, even if you are just stopping off for a lunch-time snack.

If you are not the adventurous type when it comes to food, then there is the usual array of fast-food and burger joints in the major tourist resorts where you can stick to tried and tested formulae. The food in most large hotels catering for package-tour holiday-makers is also more likely to be a choice of international foods (i.e. lots of chips and salads) than traditional Portuguese home-cooking. Don't be put off, especially in the Algarve, by the appearance of restaurants from the outside. Often the most grotty-looking shacks turn into charming, well kept tavernas once you open the door, and the food bears no relation to the outside appearance of the place.

A continental breakfast is the most usual start to the day in large establishments, with bread, jam and butter. The bread is usually freshly baked every day and comes in the shape of a *papo seco*, a crisp breakfast roll. As for beverages, you will have the choice between tea and coffee. Although the British think that no one can make a cuppa like them, the Portuguese discovered tea at the time of the Great Discoveries, so they have had a couple of centuries to refine the tea-making technique. The result is much better and more flavoursome than the usual sorry-looking imitations of the real stuff that are dished up in most Mediterranean countries. As for coffee, a *bica* is a cup of strong, black coffee (rather like expresso), and *galão*, a glass of milky coffee. *Bica* can be really strong, so look out if you intend to drink a lot.

Lunch and dinner are the main meals of the day. Lunch is usually available from 12pm to 2.30pm and there are a number of places where you can have a midday snack or meal. If you just want a bite to eat, look out for cafés which generally put on a good show of sandwiches, or *tascas* (bar-restaurants), which usually offer a wide variety of food ranging from snacks to three-course lunches. Otherwise, there are restaurants – the *prato del dia* (dish of the day) menu usually represents the best value. For a small cost (about 700$00) you can consume a very filling three-course meal.

Mid-afternoon, when spirits begin to flag in the heat, a reviving cup of tea can be enjoyed in the numerous little *salão de chá* (tea-salons) found in most sizeable resorts. Here, too, you can sample Portuguese-style cakes and pastries which are often very sweet, very good and an absolute killer for the waistline. Teashops are usually open all day, although the traditional tea-time for locals is around four o'clock in the afternoon.

Dinner is usually served from 7.30 to 9.30pm. As prices for eating out are extremely reasonable, there is no reason why you should not venture beyond the confines of the hotel restaurant and sample some of the local cuisine. If you are on half-board, check if your meal is flexible and may be taken either at lunch-time or dinner-time. As a rule, the service charge is included in the cost of the meal, so additional tips are left entirely to the individual's discretion.

Of the food itself, there are not really too many regional variations – so whether you're in the Algarve or the Costa Verde, you're likely to be eating the same kinds of dishes. Garlic and olive oil are included in most recipes, although the result is not usually as heavy and oily as Spanish or Italian dishes.

To start off with, then, there are a good range of hearty soups to choose from. *Caldo verde* (potato, shredded kale, and slices of sausage) is the most well-known but *sopa riça da peixe* (a fairly rich, strongly flavoured fish soup) is also popular, as is *sopa de pedra* (mixed pork, red beans). It's best to avoid the latter if you have a weak stomach.

As regards main meals, not surprisingly for a nation of seafarers, seafood and fish are the basis of many dishes. *Bacalhau*, or salted codfish, is the Portuguese people's staple diet and there is a frequently quoted myth that there are 365 methods to prepare *bacalhau* – one for every day of the year! The average tourist is not likely to have the dubious pleasure of sampling this fish's numerous guises, but you will come across some of the more popular *bacalhau* dishes on restaurant menus; *assado* is straightforward roast cod, and *gomes de sá* is the fish baked with potatoes, olive oil, eggs and garlic. *Caldeira da de peixe* is another traditional fish dish worth trying; this is really just a hotchpotch of fish pieces casseroled together – the result is very fishy and quite delicious. Some of the tasty fish chowders need ordering a day in advance, so bear this in mind if you have a local restaurant. Equally tasty are the sardines roasted over braziers in the streets (especially in Lisbon) which are best eaten hot with your fingers.

Unfortunately, shellfish is quite expensive to eat in most large tourist resorts. Prices for crab and lobster dishes are often not quoted on the standard restaurant menu and, if this is the case, be sure to enquire what the cost is before you order or else you might find yourself in for an unpleasant surprise when the bill is presented. For cheaper seafood restaurants, it is worth searching out a quieter fishing town along the coast. The restaurants there will not only be more reasonably priced, but the chances are the food will be better, too.

Meat is not eaten widely, although pork is more popular than beef – especially in the South which is the main pork-producing area. Here, you can find dishes such as *lombo de porco com amêijoas* (loin of pork with mussels) or *iscas com elas* (pig's liver in wine). If you're after something more unusual then *cabrito assado* (roast kid) is available in many northern restaurants.

Desserts are not very elaborate and are usually based on a mixture of sugar, eggs and almonds. Some of these sweets are worth tasting just because of their bizarre names; *barrigas-de-freira* ('nun's bellies'), *papos-de-anjo* ('angel's stomach') and *gargantas-de-freira* ('nun's throat') are all popular among holiday-makers. Otherwise, milk puddings are common, especially *arroz doce* (rice pudding flavoured with cinnamon) and *pudim flan* (creme caramel).

Portuguese cheeses are no great shakes. They are mostly made from goats' or sheep's milk, and usually come in the shape of cheddar-type cheeses. One of the most tasty, but also the most expensive, is the *queijo da serra*, a soft brie-like cheese made in the mountains from sheep's milk.

As far as drinks are concerned, the choice of wines available in Portugal is excellent. The most well-known export is *vinho verde*, a light, green-tinted wine made in the North of the country; however, there are many regional and local varieties which are just as good. Among those available are *Dão*, grown in the Costa Verde, *Bairrada* from the Costa de Prata, *Carcavelos*, *Bucelas* and *Colares* grown near Lisbon, and *Setúbal* from the Lisbon coastline. Apart from these, there are literally hundreds of locally produced varieties. These are often high quality and very cheap (less than 500$00 a bottle), so there is plenty of opportunity to find a wine that suits your taste and pocket. Brand names from home are *not* cheap, so either drink the local stuff, or take your own in as duty free. Portugal's most famous export is port wine made from grapes grown in the Douro Valley near Oporto. Three kinds are available, ruby, tawny and white port. If you are a devotee, it's a good idea to take a couple of bottles of the white back with you, as it is not widely available and is expensive to buy in this country. The fortified Madeira wine is also one of Portugal's more renowned exports and there are three varieties to choose from: the aperitif wines, *Sercial* and *Verdelho*, and the after-dinner drink, *Malmsey*. Less well known are the Portuguese brandies. The best ones are the *Aguardentes* brandies, which are quite acceptable as a mellow evening liqueur. Other varieties, called *Bagaceiras*, are only for the hardened drinker. Made from the stalks and skins of the grapes, a couple of drinks of this stuff have enough kick to put you well into next week! For less potent brandies, try *Medronho*, from the distillation of red berries grown in the Algarve, or *moscatel* produced in the Setúbal area. Other traditional liqueurs are *ginjinha*, made from cherries, or the refreshing *anis escarchado*. Remember, it is much cheaper to sample the local liqueurs and spirits as you will have to pay through the nose for imported bottled drinks.

Portuguese beer (*cerveja*) is a good, light beer, excellent for drinking in the hot, dry climates of the South or in areas where you are not sure if the water is safe. The usual carbonated drinks are on sale and mineral water is also widely available. If you're really keen on going Portuguese, try the bottled mineral water from one of Portugal's many spas.

Food and drink are very competitively priced in Portugal. A snack lunch can be had for about 600$00 and a fully cooked meal costs around 700$00. A three-course meal with wine will set you back 1000$00–2500$00.

A high proportion of accommodation in the Algarve is self-catering and there are plenty of supermarkets and cornershops where provisions can be bought. Supermarkets, especially in the larger resorts, have extended opening hours during the summer months. Another more colourful alternative is the open-air markets, held weekly in most towns and villages. On the Algarve coastline, larger markets are held in **Portimão**, **Faro**, **Albufeira**, and **Vila Real de Santo Antonio**. Here, you will find fresh meat and fish stalls, and masses of fresh fruit and vegetables. A large range of cold meats and spicy sausages are available – for example, *chouriço*, spiced pork sausage; *fiambre*, cold ham; *presunto*, ham coated in paprika. A selection of these, coupled with crusty bread, fresh fruit and a bottle of cheap vinho and you are set for picnics. You'll have to go early if you want to get the best buys though – Portuguese housewives do their shopping here, too.

Night-life

The disco and night-club scene is fairly tame, but they are an up and coming mode of entertainment – partly because the tourist industry has realized that night-club facilities attract the young, affluent holiday-maker to Portuguese shores.

If you're based in a main resort, there are likely to be a couple of discotheques in the town centre, otherwise the best place to look to for night-time activity is the hotels themselves. Most hotels put on some kind of entertainment for guests. This is usually nothing ambitious – normally a second-rate cabaret or a weekly dance – and a bit of a dead loss for those with a lot of party spirit. However, the more up-market establishments often have glitzy night-clubs and these are usually open to non-residents.

The liveliest resorts are to be found in the South on the Algarve coastline, and some of the prime night-life spots are **Albufeira**, **Vilamoura** and **Quarteira**. On the Estoril Coast, head for the major resorts of **Estoril** and **Cascais**. **Lisbon**, as a major capital city, tends to be more cosmopolitan than the rest of Portugal, so here you will find the best choice of discos, night-clubs, bars, cinemas and restaurants.

Away from the disco-scene, most night-life is centred around the bars and restaurants. These often have jazz or traditional music playing. *Fado* singing (see page 30) is a popular form of entertainment among locals and if you find a good show you'll understand why . . . these melancholic songs, dealing with the tragedy of lost love, can pull a heart-wrenching, tear-jerking punch!

Films are another option for night-life. There is a cinema in most large towns, and more than one in the major cities of Lisbon, Faro and Oporto. Most films being shown are English, with Portuguese sub-titles, so you should have no problems with the language-barrier. Similarly, if you are based near Lisbon or Oporto, you will have the opportunity to go to the opera or classical music recitals. Theatre is another possibility, although you might find it hard-going unless you speak fluent Portuguese.

The festivals held throughout the summer are often colourful, exuberant events, with music, dancing and eating, which go on right through the day and well into the night. In addition to the major festivals (see The Socialite, page 29), if you're staying two weeks in one place, then there should be at least one (often more) carnival taking place within the immediate environs. For details, apply to the local tourist office, or obtain the booklet 'Festivals, Fairs and Folk Pilgrimages' published by the Portuguese National Tourist Board in London.

Communications

There are no real problems keeping in touch with home from Portugal. International telephone calls can be made direct from most central post offices and it is equally possible to write, telegraph or telex to Britain. The mail service between Portugal and Britain is reasonably efficient – the delivery time is about four to five days – but this obviously is not much good if you run out of money half-way through your holiday and have to wait for extra funds to be mailed. It's a far better idea to avoid this situation altogether by taking an emergency fund with you in the first place.

POST OFFICES

Post offices (*correio*) open from 9am to 6pm Mondays to Fridays. In main towns and large tourist resorts, opening hours are extended to 7pm and 9am to 12.30pm on Saturdays. International telephone booths are located inside major post offices and these are usually open late, closing at 11.30/12 at night.

POSTE RESTANTE

Mail can be held at central post offices. You will be required to produce your passport as proof of identity when collecting your correspondence. The Portuguese representative of American Express, **Star Travel**, will also hold mail for card-holders. Offices can be found in all major cities.

TELEPHONES

International telephone calls can be made from some public telephone kiosks in major cities or from booths in central post offices. There are direct dialling links between Britain and Portugal, so there is no need to go through the operator.

To telephone home, dial '00' for an international line, followed by the country code. For Britain this is '44' and '1' for the USA and Canada. Then dial the area code, and if you're phoning Britain, omit the initial '0'. So, for example, to phone London the number would be 00 44 1.

You can arrange to phone home from your hotel room, by going through the hotel switchboard. Don't do this if you can avoid it, as an extra charge is levied for this service.

The phone number for the emergency services in Portugal is 115. Calls are free. General Information can be obtained by dialling 16.

Moving Around the Country

There are a number of ways for the independent traveller to move about the country. Train, local bus services, express coaches, coach tours, and car-hire are all possible modes of travel for those who want to spend a few days away from the sun and surf of a beach holiday.

Undoubtedly, public transport is the cheapest way to go. Local buses are a good way to travel if you are based at one of the coastal resorts and want to have a day out at one of the inland market towns. Train travel, too, is only really suitable for short-haul journeys. The network does link up the main centres of population (i.e. Lisbon, Faro and Oporto), but the trains are notoriously slow and antiquated. For longer trips, try one of the express coach services. These are reasonably cheap and the service offered is more or less on a par with that of similar British companies. Coach tours are the obvious choice if you want to do a job-lot of the area's famous sites in a day or half-day. However, if you don't fancy the wide-eyed tourists-on-a-bus-bit, then car hire is another option. This needn't work out massively expensive; in fact, if two or three of you are sharing the hire and petrol costs per day, it could easily work out cheaper than going on a £30 per head bus tour. Roads are fairly good if you're travelling near the coast, although standards do deteriorate the further inland you go.

CAR HIRE

There are a number of local car-hire firms in Portugal itself, but it usually works out cheaper – and safer – to book before you go, either through one of the international car-hire firms or your tour operator. If you hire in this country in advance of your holiday, you will be paying a fixed price which is not dependent upon currency fluctuations. Renting through a local hire firm, especially at peak season, prices will be high and subject to change. Reserving ahead also means a car is assured when you arrive in Portugal, whereas by waiting until you get there, you may well find that, during peak-season, the car-hire firms are busy and no cars are available.

If you're hiring ahead in this country, there are two options open to you – to go through your tour operator or to book ahead with a large car-hire company, such as Hertz or Avis. Most of the major tour operators now offer car-hire facilities. Often the prices quoted are at specially negotiated rates with local car-hire firms and are much cheaper than could be obtained if you were shopping around by yourself. Usually, the cost of car hire through tour companies includes local taxes, unlimited mileage, delivery and collection to and from your hotel, and some kind of insurance policy. The disadvantage of booking with tour operators is that this facility is inflexible; you often have to reserve your car either when you book your holiday or at least a month in advance of arriving in the country.

By contrast, major car-hire companies only require bookings of up to seven days in advance: before supplying you with a car in Portugal. Car hire generally works out more expensive with a major car-hire firm – primarily because their prices exclude local tax charges. However, on the plus side, you do have the back-up and facilities of an international company. Obviously the rates and services available differ from firm to firm, but, usually, if you hire through one of the international firms, you get unlimited mileage, third-party insurance and an emergency break-down service. There is normally no charge for delivering cars to a different town, as long as the car-hire firm operates there, otherwise you will be expected to pay for collection expenses. As with tour company car hire, petrol and fines for driving offences are the driver's own responsibility.

The 'big four' car-hire companies each offer competitive rates to Portugal, with seven days' hire of a small car in peak season starting at about £120. This price includes unlimited mileage, car insurance and local tax. Personal accident insurance is extra.

Europcar Super Drive requires just 24 hours' notice for booking, while Budget's Leisure Drive, Avis Supervalue and Hertz Europe on Wheels need between three and seven days.

Also worth considering is the Suncars package, which compares well with the larger 'name' companies above. Further details are available from your travel agent or by writing to Suncars Ltd at 'Sandrocks', Rocky Lane, Haywards Heath, West Sussex RH19 3QS (Tel: 0444 456446).

As regards documentation, British and International driving licences are valid. Application forms for International licences can be obtained from AA or RAC offices. Minimum age for driving a hired car in Portugal is usually twenty-three, and you must have held a full licence for one whole year. Rates are usually inclusive of third-party insurance and collision damage waiver, although, if you are freelancing with a Portuguese firm, you should make sure you know what kind of insurance cover is included in the basic price. Car-hire companies usually ask for a refundable deposit to be paid in advance.

Petrol comes in two grades, super (4-star) or normal (2-star), and is sold by the litre. On the motorway sections, there are special orange coloured phones for use in emergencies. Otherwise, if you are involved in a serious accident phone 115 for emergency services. For more details, see By Car section of Independent Means (page 123).

TRAINS

Train services leave a lot to be desired. They are frustratingly slow and often very crowded during the summer. The rail network is chiefly concentrated along the coastline, so this mode of travelling is not much good for those who want to tour the interior extensively. However, it's a useful means of transport between the major cities if you pay a supplement and take the fast rapido trains.

Reservations are not necessary on inland trains, and on express trains they are free, providing you book the day before departure. The cost of reservations is small and, as the trains are busy, they're well worth the extra cost to make sure you get a seat.

BUSES

There is an extensive network of bus services, connecting even the smallest country towns with the main cities. The local buses, run by RN (Rodoviaria Nacional), are a good way to see the countryside, or for short trips to the more remote hamlets in the surrounding area. Bus timetables are available from the local tourist office or from the nearest bus station. For quicker links between major centres of population (e.g. Faro, Lisbon and Oporto) there are a number of companies who run luxury coach express. Details of these can be obtained at the local tourist office.

Fares are low, so bussing it is a relatively inexpensive way to move about the country. It's a good idea to make sure that you are at the bus station well in advance of the departure time, as buses are often busy and rather chaotic – especially in mid-summer. For long-haul trips on express coaches, it's worth checking whether reservations can be made in advance – this way you are not only assured of getting a seat, but, also, if you book early enough, you can specify whether you want smoking or non-smoking seats.

For coach trips which take in several places of interest, it is best to take a planned day or half-day excursion. These can often be arranged through the tour operator rep at your resort, otherwise details are usually available from local travel agents or tourist information offices.

TAXIS

Taxis (distinguished by their green and black colour) are cheap in Portugal, and thus a good way to travel short distances around town. They can be ordered from your hotel, hailed in the street, or in larger resorts, picked up at the taxi ranks. If you are travelling one-way outside the city limits, the taxi driver is allowed to charge the price of the return journey. A supplementary fare can also be levied if passengers are travelling with several items of heavy luggage. If this applies to you then it is worth enquiring how much this extra charge will be before you set off. Fares go up by 20 per cent between 11pm and 6am.

Taxis should be metered or have a list of fares written in French and English on hand for passengers' inspection. If neither of these tariff-indicators are available, negotiate your fare before you start off, and hold the driver to it. Small tips are customary.

Problems/Emergencies

MEDICAL

If it's a minor problem, head for a chemist. *Farmacias* should have the name and address of the nearest all-night chemist clearly displayed in their windows. If it's more serious, get to a hospital or phone an ambulance (dial 115), and remember British citizens with an E111 certificate are entitled to free emergency hospital treatment (see Health, page 49).

POLICE

The police (*Policia de Segurança Pública* or PSP) must be contacted if any of your belongings have been stolen. Insist on a copy of your statement – insurance companies often require this as proof of theft before they will reimburse you. It is also a good idea to inform your travel rep. Telephone 115 in emergencies.

EMBASSIES AND CONSULATES

The British Embassy is at Rua São Domingos à Lapa 37, Lisbon 1200 (Tel: 661191). The British Consulate in **Oporto** is at Avenida da Boa Vista 3072 (Tel: 684789); in the Algarve, 21 Rua de Santa Isabel, **Portimão** (Tel: 23071), and Rua General Humberto Delgado 4, **Vila Real de Santo Antonio** (Tel: 43729); the Costa de Prata, Quinta de Santa Maria, Estrada de Tavereve, 3080, **Figueira da Foz** (Tel: 22235); on Madeira at 14, Rua da Sé, **Funchal** (Tel: 21221); the Azores, at 26, Rua Dr Bruno Tavares Carreiro, 9500 **Ponta Delgada**, São Miguel (Tel: 252 15/6).

WORK

Unemployment is high in Portugal so there are not many opportunities for long-term work, apart from teaching English to Portuguese students. To do this you usually need a TEFL or equivalent qualification, and a work permit. Prospective employers are responsible for arranging employees' work permits through the Ministry of Labour. Otherwise, there is the usual selection of low-paid, hard-worked seasonal employment to be found in most major cities and tourist resorts. Bar and hotel work in the Algarve during the peak-season months constitute the best opportunity for casual work in Portugal.

WOMEN

Portugal is a Roman Catholic country and although among the younger set this may be nothing more than a convenient label, centuries of devout religion have left their marks and one of these is that Portuguese women are much less independent and liberated than their counterparts in Northern Europe. Especially in the North of the country, young Portuguese women will rarely travel alone. Having said that, the potential problems the lone woman might be faced with are no greater in Portugal than in the rest of Europe. In fact, Portuguese males are a lot less unbearably intrusive than would-be Spanish and Italian romeos. If you follow the usual principles of not courting trouble by walking home through ill-lit streets, etc, you should have no problems.

In the main resorts, where there are probably more holiday-makers than Portuguese, there are no strictures about what kinds of clothes you wear, although churches often require that visitors be dressed 'respectfully', which usually means no shorts and skimpy T-shirts. In the rural districts of Northern Portugal, you might find that similar attire gets you a few stares from the local lads, but that, usually, is as far as it goes. If anything nasty starts to develop, get hold of a policeman – or make as much noise as possible.

A Potted History of Portugal

Portugal's past has often been overshadowed by the turbulent and colourful histories of its larger neighbours, Spain and France. Nevertheless, this small country, which enjoyed two centuries of great maritime voyaging, was instrumental in pushing back the geographical boundaries of the known world throughout the Middle Ages and, consequently, became the centre of one of the largest empires the world has ever seen.

The first known influx of settlers into the Western part of the Iberian peninsula were the Celts around 700 to 600 BC. Their main legacy to modern-day Portugal are the remains of the large *citanias*, or fortified towns which are scattered across the North of Portugal, the most notable of which is Citania de Britaras located near the towns of Guimarães and Braga. After the Celts came a number of famous peoples, who established bases for a brief time in Portugal before history took its course and replaced them with another more powerful race. The Phoenicians, the Romans and the Visigoths all left the traces of their civilizations and cultures, but the people who had the single greatest influence on the Iberian peninsula were the Moors, who made incursions for a period of 150 years beginning in the eighth century. With them, the invaders brought the sophisticated Moorish culture and sense of refinement. While the rest of Europe groaned under the yoke of the Dark Ages, Southern Spain and Portugal developed, under the influence of the Muslims, advanced agricultural and architectural methods, and benefitted culturally from the delicacy and beauty of Moorish art. The far-reaching effect the Moors had on the Iberian peninsula can still be seen today, in the old Moorish quarters of many southern towns, and the intricate geometric designs which adorn much of the hand-crafted tile and filigree work. Indeed, the place name 'Algarve' is derived from the Arabic, meaning 'a place beyond'.

The movement to re-Christianise the peninsula became a potent force in the tenth and 11th centuries, and eventually the kingdoms of Galicia and León were seized from Moorish domination. At this point, there was still no separate Portuguese dominion. What did exist, however, was a province around the banks of the river Tagus, called Portucale.

In 1095, the King of León, Castile and Galicia gave his daughter Teresa in marriage to a French nobleman called Raimundo, as a gesture of thanks for the help France had given him in his Moorish campaigns. With Teresa went a generous dowry of the lands of Portucale. This province rapidly expanded its administrative centre and structure and, in 1140, Teresa's son Afonso Henriques proclaimed himself the first king of Portugal. Over the next two centuries the kingdom extended its boundaries southwards, until eventually it occupied roughly the same geographic boundaries as modern Portugal today.

There followed a phase of peace and embryonic economic development. It was during this time that Portugal signed its historic trade agreement with England, an alliance which has lasted up to the present day and is, thus, one of the oldest allegiances Europe has ever seen. The ensuing period was marred by strife between Castile and Portugal, as the Castilians tried to regain control of the fledgling nation, but this ended in 1387, with victory for Portugal.

With political stability established at home, Portugal turned its attention outwards over the largely uncharted, undiscovered seas to the prospects of new worlds. Falling incomes from land revenues and the scarcity of land to supply all members of the aristocracy contributed to the Great Sea Voyages, which enjoyed royal patronage. This, coupled with the nation's great tradition of seafaring, gave the impetus for the course of maritime discoveries which was undertaken and continued through the next two centuries.

The role of Prince Henry the Navigator as a real visionary in the development of these sea voyages cannot be understated. Under his guidance, a navigational school was set up at Sagres, which taught such great names as Vasco da Gama and Christopher Columbus. Ship-building techniques were also improved and perfected and this culminated in the famous Portuguese *caravels*, vessels especially designed to weather the dangers involved in lengthy sea journeys. These ships voyaged around the previously uncharted tip of Southern Africa, monopolized the trade routes from the coast of Africa and eventually reached India, a much sought-after pearl because of her wealth of spices, silks and precious stones. In 1494, a conflict of interests arose between Portugal and Spain, the other nation actively pursuing a policy of sea-discoveries. This dispute was solved by the arbitrating power of Pope Alexander II. So there would be no further quarrels over sovereignty, the two countries agreed to split the world into two hemispheres vertically. Included in Portugal's half was the wealthy, but as-yet undiscovered Brazil.

Colonization followed as a consequence of the discoveries and in a short space of time Portugal established colonies in Africa and as far afield as Japan. In worst tradition, the country milked its colonies of their natural resources in order to finance an ailing economy at home. In Portugal itself, the peasants saw little of this phenomenal wealth and there were sharp contrasts between the well-hecled merchants, the *ancien régime* of the aristocracy, and the impoverished condition of the ordinary people. Economically, there remained an overdependence on small unproductive unit-farming and a shortage of skilled labour.

By the beginning of the 17th century, Portugal's golden era began to wane. The death of the monarch, Dom Sebastião, in 1578, while pursuing a fruitless and expensive campaign in North Africa, left the Portuguese throne vulnerable to Castilian domination. This threat was staved off briefly when the elderly Cardinal Henrique was placed on the throne, but was renewed again following his death.

The pressure exerted by Castile proved to be irresistible. Philip II of Spain was crowned Felipe I of Portugal and this began a 60-year rule by the Castilian sovereigns. At first, the separate Portuguese institutions, systems, and cultures were respected by the Castilian monarchs. However, after a lapse of a few years, it became clear that Portugal was worse off than ever before under Castilian rule. Heavy taxes were levied, there was greater intervention in Portugal's internal affairs, and the influence of Castilian culture was pervasive and corruptive to Portuguese traditions. Abroad, the situation could not have been worse; continuous guerrilla warfare was being waged as the colonies moved closer and closer to independence. All these factors acted as a catalyst for a revolution. And indeed it came, in 1640 – although it was not until 1668 that Portugal finally managed to shake off the mantle of Castilian domination.

There followed a brief period of renaissance in Portugal's fortunes. The nation's power in the East had all but disappeared, but it was Brazil in the West who was to prop up the country for a while, with the income gleaned from its vast natural resources of tobacco, cotton and minerals. This influx of wealth brought about renewed activity in the country. Progress was made in modernizing agricultural methods, the famous port wine monopolies were created, advances were achieved in ship-building, there was an upsurge in manufacturing and a revival in cultural activity.

This forward-looking momentum was somewhat abated at the end of the 18th century, with the break-up of the country's fragile political stability. European events impinged. Napoleon invaded, the monarch disappeared to Brazil, and Portugal was once again plunged into a state of national crisis. The Napoleonic threat was eventually staved off with help from the old ally, England, but the ideology and example of the French Revolution had struck a resonant chord among a people where the majority of the population lived in poverty while the nobles 'ate cake' and enjoyed a life of luxury. All these conditions prompted the drawing up of a constitution in 1820 whereby the monarch was required to relinquish his executive power, and the traditional powers of the nobility were substantially weakened.

This step was significant because it represented the first formalized statement of the new spirit of democracy which was germinating in the country. However, the path to a democratic state was fraught with obstacles and in the period between 1822 and 1908, the country veered between a return to absolutism, as embodied by the monarch's rule, and the new-found sense of democracy. This was also a time of economic disarray, although in the intervening periods of peace, considerable social advances were made, such as the abolition of slavery and the death penalty, and the establishment of compulsory primary school education.

In 1910, following a military coup, the first democratic republic was established. However, despite professed egalitarian policies, there was over-optimism about what could be achieved in a short time and the changes felt at grass-roots level among the ordinary Portuguese people were minimal. In the war-years of 1914 to 1919, Portugal sided with the allies, but emerged from the war with the economic clouds darkening at home. The democratic spirit faltered and a military coup overthrew the government in 1926. This was immediately followed by another revolt, led by General Carmona. A dictatorial regime was subsequently instigated with all the trappings of a one-party state; official censorship of the media, suppression of workers' rights, a police force modelled on the Gestapo. Under the directorship of Prime Minister Salazar, this autocratic rule continued until 1968, when the iron-grip of the leader was loosened following an accident which caused him brain damage.

Two main factors gave rise to the huge welter of dissatisfaction among the military and the ordinary people: the pointlessness of a thirteen-year war being waged in Africa, which no one believed in any longer – not even the soldiers who were doing the fighting; and the lack of any change in the harsh, repressive regime which was being operated at home. When the new prime minister who replaced Salazar failed to address these problems in any constructive fashion, the sense of disillusionment and betrayal grew. After one abortive attempt, there was eventually a successful bloodless coup on 25 April 1974. The action was initiated by the military in Lisbon but, with popular support throughout the country, the revolution snowballed, until the government and all its administrators were deposed without opposition. This event is vividly remembered in modern-day Portugal, and 'lest we forget', the Portuguese authorities name bridges after the date of the revolution, while the young people remember it in spray-can graffiti on city walls.

After the overthrow, it was more or less obligatory that a multi-party system be set up. With the wind of change blowing, social policy, restructuring of the industrial infrastructure, and the fairer distribution of wealth among people became the aspirations of those involved in the new system. Not that everything was plain sailing; for a time there existed a deep ideological divide between the communist spirit in the South, and the deep conservatism of the North – with the instigation of a democratic state the Portuguese people were entering largely uncharted waters.

For several years following, the country was in a state of flux. A number of governments were elected for a short period of rule and countless political parties rose with meteoric public support only to disappear within a matter of months. So far, despite the extremist tendencies which were prevalent immediately after the revolution, only moderate left-wing governments have been voted into power. For the 11 years following the revolution, the president of the new republic was ex-soldier Eanes. Although required by the constitution to step down from his presidency in 1986, Eanes has emerged as a figure of stability in the mercurial political climate. As such, he enjoys vast popular support among the Portuguese people and looks set to remain an important figure in Portuguese politics for some time to come.

At elections in October 1985, Dr Cavaco e Silva led his Social Democrat party to victory. In 1986, Portugal became a member of the EEC. As part of the community, it is hoped that the country will see an upturn in its economic output, particularly in the agricultural sector. Today tourism is one of the most quickly growing industries in Portugal. Over a period of twenty years, the number of holiday-makers coming to Portugal has tripled and that trend looks set to continue. As more people drift away from the likes of Spain or Greece, in search of a new, more exotic holiday destination, Portugal is just beginning to open up to tourism. Although the golden beaches and guaranteed sunshine of the Algarve have made it a favourite haunt among holiday-makers for a number of years now, the beautiful landscapes of the North and charming old capital Lisbon are attracting more and more fans each year and tour operators are increasingly offering packages to these destinations. But it is not just the climate that brings people back to Portugal. British people in particular find the 'olde worlde' atmosphere and friendliness of the people very reminiscent of all the best that Britain has to offer – and that's a holiday attraction that no amount of mass tourism can alter.

Part Four

THE COUNTRY

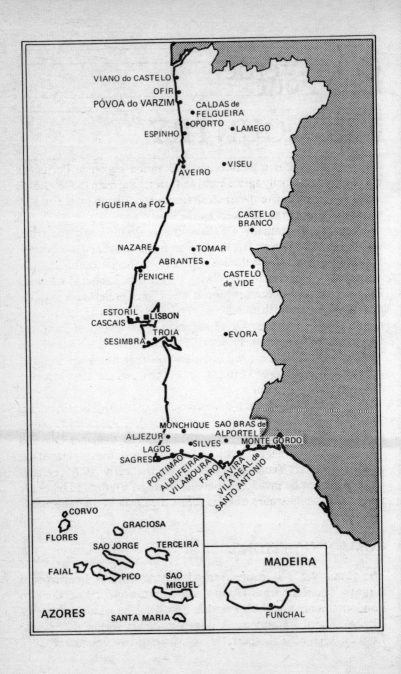

VIANO do CASTELO
OFIR
PÓVOA do VARZIM
CALDAS de
FELGUEIRA
OPORTO
LAMEGO
ESPINHO
VISEU
AVEIRO
FIGUEIRA da FOZ
CASTELO
BRANCO
NAZARE
TOMAR
ABRANTES
PENICHE
CASTELO
de VIDE
ESTORIL
LISBON
CASCAIS
TROIA
EVORA
SESIMBRA
MONCHIQUE
SAO BRAS de
ALPORTEL
ALJEZUR
SILVES
MONTE GORDO
LAGOS
SAGRES
PORTIMAO
ALBUFEIRA
VILAMOURA
FARO
TAVIRA
VILA REAL de
SANTO ANTONIO

CORVO
GRACIOSA
FLORES
SAO JORGE
TERCEIRA
MADEIRA
FAIAL
PICO
SAO
MIGUEL
AZORES
SANTA MARIA
FUNCHAL

Costa Verde

HISTORY

The Costa Verde is a picturesque and varied region in Portugal's north-east, principally agricultural and stretching from the south side of the Douro Valley to the Spanish frontier, bordered on the east by the mountains and on the west by the sea.

This area was initially a Palaeolithic civilization and the tribal isolation it enjoyed gave rise to some art forms peculiar to the region. It was later overrun by the Romans and in the 1st century BC the settlement of Bracara became Bracara Augustus, capital of a Roman Province. In the 6th century, Iberia was unified under the Visigoths, and in 716 the Moorish invasion reached the Costa Verde, followed by the Christian reconquest and the creation of the county of Porto and Cale which was to become Portugal. The nation's roots lie in the Costa Verde: it was from the town of Guimaraes that Afonso Henriques, self-proclaimed King of Portugal, set out to expel the Moors; and in 1140 Portugal was born.

The 15th and 16th centuries saw many scuffles with neighbouring Spain. It was during this period that Portugal became a major world power and the Age of Discovery (with men like Bartholomeu Dias and Vasco da Gama) brought wealth and importance to the seaports of the region, such as Viana do Castelo. In the early 19th century, Napoleon's armies invaded, following Portugal's refusal to blockade British ports, and armies trekked across the Costa Verde once more.

COMMUNICATIONS

The Costa Verde is easily reached. Pedras Rubras International Airport, ten miles from Oporto, has international connections to London among other cities, and is linked to the wider contacts of Lisbon. There are also many domestic flights within the region. Leixões, the main seaport, is not particularly important as a

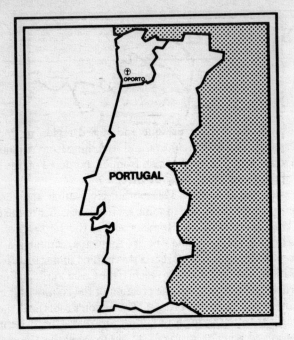

passenger terminus. Within the region there is a comprehensive bus system and the railway network connects all places of importance and eventually crosses the Minho into Spain.

CLIMATE

The climate is mild, thanks to the moderating influence of the Gulf Stream. The mean summer temperature is 68°F (20°C); however, the sea temperature in the same season is a chillier 61°F (16°C). The factors responsible for these temperatures are also the cause of the name 'Costa Verde' or 'Green Coast' – the luxuriant vegetation is the result of a relatively high annual rainfall. Summer is generally dry, but a visit to the Costa Verde in the off season has some of the characteristics of August in Cornwall!

SPECIALITIES

Regional specialities are mostly of agricultural origin, such as fishermen's sweaters, carved ox yokes and kitchenware, often

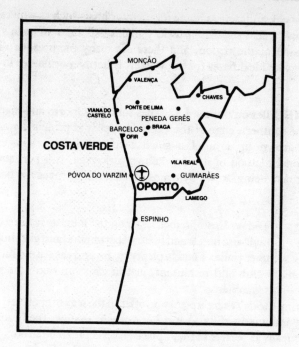

decorated with traditional patterns. Skilled gold- and silversmiths produce delicate filigree work, and the strongly religious nature of the people has perpetuated the making of religious statuary.

Regional gastronomy puts particular emphasis on seafood of all kinds, often cooked to a 'secret' local recipe – among the more unusual dishes are lampreys (spitted or stewed), eels and octopus. Ham and sausage are typical products along the Spanish frontier.

More than its food, the Costa Verde is known for its wines. Port is produced in the Douro Valley and is drunk all over the world, and vinho verde, the slightly sparkling table wine, also comes from this part of the country.

WHERE TO GO FOR WHAT

Just inside the region lies Portugal's only National Park, the Gerês. This is a wilderness bordering on the mountains, mainly luxuriant forest of oak and pine, a home for many animals such as wolves, wild boar and wild cats. Prehistoric remains tell tales of man's early occupation of the region, and there are many picturesque villages which make ideal bases for the walker, fisherman or nature lover.

ESPINHO lies on the coast 12 miles south of Oporto and marks the extreme southern edge of the Costa Verde. It is principally a resort town, grown up around a small medieval fishing village. The traditional method of fishing, known as *xavéga*, still persists, with fishing nets being drawn by teams of oxen which cover the beach.

Today, Espinho focuses upon the tourist. It has a core of high-rise hotels and luxury apartments, and gift shops do a roaring summer trade. There's plenty to do, and the casino incorporates a night-club and restaurant, just in case you don't fancy your chances as a gambler.

During the day there's plenty on offer in the way of sport, especially sailing and windsurfing. A word of caution, though: the beaches are by no means as perfect as they appear. Currents can be strong, so take notice of the warning flags. Add to that the fact that the beaches south of Oporto are becoming increasingly polluted and you may think twice about sea bathing. Only one hotel, the **Praia Golfe**, has a pool, though there are hot sea water baths whose medicinal properties are reputedly good for rheumatism. You can always sunbathe, and there's an eighteen-hole golf course.

Out of season, the wide boulevards are much quieter. It's possible to view the town without being caught up in the frantic rush, and to absorb some of its history. The town has a world famous violin workshop, and is well known as a furniture centre. There are plenty of hotels, such as the **Praia Golfe** and the **Mar Azul**, and many inexpensive pensions, while restaurants include the **Marisqueira**. Thirteen miles inland there is the village of RIO MEAÕ, which has a 16th-century parish church, although most of it dates from 200 years later. There is also a campsite here (Tel: 723718) and an apartment complex, **Apart Hotel** (Tel: 72334). If you don't feel like cooking for yourself, there is a restaurant. They also provide a babysitting service.

OPORTO, Portugal's second largest city, dominates the north of the country. In world rankings of tourist cities it doesn't rate very highly: its sights are limited and its charm not immediately apparent, but it is, and has been for centuries, the commercial centre of the country, giving its name to the world famous port wines.

The city is located on the north bank of the Douro, a river whose impressive gorge is spanned by three no less impressive bridges – the **Maria Pia** railway bridge designed by Gustav Eiffel (better known for the Eiffel Tower); a more utilitarian-looking concrete motorway bridge, and the two-storey **Ponte de Dom Luis**. All three connect the city to Vila Nova de Gaia.

An old and oft-repeated saying in Portugal comments on the major cities: 'Coimbra sings, Braga prays, Lisbon shows off and Oporto works'; and Porto is indeed a functional city, as its commercial status testifies. First impressions are almost always a little unfavourable, with later ones often discovering the value of hidden worth rather than outward show. Dull at first sight, the city is currently in the process of urban renewal – often a troubled process, but in this case having surprisingly tasteful results.

The waterfront is typical of the city. The Douro is known as the 'golden river' and along its north bank, as well as from the bridges spanning its gorge, the city can be seen at its most striking. The bridges are breathtaking and the waterfront lively and colourful. It is this part of the city that Prince Henry the Navigator, inspiration behind Portuguese expeditions in search of the New World, was born. The river itself, though crucial to Oporto's development, is unsafe, gradually silting up and given to flooding. As a result, many maritime functions have been transferred to LEIXÕES, where an artificial harbour and an industrial complex have been built.

Most of the tourist's attention, however, will be focused on the tiny, cramped city centre, stretching inland from the river in a maze of one-way streets which could have been designed to pose problems for the motorist. The centre is full of atmospheric bars and cheap seafood restaurants, as well as a daily market on the waterfront. Beyond, Oporto sprawls up the valley sides in the neat patterns of suburbia.

Oporto's origins are pre-Roman. As the settlement of Cale, it developed under the Roman Empire into the commercial settlement it has been ever since. Later waves of invaders swept across Iberia, but Oporto remained a stronghold of Christianity against the Barbarians and the Moors. Lying as it does in the region between the Douro and the Minho rivers, it was the chief town of the estates given as dowry to Princess Teresa of Burgundy and the heart of the new nation liberated from the Moors by her son, Afonso Henriques – the nation whose name derives from the ancient and modern names for the city, Porto and Cale.

In the 10th century, a crusader was rewarded for his part in the struggle to recapture Jerusalem with a parcel of land in the Douro Valley, which he planted with vines transported from his native Burgundy – vines which, thriving in the fertile soils and summer heat, became the port wine which has long been the country's most famous export. The trade has always been particularly connected with England, Portugal's longest-standing ally, as English monarchs developed a taste for the wine. As a result, many English families emigrated to Oporto, and many companies bear English names.

Despite being the traditional centre for port wines, Oporto has lost much of its activity to **VILA NOVA DE GAIA** on the opposite side of the river, where almost all the great port wine companies now have their headquarters. It is there that the grapes are brought in spring, and from there that the wine is eventually taken.

Port is a fine rich wine, and accompanies the city's equally rich cuisine. The traditional dish is tripe, the least romantic-sounding of all dishes, cooked with chicken and sausage. The reason for this is that, in order to supply the voyages of discovery, almost all the livestock was slaughtered and salted, with only the offal remaining in the town. Other local specialities include *caldo verde*, a thick soup, as well as fish and seafood.

As might be expected of so large a city, Oporto is not short of accommodation, although it is equally to be expected that standards and prices will show great variation. Examples range from the luxury **Meridien** (Avenida Boavis, Tel: 66896) to the smaller, more reasonably priced **Imperio** (Praça da Batalha, Tel: 26861) with numerous pensions and residencias such as the **Pensão do Brasil** (Rua Formosa, Tel: 30516) and the **Pensão França** (Praça Gomes Teixeira, Tel: 22791). There is also a youth hostel for which advance booking would be wise. A word of warning here – Oporto's main festival, the Feast of St John, occurs at the end of June, so arriving and expecting to find instant accommodation isn't wise at this time.

There's no shortage of places to eat and drink in the city centre, although out towards the suburbs the choice is more limited. The centre has everything from restaurants such as the **Taberna Bebedos** (Cais de Ribeira) serving huge, cheap portions of local and regional specialities, to international menus in hotel restaurants. Bars vary from the sleazy to the sublime, and many of the cafés serving coffee and glasses of port are worth a visit. They are often panelled in rosewood or mahogany and have interesting interiors (a taste acquired from 18th-century British immigrants). Of these, the **Imperial** and **Majestic** are the best known.

This predominantly commercial city has, on first acquaintance, little to see other than the three majestic bridges spanning the Douro, and little to do beyond crossing them to taste port in Vila Nova de Gaia. Although Oporto is certainly devoid of the extravagant splendour of Lisbon, it has plenty of character and history, and many of its old buildings are worth seeking out.

The *sé*, or cathedral, stands in the Morro da Sé on top of the cliffs above the Douro gorge. Founded in the 12th century, it is a dark and austere structure with fortifications reminding the visitor that its origins lie in the most turbulent part of the nation's history. (It was from the cathedral steps in 1147 that the Archbishop berated a sheepish populace and exhorted them to join Afonso Henriques in his quest to free Lisbon from the Moors.) Inside is a beautiful cloister, Gothic in style, dating from the 14th century and brightened by a depiction of the Song of Songs, while the side chapel of **São Vincente** has a baroque façade. The *sé*'s altarpiece is silver, and only escaped looting by Napoleon's armies through being whitewashed!

Oporto is rich in churches. The church of **São Francisco**, close to the *sé*, was built in 1416 but most of its interior decoration dates from the 17th century. It appears relatively simple on the outside, but as you enter, a riot of rococo style emerges, all gilt cherubs and intricate decoration. It is the finest of all the city's churches, owing its richness to a curious fashion among noblemen who paid to be buried within its walls – curious, because Francis is the patron saint of the poor. Oldest of the churches is the **Cedofeíta**, which just predates the *sé*, and in the **Misericordia** church is a beautiful painting of Christ on the cross, claimed by art historians as being the work of Hans Holbein or Jean de la Pasture.

The **Torré dos Clérigos**, built by the Italian, Nicolas Nasani, is the tallest structure in Portugal and provides an unparalleled view of the city. There are three good museums. The **Ethnographic Museum**, close to the Torré dos Clérigos, focuses upon the tradition, folklore and history of the province, while the other two are named after **Guerra Junqueiro** the poet, and the sculptor **Soarés dos Reis** respectively. The former is the poet's home with all its contents, including some particularly fine examples of furniture and silver, while the latter, in the **Palaçio das Caranças**, contains sculptures (many by dos Reis himself) and some antique English furniture. The building was used as Marshal Sault's headquarters during the Peninsular War.

Also not to be missed is the **Babsa**, Portugal's Stock Exchange, built in the 19th century. Guided tours are available and will take you into the wonderful **Arab Hall**. The 14th-century **Casa do Infante**, close to the waterfront, is reputedly the birthplace of Henry the Navigator.

On the coast road to the North lies a Gothic church at **Leça do Balio**, site of the wedding of Dom Fernando and Leonor, the queen who was to prove faithless to him – an interesting afternoon trip.

VILA NOVA DE GAIA is on the south bank of the River Douro, remaining separate from Oporto, although connected to it by three bridges and technically a part of suburbia. This is the centre of the port industry where most of the port 'lodges' promote an informal family image. Many are open daily, offering free tours and tastings to the visitor. Although the traditional image of port is of a red wine, it is possible to buy a white variety. The wines are either blended or, in good years, left unblended, when they are considered to be vintage.

Vila Nova de Gaia is noted for more than just port, being the birthplace of the noted Portuguese sculptors, Soarés dos Reis and Teixeira Lopes. It also has a circular church, that of **Nossa Senhora do Pilar**, used by Wellington in the Peninsular War and now a barracks with a superb view across the Douro.

Boat trips leave every hour from the quay, taking visitors up the gorge of the fickle river and under the three bridges.

MATOSINHOS lies on the coast just outside Oporto. Its beaches are both good and extensive, but its proximity to the industrial complex at Leixões has caused heavy pollution, so swimming and water sports are not advisable, although there are plenty of swimming pools. The town is principally a resort and provides all necessary facilities for holiday-maker and day-tripper alike.

Like most of the coastal resorts, Matosinhos was originally a fishing village and has now been overtaken by the tourist industry, although remaining a base for a fishing industry whose catch of sardines is canned nearby. Town and beach are backed by pine-woods which contain a well-run campsite, with hotel accommodation relatively easy to find, depending on the season.

In the town itself, the 18th-century church of **Senhor Bom Jesus** is worth a visit and the **Quinta da Conçeicao** (municipal park) has a doorway in the Manueline style.

Close to Matosinhos, at **SÃO MAMEDE DE INFESTA**, is the **Salazar Museum**, which houses artefacts from Portugal's recent past, while at LEÇA DE PALMEIRA, just to the north, is the 17th-century castle of **Nossa Senhora das Neves**.

VILA DO CONDE, lying on the coast ten miles to the north of Oporto, is a quiet fishing village at the mouth of the River Ave. Although it is actually included in the metropolitan district of Oporto, it is in reality a peaceful settlement with beaches less polluted than those further down the coast.

The town has some fine monuments and a bustling medieval quarter of narrow, crowded streets. It is dominated by the **Convento da Santa Clara**, which dates from the 14th century and is now an orphanage, although it has an elegant cloister and incorporates a parish church.

Well known for traditional crafts, Vila do Conde remains a lacemaking centre and is also known for its embroidered woollen jumpers. Some boats are still built here and maritime traditions are reflected in the wide choice of fish and seafood on offer in local restaurants which, like the casino, have sprung up to cater for the holiday-maker. Accommodation is available but can be quite expensive and in high summer the town may be full; however, most of the small outlying hamlets have at least one pension.

Although there are perhaps few significant monuments in the

town itself, some of the surrounding villages can boast buildings of note. At AZUARA, just outside the town, is a 16th-century parish church and the **Capuchos** monastery, while five miles to the north-east at RIO MAU is the 12th-century church of **São Cristovão**. At VAIRO, three miles to the south-west, the monastery of **São Bento** was the source of the first document to be written in the Portuguese language.

PÓVOA DO VARZIM lies three miles north of Vila do Conde and, despite similar origins, has now outstripped all neighbouring resorts. Although the southern part of the town still concentrates on fishing, the activity which is its major economic mainstay (there is a daily fish auction), the main business is tourism and it is now a leading tourist resort, making the most of its dune-backed beaches. The northern part of the town has been highly developed, with facilities including luxury hotels and a casino.

The town is very much a summer resort and in winter becomes the preserve of the locals, who continue to fish and tend the vines growing in sheltered depressions in the dunes.

Like its close neighbour Vila do Conde, Póvoa do Varzim has a long tradition of local handicrafts, especially fishermen's sweaters (embroidered or plain) and silver and gold ware of the highest quality and intricacy. Its gastronomic delights are seafood, especially the ubiquitous sardine and a local method of cooking hake.

As in all resorts, accommodation is plentiful, but booking at the height of the summer is a useful precaution. Although many of the hotels are soulless seafront tower blocks, they are well equipped and usually good value, such as the de luxe **Vermar Dom Pedro** in the Avenida de Mar (Tel: 68 34 01). Small, cheap hotels are relatively scarce and some of the restaurants are over expensive, so take care.

There is little to see in the town, although the harbour is dominated by the ruins of a small castle, **Nossa Senhora de Conçeicao**, dating from the 18th century, and there is also a good local history museum. There is plenty to do other than sightsee, since the town is adequately provided for in terms of beach and night-life. Close by, the village of RATES contains the 12th-century church of **São Pedro**.

FAO is eleven miles up the coast on the estuary of the River Cávado and with its close neighbours Ofir and Esposende forms a trio of small, well-equipped resorts. Like so many others, it is a fishing village turned summer boom town. The seaweed gatherers pursuing their traditional occupation look oddly out of place on the sandy stretches thronging with holiday-makers.

The beaches are good, backed by dunes and pine-woods, and ideal for camping; many water sports are also available. There is a fine 18th-century church, **Bom Jesus**, and excursions are possible to the archaeological site of CITANIA, four miles away. Specialities are fishermen's sweaters, statuary and basketry. Accommodation is plentiful and usually cheap, and seafood restaurants abound, with grilled sardines again a local speciality.

OFIR lies on the coast while Fao, less than a mile away, is on the river estuary. This fact apart, the two resorts could be twins, each with the same to offer in the way of beaches, food, accommodation (try the **Hotel Ofir**, Tel: 96 13 83) and souvenirs.

ESPOSENDE is on the north bank of the Cávado estuary, a couple of miles from Fao. Again the pattern recurs – traditional fishing village becomes tourist resort thanks to sandy beaches and fringing pine-woods. Yet with all the facilities and extensive hotel development, the town has a little more to offer than most. Recent archaeology has revealed the remains of a sizeable Roman settlement, although much of it is still buried, and there is the castle of **São João Baptista**, built during the 17th and 18th centuries. The *Igreja Matriz* (parish church) in the town centre dates from a hundred years earlier.

VIANA DO CASTELO is the major resort town on the Costa Verde. Forty-five miles north of Oporto on the north bank of the River Lima, this fortress town has a long history. The river itself was named by the Romans after the Lethe, the mythical River of Forgetfulness. Sometimes known as 'The Princess of the Lima', the town is neatly placed between the sea and the hills rising behind it and is a bustling tourist centre, well supplied with shops, night-life and sports facilities, as well as retaining an active commercial harbour.

Viana do Castelo has its origins in prehistory, but it was under the Romans that it developed as an important port, visited by ships from Genoa and Venice. Its renown continued to increase throughout the Middle Ages until, by the 16th century, it was rivalling Oporto as a maritime centre and was the major outlet for the shipment of port to

England, later declining as its rival grew. It was still important enough, however, to be besieged in 1827.

Its status as a historic trading port has today made Viana do Castelo a centre for the folklore and tradition of the Minho. Pottery and regional handicrafts such as jewellery and embroidery are important and the town is particularly famed for regional dress. On the weekend closest to 20 August it is caught up in the festival of Nossa Senhora de Agonia – as much a regional as a religious celebration.

As is usual in such resort towns, there is no shortage of accommodation, with the usual variations in quality and price. As well as luxury hotels such as the **Afonso III** in Avenida Dom Afonso (Tel: 2 41 23), there are several smaller hotels and pensions, including the **Pensão Dolce Vita** in Rua de Poco (Tel: 2 48 60).

Its long and prosperous history has left Viana do Castelo with an array of monuments. In the Praça de Republica there is an arcaded *misericordia* (alms house) dating from 1598, and the town hall is of similar style. The square itself is in the Manueline style, with a beautiful 16th-century fountain. The *Igreja Matriz*, the town's parish church, which was begun in 1285 under João I, and completed 148 years later, is starkly Gothic on the outside but with a beautifully carved interior. The **Tavoras Palace**, dating from the 16th century, was occasionally used as a residence by King Manuel, while another palace, the **Barbosa Macieís**, is now the town museum.

There are one or two sights of interest in the immediate vicinity of the town. Pinning the buildings against the shore is the hill of **Monte Santa Luzía**, pleasantly wooded and topped by a basilica, with Celto-Iberian remains dating from 500 BC. It can be reached by foot or by funicular railway. PRAIA DE CABADELO is an excellent beach, reached by bridge or ferry from the town itself, and has good breakers for the surfing enthusiast, while the village of MAR, about five miles to the south, is a pleasant place to stop and camp.

AFIFE lies about six miles north along the wooded coast road. It is a tiny, unspoiled village set among coastal dunes and provides a useful stopover for the weary traveller, with a small pension and a café-cum-shop.

VILA PRAIA DE ANCORA, three miles north of Afife, occupies a sheltered site on the shore of a safe but small estuary. It is purely a resort town, living on the strength of its safe swimming and good sandy beach. Much favoured as a weekend destination, especially by urban dwellers, the town has plenty of restaurants, although hotel accommodation is more limited.

MOLEDO is another small family resort nestling among the dunes and pine-woods, given an old-world atmosphere by the half-ruined fort standing on a sandy spit. It is an ideal site for swimming and there are café facilities and limited accommodation.

CAMINHA is a frontier town first and foremost, at Portugal's extreme north west, facing Spain across the River Minho. It is a quiet river port, historically – and currently – a haven for smugglers, for whom the shallow, sluggishly-moving Minho caused few problems. The main square has a battlemented town hall and a 14th-century *campanile* (clock tower). Many of the buildings date from the town's period of prosperity in the 15th and 16th centuries.

The *Igeja Matriz* stands within the town walls. It was built in the 15th century and displays traces of Moorish influence in the architecture and decoration, especially the carved ceiling. Other buildings of note are the 15th-century mansion **La Solar dos Pitos**, and a number of 17th-century houses within the town walls. The **Insua** fort dates from the 16th century and the days when Portugal nursed no friendship for her close neighbour, Spain. A small ferry runs across the Minho to La Guarda in Spain – where clocks are an hour ahead, so make sure of the return ferry times before leaving.

Local handicrafts are artefacts and ornaments in copper and brass. Special delicacies served in the restaurants are lobster and lamprey, as well as sausage and roast kid.

VILA NOVA DE CERVEIRA is ten miles inland on the Minho river and is a typical walled frontier town, although it has no crossing point to Spain. It is a quiet settlement, ideal for an overnight stop, with a number of good value pensions.

VALENÇA is the next town along the Minho valley, and the second at which it is possible to cross to Spain – the **International Bridge** spans the river, one end in Valença and the other in the Galician town of Tuy.

Valença is the ideal, almost perfectly-preserved 17th-century town, neatly hemmed in by restored ramparts and with fine views over two countries. In some ways it is almost too perfect and quaint for comfort. It was besieged by the Spanish in the reign of Afonso III, but most traces of this period of turbulence have been replaced by tranquillity. Both the *Igreja Matriz* and the old fortress, however, have 13th-century origins.

The maze of narrow streets is cobbled. The day-time atmosphere is one of continuous activity but at night the gift shops close and virtually all that activity ceases. However, there are plenty of good walks in the town itself and a day-trip to Spain can be tempting. Accommodation is limited but not totally lacking, and one or two good restaurants provide local gastronomic treats such as eels and lampreys.

MONÇÃO lies ten miles upriver from Valença. It, too, is a former frontier town, larger, older and more historically important than its neighbour, although it no longer has a crossing point to Spain. Its ramparts stand tall and within the walls are many monuments dating from the wars with Spain. In the 13th-century *Igreja Matriz* can be seen the tomb of Dieu-la-Dieu, a local girl who, according to legend, saved the town from a besieging Castilian army in 1638. As the townspeople began to run short of food, she baked cakes and sent them out to the Castilians who, assuming that the defenders had plenty to eat, packed up and went home! Dieu-la-Dieu is remembered everywhere, in statues, postcards and a local cake named after her.

Monção is also a spa town, its waters reputedly beneficial for those suffering from rheumatism and skin diseases. It also has a pleasant riverside park. The town is also a local centre for the region's agricultural produce, especially the fresh light wine known as vinho verde, which is a particularly good accompaniment to the trout, salmon and lampreys taken from the Minho.

Close by is the tiny hamlet of BARBELTA, where a 13th-century bridge over the River Douro was the site of a meeting in 1386 between John of Gaunt, the English Duke of Lancaster, and João I, King of Portugal. This had farreaching effects – the marriage between João and Philippa, Gaunt's daughter, further cemented an alliance between nations which is now the oldest in Europe. At nearby LONGOS VALES, there is the 12th-century church of **São João**.

MELGAÇO lies sixteen miles east of Monção. It does not stand on the Minho itself and was never a frontier town, but, nevertheless, was not untouched by the armed strife of the region's past, as its fortifications indicate. An ancient town, Melgaço has a ruined castle and a church, **Nossa Senhora do Orada**, both of which date from the 12th century. It is also a notable spa town.

Other than this there is little reason to stop, unless to buy some of the locally produced smoked hams or Alvarinho wines. It is only five miles to the frontier post at SÃO GREGORIO.

PONTE DA BARCA is a small town lying twenty-five miles south of Monção in the heart of the agricultural region of the Minho. There is little to see here other than a vision of pastoral calm and the bridge spanning the Lima, the supposed River of Forgetfulness, which gives the town its name. There is accommodation, but little in the way of places to eat out, although there is a bar at nearby BRAVÃES, which is also worth visiting for the 12th-century church of **São Salvador**.

PONTE DA LIMA was a Roman outpost commanding the valley of the Lima between Ponte da Barca and Viana do Castelo: the bridge is partly Roman and partly medieval. On Mondays there is a weekly market by the river – the oldest in Portugal, begun in 1125.

The town has a striking air of the medieval, its centre is full of whitewashed 16th-century houses and it has an old castle keep which was used as a prison in the 1960s. The monastery of **São Antonio dos Capuchos** is reached by a walk between the plane trees and has a small museum tucked away in the church. The *Igreja Matriz* in the town dates from the 15th century.

There is some accommodation available, although it is wise to book first around the time of the annual festival on 1–2 September. There is also a restaurant, the **Monte da Madalena**. The local delicacy is spitted lampreys.

At FREIXO, six miles to the south, the picturesque 14th-century **Castelo do Corutelo** can be seen.

BRAGA is the Portuguese Rome – or so the locals like to call it. The provincial capital of the Minho, thirty miles south east of Viana do Castelo and the same distance north-east of Oporto, it is also the ecclesiastical capital of the entire nation. It is a city of squares and parks, churches and coffee houses.

Braga is an old settlement: its Celtic name was Bracara and under the Roman occupation it became Bracara Augustus after the then

Emperor, assuming great commercial and military importance on account of its location at the junction of five strategic routeways. It was occupied by the Visigoths and later, after a long struggle, by the Moors in 716, being recaptured in 1040. For all of these changes it retained its importance as a religious centre until, at the end of the 11th century, the Bishops of Braga were laying claim to the 'Primacy of the Spains'. It is one of the oldest Christian cities and has its own liturgy. Throughout the Middle Ages its wealth and power increased and by the 16th century, the city's Golden Age, the Archbishops of Braga were sometimes as influential as the kings they supposedly served.

Although the city's influence then declined, it remained a centre of reactionary politics well into the 20th century. It was from here that the right-wing coup was launched in 1926, and forty-nine years later, after the almost bloodless revolution which brought the Socialists into power, the Archbishop exhorted a mob to attack the offices of the local Communist Party.

As is to be expected of a cathedral town, local specialities are statuary, vestments and other religious paraphernalia. To this can be added the specialist handicrafts of an agricultural region. Pottery is produced, as are articles made from wickerwork and straw, and the usual rural decorations like embroidery and lace.

Braga has plenty of available accommodation of all types and prices, from the expensive and comfortable **Hotel Turismo** in the Avenida João XXI (Tel: 2 70 91) with its rooftop swimming pool, to the much cheaper **Pensão Francfort** (Avenida Central, Tel: 2 26 48). There are also pensions, such as the **São Marcos**, in the street of the same name (Tel: 7 71 77), and the **Pensão Comercial** (Rua dos Chãos, Tel: 2 26 28). Many have restaurants. A useful point for the impecunious traveller is that the city contains one of the only two youth hostels in the Costa Verde (the other is in Oporto). Further information regarding current prices is available from the tourist office.

There are also plenty of restaurants in Braga, again of varying price and quality, such as the **Inácio** in the **Campo das Hortas**, serving good regional dishes. These include such delights as pork titbits (*rojões do porco*) and pig's blood stew (*papas de sarrabulho*), as well as dried salted codfish and roast kid. Wines are from the surrounding region, producing vinho verde.

Braga has much to show. In the centre is the *sé*, begun in 1070 and intended as a Romanesque monument, although it incorporates Gothic, Manueline and baroque architecture, and was not finally completed until the 16th century. Inside can be seen the tombs of Count Henry of Burgundy and his wife Teresa, parents of King Afonso Henriques and founders of the cathedral.

The interior of the *sé* was originally austere in the extreme, but was relieved by the embellishment of later periods and the decoration is profuse, notably in the **Capelo da Gloria**, built in 1330, while the **Capelo de São Giraldo** contains intricate wrought-iron tracery. The **Treasury** (a small fee is charged for entry) contains works of art, vestments and some 18th-century carved choir stalls.

Opposite the *sé* stands the **Archbishop's Palace**, a mixture of Gothic and baroque insensitively restored, now containing a library and an ecclesiastical museum. The town centre is full of mansions built in baroque and rococo styles, the most notable among them being the **Paláçio do Raio**. A former nobleman's house, the **Casa dos Biscaínhos** now contains an ethnographical and archaeological museum. Almost all the churches are worth a visit. The oldest monument of all is the **Fonte do Idolo**, a Roman fountain.

Two miles to the north west, at TIBAES, are the remains of a monastery with only its abbey church maintained – hard to believe that this was once one of the grandest monastic foundations in the land. Half a mile further at SÃO FRUTOSO lies another church, which was founded in the 7th century and rebuilt 400 years later after having been used by the Moors. It stands next to an 18th-century church whose baroque splendour contrasts starkly with the simplicity of the older building.

BOM JESUS DO MONTE, two miles from Braga and visited by buses every half hour, is a spectacular place for a picnic or a half-day visit. It is a noted place of pilgrimage for the Portuguese, but you can equally go and enjoy it for the wooded gardens and grottoes, fountains, streams and boating pools. Plenty of cheap restaurants are to be found here for those who wish to satisfy curiosity as much as to make a pilgrimage.

There's no getting away from the fact that the shrine of Bom Jesus is something of an oddity. It is reached either by a funicular railway or by a huge, fan-shaped staircase with 365 steps. Those who take the latter ascent are treated to a spectacle of 18th-century baroque at its most exotic. The granite staircase is a huge allegory, each landing has a fountain, and a representation – the first of Christ's wounds, the second to the sixth being the five senses, the seventh, eighth and ninth representing the human virtues, and so on. Many pilgrims still make the climb on their knees, but, whatever your feelings, a visit will be richly rewarded by the view from the top.

Exactly why there is a shrine here is unclear: it seems that the place of pilgrimage was the brainchild of an Archbishop of Braga some time in the early 18th century. Close by there are two other shrines to the Virgin, at SAMEIRO and SANTA MARIA MADALENA.

BARCELOS is the town which gave Portugal its national emblem, the cockerel. Almost equidistant from Braga and Esposende, it lies on the north bank of the Cávado at the centre of a rich agricultural region. In this medieval market town, the stallholders still often sit with their wares spread out on the ground in traditional fashion, concentrating on one item such as cheese or vegetables. The town has no single outstanding feature, although as an example of a typical old Portuguese market town it is well worth a visit.

The history of Barcelos is that of almost every other old market town. A castle was built by the dukes of Bragança in the 15th century to guard the river crossing, but it witnessed nothing more serious than a few skirmishes. The most famous episode connected with the town can hardly be said to be history, although it is told locally as though it were true. A tinker, who was condemned to death, protested his innocence to the magistrate (who was dining at the time) by saying that he would be hanged if the cock (currently being served up) didn't crow. The cock, of course, did just that; and the tinker's conviction was quashed.

The same tale is told in many towns, and not only in Portugal, but it is only in Barcelos that the cockerel has attained celebrity status, reproduced in virtually every medium – basketry, embroidery and, especially, the earthenware ceramics for which the town is well known. Pottery is the main crafted item and articles both decorative and utilitarian can be bought.

There are plenty of places to stay in Barcelos: again, a full list can be obtained from the *Turismo*. Among the best are the small pensions, such as the **Pensão Bagoeira** in the Avenida Dr Sidonio Pais

(Tel: 82236). Many also have their own restaurants.

Chicken (not surprisingly, perhaps) is on the menu in most Barcelos restaurants, served with rice. Other delicacies are regional rather than specific, including pig's blood stew and stewed lampreys. Many establishments, notably the **Turismo** restaurant, serve these. Barcelos is also noted for vinho verde.

The main square is the **Campo da República**, site of the Thursday market. At one corner is an old 15th-century castle, now a ruin, and the *Igreja Matriz* which stands nearby is built in the austere style of the 13th century, with later additions: its Gothic façade is a startling contrast to its baroque altar.

There are two other churches worthy of note. The **Igreja do Terco** stands in the main square, an 18th-century building once part of a Benedictine convent. **Nossa Senhora da Cruz** was built in 1708, an octagonal construction with a heavily-gilded pulpit and a sumptuous interior which was to set a style throughout the region.

There is also an interesting pillory and the **Senhor do Galho** cross, depicting the legend of the cockerel. The 15th-century bridge is fronted by gardens, and the **Palace of the Dukes of Bragança**, built in 1786, is now a ruin housing the ceramic and archaeological museums.

CITANIA DE BRITEIROS lies between Braga and Guimarães, not a town but a Celtic hill settlement which was reputedly a last stronghold against the invading Romans. The site consists of about 150 huts, paved streets, town walls and cisterns. It shows little sign of Roman influence, but appears to have been occupied as late as 300 AD.

For the sightseer without a car, Briteiros is difficult to reach, since it is well away from main roads. There are two buses a day from Braga, however: one first thing in the morning and one in the evening. The site is open from 9am until dusk.

GUIMARÃES, fourteen miles south of Braga, lays claim to being the 'cradle of Portugal's nationhood'. In 1106, a son was born to Count Henry, Duke, through his wife, of Porto and Cale. The child was Afonso Henriques, who was to lead the reconquest of Portugal from Moorish domination and make Guimarães the first capital of Portugal. Some would have it that the town's regal connections are older still. Wamba, a Goth, was elected king and was in Guimarães when the news came. Reluctant to take on such a burden, he thrust his staff into the ground and declared that he would only take on the kingship when the staff sprouted. Almost at once it did just that: and Wamba ruled happily ever after.

These connections are tenuous: the childhood of Afonso Henriques is history. He was born in the castle built by his father, with its huge, square crenellated towers and supposedly baptised in the church of **São Miguel**, inside the castle. Although the church itself is 13th-century, the font may well be that which was used.

Away from the castle, the town is one of small squares and narrow streets with the **Rua de Santa Maria** almost unchanged since the Middle Ages. The collegiate church of **Nossa Senhora de Oliveira** dates from the 10th century, but has since been restored three times – most recently in the 19th century. This church contains the tunic supposedly worn by João I at Aljubarrota, the battle which finally separated Portugal from Spain. It was at the spot immediately outside that Wamba's acceptance of the crown is said to have taken place.

The 15th century **Palace of the Braganças** has been heavily restored: it was formerly an official residence of Dr Salazar and now contains tapestries, hangings and foreign treasures. The **Museu Martin Sarmento** contains prehistoric remains, including the huge granite figure known as the Colossus of Pedralia. This is in the church of São Domingos. The 17th-century church of Santa Cruz is now the **Museu Alberto Sampaio** and contains the treasures of a former monastery and mementoes of Aljubarrota.

The town is known for its handicrafts, notably pottery, statuettes, embroidery and linen, while pig's trotters are a particular local delicacy.

Accommodation is plentiful and, for those who can afford it, can be an experience in the luxury hotel, **Pousada de Santa Maria**, an 18th-century palace in Rua de Santa Maria (Tel: 412157). This elegance is not cheap, but there are plenty of inexpensive hotels and pensions to choose from, such as the **Hotel do Toural** in the Largo do Toural (Tel: 411259).

PENAFIEL is twenty-two miles from Porto, an old town set in vineyards and producing a light table wine. It has a fine old 16th-century parish church, **São Martinho**, and a museum, the **Museu Sobral Mendes**.

A number of interesting monuments can be found in the countryside close to Penafiel, such as the 12th-century churches of BOELHA, EJA and FERREIRA, while a monastery of the same period can be found at CETE. At SANTA MARTA, there is a dolmen, a relic of neolithic times.

AMARANTE lies on the River Tamega, to the north of the Douro Valley, forty-one miles north-east of Oporto. It is a pleasant town, its houses having picturesque balconies, and its streets are full of bars and cafés.

The most notable sight is the **Convento do São Gonçalo**, built in the 16th century. Gonçalo, the town's patron saint, is the protector of old maids and young widows and is the centre of a strange fertility cult – on the first Saturday in June, young people exchange phallic-shaped cakes. Touching the saint's tomb is said to promote a swift marriage!

The former monastery is now a museum of modern art, and the convent is lavishly decorated with all the excesses of the baroque style.

In the 16th century, Amarante was a Jewish stronghold and many Jews clung to their faith despite a pretence at being converts to Catholicism. This gave rise to a mongrel cult, neither Jewish nor Catholic, which still persists.

Amarante, a market town, is the centre for many agricultural products. It is widely renowned for its confectionery, especially *doce de São Gonçalo*, a small jelly made from eggs and sugar.

There are several hotels, largely inexpensive, such as the **Hotel Silva** in Rua Candida dos Reis (Tel: 423110). There are few restaurants, although café-cum-bars are a feature of the town.

An excursion to TRAVANCA, about ten miles away, will be rewarded by finding a 12th-century church, all that remains of a Benedictine monastery. From the town it is just a short distance to the rugged mountains of central Portugal.

VILA REAL lies in the extreme south-east of the Costa Verde, on a hilly plateau in the foothills of the Serra do Marao, backed by waterfalls where the gorges of the Cabil and Corgo rivers join. Buildings are old, and decorated, their character somewhere between that of the mountain and valley dwelling. The Gothic **Sé de São Domingo** stands in the town centre, with the **Igreja São Pedro**, famous for its beautiful ceilings, nearby. The **Casa do Diogo Cão** is supposedly the birthplace of the discoverer of the Congo.

The local souvenir is the 'black pottery' produced in the area. This can be bought most cheaply at the annual St Peter's Fair, which takes place on 29 June.

As a regional centre, Vila Real is well provided with hotels, such as the **Mira-Corgo** in Avenida 1 de Maio. Prices tend to be reasonable and services good. There are also a couple of reasonably-priced restaurants.

Costa de Prata

The Costa de Prata comprises the coastal strip from Espinho southwards to beyond Peniche, marked on the inland side by the foothills of the mountains. The region has both sandy beaches and dramatic cliff scenery interspersed with sunny coves. It has luxuriant pine-forests and vast stretches of agricultural land – variations in scenery to suit almost any visitor.

COMMUNICATIONS

The Costa de Prata is easily accessible. International flights arrive at Lisbon from all over the world and the southern part of the region is within easy reach of the capital. From Lisbon to Oporto there are two main railway lines – an express line and a slower one which follows the coast route and stops at or near many coastal resorts. A secondary line goes to the university city of Coimbra and bus services run to those towns not on the rail network.

CLIMATE

The climate of Portugal is mild, as might be expected from a coastal nation. Average temperatures are around 77°F (25°C) in July and 55°F (13°C) in January, although inland they can be more extreme. Some rain can be expected, but not nearly as much as in the north or the mountains, and sunshine totals are ideal for the holiday-maker wishing to tan on the beaches of São Martinho or Figueira da Foz.

Historically, this is the region where modern Portugal can be said to have been founded. It was at Aljubarrota that the decisive battle which freed Portugal from the power of Spain was fought in 1385. Today the battlefield is flanked by two great monasteries, the first fulfilling a vow made by João I after the battle, the second satisfying a similar vow from Afonso Henriques after the Reconquest. It is in this area, too, that many battles of the Peninsular War between England and France were fought.

SPECIALITIES

A regional speciality is fish – off the coast lie some of the richest fishing grounds in Europe. Apart from the sardines, mackerel and red mullet, there are some less likely marine treats. Squid, tuna, octopus and even barnacles join the usual menu of lobster, crab and shrimps. Non-fish dishes are fewer, the most notable being spit-roasted sucking pig. The region's wines are not as famous as those of the North, but are nonetheless pleasant and cheap.

Souvenirs are mostly traditional crafts and decorated utilitarian items tend to be the best buy. Embroidery is of high quality, as is lace, especially around Peniche and Nazaré.

VILA DE FEIRA lies at the northern edge of the Costa de Prata, not so much a town as a medieval castle dominating a small village. The castle is 11th-century with later additions and is among the best-preserved fortresses in Portugal, set against a background of trees. The village itself has both accommodation and restaurants.

OVAR is a market town (formerly a port, but blocked by sand which choked the mouth of its river) and is primarily a centre for livestock breeding and dairying. It has a chapel, **Calvaírio**, which attracts many pilgrims. There is also an ethnographic museum specializing in pottery, clothing and folklore. Restaurants serve the local speciality, lobster.

Two other towns share Ovar's loss of maritime support. MURTOSA is now a mile inland as the lagoon continues to silt up, while ILHÁVOS recalls its maritime traditions through its museum of the sea.

TORREIRA is a small but lively settlement from which a ferry runs to the regional capital, Aveiro. It is principally a fishing village and some of its houses are peculiarly distinctive, being made from the hulls of old fishing boats. Close by, on the end of the spit enclosing a huge lagoon, lies the beach of SÃO JACINTO. The beach has one or two cafés and is safe for swimmers. There is also good camping.

AVEIRO, which lies on the lagoon (enclosed by a sand bar) which ponds up the river Vouga, is known as the 'Venice of Portugal'. The town is built over a network of canals crossed by low-arched bridges. On the lagoon, the town's fishermen guide the flat-bottomed swan-necked boats (called *barcos moliceiros*) through the reeds in search of eels. The town survives mainly upon fishing, seaweed (gathered for fertilizer) and salt, which is collected from salt pits drying out in summer, the salt being gathered into heaps to crystallize in the sun. An industrial estate outside the town represents a less romantic side of the town's economy.

Although currently a low-key resort town, Aveiro has an antiquity stretching way back. It became prominent during the Age of Discovery, especially after the opening up of the Grand Banks, the fishing grounds off Newfoundland, which were worked by local boats. This importance was lost when the Vouga silted up in 1575, causing outbreaks of fever from the stagnating lagoon. In 1808 the bar was breached by the sea and the marshes drained, allowing the limited rejuvenation of the fishing industry.

When stewed, the eels which are trapped in this lagoon form a local delicacy to which bairrada wine is a good accompaniment. There are also sweets, called *ovos moles*, made from eggs. However, there are very few good restaurants, perhaps the best of them being the **Centenário**.

There are plenty of places to stay in the town. Large hotels include the **Afonso V**, and there are also several good-quality pensions such as the **Pensão Beira**, in Rua José Estevâo (Tel: 24297). Camping is possible on the dunes and beaches of the coast, only a short distance from the town.

In the Praça do Milenário is the **Convento de Jesus**, reputedly one of the finest pieces of baroque architecture in the country. It was formerly the home of the Infanta Joana, who was forbidden by her father to become a nun but eventually took the veil in 1472. Her tomb is in the convent, part of which is now a museum containing many 15th-century paintings, especially royal portraits.

The 15th-century **Igreja São Domingo**, nominally a church but actually a cathedral, is also worth a visit for its blue and gold altarpiece. The octagonal chapel of **Senhor das Barrocas** dates from the 1720s.

The visitor to Aveiro during the last two weeks of August will be treated to the Festa da Ria, a local festival with racing and dancing, culminating in a carnival. During July and August, some of the fishermen find it profitable to run boat trips to the tranquil parts of the lagoon; these are bookable at the tourist office.

At VISTA ALEGRE, the visitor can go on a guided tour of the china works which was established in 1824 and now makes quality porcelain. Just outside Aveiro itself there are many safe beaches, although one or two can be a little overcrowded.

MIRA lies eighteen miles south of Aveiro along the nearest thing in the Costa de Prata to a coast road, although only two side roads actually meet the sea between Aveiro and Figueira de Foz. Mira is at one of these points and although two miles inland has easy access to a good beach and some development as a not-quite-coastal resort.

There is limited accommodation, for this is principally a fishing village, where some homes are made from upturned boats. Traditional methods of fishing still survive, with the boats being dragged up the coast on rollers in the absence of a proper harbour. Locally, the seafood is excellent.

FIGUEIRA DA FOZ, forty miles south of Aveiro and thirty-four miles north of Leira, is the largest and most important resort on the Costa da Prata, as well as being the oldest and the best known. It has a particularly good climate, which the visitor can make the most of on the huge – but often crowded – beach, the 'beach of brightness', as it is called.

The town is characterized by its tall old buildings and apartment blocks, as well as the old-fashioned cafés and the familiar trappings of the former fishing village. However, apart from fish, the town has little that is unusual to offer in the way of either food or souvenirs.

As a large and important resort town, Figueira da Foz can be expected to provide accommodation in all categories and this is indeed the case. The de luxe **Grande Hotel**, in the Avenida 25 de Abril (Tel: 22146), also owns some service apartments facing onto the Atlantic. Recommended pensions are the **Pensão Central**, in Rua Bernardo Lopes (Tel: 22308) and the **Pensão Europa**, in the Rua Candido dos Reis (Tel: 22265).

The sights of Figueira are few. Basically it consists of the port, a small marine enclave within the resort, full of old cafés, tiny restaurants, open squares, parks and streets. At the northern end of the town is the village of BUARCOS, which has been absorbed into the physical extent of the resort, yet remains a distinct village-within-a-town. There is a museum in the **Casa da Paco**. This is of limited interest unless you like delft tiles – there are 7000 of them there – but the building itself is interesting, as it was formerly the palace of Dom Carlos I.

All in all, Figueira da Foz is famed for its happenings rather than its sights. There is a film festival which takes place in the casino in September, and in season there is bullfighting in which the bull is not killed (publicly, at least). There is a lively night scene with bars, pubs, discos and the casino, while during the day, facilities are available for windsurfing, fishing, tennis and water-skiing.

For the holiday-maker who needs, once in a while, to be alone on a good beach, QUIAOS and TOCHA lie further up the coast, four and ten miles away respectively. Access is difficult, but the dual requirements of beach and solitude will certainly be met. Alternatively, for the more active, SERRA DE BOA VIAGEM lies just outside the town – a hill, not too strenuous to climb, with rare plants, natural springs and a good view of the coast.

MONTEMOR-O-VELHO lies between Figueira da Foz and the city of Coimbra, ten miles up the Mondego river valley. It is dominated by the castle built by Sancho I in the 12th century, but now a ruin towering over the narrow cobbled streets of the walled medieval town. It was here that Afonso IV sanctioned the murder of his son's mistress, Inês de Castro, a vital part of Portugal's greatest love story.

MARINHA GRANDE is an uninspiring industrial sprawl thirty-four miles south of Figueira da Foz. Its industrial history dates back to the middle of the 18th century, where the Stephens brothers from England set up a glass factory which, in its heyday, was one of the leading producers in Europe.

SÃO PEDRO DE MOEL lies on the coast six miles west of Marinha Grande, on an exposed cliff top swept by Atlantic winds. A rash of new villas have recently sprung up around the old cobbled quarter. At the bottom of the cliff path there is a good sandy beach pounded by the surf, and the dramatic coastline is ideal for fishing and diving. At the lighthouse a mile north of this new resort you can enjoy dramatic coastal views.

NAZARÉ is an oddity among resorts. It is marketed by tourist authorities as the ideal Portuguese fishing village; historic and unspoilt. Men wear traditional clothes, women often go barefoot and the whole centre remains exactly as it was centuries ago. Around it, however, new developments have sprung up since the 1960s and Nazaré is now a curious paradox – a resort in summer and a fishing village in winter.

Historically, it is believed to have been an important trading point for the Phoenician civilization, existing in its own tranquillity until, in recent years, its fame caught up with it.

One or two hotels are located in the clifftop village, but most are in the new development which flanks it or close to the beach. There are a few high-powered luxury hotels, such as the **Hotel da Nazaré** in the Largo Afonso Zuquéte (Tel: 46311), but the majority are in the inexpensive and simple style which is Nazaré's main selling point. Examples are the **Pensão Beora Mar** in the Rua dos Lavradores (Tel: 46458) and the **Pensão Ideal** in the Rua Adrao Batalha (Tel: 46379). There are one or two reasonably-priced restaurants, especially seafood establishments.

Nazaré is in itself a 'sight': even the most mundane tasks and objects, because of their timelessness, are interesting to watch and see. The main part of the village lies on the clifftop: whitewashed houses and cobbled streets shine in the sun. It is known as Sítio and is almost exclusively residential, except for a few handicraft shops and restaurants. Saturday bullfights take place throughout the summer.

In Sítio is the church of **Nossa Senhora do Nazaré**, and there is an annual pilgrimage 8–10 September. It dates back to shortly after the Reconquest of Portugal under Afonso Henriques: Fuas Roupinho, who had fought beside the king, was out hunting on the cliffs when a thick mist came down. Suddenly his horse halted and he saw a vision of the Virgin Mary. Roupinho dismounted to pray, only to find himself kneeling on the edge of the cliff . . . saved from a fall certain to have caused his death.

Away from the Sítio is the colourful harbour and the wide sweep of cliff-foot beach. The beach itself is lovely to look at, but the breakers which pound against it are the product of dangerous tides, so those warning flags should be taken seriously.

Ten miles away at COZ, a quaint Bernadine church provides a break from the bustle of high summer crowds. It is baroque in style, perfectly preserved with gilded woodwork and 17th-century statuary – well worth an afternoon trip.

SÃO MARTINHO DO PORTO is the second major resort on the Costa de Prata, ninety miles south of the more important Figueira da Foz. It lies on a seashell shaped bay, where a tiny river enters the Atlantic. The bay itself is sheltered and its shallowness gives it a startling colour. The dunes at the river mouth provide a perfect picnic area.

Several of the hotels in São Martinho have facilities such as tennis courts and swimming pools: many, such as the **Hotel do Parque** in the Avenida Maréchal Carmona (Tel: 9 85 06), also have their own discos. There are self-contained apartments for rent and a youth hostel – in short, a plethora of accommodation for all budgets.

There is little to see in the town other than the tiny fisherman's quay, the sandy beach and the dunes. Having said that, though there are no specific sights, the town remains picturesquely untouched by the developers and it has a pleasant atmosphere. For the active, there is plenty in the way of things to do: water-skiing, windsurfing, land-based sports such as tennis, and active night-life.

PENICHE is a ramparted and busy fishing port (the fourth largest in Portugal) lying on a peninsula of the same name: a combination of cliffs and sandy beaches. Its name is a corruption of the word peninsula, an apt description of its rocky site.

Today it is a fishing port with large docks and a canning factory to handle the sardine catch.

Like many other fishing ports along this stretch of coast, Peniche owes its importance to a combination of the rich fishing grounds which lie offshore and the early visits from the Phoenicians, who established the town as a trading post. Until the 12th century, Peniche was a rocky island, but a combination of geographical factors has ensured that it is now firmly attached to the mainland. In the 16th century, it fell into the hands of the Spanish and was subsequently raided by our own Sir Francis Drake. Since then, Peniche's way of life has remained largely undisturbed.

All the usual handicrafts are to be found, but the speciality is lace (both hand and machine made) and there is an exhibition of it in the town. Peniche is known for fish – not surprisingly dishes of sardines, which are canned here – and the mackerel and red mullet which can be seen a-plenty when the fishermen bring in their catch.

Peniche is not a wildly popular resort, but there are reasonable places to stay, such as the **Pensão Felita** in the Largo Prof. Franco Freire (Tel: 991 90).

The castle and ramparts were built to defend Peniche against the Spaniards. Construction of the *fortalezza*, or citadel, took place 1557–70; it is still in good condition and worth a look. Under the Salazar regime it was used as a prison by the secret police and it was from here that the leader of the Communist Party escaped in 1960. After the 1974 revolution, it was used as a temporary home for Angolan refugees.

The church of **São Pedro** dates from the 16th century and has three wide naves along its length. The other church of interest is **São Leonardo**, which originated in the 13th century in the Romano–Gothic style. It has many 16th-century paintings and a 14th-century nativity relief.

Ten miles offshore lie the ISLAS BERLENGAS, a rocky archipelago which acts as a national bird reserve. Only a mile square, the main island contains marked paths and is looked after by a warden. Naturalists can stay in the small campsite there: also there are the ruins of the **Forte de São João Baptisto**, destroyed by the Spaniards in 1666. The island can be reached by ferry from Peniche.

From CABO CARVOEIRA, three miles east of Peniche, there are good views of the rocky coastline. There is a lighthouse, built in 1779.

SANTA CRUZ is the popular resort for the town of Torres Vedra. It boasts a good safe beach, some twelve miles south of Peniche, and has an atmosphere which is friendly and lively. Accommodation is cheap, but be warned – there is only one hotel and one pension, so it is probably better to stay at Torres Vedra, four miles inland.

TORRES VEDRA is probably best known as the battlefield in the Peninsular War where Napoleon's armies were defeated and the French finally halted. However, there is more to the town than the still-visible battlefield. The 12th-century castle was regularly occupied by royalty for 400 years and there is also a convent, the **Graça**, whose cloisters are worth a visit for their paintings. The convent stands in the town square and in front of it is a monument to the Duke of Wellington. The small town museum details the campaigns of Wellington in the area. At ZAMBURGAL there is a prehistoric monument.

ERICEIRA lies on the coast thirteen miles south-west of Torres Vedra – another in the string of gleaming beach resorts on the rocky coast, and another village whose importance as a fishing port is gradually declining as tourism takes over. There is a small chapel to **Santo Antonio** and a hermitage to **São Sebastião**, which was built in the 17th century and has a beautifully decorated interior. It was from this port that the last king and queen of Portugal fled in 1910.

OBIDOS, lying fifteen miles east of Peniche and fifty-nine miles north of Lisbon, is one of the loveliest towns in Portugal. Set on a hilltop, with its medieval fortress dominating the surrounding vineyards, it was one of the seven key fortresses taken by the Moors and later recaptured by Afonso Henriques.

In the 12th century, Dom Dinis was passing through Obidos with his bride. She expressed particular delight with the town, so he gave it to her as a wedding present. Since then, it has traditionally been the wedding gift of Portuguese kings to their wives – a tradition ceasing only with the overthrow of the monarchy.

The town's royal connections are more extensive than this. In 1444, Afonso V married his cousin Isabella, when he was ten and she only eight years old. The wedding took place in the **Igreja Santa Maria**, rebuilt in the 17th century, and probably the loveliest of Obidos's many churches. The oldest among them is **São Martinho**, in simple

Gothic style. Outside the walls is the octagonal church of **Senhor da Pedra**.

The museum specializes in 17th- and 18th-century statuary, especially that by Josefa d'Ayala, the 17th-century sculptress who was born in the town (her home can still be seen). There are also many exhibits relating to the Peninsular War.

The castle is now a tourist inn, small, expensive, but well worth the cost, offering comfort and style. (Other hotels tend to be expensive, anyway.) In the height of the tourist season, accommodation can be difficult to find, so arrive early or book ahead.

Obidos is known for its agricultural products, especially apples, and potential souvenirs are rugs and local lace. It also produces fish dishes, especially eels, since it is less than ten miles from the sea and close to a tidal lagoon, the Lagoa do Obidos. This proximity to the sea gives good access to the beaches at FOZ DO AVELHO and PRAIA DO REI CORTICO.

A useful tip for the visitor who comes by car is to leave the vehicle outside the town walls, both to avoid the chaotic traffic and to appreciate the town's character to the full – something best achieved on foot.

CALDAS DA RAINHA is a spa town five miles north of Obidos. Its name means 'Queen's spa' after Dona Leonora, who was travelling in these parts when she saw beggars bathing in sulphurous smelling pools. Upon enquiring about this and being told that they gained relief from their illnesses, she decided to follow suit. So beneficial was the effect that Leonora founded a hospital there in 1484, and the town continued to gain note for its spa quality, reaching its zenith as a social and medical centre in the 19th century. The spa waters can still be visited. Heavily impregnated with calcium sulphide, they are an effective weapon against respiratory ailments and rheumatism.

Little is now left of the town's former wealth and today it is nothing more than a brief stop on the road to Nazaré. There is a fruit market every morning, selling local produce.

The **Museu Malhoa** in the town is devoted to ceramics, sculpture and paintings, especially by the local 19th-century artist José Malhoa, after whom the museum is named. The chapel of **Nossa Senhora do Populo** contains 17th-century tiles.

RIO MAIOR is an agricultural town ten miles from Caldas da Rainha.

It is of little note, although many prehistoric artefacts can be found around it. From here it is six miles to the Gruta das Alcobertas, a cave in the SERRAS DAS CANDIEIROS.

ALCOBAÇA lies eight miles south-east of Nazaré at the confluence of the Alco and the Baça rivers. It is a town of quiet narrow streets, which played an important part in Portugal's history, as well as being the setting for the final part of the love story of Dom Pedro and Inês de Castro.

Alcobaça was the site selected for a monastery built by Afonso Henriques in 1153, the fulfilment of a vow he made before conquering the Moorish stronghold of Santarém. In its heyday, the monastery was the seat of the Cistercian order, and governed thirteen towns (including Alcobaça itself, which grew up as a town to supply the monastery) and three seaports. Under Spanish rule it declined, but was restored in the 18th century only to be damaged again in the Napoleonic Wars.

In the heyday of the abbey, travellers raved about the lavish hospitality they received from the monks. Today the visitor has to be content with the town's hotels: not nearly so extravagant, but very reasonably priced. A couple of suggestions are the **Hotel Santa Maria** in Rua Dr Zagalo (Tel: 43295) or the **Pensão Mosteiro**, in the Avenida João de Deus (Tel: 42183).

The abbey is not just Alcobaça's main sight: it is its *raison d'être*. Built in the twelfth century, its exterior is austere and majestic and it is considered to be the finest example of medieval church architecture in Portugal. Inside, the ceiling soars to a height of seventy feet; the abbey church is the largest in the country. In the **Sala dos Reis** stands a statue of every king of Portugal, while the **Cloister of Silence** was added in the reign of Dom Dinis, the 'poet king' who set up a literary colony in the abbey. The dormitory and refectory are splendid in their vastness and simplicity.

It is in the south transept of the Gothic abbey that the most well known monument is to be found – the tombs of Dom Pedro and his 'queen' Inês de Castro. Before his accession, Pedro fell in love with Inês, one of his wife's ladies-in-waiting. They became lovers and she bore him, in secret, three children. Upon learning of the affair, Pedro's father had Inês murdered. When Pedro finally succeeded to the throne on the death of his father, he put two of the murderers to death (a third could not be caught). Inês was exhumed and the still-besotted Pedro had her brought to Alcobaça and crowned as his queen in the abbey – a grisly ceremony, with the courtiers forced to kiss her decaying hand as a token of homage. They lie buried in ornate tombs, foot-to-foot so that when they rise on Judgement Day the first thing they see will be one another.

Between Alcobaça and the site of a second great monastery, Batalha, lies the battlefield of **Aljubarrota**, where in 1385 João I defeated the Castilian army and founded modern Portugal.

MIRA DE AIRE lies thirty miles from Alcobaça by road, set in the foothills of the interior. It is an uninspiring textile centre, but close by are the caves of **Grutas do Mira de Aire**, Europe's deepest caves. They are 110 metres below ground and were discovered in 1947. They can be very cold, so do take a heavy jumper or cardigan. There are also caves at **Santo Antonio** and **Alvados**.

PRIVATE. Keep Out **PORTO DE MÓS** lies five miles south of Batalha. This uncommercial town contains a 13th-century castle built by the order of Knights Templars. From here, buses run to the caves at **Mira de Aire**; and there are plenty of cafés and restaurants, making it a useful stop for the hungry or thirsty traveller.

BATALHA lies thirteen miles north of Alcobaça. Not so much a town as a small settlement with a luxury hotel, it has a couple of pensions and a magnificent abbey. Like Alcobaça, Batalha was the result of a vow made by a Portuguese king, this time the twenty-year-old João I. As at Alcobaça, the vow was connected with a battle crucial to the nation's history; this time Aljubarrota. In 1385, João destroyed the Castilian army despite being heavily outnumbered and began to fulfil his vow – the construction of an abbey close to the site of the battle.

The only thing to see in Batalha is the abbey. The battle took place on the Feast of the Assumption: in consequence, the church is dedicated to the Virgin Mary and called **Santa Maria da Vitoria**. The building is Gothic in style, but with an English influence thanks to João's marriage to Philippa of Lancaster. The couple are buried in the **Founder's Chapel**; so are their sons, including Henry the Navigator.

After João's death, his son Duarte continued the building, as did the next in line, Manuel. Manueline architecture appears in the **Royal Cloister**, which was intended to be simple in style, but which was decorated with luxuriant carved vegetation running riot throughout, as well as motifs such as anchors and seamen's knots, reflecting the growth of Portugal's empire.

The **Chapter House** is a miracle of mathematics, built to a design so apparently unstable that its architect was forced to sleep underneath it to prove that it was safe. It contains the **Tombs of the Unknown Soldiers**, one from the battlefields of Europe, the other from Africa.

The abbey is not complete. Duarte's dream had been to create a chapel for the Aviz dynasty behind the altar, but successive kings either ran out of money for the project or had vows of their own to fulfil. Going out through the Manueline doorway at the east end of the church brings the visitor into the **Unfinished Chapels**, all of which are roofless.

An interesting excursion from Batalha is to ALJUBARROTA itself, the battlefield that was the motive for the abbey, which lies seven miles south. Some sources have it that the site for the abbey was selected by the victorious king throwing a spear – which would have been a remarkable feat if it were true! At the battlefield is the small chapel of **São Jorge**, where a jug of fresh water can always be found. João's friend and comrade-in-arms, Nun' Alvarez Pereira, was taken by a sudden thirst during the battle and vowed that there would always be water at the spot for the future.

FATIMA, twelve miles west of Batalha, is the main centre of religious devotion in Portugal and one of the most important in the Roman Catholic world. On 13 May 1917, as Europe still struggled in the throes of the First World War, three children – Lucia Marto and her younger brothers, Jacinto and Francisco – were watching sheep on a hillside when they saw a vision of the Virgin Mary. This vision was repeated on the 13th of each month until October, when a crowd of 70,000 turned up to see a strange display of lights in the sky. Yet only the children saw the vision and only Lucia could speak to her. At this, the so-called 'Miracle of the Sun', the vision divulged three secrets. The first was a tale of peace and a vision of hell, the second dealt with the conversion of Russia and the third was considered by the Pope to be so appalling that it has never been made public.

Fatima is the creation of this vision – a huge shrine swamped with pilgrims in mid-May and mid-October, yet somehow retaining its sincerity in an oddly uncommercial manner. The **Chapel of the Apparitions** has a huge 65-metre tower topped by a cross. This replaces the original chapel, which was destroyed by anti-Catholic activists in 1922. In front of the chapel, surrounded by numerous religious hostelries catering for pilgrims, is a collonaded square capable of holding up to a million people. On the fiftieth anniversary of the apparition, Fatima was visited by the Pope, as well as by Lucia Marto, the only survivor of the three children, who is now a nun. The other two are buried inside the basilica.

Fatima has excellent accommodation, mostly run by religious houses, but it also receives huge numbers of visitors and it's virtually impossible to find a room in mid-May or mid-October. There is no shortage of places to eat and there are numerous shops selling statues, rosaries and candles. The village is within easy reach of Tomar or Leira.

In the nearby hamlet of ALJUSTREL, the house of the three children can be seen. The beatification of Jacinto and Francisco is in progress.

VILA NOVA DE OUREM, two miles north west of Fatima, is a market town of little importance other than for the fact that the wife of Sancho I was kidnapped and brought here by rebel barons in 1246.

TOMAR lies on the River Nabão, twelve miles east of Vila Nova de Ourem. Originally a small medieval town, it is now a market centre with lashings of traditional charm in its whitewashed cottages and beautiful 17th-century town hall and square.

Tomar's history is inexplicably linked with the controversial and colourful order of Knights Templar, a group of noblemen who banded together to fight against the Muslim faith and promote the triumph of Christianity. Many were leaders in the crusades, later carrying their mission to the expulsion of the Infidel from Iberia. They numbered many members of European royal houses among their ranks and had an elaborate series of rites and rituals. Eventually, however, they became so rich and powerful that they threatened and antagonized the kings they supposedly served.

In 1190, the Knights repulsed the Moors from Tomar where they had a sanctuary, built twenty-eight years previously, and from where they carried on their Holy War. Tomar was both the military and spiritual centre. As a result of the Reconquest, the Order became immensely rich, but the power that accompanied such riches, together with their unorthodox methods, became a threat throughout Europe, not least to the church to which they belonged. In 1314 they were officially suppressed and the Order was cruelly persecuted, its surviving adherents finally taking refuge in Portugal.

Here they found support and encouragement. Even when King Dinis eventually bowed to Papal pressure and outlawed them, they emerged unscathed under another name – the Order of Christ. From 1417 to 1460 Prince Henry the Navigator was Grandmaster of the Order, and it was their wealth which helped to finance the great expeditions of the Age of Discovery. The order eventually lost a lot of its influence and petered out.

Tomar is an ideal place to stay; there are hotels of all standards, such as the expensive but comfortable **Hotel dos Templarios** in the Largo Candido dos Reis (Tel: 33121) or the less expensive **Pensão Nuno Alvares** in Avenida D. Nuno Alvares Pereira (Tel: 32873). Riverside restaurants serve cheap food and local wine.

There is a tourist office on Avenida do Dr Candido Madureira (Tel: 33095) and another in the Parque Municipal (Tel: 33750). The main sight of the town is the citadel, known as the **Convento do Cristo**. Its centre is the **Charola**, or temple, a sixteen-sided church built in the 10th century and based upon the church of the Holy Sepulchre in Jerusalem. The architecture is largely Manueline, an explosion of decoration, and the extensions were carried out to the specifications of a succession of kings, Manuel I prominent among them. His desire was that Tomar should be an expression of Christianity triumphant.

There were no fewer than seven sets of cloisters built in the convent between the 12th and 17th centuries. They were not built for meditation, but for the glory of God; yet much of the decoration involves the flamboyant and decidedly unChristian motifs and forms of Byzantine art. The stained glass window in the **Chapter House** is a pictorial record of the Discoveries. Under João III, the convent once again became home for a practising monastic order and two much more simple and dignified cloisters were added. Today, the building contains a seminary and – appropriately – a military hospital.

In the town itself is the church of **Nossa Senhora da Conceicão**, which has an extravagantly-pillared interior and dates from the 16th century. Close by is the Gothic church of **São João Baptista**, dating from a hundred years earlier. See, too, the 14th-century **synagogue**, the best-preserved in the country: it contains many Hebrew inscriptions and is now a museum. Off the Fatima road lies the **aqueduct** of Pegões Altas.

LEIRIA is situated twenty miles from Alcobaça on the main road to Coimbra. It lies on the banks of the River Liz, a town of squares, narrow streets and gardens around a volcanic hillock. Flanking it is the **Pinhal dos Reis**, the oldest state forest, which was planted on the instructions of Dom Dinis in order to stabilize the sand dunes and is still managed for that purpose.

Like so many other towns, Leiria was held by the Moors, defended from the castle they built on top of the hill. In the 12th century it was one of the seven major fortresses captured by Afonso Henriques during the Reconquest. The town subsequently changed hands twice before the town's politics stabilized.

Situated on the main road between Lisbon and Coimbra, Leiria is a conveniently placed and well equipped overnight stop. There are hotels ranging from the **Eurosol** in the Rua D. José Alves Correia da Silva (Tel: 24101), to the less expensive but equally pleasant **Pensão San Francisco** in the Rua de São Francisco (Tel: 25142). There is also a youth hostel. Restaurants such as the regional **Vinho Verde** serve good, if plain, food.

The **Castelo do Leiria** dominates the town from its volcanic outcrop. It was originally constructed by the Moors, but eventually became the home of Dom Dinis and his wife Isabella, later Santa Isabella. The exterior has been restored and has beautiful Romanesque arcades. The castle church is Gothic in style, and from here there are views over the surrounding town and country. The **Igreja São Pedro** dates from the 12th century and is Gothic in style. The *sé*, on the other hand, is 400 years more recent and relatively plain for its period. Also to be visited, if only for the fine views, is the **Nossa**

Senhora da Encarnação, a sanctuary set on top of a smaller hill. There is also a small museum in the town, in case you hit a wet day.

POMBAL, seventeen miles north of Leiria on the road to Coimbra, takes its name from the Marquis of Pombal, the statesman who was responsible for the rebuilding of Lisbon following the earthquake of 1755, and who died here. It has a 12th-century castle of the Knights Templar, which has been recently restored and which is a good viewpoint.

COIMBRA, which lies on the River Mondego, is one of the most historic cities in the country. It is the premier university city in Portugal, allegedly the most romantic of its towns or cities, and the university itself, founded in 1290, is the second oldest in Europe. It is a city of tangled streets and alleyways, old world charm and outstanding sights. In term time the city is full of students, who have their own behavioural code – although it seems to make little difference to their actions! (For a long time the university had its own jails and enforced its own discipline.) Many of the traditions still persist: students still wear capes and many can be found in cafés and bars, strumming guitars and singing old sentimental ballads in the courtyards.

Coimbra's importance is deeply rooted in history, succeeding Guimarães as capital city in 1139 and remaining so until Aljubarrota in 1385. It was during this period that the university was founded; it was firmly established by the 16th century and remains the focal point of the city today.

While in Coimbra be sure to take in a *fado*. This traditional music of Portugal has its own variant in Coimbra – all very romantic!

High though it ranks as a tourist attraction, Coimbra is singularly ill equipped when it comes to accommodating tourists. There are hotel rooms to be had, and they are usually reasonably cheap – for example, the **Avenida** in the Avenida Emidio Navarro (Tel: 25503) or the **Hotel Mondego** in Largo das Ameias (Tel: 29087) – but they *are* scarce and there are not too many pensions (try **Pensão Jardim** in the Avenida Emidio Navarro, (Tel: 25204)). One good new addition to the hotel scene is the three-star **Hotel D. Luis** with 102 rooms and 2 suites all with private facilities (Tel: 841522/841510). The same drawback applies to restaurants, although one or two, such as the **Pinto d'Ouro**, may be recommended.

Not surprisingly, Coimbra's main sight is the university. The main buildings, close to the **Arch of Almedina**, date from around 1537 in the reign of João III. The centre of the university lies through the gate known as the **Porta Ferrea** and was formerly the palace of João III, a gift from a king to a royal seat of learning. Inside is the **Cabra**, or clocktower, and the **Sala dos Capelos**, where graduation ceremonies are held. Ex-students of the university include St Antony of Padua, Camões (the country's most famous poet) and the exiled dictator, Dr Marcelo Caitano.

The chapel stands next to the library, a baroque building by an unknown architect. Its interior is extravagant to say the least. It was built between 1716 and 1723 under the auspices of João V and contains a million books. From the square outside there are magnificent views of the Mondego valley.

Coimbra has two cathedrals. The older, predating the university by 120 years, has many associations with St Antony of Padua and contains a beautiful Flemish altar and crucifix. The building is simple, but severe in style: its 16th-century successor is neoclassical.

Older than either cathedral (although extensively restored in the Manueline period) is the 12th-century monastery of **Santa Cruz**. Its sacristy, cloisters and choir are particularly fine and the church contains the tombs of Portugal's first king, Afonso Henriques, and Sancho I, his son and successor. Some sources have it that this church was the site of the grisly coronation of Pedro and his dead queen Inês, as it was at Coimbra that she was killed.

On the left bank of the river stands **Santa Clara a Velha**, where Inês is said to have been buried. It was also the burial place of Dom Dinis' wife, the saintly Isabella. The convent itself stands partially submerged and the palace which was beside it is now totally destroyed. Isabella's body was removed to a new building, **Santa Clara a Nova**, where her silver tomb lies in baroque splendour.

Back in the city, the **Museu Machada de Castra** contains some fine ecclesiastical sculpture, for which Coimbra is renowned; it stands on top of what is thought to have been a Roman granary.

Alongside the Mondego, gardens provide a welcome relief from the claustrophobic city centre. It is here that Inês de Castro is said to have been murdered. Also in this area is **Portugal dos Pequeninos**, a model village containing amusing, if not necessarily accurate, representations of all the major buildings in Portugal and her foreign territories. It is near the **Botanical Gardens**.

Ten miles south-west lies the largest Roman site in Portugal, at CONIMBRIGA. Although its origins are possibly pre-Roman, the best remains are those of the 2nd to the 4th centuries, when it was a major stop between Lisbon and Braga. The site is divided by a swiftly constructed wall around which most of the excavation has taken place. Much of the site, including the forum, remains buried. Houses, pools and baths have been uncovered and some exposed mosaics are almost perfect.

Seventeen and a half miles from Coimbra, Carmelite monks seeking seclusion founded a monastery in 1628. BUCACO lies in a forest, where the monks cultivated exotic species such as cypresses and cedars. In 1643, excommunication was threatened to anyone who destroyed it; although the forest later became a battleground where Wellington emerged victorious over the French. The abbey was later turned into a royal hunting lodge. There is a small museum there, with exhibits from the Peninsular War.

MEALHADA lies thirteen miles north of Coimbra in the foothills of the Serra do Caramulo. It is known for one thing only – roast sucking pig. Exactly why this delicacy should be as strongly connected with this town is unclear: the fact remains that inns and restaurants serving the dish abound, the most popular being **Pedro dos Leitões**, on the main road through the town. Do be careful when eating it, however, as even Portuguese stomachs find it very rich.

LUSO is a spa town two miles from Buçaco. In the season (June–September) there are festivities and sports. There is a casino, with a night-club and two swimming pools, set in countryside ideal for walking and fishing.

The Mountains

HISTORY

The Mountains region of Portugal is one of the largest and yet it remains one of the least visited and relatively under-developed areas of the country. Much of the area is quite sparsely populated and some of the most remote parts have only recently been discovered by the more commercial kind of tourism. It is a part of Portugal that will suit those who want to get off the tourist-beaten track and see something of the simple reality of the country and its people.

The region encompasses the remote north-eastern historical province called TRÁS-OS-MONTES (Over the Mountains), which stretches to the Spanish border in the North and includes the upper valleys of the River Douro, home of Portugal's most famous product – port wine. An area of vast plateau and deep valleys, Trás-os-Montes is scattered with small, traditional settlements and grey, border stronghold towns whose people retain many ancient customs and traditions, as well as a distinctive local dialect.

To the south and west, through the valleys of the lower Douro and the Modego rivers, are the wooded highlands of the BEIRA ALTA, with extensive farming in poor, rocky soil. The region produces wine, too, including the popular and well-known Mateus Rosé. Summers here are often very hot, but winters can be harsh and cold. The visitor can sample local customs and cookery and admire ancient monuments to Portuguese history.

The Beira Alta area stretches to the foothills of the SERRA DA ESTRÊLA, the massive, storm-battered granite ridge extending for some sixty miles south-west from Portugal's highest town, Guarda. The range also takes in the nation's highest peak, Malhão da Estrêla, which rises to some 6532 feet (1991 metres) and includes the country's winter ski resort at PENHAS DA SAÚDE. The small country villages around these mountains produce cream cheese, and sheep's milk cheese, and a woollen industry has been established.

From the south-east edge of the Serra da Estrêla, the Mountains region extends further south, across the infertile plains of the BEIRA BAIXA province as far as the ancient but busy town of Castelo Branco. Although not as remote as the more northerly parts of the Mountains region, this area could scarcely be called commercialized and often retains as much tradition and unspoilt charm as can be found elsewhere in the region.

COMMUNICATIONS

As with any remote area, the communications in the Mountains are not of the same standard that might be expected in the more populous modern parts. The roads in the region tend to be mostly second- or third-class in nature and a number of them are of fairly recent construction since much of the region was relatively late in being integrated into the country's national road network. However, given the fact that the mountains are, in general, quite sparsely populated, the traffic on these roads is unlikely to be heavy.

The rail network is limited but adequate, allowing connections to most places of any size or significance. Steam trains are run on the historic Tamega line between Livração and Arco de Baulhe on the western edge of the region where it meets the Costa Verde.

There are also buses, of course; the State's national network providing a similar standard of service to that which it provides in the rest of the country.

CLIMATE

The Mountains region is extremely large and the climate varies considerably from one part to the other. Like most of Portugal, the region is in general quite warm from April to October, although less predictably so than in, say, the Algarve. In the north-east, around the Douro, temperatures at the bottom of the valleys can reach 100°F (38°C), whilst higher up it can be just warm.

Obviously, higher regions are cooler and temperatures in the Serra da Estrêla rarely rise above the mid-60s Fahrenheit; so, do not come here in search of endless baking sun – the region's charms lie elsewhere. The Serra can also be quite wet at times, with considerably higher rainfall (and snowfall) than elsewhere in Portugal. The north-east, however, is protected by the 'rain-shadow' of the mountains.

In short, the visitor to the Mountains can expect to find generally comfortable, warm weather with limited rainfall for most of the typical holiday months, but should not expect the sort of weather beloved of those who prefer to spend their time on a beach.

SPECIALITIES

Although not renowned for high cuisine, the Mountains have a number of specialities to offer. Several towns are well known for their dried or smoked ham, including Lamego and Chaves. Lamego is also responsible for *Raposeira*, a sparkling white wine similar to champagne.

The town and villages of the Serra da Estrêla produce a creamy mountain cheese from ewe's milk, called *Queijo da Serra*. The Serra da Estrêla is also known for fresh trout (*trutas*).

The sweet tooth of the Portuguese is satisfied by the sugared almonds of Torre de Moncorvo.

Undoubtedly the most famous product of the region is port, which is produced in the vineyards around the River Douro close to Vila Real, in the Trás-os-Montes province, and is a strong, fortified wine made with three parts wine and one part brandy.

The well-known wine Mateus Rosé is also produced in this region. Other wines from the mountains of Portugal include the light, sparkling vinho verde and the ruby-red or light-yellow Dão wines of the Dão and Mondego river valleys.

Vidago, a spa town in the region, is one of the nation's sources of table water.

WHERE TO GO FOR WHAT

The Mountains are relatively undeveloped as a commercial tourist area. As such, they have considerably more to offer the sightseer and nature lover than the socialite, who might be well advised to go elsewhere as night-clubs and bars are *not* commonplace.

Sightseers should be in their element throughout the region. Particularly attractive to them will be the gardens of **Castelo Branco**, the church and pilgrims' staircase at **Lamego** and, for the more adventurous, the simple charm of the **Corgo railway line**.

The recluse will find a number of quiet and remote places to his or her taste – especially in the Trás-os-Montes province in the north-east. There is also ample opportunity for healthy holidays, with spas at **CALDAS DE FELGUEIRA, CARAMULO** and **VIDAGO**; and skiing in the winter at **PENHAS DA SAÚDE**.

The nature lover should also find much to enjoy in the unspoilt countryside of the Biera Alta and Trás-os-Montes provinces.

Sun worshippers are not particularly recommended to come to the

Mountains – it is not a cold or unpleasant climate, but nor is it the Algarve.

The Mountains can, for simplicity, be divided into two large areas, north and south of the major road between the towns of Viseu and Guarda. North of this line lies Trás-os-Montes and most of the Biera Alta province.

Northern Mountains

The largest of the towns of the northern area is **VISEU**, a quiet and historic town, lying amidst woods on a high plateau cut by the River Paiva, in the region which produces Dão wines.

In the 16th century, the town was the centre of a great Portuguese school of painting, whose most famous exponent was Vasco Fernandes, known as Grão-Vasco. Examples of paintings from this era are displayed on the third floor of the Museu de Grão-Vasco, housed in a former Renaissance palace, the **Paco dos Três Escaloes**. The museum also houses sculpture from the 13th to 16th centuries, paintings by Dutch, Spanish and French masters, and a collection of 19th- and 20th-century works by Portuguese artists.

Close by the Museu de Grão-Vasco is Viseu's cathedral (*sé*), dating from the 12th century, in a combination of Romanesque and Gothic styles. The interior was rebuilt in the 18th century and the high, arched vaulting is from this time. A massive baroque altar supports a 14th-century figure of the Virgin. The cathedral can be found in the large but rather unwelcoming **Praca de Sé**, in the centre of Viseu, and its upper windows offer an excellent view of the old town's cobbled, twisting streets and overlapping roofs.

An interest in churches may be of use to the visitor to this part of Portugal, as they are a somewhat ubiquitous presence on all lists of what to see here. As well as the cathedral, Viseu also offers the baroque church of **São Bento** on the east side of the old town, which features attractive 17th-century glazed tiles – *azulejos*; and the **Church of the Misericórdia**, a pure example of baroque architecture with an impressive white frontage.

Around the town's ancient heart, new, modern surroundings have been created with hotels, shops and restaurants. For tourists in search of souvenirs, there are a number of antique shops.

On the northern edge of Viseu is a park, occupying the site of what was once a Roman and Lusitanian encampment. The Iberian rebel Viriatus, who led an uprising against the Romans, is thought by some to have camped here, but there is little to be seen other than his statue.

The visitor will find a number of hotels and guest houses in which to stay, including the four-star, motel-style **Grão Vasco** hotel on Rua Gaspar Barreiros in the centre of town. It offers modern accommodation and acceptable cuisine in a garden setting. (Tel: 235112 3.)

The smaller **Hotel Avenida** is notable for the owner's collection of African and Chinese antiques. (Tel: 234323 4.)

To sample the local cookery in a comfortable setting, the **Conitco** restaurant at 47 Rua Agusta Hilario is worth trying. Remember to order local Dão wine to accompany your meal. (Tel: 23853.)

The tourist office on Avenida Gulbenkian will be pleased to provide maps and information – including details of the annual fair in September, the **Fiera de San Mateus**, which is primarily an agricultural event, but includes some bullfights and folk dancing.

From Viseu, major roads lead to the rest of the Biera Alta province. South-west, through the beautiful hills of the Serra do Caramulo is the health resort of **CARAMULO**, set on a hillside at a height of 2,625 feet (500 metres). Here, one can find a museum with an impressive collection of medieval art, porcelain and pottery, tapestries and furniture, as well as paintings by artists as significant as Picasso, Dali, Miro, Chagall and Leger. There is also an exhibition of vintage cars.

Accommodation in Caramulo, which provides a good base for walkers, includes the small **Pousada de São Jeronimo**, surrounded by trees and with good views of the Do valley. The air is clear and invigorating.

South-east of Viseu, near Nelas, is the spa of **CALDAS DE FELGUEIRA**, with the large **Grand Hotel das Caldas**, offering a sauna and pool. In addition to the alleged cures for skin, circulatory and respiratory problems, there is fishing and bathing on the River Mondego in an attractive area amid pine-covered hills. (Tel: 942001 9.)

The road north of Viseu runs through the high, rough and sparsely populated landscape of the SERRA DO MONTEMARO, with few settlements except for the unremarkable little mountain village of CASTRO DAIRE, which has a fourteen-room guest house if you have to stop here.

About thirty miles on, as one approaches the richer agricultural land around the River Douro, one comes to **LAMEGO**. A small town, which is both affluent and elegant, it spreads out over the surrounding slopes of Monte Penude. An important market town since medieval times, it offers the local specialities of dried ham and a sparkling wine, *Raposeira*, a sort of Portuguese champagne. It is possible to visit the **Caves Raposeira**, just outside town, where the wine is produced.

The most notable site to see is the church of **Nossa Senhora dos Remédios** (Our Lady of the Cures), an elaborate 18th-century construction which lies on the summit of the Monte de Santo Estevão hill. It is reached by an impressive baroque staircase, with fourteen 'stations of the cross' on the way up, which are extensively decorated with fountains, statues and *azulejos*. Every year on 5 September, thousands of pilgrims climb to the top of the stairs on their knees, an event accompanied by considerable celebrations. There is a magnificent view from the terrace of the church itself.

Also to be seen in Lamego is the Gothic cathedral on the **Largo de Sé**, which has a 12th-century tower and attractive cloister. The interesting **Museu de Lamego** is housed in the former Bishop's Palace and displays tapestries, Portuguese paintings – including some by the aforementioned Grão Vasco – and sculpture.

From the Praça do Comercio, you can climb up to the *castelo*, passing other churches on the way. The castle is Moorish in origin and includes a 13th-century keep and cistern. Now used as the local scout hut, it is still worth a visit.

If you are still well disposed towards churches, the oldest in Portugal is the Visigothic foundation of **São Pedro de Balsemão**, which dates from the 7th century and is two miles to the north-east of the town.

There is no particularly distinguished accommodation in Lamego, though there is a four-star hotel, the **Estalagem de Lamego** (Tel: 62161) and a good guest-house, the **Residencial Solar**, at Largo de Sé – breakfast only (Tel: 62060).

A minor road leads off to the east of Lamego along the southern banks of the Douro. Eleven miles (18km) on is the attractive little town of RESENDE, with an excellent view from the Romanesque church of **São Salvador** above the town. Nearby is the reservoir of **Carrapatelo**.

A little further on is CINFÃES, a small country village famed for its vinho verde. There is an 18th-century house, too, the **Quinta da Feruanca**.

Also close to Lamego is the small spa of CALDAS DE AREGOS. Attractively situated on a hill above the Douro Valley, there are hot sulphur springs and a pleasant park. Cures are claimed for respiratory, skin and gynaecological complaints, though we have no evidence of their efficacy! There are as many as five hotels available to the visitor.

Directly north of Lamego, nine miles (15km) on is PÊSO DA RÉGUA. Here, the Corgo and Baroso rivers join the Douro in a small village which is at the heart of the 'land of wine', and which is especially busy during the vintage in September and October.

Continuing northwards, across the Douro and on the north edge of the Serra do Marão, is **VILA REAL**, the most accessible and largest of the towns of Trás-os-Montes province. In a setting of orchards, vineyards and waterfalls, it is an averagely attractive town of 14,000 people, famed for its fine black pottery. There are no outstanding sights, but visitors might be interested in the Italian Renaissance style house at Number 11, Avenida de Carvalho Araujo, which is the birthplace of the navigator Diogo Cão, discoverer of the Congo River.

The 14th-century Gothic cathedral of **São Domingo** retains the original Romanesque capitals from the first church on the site, and the church of **São Pedro** is expensively decorated with 17th-century *azulejos*.

If you happen to be in the town on 29 June, the **Fair of St Peter and St Paul** is held then. Among the goods on offer are examples of the local pottery.

There are three main hotels in the town, including one not particularly special four-star, as well as a number of fairly poor guest-houses. The tourist centre, in an interesting building, is on Avenida Carvalho Araujo.

The baroque country house, **Solar Mateus**, two and a half miles (4km) out of Vila Real on the road to Sabrosa will be familiar to those who enjoy the wine Mateus Rosé, since it is shown on every one of the thousands of bottles sold. A tour of the house, once the home of the Counts of Vila Real, is available but cannot, unfortunately, be recommended very highly, as it is rather dull.

For those intent on exploring the surrounding countryside, the little village of PINHÃO, further to the south-east, has a good two-star guest-house.

The main road north of Vila Real runs parallel with the Corgo railway line in the valley of the River Corgo, through countryside with an ancient, untouched air. Terraces are carved from the hard rock above the winding river and, on higher ground, these give way to fir trees which scent the air with pine. They grow in a tough landscape of granite, huge chunks of which have been hewn by the local people into water troughs, grain shelters and even used to construct simple homes.

The railway is primitive and charming; the trains have only three carriages, open at either end, and will stop at points along the route where there is only a narrow track leading off into the mountains. The visitor should not miss a chance to try this trip.

On the route north is VIDAGO, a famous spa town with hot springs which locals claim spew forth from the depths of the underworld itself! Cures are claimed for dyspepsia, allergies and 'metabolic disturbances'. There are a number of hotels and guest-houses and visitors can enjoy swimming, bathing, tennis, horseriding, fishing and clay pigeon shooting, as well as a night-club of sorts – a comparative rarity in northern Portugal.

The Corgo line ends at the town of **CHAVES**, about fifteen miles from Vidago and just seven miles (10km) from the Spanish border. An ancient border stronghold lying in a wide, green valley, it is also a market town famous for its smoked ham and also offering a strong, red local wine.

The *castelo*, rebuilt in the 13th century and founded on the remains of a Roman fortress, testifies to the closeness of the frontier. All that is left now is the outer wall and the impressive, strangely-designed keep, four floors of which house a military museum with ancient weapons, and reminders of the First World War.

Other sites include the baroque church of **São João de Deus**, an octagonal building with an attractive façade of granite; and the originally Romanesque parish church, which has impressive large blue and white *azulejos* covering its interior, depicting biblical scenes, and fine 18th-century ceiling paintings.

The Tamega River is spanned by a Roman bridge with twelve arches dating from the 2nd century AD.

If eating out, try the **Arado** restaurant on Ribeira do Pinheiro. Popular with local people it offers good regional cookery and wine, with fine views (Tel: 21996). Accommodation is somewhat restricted and basic, but try the **Hotel Trajano** on Travesso Candido dos Reis (Tel: 22415), which is simple and hospitable and offers good local cooking.

A minor road south-east from Chaves leads to **MIRANDELA**, more than twenty-five miles (40km) away. The road passes through RIO TORTO, which has a four-star guest-house, the **Estalagem de José**, if you have to pause on your trip.

Mirandela is an isolated but pleasant town on the edge of the River Tua. The 18th-century **Paco do Tavoras** with a façade of granite, is now the town hall and there is an old medieval bridge with eighteen arches to be seen.

Twenty miles south-west, back towards Vila Real, is the gloomy little town of MURCA, famous for a granite figure of a wild boar from the 7th century.

MACEDO DO CAVALEIROS is a small, pleasant place with a four-star hotel on the route north-east of Mirandela, through the mountains to Bragança.

The ancient and atmospheric capital of Trás-os-Montes, **BRAGANÇA** lies in the extreme north-east of Portugal, close to the Spanish border. Originally the seat of the rulers of Portugal from 1640 to 1910, the town dominates the surrounding area, which is mainly agricultural in nature.

Above the town is the *castelo*, an impressive outpost, once regarded as impregnable, and surrounded by double walls, the remains of which still stand – though the town grew beyond them centuries ago. Within the walls lies an imposing keep, the **Torre de Menagem**, together with a statue of Dom Fernando, Duke of Bragança; the 16th-century church of **Santa Maria do Castelo**; and the **Ducal Castle**, set in attractive gardens.

Perhaps the most fascinating building in the town is the *Domus Municipalis* (town hall), a 12th-century granite construction in the shape of an irregular pentagon. Inside is a cavernous hall lit by small round arches. Visitors can obtain the key from 40 Rua Dom Fernão o Bravo da Cidadela-Bragança, no less. In front of the building stands a pillory, the symbol of municipal authority, rising from the back of a prehistoric pig, a traditional fertility symbol. Walking the narrow streets around this building on Ash Wednesday, the unsuspecting visitor may be shocked as he is confronted by the figure of Death. Every year a local dressed in a skeleton costume and cape walks the streets as children throw stones in a somewhat macabre local custom.

The local restaurant, **Machado Cure**, is cheap, welcoming and can be recommended.

Three miles from the town is **Capela de São Bartolomeu**, which allows a superb view of both castle and town.

PRIVATE.
Keep Out
From Bragança, the roads south-east lead to the frontier town of **MIRANDA DO DOURO** on the upper reaches of that river. On the way is VIMIOSO, with the ruins of a castle, destroyed in the 18th century. Miranda do Douro is a quiet, remote, grey old town on a hill above the Douro, which is dammed close by. Although it lies on the Spanish border, there is no crossing here.

The remoteness of the place has meant that ancient customs, and the local dialect, somewhat like vulgar Latin, have been preserved. Every August, on the third Sunday of that month, men dance the dance of the *pauliteiros* (wooden stakes) in a costume of woollen kilts, striped socks and hats decorated with flowers. There is not, however, a great deal to see here. The 12th-century *castelo* was destroyed by an explosion in 1760, leaving only its watchtower, but there is a 16th-century cathedral with a broad W-shaped front, supported by towers. The terrace provides good views of the Douro Valley.

The nearby **Pousada de Santa Catarina** overlooks the Picota Dam on the edge of a gorge and provides the usual excellent standards of all *pousadas.*

A few miles on from Miranda, and deeper into this remote area,

MOGADOURO is a pleasant town surrounding a ruined castle, with attractive little cottages and – somewhat surprisingly – a good French restaurant.

About thirty miles (50km) south-west of here is TORRE DE MONCORVO, lying in dry, poor farming land producing fruit and vegetables. The parish church, a Renaissance foundation, has attractive *talha dourada* decoration and the *Misericórdia* church has a beautiful carved granite pulpit, of Gothic origin. Sugar-coated almonds are a local speciality.

To the north-east and north-west of Torre de Moncorvo, respectively, are the little towns of ALFÂNDEGA DA FÉ and VILA FLOR, the latter with an 18th-century palace, old town hall and a 16th-century church decorated with *azulejos*.

Travelling southwards, back through the Beira Alta region, **FIGUERA DE CASTELO RODRIGO** is a beautiful frontier town set on a plateau and surrounded by a number of fruit orchards. The original *castelo* stands on a hill above the town. *En route* to Figuera from the North, the village of ESCALHÃO has a small guest-house which may provide a useful stop-off for the weary traveller.

Onwards from Figuera, to PINHEL, in the east of Beira Alta, close to the border with Spain, which to this day is enclosed by the old defensive walls from its violent past. There is another ruined castle, and the 14th-century church of **Santa Maria do Castelo**. A three-star guest-house, the **Pensão Falcao** can accommodate visitors in reasonable comfort (Tel: 42104).

A minor road from Pinhel takes us on to **GUARDA**, on the edge of the Serra da Estrêla. Described by the Portuguese as cold, rich, strong and ugly, Guarda at a height of 3,400 feet (1,057 metres) is the highest city in the country, more than half a mile above sea level. It has been an important stronghold town since Roman times; it took part in a rebellion against Rome in 80 BC. Later it was devastated by the Moors before being rebuilt by Dom Sancho I in medieval times.

The traditional description of Guarda as ugly is a little unfair – in fact it has considerable historical charm. The cathedral in the centre of the town is an interesting jumble of several architectural styles, with an almost castle-like façade, complete with crenellations. The interior is magnificent and affords access to the roof terrace which gives superb views across the town to the Serra da Estrêla.

There is not a great deal else to see here, however. The old Bishop's Palace houses an uninspiring regional museum with pictures, photographs and archaeological specimens. Little remains of the ancient fortifications, except the 12th-century keep, the three town gates and remnants of the surrounding walls.

There is a pleasant market next to the fairly good **Hotel de Turismo** (Tel: 22205) and here you can buy some *Queijo da Serra*, the local cheese made from ewe's milk.

The **Telheiro** restaurant outside the city has good local cuisine, panoramic views and can be recommended (Tel: 21356). For information, try the tourist office, behind the cathedral on Praça Luis de Camões (Tel: 66205).

On the road from Guarda, back towards Viseu in the West, the town of MANGUALDE is the location of an extravagant 17th-century palace of the Counts of Avenida, which is set in a lovely park. Conducted tours are available.

Southern Mountains

The south of the Mountains region, beyond the Viseu–Guarda line, is composed mainly of the BEIRA BAIXA province, together with the mountains of the Serra da Estrêla. In contrast to the often great beauty of Beira Alta and Trás-os-Montes, the Beira Baixa is a region of flat, monotonous parched plains, with only a few cork trees and the occasional orchard to relieve the landscape. There are only a few places of interest here and only one of any great size – Castelo Branco.

CASTELO BRANCO, which has a population of 15,000, is an attractive, busy and prosperous border town close to the eastern frontier with Spain. It takes its name from the 'White Castle', now ruined, which stood above the town and reminds us of its former strategic importance. The place has lost some of its old grandeur and what is left of the old town can mainly be found around the castle ruins.

The modern town is not, however, unattractive and is built around wide avenues, broad squares, parks and gardens. The most notable sight is the **Antigo Paço Episcopal**, or

Bishop's Palace, and its baroque gardens. These terraced gardens have a deservedly high reputation and are a monument to extravagant design. Baroque sculptures of archangels, apostles and life-size kings are set amid clipped hedges and shrubs. The complete set of Portuguese kings ascend a flight of steps. The statues of the detested Spanish rulers Felipe I and II are contemptuously smaller than the rest.

The Palace itself houses the regional museum with a fairly ordinary collection of local artefacts, armour and archaeological finds. It also has examples of the famous *colchas*, embroidered bedspreads sewn by young girls in preparation for their wedding nights.

Above the town are the castle ruins and its associated church and from here you can ascend a flight of steps to the **Miradouro de São Gens**, a viewpoint which provides a superb panorama of the town and the surrounding countryside.

There are, somewhat surprisingly, no hotels in the town, though there are a number of guest-houses. Restaurants are not especially notable either, but try **Arcadia** on Avenida da Liberade for good regional cooking (Tel: 21933). Also, **Ti Lourdes**, on Estrada Montahao, serves fresh shellfish (Tel: 21006).

The local tourist office is in a small park, off the Alameda da Liberade, in the town centre (Tel: 1002).

Minor roads from Castelo Branco lead to the remarkable village of **MONSANTO**, about thirty miles (50km) to the north-east. Here, one finds a place scarcely touched by modernity; a village that time forgot. Hiding under a granite outcrop, it is a poor and simple place, apparently hewn from the grey rock. Some of the houses have been whitewashed to relieve the general greyness of the granite. Flowers adorn the narrow little streets. There is also an impressive but ruined castle nearby. A fascinating place to visit, a trip to Monsanto is like stepping into a different time.

North of Castelo Branco, nineteen miles (30km) over the stony plains is ALPEDRINHA, an attractive town dating from Roman times. There is a pleasant walk to the hermitage, the **Penha de Senhora da Serra**, from where there is an excellent view. Also, you can see the nearby remains of a Roman road.

The road now twists its way further north, through more fertile countryside to **COVILHA**, on the south-east slopes of the Serra da

Estrêla. This is a pleasant hill town, in a woody setting, which is often used as a base for exploring the Serra. It has a 15th-century church, **Santa Maria**, which has an *azulejo* adorned façade. There is also a park with good views of the town.

Covilha serves as a base for users of Portugal's only ski resort at nearby PENHAS DA SAÚDE, with skiing on the high plateau of the country's highest peak – Torre.

There is a tourist office on the Praça do Municipio (Tel: 22170).

Most of the remaining places of interest in the southern mountains lie on the opposite side of the Serra from Covilha. GOUVEIA is a little town close to the Mondego River and is another popular location for exploring the Serra da Estrêla. A few miles closer to the mountains is MANTEIGAS, a pretty if unremarkable market town with a couple of guest-houses.

South-east of Gouveia is SEIA, another small place with a pleasant view over the surrounding countryside from the parish church. The nearby NOSSA SENHORA DO ESPINHEIRO has one of the most pleasant of the shepherds' *romarias* celebrations, with a pilgrimage dedicated to a uniformed Child Jesus.

Further on are OLIVEIRA DO HOSPITAL, with a two-star hotel and guest-house; COJA, and ARGANIL, each with one small guest-house. All small and unremarkable places useful for a short break in a journey *if* you need to stop.

PÓVOA DAS QUARTAS, on the edge of the Mountains region, is in a high, scenic location and offers the **Pousada Santa Barbara**, with sixteen rooms and superb views of the countryside (Tel: 52252).

The Plains

HISTORY

Portugal's largest region, the Plains takes in a vast expanse of the country. Stretching from the Spanish border in the East, to the

Atlantic coast in the West, and bordered by the Mountains region in the North and the narrow strip of the Algarve in the South, the region comprises well over a quarter of the country's land mass. The Plains are, however, sparsely populated and have seen relatively little development. Much of the region is composed of an endless, rather featureless tableland which some tourists may find rather monotonous and uninteresting. These flat expanses of the old ALENTEJO province are primarily agricultural and rural in nature. Here, the visitor will find the storehouse of the nation, where wheat, olives and two-thirds of the world's supply of cork are grown, often on vast estates called *montes*.

Although for many travellers the Alentejo is simply *en route* to the Algarve, it is not without interest. It is a region of ancient settlements and there are several Roman, Moorish and Stone Age remains to be seen in its historic towns and villages, which are set fairly wide apart in the sparse landscape.

The Alentejo also has a fifth of the Portuguese coastline, with some fairly good beaches. Whilst the waters of the western Atlantic may not be quite as warm as those off the Algarve coast, the beaches are much quieter – ideal for those in search of quiet sunbathing.

The north-west of the Plains region takes in the ancient province of the RIBATEJO. Much of this area of Portugal is considerably more fertile than its neighbour the Alentejo. The uplands in the north of the province are intensively farmed, with figs, olives and citrus fruits being grown. In a strip along the banks of the River Tagus are water meadows which are flooded each spring, providing suitable conditions for the locals to cultivate rice. Horses and cattle are also reared here – including fighting bulls – and mounted cattle-herders, *campinos*, with traditional costumes and long lances can still be seen working with their animals.

To the south, the Ribatejo runs into the Upper Alentejo province, the fertile lands of the Tagus giving way to the flat plains, sun-baked in summer, with their characteristic large farming estates.

The Plains remains a region relatively untouched by tourism and, for this reason, retains considerable interest and charm – particularly for those keen to escape from the more well-trodden paths of the less adventurous kind of tourist.

COMMUNICATIONS

Communications in the Plains are adequate and unremarkable. Three major roads cross the region from east to west, dividing it into four broad 'chunks', and are inter-connected by a number of second-class routes running north to south. Some of the more remote villages of the interior are reached along local roads of variable but more or less acceptable quality; remember, however, that much of this region *is* rural.

Both buses and trains provide basic or better services throughout the region.

CLIMATE

The climate throughout most of the interior of the region is basically Mediterranean, with a cold winter without snow and hot, dry summers. Spring is short and in the autumn there are frequent rain showers. Overall, rainfall is low, with an annual average of around 24in or 600mm.

Summer temperatures may reach the mid to high 70s°F or occasionally higher. The coast has slightly lower temperatures – in summer low to mid 70s°F – but is still relatively warm and dry throughout the summer holiday period.

SPECIALITIES

Culinary specialities of the region include pork – this being an important livestock rearing area. This is most often served fried with clams. Another popular speciality is the cold soup *gazpacho*.

ELVAS is well known for its candied plums, grown locally, and gammon and smoked sausage are a favourite throughout the Alentejo. SERPA and TOMAR both produce speciality cheeses.

WHERE TO GO FOR WHAT

The Plains is a vast region and much of it is flat tableland of no interest whatsoever. There are, however, a number of places of interest in this desert of rural tedium.

Sightseers will enjoy the major attraction of ÉVORA, with its numerous monuments – especially the Roman temple and the Chapel of Bones, another example of which can be seen at CAMPO MAIOR. **The Castle-Convent of the Knights of Christ** at TOMAR is an outstanding sight which should not be missed by anyone with any interest in history, architecture or religion. **Almourol Castle** near ABRANTES should also be of great interest to the sightseer. There are, in addition, many interesting castles, churches and museums to be seen throughout the region.

A number of places should suit the recluse. The sleepy market town of MARVÃO in the north of the region and the remote, unspoilt village of MONSARAZ in the south should both interest this sort of visitor. Also, the *pousada* at SANTA CLARA-A-VELHA provides a suitable setting for a tranquil vacation.

For the sunseeker, the Alentejo coast provides a number of excellent, unspoilt and, above all, quiet beaches at LAGOA DE SANTA ANDRE, MELIDES, and ILHA DO PESSEGUERRO. VILA NOVA DE MILFONTES is another good beach resort but is not quite so quiet.

The spa town of CASTELO DE VIDE may be the setting for a healthy holiday.

Évora

Perhaps the most outstanding attraction of the Plains region – lying almost at its centre – is the old capital of the Alentejo province, the city of **ÉVORA**. If you visit one town in the region, make it this one.

An ancient settlement, dating from pre-Roman times, and one of the oldest trading posts in Portugal, Évora is an atmospheric place, laden with historic monuments and places of interest. It lies on a small hill amidst the rolling tablelands of Alentejo and still retains flavours of its Roman, Moorish and medieval pasts amidst its narrow cobbled lanes and streets – some with surprising names such as the Alley of the Sulking Child and the Square of Our Lord of the Earthquake.

In the centre of town is the **Praça do Geraldo**, a central square, partially surrounded by arcades, and a place of numerous cruel executions during the Inquisition. Among the sites here are a marble Renaissance fountain of 1570 and the collegiate church of **Santo Antão**.

To the east of the square is the cathedral (*sé*), an early Gothic edifice completed in the 14th century. Two asymmetrical towers guard the vast entrance on which stand the twelve apostles – fine examples of Portuguese Gothic sculpture. Excellent views of the town can be had from the roof. The interior is simple but attractive with a beautiful cloister and an interesting museum in the form of the Cathedral Treasury. Here, one finds valuable gold, silver and enamel ware and a 13th-century ivory triptych of the Virgin and child.

Close by the cathedral is Évora's famous **Roman Temple** – often wrongly referred to as a Temple of Diana. Dating from the 2nd century AD, this is an excellently preserved Roman monument – perhaps the best in Portugal. Once disrespectfully used as a slaughterhouse, the temple still retains fourteen of its eighteen Corinthian columns and a section of the architrave. The effect of this historic grandeur can be somewhat spoilt by the cars that are permitted to park around the temple's base.

Adjacent to the temple is the **Church of Lóios**, a 15th-century building with typical Portuguese *azulejo* tiles. Now converted into a *pousada*, the 'church' provides some of the most outstanding accommodation in the town – if somewhat expensive. Guests can stay here amid carefully restored historic grandeur and can dine under the arches of the former cloister. Previously used as a school, barracks and telegraph office, the *pousada* has been beautifully fitted out. Meals are also available to non-residents and are of the same high standard as the accommodation (Tel: 24051).

Not far from the *pousada* is the **Old University**, founded in 1551 as a Jesuit college and closed in 1759 when the Jesuits were banned in Portugal. Built in Italian Renaissance style, it is open to visitors during the holidays of the school-children now taught there.

South of here is the charming **Largo das Portas de Moura** square in which can be found the **Casa Corodovil**, a 16th-century Moorish and Manueline palace; and an attractive fountain featuring a symbolic globe, heralding the dawning of a new age (*c*.1556).

Still further south in the city is the church of **São Francisco**, one of the best Manueline buildings in Portugal. Of particular interest here – especially to those with a morbid nature – is the **Casa dos Ossos** or Chapel of Bones, off the south aisle. This 17th-century charnel house has a grim display of the bones of more than 5000 monks. A sign above the door warns, 'We bones here are waiting for your bones . . .'

Close to the church of São Francisco is the *Jardim Publico* (municipal park), with a **Museum of Decorative Art**, which is worth a glance at least; and the remains of the **Palace of Manuel I**.

Continuing southwards, the visitor will find another Gothic edifice erected in thanks by survivors of the plague. The **Ermida de São Brás** (Hermitage of St Blaise) is a morose building with a crenellated roof and a number of conical decorations on each side.

In addition to the Pousada dos Lóios, there is a fair amount of reasonable accommodation in the town. There are a couple of average hotels, but the four-star **Pensão Riviera** at Rua 5 de Outubro is possibly better value (Tel: 23304). It is simple but well maintained and has a conveniently central location – though only the hotels and *pousada* have bars.

Just outside town (2 miles/4km on the road to Alçacoves) is the **Estalagem Monte das Flores**, a charming hotel in a converted stable block offering amenities which include horseriding and a private lake. An attractive dining terrace provides a pleasant location for an outdoor meal of good local cookery (Tel: 25490).

For restaurants, try the **Cozinha de St Humberto**, at 39 Rua da Moeda (Tel: 24251). This atmospheric place is rustically decorated and offers excellent local cuisine. Also, **Fialho**, at 14 Travessa Mascarenhas (Tel: 23079) with excellent food in a pleasant interior which belies the rather unattractive entrance. A local speciality is fried pork with clams.

In the surrounding countryside, twelve miles to the north-west, is the interesting **aqueduct of Sertorius** (1552) built on Roman foundations; and twenty-two miles (35km) to the north-east is the imposing ruin of **Évoramonte Castle**, with a magnificent view.

North of Évora

Across the Plains, to the north-east of Évora and across the Serra da Ossa, lies **ESTREMOZ**. A small old town with Moorish overtones, it is a place of narrow lanes and whitewashed, traditional houses. Still enclosed in 17th-century Vaubanesque fortifications, with a number of impressive towers, the town stands on a hill above the plain, in the shadow of the *castelo* (13th century), which was once the residence of King Dinis I, but is now in decay. The local buildings make much use of a bright, white marble.

Sights include a number of Gothic and Manueline burghers' houses in the older, upper town and the church of **Santa Maria do Castelo**, which has two El Greco paintings of the Virgin Mary.

Also to be seen is the town hall (1698) which houses the **municipal museum** with a fairly standard collection of pottery, *azulejos*, pictures and armour. More *azulejos* can be seen in the 17th-century **Tocha Palace** on Largo do General Graca.

The town is well known for its earthenware pottery and the factory workshops are open to tourists. One notable object produced is a jar with one handle and two spouts, inlaid with marble, called a *moringue* – these jugs are associated with royalty.

In the lower, more modern part of town there is a weekly market in the Praça do Marquês de Pombal.

The 14th-century Royal Palace is now the **Pousada da Rainha Isabel** (Tel: 22618) and is within the castle. The *pousada* is decorated in sumptuous style with gold leaf, velvets, marble and antique furniture. There is an excellent view from the keep. The price of accommodation is in keeping with its grandeur and it is one of the more expensive of Portugal's *pousada*s. It is also open to non-residents who want to look around and admire the décor.

An excellent restaurant is the **Aquías d'Ouro** (Golden Eagles) at 27 Rossio do Marquês de Pombal. Diners seated in comfortable leather armchairs are served from an à la carte menu which includes pork, clams and partridge. Chocolate mousse is a speciality dessert.

Further north from Estremoz, more than twenty-five miles (40km) distant, towards the Spanish border, is **PORTALEGRE**, capital of the upper Alentejo province. A town of 13,000 people, its streets are lined with traditional white houses which cling to the steep sides of the hills. There are a number of attractive burghers' houses and some good examples of baroque architecture, as well as the fascinating local tapestry workshop.

The 16th-century **cathedral** (*sé*) has a Renaissance interior and the sacristy features an *azulejo* rendition of the Flight from Egypt. There are fine views from a nearby terrace. Close to the cathedral is the **municipal museum** with an excellent display of ceramics from Portugal, Spain, Holland and Italy, together with more ordinary armour and archaeological exhibits.

To the north of here is the **Palácio Amarelo**, or 'Yellow Palace'. This features beautiful 17th-century ironwork.

Just outside the town, in the **Parque de Miguel Bombarda**, is a former Jesuit convent which houses the tapestry workshops. Here, local girls use over 5000 different shades of yarn to produce copies of cartoons by the Frenchman Lurçat. The workshops are open from 11 am to 12.30 pm and from 2 pm to 6.30 pm (closed Sundays).

The Convent of São Bernardo, north of the park, is now a barracks but may be seen on request. It houses the tomb of Dom Jorge de Melo. To the west of the park is the *Rossio* – the main square in which can be seen the **Hospital of the Misericordia** – with an 18th-century façade. Above the town are the ruins of the obligatory *castelo*, which are of no particular significance.

The one hotel, the **Dom João III**, on Avenida da Liberdade (Tel: 21192) has 112 modern, spacious rooms, all of which have balconies looking out over the park. There is also a bar and shop. Alternative accommodation can be found in any one of four unremarkable guest-houses.

Alpendre, 21 Rua 31 de Janeiro is a fine local restaurant, air-conditioned in the hot summers, which offers the local speciality of pork with clams.

South-west of Portalegre is ALTER DE CHÃO, a small village close to the national horse breeding centre. There is not much here but if you have to stop, a single one-star guest-house provides reasonable accommodation. There is a tourist office in Portalegre which will be pleased to deal with any enquiries – Rua do 19 de Junho.

PRIVATE. Keep Out A little way north of Portalegre is the sleepy market town of **MARVÃO**, virtually on the Spanish frontier. Lying in a remote position, high on a rocky spur, the town is reached via a road along a promontory. The steep, narrow streets are lined with whitewashed houses, decorated with flowers, and the town is still ringed by the original medieval walls. The 13th-century *castelo*, standing above the town, offers excellent views in all directions from its keep.

Aside from the unspoilt, ancient atmosphere of the place, there is little else of note. The **Convent of Nossa Senhora da Estrêla**, outside of town, is now a hospital.

 There is a small, pleasant *pousada* with nine double rooms (Tel: 93201).

Seven and a half miles (12km) north-west is **CASTELO DE VIDE** – a maze of narrow streets, squares and alleys on the north-west side of the Serra de São Mamede. The town has retained much of its ancient character and charm and is dominated by the ruined 14th-century **Castelo de São Roque**, with its impressive keep from which there are fine views.

Castelo de Vide is a spa town with cold mineral springs containing Glauber's salts. Visitors still come to take the cure. The square in the centre of town, the **Praça de Dom Pedro V** has a number of churches, the town hall, and a few examples of baroque architecture – including the church of **Santa Maria**, which has a pyramidal tower.

The charming Jewish quarter is an atmospheric tangle of lanes and is populated by a large number of cats. There is also a synagogue to be seen here. The church of **Nossa Senhora da Alegria** is within the castle and features 17th-century *azulejos*.

There are a couple of hotels here, including the three-star **Hotel Sol e Serra** with 102 rooms, a pool, fine cuisine and bar. This can be found on Estrada de São Vincente (Tel: 91301).

The **Dom Pedro V** restaurant, on Praça Dom Pedro V, is the best place to eat out. It offers a full menu of regional dishes at reasonable prices and has a bar and – an unusual feature in this part of Portugal – a disco.

Back south-east (and almost directly east of the aforementioned Estremoz) is the attractive border stronghold town of **ELVAS**. It stands on a hillside less than ten miles from its Spanish counterpart of Badajoz and was built to defend the country from attacks from that town. From medieval times and onwards, the town was reinforced and fortified to provide a defence against attacks from Spain. The *castelo* above the town is 13th-century Moorish and offers fine views over the town.

On Elvas' **Praça de Dom Sancho III** the visitor will find the town hall, and the cathedral (*sé*), a mixture of late Gothic and Manueline styles. The interior of the cathedral is beautifully decorated with *azulejos*. Also to be found in Elvas is the church of **Nossa Senhora da Consalção**. Founded in the 16th century, it has an unusual design with an octagonal interior and a dome supported by high, *azulejo* encrusted columns.

In the north of the town is another example of the frontier defences – the 18th-century fort of **Nossa Senhora da Graça**, also known as **Forte Lippa**. The **Fort Santa Luzia** is a 17th-century foundation in the south of the town.

Another worthwhile place to visit is the **Museu de Antonio Tomás Pires**, which has examples of religious art, coins, pictures, sculptures and archaeological artefacts.

There are a couple of hotels in Elvas, as well as the excellent **Pousada de Santa Luzia**, which has a large number of antiques on display – many of which are for sale. Ask to see the dungeon crypt; this is also laden with antiques. Other hotels include the **Estalagem Dom Sancho II** in the main square (Tel: 226869). This has a very good dining room and a bar.

The **Don Quixote** is a pleasant, air-conditioned restaurant which serves both regional dishes and continental meals, as well as shellfish. A cheaper alternative is the **Café-Restaurant Marisqueira** at 33 Rua da Cadeia. It serves good local food in pleasant, quiet surroundings. A local speciality in Elvas is locally grown candied plums.

Four miles (7km) from town is the **Aqueduto da Amomeira**. Over 800 arches in up to four tiers still carry water to the 17th-century *Misericórdia* fountain in the town. Unfortunately, the aqueduct is rather unattractive.

It is twelve and a half miles (20km) north-east from Elvas to the border village of **CAMPO MAIOR**, which is still surrounded by a full, unbroken ring of defensive walls. The *castelo*, a 14th-century example built by King Dinis, is now ruined but has excellent views.

The most interesting site is the **Capela dos Ossos** – a chapel of bones on the same lines but on a smaller scale than that in Évora, which stands next to the parish church on the Rua I de Maio. Its walls are covered in bones, with two complete skeletons hanging up and rows of skulls arranged on the window ledge. The key to this grim relic can be had from the church. It is thought that the bones may have been provided by a disaster in 1732, when a powder magazine in the *castelo* was struck by lightning, resulting in the deaths of 1000 or more people.

On the other side of the country, on the very edge of the Plains region where it adjoins the Costa de Prata, is **SANTARÉM**, in the ancient province of the Ribatejo.

A beautiful and interesting place of some strategic significance, Santarém stands on a rocky spur above the banks of the Tagus. In the centre of town is the Praça de Šá da Bandeira, on the west side of which is the **Seminary Church** with excellent 17th-century *azulejo* decoration. Also in the square, which was the site of a famous execution in 1357, is the church of **Nossa Senhora da Piedade** – although it is not especially remarkable.

In the south-east of Santarém is the church of Sao João de Alporão, in Gothic and Romanesque style, which houses the **Archaeological Museum**, as well as the Gothic **tomb of Duarte de Meneses**, who was killed by the Moors, in Morocco, in 1458. So savagely was Duarte killed that only a single tooth remained to bring back to Portugal for burial. Close by the church is the **Convento da Nossa Senhora da Graça**, which has yet another late Gothic church inside.

In the north of the town stands the tall landmark of **Torres das Cabeças**, thought to have been originally a minaret. It contains an unusual clock. Also worth seeing, or seeing from, is the **Portas do Sol** (Gates of the Sun), an excellent lookout point to the south-east of Santarém. A small restaurant of the same name, standing in the gardens (Jardim das Portas do Sol) serves good regional food and wine, with the bonus of excellent views.

For accommodation, try the three-star **Hotel Abidis**, on 4 Rua Guilherme de Azevedo, a hospitable establishment with an excellent tavern style restaurant (Tel: 22017). The **Victoria** guest-house, 21 Rua 2 Visconde de Santarém (Tel: 22573) has sixteen simple rooms and provides good accommodation at the cheaper end of the market.

There is a tourist office, with helpful staff, on Rua de Capelo Ivens (Tel: 23140).

Santarém also plays host each year to the **Great Annual Ribatejo**

Fair, which lasts two weeks, starting on the fourth Sunday each May, and is worth a visit if you are in this vicinity.

En route between Santarém and Tomar is **TORRES NOVAS**, a small place with a ruined 14th-century *castelo* and three beautiful churches. The most interesting of the churches is the *Misericórdia*, which has some excellent *azulejos*. There are two guest-houses providing adequate rooms for the weary traveller.

Also *en route* is ENTRONCAMENTO, an unremarkable little stop-over with one small, basic guest-house.

Continuing east from here, rather than turning north off the main road to go to Tomar, one comes to **ABRANTES**, an ancient town that was a key point in the defence of the northern provinces. Standing high and exposed above the northern banks of the Tagus, Abrantes is a pretty town of white dwellings and flower-decked streets. The *castelo*, built in 1313, was subsequently flattened by the French in the 19th century. From the keep of this ruined fortress there are excellent views of the river and the surrounding countryside.

There are three churches of note in Abrantes. Within the ruined castle itself, the church of **Santa Maria** (1215) houses the **Museu Dom Lopo de Almeida** with *azulejos*, sculpture and two 1st century AD Roman statues amongst its motley exhibits. The church of **São João Baptista**, built in the 14th century, has a Renaissance coffered ceiling and interesting wood carvings. The *Misericórdia* offers a Renaissance doorway and 16th-century Portuguese paintings. Also to be seen is the **Convento de São Domingos** which has an impressive two-storey cloister.

The most interesting site for which Abrantes is known is, however, ten miles (15km) from the town. Built by the Templars, **Almourol Castle** stands alone on a small island in the Tagus and has an air of fantasy about it. It never saw military action and is almost perfectly preserved, with ten small towers and double outer walls. Two ferrymen will row visitors out to the island for a small charge and will drop you off at a tiny beach from which you are free to explore the island and the castle for as long as you like.

Abrantes provides an excellent base from which to travel to Almourol Castle. A good place to stay here is the three-star **Hotel Turismo**, off Largo de Santo Antonio (Tel: 21261). There are forty-eight rooms with baths, a currency exchange and bar. Otherwise, Abrantes offers three small guest-houses.

There is a good cheap restaurant if you want to eat out – the **Restaurant Huambo** on Largo Avelar Machado – but one should not expect international cuisine in Abrantes; it doesn't exist.

The tourist office (Tel: 555) is on Largo da Feira.

A little way along the main road which runs through Abrantes is an alternative stop-over – with nothing else, in particular, to recommend it. ROSSIO AU SUL DE TEJO has a single three-star guest-house with thirty-two rooms and a good restaurant called **Pensão Vera Cruz** (Tel: 31250).

South of Évora

PRIVATE.
Keep Out

There are strangely very few places of interest in the rolling, sun-baked plains south of Évora – and only one major attraction, Beja. One of the places that is worth a visit is **MONSARAZ** – a village of stunning simplicity. It has only seventy or so houses and lies, extensively fortified, just five miles from the Spanish border. The Portuguese call it *Ninho de Aguias*, or Eagles' Nest.

It is a somnolent, remote place with just one real street in which the thirsty traveller will find the one bar. The square at the end of this street has an 18th-century pillory topped off with a 'sphere of the Universe'. The *castelo* at one end looks out over neat, sun-drenched fields which stretch for miles in all directions, dotted with the occasional cork-oak.

Many miles to the south-west of Monsaraz (but *much* easier to reach directly from Évora) is the only major town in the southern plains region – **BEJA**, the former capital of the southern Alentejo province, which has a population of 20,000. It stands, oasis-like, on a hill above the rolling wheatfields and dates from Roman times, or earlier.

The obligatory *castelo* above the town is another of King Dinis' 14th-century edifices and was built on the remains of a Roman fortress. There is an excellent view and, in the lower courtyard, the **Museu Militar do Baixo Alentejo** (military museum), but it is of only slight interest. There is another **museum** – a Visigothic one – nearby in the Romanesque church of **Santo Amaro**. Below the castle, in the south-east of the town is a former **cathedral** in Renaissance style.

In the town itself there are a number of handsome burghers' houses amid the more ordinary dwellings – in some of whose doorways women still cook on old fashioned braziers. In the **Praça da República** is the church of the *Misericórdia* (1550) which was built as a market hall. The original function is still evident from the interior design. Also in the square is a Manueline pillory column.

To the south-east is the **Praça da Conceiçao** with the **Convent of the Conception**. The convent has 16th-century Manueline features and an attractive *azulejo*-decorated cloister, as well as housing the **Museu da Rainha Dona Leonor**. Exhibits include religious art, coins, *azulejos* and paintings. There is also a panoramic view from its turret. The convent is most famous, however, for being the home of a 17th-century nun alleged to have fallen in love with a French cavalry officer. Her letters to him – the *Five Love Letters of a Portuguese Nun* – were first published in Paris, in 1669.

Opposite the convent is the church of **Santa Maria**, an unusual light-coloured building with five towers.

An annual event in Beja is the **Feira de São Lourenço e Santa Maria**. Held each August, it is an enjoyable fair with various events including bullfighting.

Strangely for such a comparatively large place, Beja has no hotels, but there are a number of basic guest-houses of which the **Pensão Santa Barbara** at 56 Rua de Mentola (Tel: 22028) and the **Pensão Cristina** at No.71 in the same street (Tel: 23035) can be recommended.

A basic restaurant, with a tourist menu, is the **Luís da Rocha**, on Rua Capitão João (Tel: 23267).

PRIVATE. Keep Out — For those in search of tranquillity, try the nearby village of SANTA CLARA-A-VELHA. Remote and attractive, it offers a small *pousada* (Tel: 52250) adjoining a dam and its associated lake.

The Beja tourist office is on Rua do Capitão João Francisco de Sousa (Tel: 23693).

Nineteen miles (30km) south-east of Beja is SERPA, another ancient settlement with narrow little streets lined with white houses. There is a 13th-century *castelo* above the town, and the Gothic church of **Santa Maria** has some interesting *azulejos*. Nearby are the ancient remains of the **Ponte de Beja aqueduct**. The **Pousada de São Gens** overlooks the town from a distance of one and a quarter miles (two kilometres) and has the same high standards as all *pousadas* (Tel: 52327).

Some distance north of Serpa, across the Serra da Adica, is **MOURA PONTE DE SOR**, a spa town standing on the left bank of the River Guadiana. Founded by the Moors, and still retaining a Moorish air, the town has several of the low white houses characteristic of the region. In the main square, the **Praça de Sacadura Cabral**, is the church of **São João Baptista** in Gothic and Manueline style, with *azulejo* pictures of the Cardinal Virtues. The town hall, with arcades, is fronted by the **Três Bicas** (three jets) fountain.

In the park lying below the *castelo* – which is unremarkable – are the alkaline mineral springs which are allegedly useful in the treatment of rheumatism.

The **church festival of Senhora do Monte do Carmo**, held each October, has a number of folk events, of which the tourist office, on the main square (Tel: 22589) will provide details.

There is just one, average hotel, the two-star **Hotel de Moura** (Tel: 22495) with seventy-four rooms.

The final place of interest in the southern plains lies many miles to the north-west at **TORRÃO**, on the shores of Lake Carrascais. Here, one finds a Manueline church, in the birthplace of the poet Bernardim Ribeiro (*c*.1482–1552). The **Pousada Vale do Gaio** (Tel: 66100) with fishing, shooting and excellent food, is nearby.

The Plains Coast

The Alentejo province has one fifth of the Portuguese coastline along which there are a number of places of interest – primarily the excellent and relatively undiscovered beaches.

The attractive town of **ALCÁCER DO SAL** (Castle of Salt) stands on the right bank of the Sado River, which broadens out at this point into an estuary. The wide salt pans along the sides of the river gave the town its name.

There are a number of interesting buildings to be seen in Alcácer, which achieved prosperity in medieval times through its salt and corn trade, and on the rice which is still grown in the marshlands at the sides of the Sado. Above the town is the *castelo*, now ruined, within which is the church of **Santa Maria do Castelo**. It has a Renaissance doorway and 17th-century *azulejo* decoration. There are excellent views from the castle out over the town and the surrounding countryside. The **Convent of Santo Antonio** (16th century) has another Renaissance doorway and, in the **Chapel of the 11,000 Virgins**, sumptuous decoration in marble. There is also an **archaeological museum**, with some Stone Age and Roman relics, plus Moorish material, housed in the former church of **Espírito Santó**.

The one hotel is the four-star **Estalagem Herdade da Banrosinha** (Tel: 62363), off the Estrada Nacional 5. It is an acceptable stop-over with twenty-two rooms and very good food.

The pleasant promenade along the waterfront has a number of good restaurants at which to eat as well as a selection of tempting cake shops.

The tourist office is on Câmara Municipal.

Some miles along the Estrada Nacional 5 is the small town of GRANDOLA, an important cork centre. There is little here for tourists, but for stop-overs there are two small guest-houses.

Continuing south, **SANTIAGO DO CACÉM** lies slightly inland in the southern part of the Serra de Grandola and is an ideal base for the excellent beaches at SANTO ANDRE and MELIDES.

The town itself has an old Templar *castelo* with attractive views and an impressive parish church with a Romanesque and Gothic style doorway. The municipal museum, housed in one of Salazar's old jails, has an unremarkable collection of local artefacts, but does preserve one of the old jail cells.

For those with an interest in ancient history, it is just twenty minutes' walk to the Roman remains at **Mirobriga**. A Temple of Jupiter has been partly rebuilt and a paved street leads to a villa complex with parts of its underground 'central heating' system still intact.

At **LAGOA DE SANTO ANDRE** and **MELIDES**, the sunseeker will find two excellent beaches: though the waters of the eastern Atlantic may not be quite as warm as those of the Algarve Coast. At Lagoa, there are only a few small wooden shacks, a number of small beach cafés and ice-cream stalls and long stretches of unspoilt sand. In both places, the visitor will find peace to relax in the sun – this coastline is completely undeveloped in comparison with the Algarve.

Another beach 'resort' is SINES. It is now best avoided as the government are currently constructing an enormous oil terminal here, carving up the countryside as they do so.

However, farther south there are more untouched beaches – one of the best is at ILHA DO PESSEGUEIRO, on the Porto Corvo road. Here, there is little except a marvellous bar-restaurant and a ruined seaside fort.

VILA NOVA DE MILFONTES is on the estuary of the River Mira. The most popular resort in Alentejo, there are more people here than in some of the beaches mentioned earlier, but it is still relatively undeveloped. Guest-houses here tend to be fully booked throughout the summer.

Lisbon

The bustling, cosmopolitan city of Lisbon has grown up around a wide natural harbour half-way down Portugal's western coast. Legend has it that Ulysses established the city thousands of years before the birth of Christ. Archaeologists date Lisbon more positively to around 5000 BC and it was certainly known to the Phoenicians before the time of the Romans, who were enchanted by her seven large hills and safe harbour. The site of the first Phoenician colony was uncovered many centuries later nestling on the hill where the Castelo de São Jorge – the oldest monument in Lisbon – now stands.

The Romans arrived in Lisbon in 205 BC and over a period of several centuries turned the city into an important western outpost linked by three great roads to what is now Merida in Spain. The Barbarians,

Moors and Christian crusaders dominated the city in turn until the mid-12th century, when the 'Portuguese era' began properly. The 16th century saw the beginnings of modern Lisbon, as we know it today, when Portugal herself was reaching the peak of her international power and domination. Portuguese ships and navigators were amongst the finest in the early modern world and Lisbon became the main stopping place between Europe and Africa, and later Asia and America as well.

Most of the modern-day Lisbon which you will see, however, is less than two and a half centuries old. On 1 November 1755, All Saints Day, the city was devastated by one of the most fearsome earthquakes in recorded history. Around mid-morning the initial tremor struck and was followed by nearly two dozen more during the next couple of days which were felt as far away as Scotland and Africa. Packed churches, hospitals, prisons, brothels, inns, shops and whole streets of crowded homes collapsed like houses of cards. Over 30,000 people were killed in the initial turmoil and as many again died in the fires and tidal waves which followed, leaving the city a charred and derelict graveyard. The great Enlightenment thinker, Voltaire, recorded that 'the sea boiled up in the harbour and smashed the vessels lying at anchor. Whirlpools of flame and ashes covered the streets and squares, houses collapsed, roofs were thrown on to foundations and the foundations crumbled.'

The city was rebuilt totally in the aftermath of the earthquake and this was when the city's famous mosaic pavements and wide boulevards were built. Years of war battered Lisbon in the couple of centuries which followed but the reconstructed city remained in essence what you'll see today.

Lisbon has a host of magnificent points of interest which you shouldn't miss. If you visit nowhere else, get to the **Castelo de São Jorge** (St George's Castle) which sits right on the highest point in the city. Older than the city itself, the castle has been added to by generations of Portuguese kings and noblemen who have occupied it over the centuries. The earliest part of the castle dates from the 5th century AD, but its most famous occupant was King João I who carried the picture of St George into battle when he fought the Spanish in the late 14th century. It's open daily from 9am till sunset.

The *castelo* is a steep walk away, so you might prefer to take a taxi up to the edge of the building's ten old towers. Once there, you'll find each of the towers linked by massive battlements along which it is possible to stroll and admire the truly stunning views over the city below you. You can still explore the remains of a medieval village between the *castelo's* inner and outer walls. An attractive animal sanctuary is home to some amazing white peacocks and flamingos.

Lying directly below you is the picturesque district of **Alfama** and as you begin your descent back down into the heart of the city you will pass the **Museum of Decorative Arts**. Built within a 17th-century palace, the modern-day museum has a fine collection of magnificent furniture dating from between the 17th and 19th centuries. Look out for the marble statue of São Vincente, Lisbon's patron saint, inside. Next door to the museum is a professional workshop where craftsmen learn how to make and repair art objects, including wood inlays, carved cabinets and gold-leaf panels.

Alfama is the oldest part of Lisbon, so bear in mind that many of the streets will be short and narrow. Some of the better known ones can become particularly crowded in the summer months. Tiny cafés and tavernas have sprung up along the sides of all the streets, so you will never be short of somewhere to sit down for fifteen minutes and enjoy a quick snack or a drink. **Rua de São Pedro** is Alfama's liveliest, and most crowded, street, littered with stall vendors selling fruit, vegetables and freshly-caught local fish. Look out for the quaint 'British Bar' near the Duke of Terrceira's statue. British beers are sold (in pints!), although the staff don't speak English.

Also in Alfama is Lisbon's magnificent old **cathedral**, actually once a fortress, built originally in the 12th century. The building has been heavily restored since then, in the Romanesque style, and the influence of intricate baroque artwork is quite striking. Several sculptures by Machado de Castro can still be seen.

Lisbon is well-blessed with fine churches and a day's exploration of these could be enjoyable on its own. **Santa Maria** has beautiful interior stonework and fine vaulting, and the **Igreja da Madra de Deus** (Church of the Mother of God) retains some magnificent 18th-century *azulejos* and decorative panels. You'll find both on the Rua da Madre de Deus. Further afield, on the Largo Trinidade Coelho, is the **Igreja do Carmo** (Carmelite Church) with some fascinating 14th-century ruins and a modest archaeological museum. On the same road is an elegantly decorated 16th-century Italian baroque style chapel, **Igreja de São Roque**, and the modern **museum of sacred art** adjoins the church.

Walking through Lisbon, you will not fail to notice several striking monuments which are well documented in the Lisbon publicity material issued by the National Tourist Authority. Without a doubt the most striking of these is the 18th-century stone **aqueduct**. Over eleven miles long, it still brings water into the city daily.

In the city's **Belem** district you will be able to see the famous **Torre de Belem**, a decorative Manueline fortress with an attractive five-storey tower located along the north bank of the River Tagus. One of the few remaining examples of Manueline architecture, the Belem Tower was one of the most remarkable survivors from the fateful earthquake in 1755. The stonework inside and around the tower is truly amazing and it is possible to climb up inside the Tower and take in the spectacular views from the balconies. Several royal tombs are inside, together with those of the medieval explorer Vasco da Gama and the Portuguese poet Camões who eventually died in poverty.

Nearby sits the **Padrão dos Descombrimentos** (Monument to the Discoveries), a relatively modern monument which was built in honour of Prince Henry the Navigator on the occasion of the 500th anniversary of his death. The peculiar stone-carved sculpture resembles either an erect sword or billowing sail, depending on what angle you happen to view it from, and juts out across the river towards the sea.

Lisbon has an abundance of fascinating museums, each totally different from the other. Most are open Tuesdays to Sundays between 10am and 5pm, and closed on Mondays and national holidays. **Museu Calouste Gulbenkian** along the Avenue de Berna was opened in 1969 as part of the Calouste Gulbenkian Foundation. It provides an elegant setting for much of the donor's massive art collection from ancient Egypt, Persia and the Orient, and the Greco–Roman Empire. A spectacular museum which deserves a full-day visit to do it justice.

Portugal's finest collection of modern art is located in the **Museu de Arte Contemporânea** along the Rua Serpa Pinto Chiado. It contains a large collection of modern Portuguese work, in addition to lesser collections of foreign paintings and sculpture.

Among the city's other museums the **Museu Nacional do Trajo**, along the Parque do Monteiro Mor, has a great collection of national dress costumes and the **Museu de Marinha** is the city's main maritime museum. Those interested in military history should head for the **Museu Militar** in the Alfama district, but if you find ancient art more your passion then the **Museu Nacional de Arte Antiga** along the Rua das Janelas Verdes will not disappoint you.

Getting around Lisbon shouldn't be too much of a problem. On the whole, buses and taxis are inexpensive, but finding one can be a nuisance at times. Walking, particularly over relatively short distances, is frequently your best option if you can cope with the staggering volume of traffic noise at peak periods. City trolley cars and buses are amongst the cheapest in Europe but can be crowded at rush hours during the summer months. The Metro system covers only a small part of the city but it is efficient if you can find it, since the large M signs are frequently inconspicuous!

Accommodation in Lisbon ranges from the magnificent to the avoidable, although virtually all the hotels used by British operators are nearer the top end of the scale because of the relatively low room prices compared with British hotels. The city's oldest de luxe hotel is the **Avenida Palace** along the Rua de 1 Dezembro. You can also expect top de luxe service at the **Ritz**, **Alfa**, **Lisboa** and **Lisboa Sheraton**. Second-grade 'quality' hotels are surprisingly inexpensive, compared with the de luxe bracket. A real gem is the **Principe Real** on the Rua da Alegria, although the **Tivoli Jardim** and **Florida** are almost as comfortable and more centrally located.

The independent traveller in Lisbon should not find accommodation a great problem as lower grade hotels and guest-houses are located all over the city. The central **Presidente**, 13 Rua Alexandre Herculano (Tel: 539501), **Embaixador**, 73 Avenida Duque de Louie (Tel: 530171), **Fenix**, 8 Praça Marquês de Pombal (Tel: 535121) or **Flamingo**, 41 Rua Castilho (Tel: 532191) should not disappoint you. The city's youth hostel at Andrade Corvo 46 is cheap and central and there is a good campsite at the Parque Nacional de Turismo e Campismo (Tel: 708384).

Eating and night-life in Lisbon are excellent and there's something to suit most pockets and tastes. The opera season lasts from December to July, at the opera house on Largo de São Carlos, and the theatre is always lively and very active. Bear in mind that drama performed in Portuguese loses a lot (unless you speak the language, of course!). Lisbon has four main theatres and the largest popular one is **Municipal Theater de São Luis**. Concerts by Portuguese and international artists are performed regularly throughout the year at the opera house and municipal theatre.

The best night-life centres around Lisbon's numerous night-clubs and bars: **Procopio** on Alto São Francisco, **Foxtrot** on Travessa Santa Terezinha, and **Mrs Breton's Pub** on the Rua Marechal de Saldanha. The Sheraton's rooftop **Panorama** is popular but expensive. Numerous '*fado* places' have grown up around the city – each offering a taste of Portugal's unique soul music with the option of a meal beforehand as well. A particular favourite with locals is **Senhor Vinho** at 18 Rua de Meio-à-Lapa.

If you are eating out in Lisbon, then none of the de luxe class hotels should disappoint you – if the price falls within your budget. The **Sheraton** has a particularly fine grill. **Restaurante Baleal**, on Rua de Madalena, serves good Portuguese meat and offers an excellent (cheap!) house white. **Canto do Carnões** restaurant (Tel: 365464) on Travessa da Espera has a good value, all round menu with the added attraction of traditional *fado* music most evenings. The ebullient head waiter – Antonio de Alreu Alves – will add to the evening's entertainment. The **Hotel Tivoli** has an expensive à la carte menu with a splendid lobster speciality. A few other restaurants of note are **Michel** near the *castelo* for excellent local cuisine, and the (very expensive) **Tayares** on the Rua da Misericórdia for truly top class Portuguese and continental specialities.

Excursions by coach, train or hire car are relatively easy across the nearby coastal and inland regions which encircle Lisbon. There are some excellent beaches along the Estoril Coast which are easily accessible, together with a host of former palaces and disused villas that were homes to countless deposed, exiled or 'retired' monarchs and noblemen. One of the best night-spots outside Lisbon's city centre is at CASCAIS, once a tiny fishing village with origins dating to before the 15th century. On a main road, bus connections from Lisbon are frequent.

Slightly further than Cascais lies the famous **Boca do Inferno** (Mouth of Hell) cave. A massive indentation on the cliffside, the cave is surrounded by the remains of old lookout fortresses decaying ever more slowly as the generations have passed. A fast and regular train service from the city will bring you down the Estoril Coast in no time at all. For details of where and when organized excursions from Lisbon are available contact the main tourist office at Palacio Foz, Praça dos Restauradores, or else at the Miradouro de Santa Luzia near the Castelo de São Jorge. There is an English telephone tourist information service available if you call 575086 or 360450 in Lisbon.

The Lisbon and Estoril Coasts

The coastal areas around Lisbon provide some excellent alternatives to the more conventional Algarve resorts for the visitor in search of sun, surf and sand.

To the west of Lisbon, along the coast, is the area known as the 'Portuguese Riviera', with the resort towns of Estoril and Cascais connected to the capital by a four-lane motorway. Here, on the Atlantic coast are some excellent beaches, backed by green hills, sheltering them from the north and west winds. These resorts are increasingly popular with tourists, though they are not yet overcrowded.

Also to be found just inland from the Estoril Coast, west of Lisbon, are the historic towns of Mafra and Sintra, with some fascinating sights, particularly in Sintra – described by Byron as a 'glorious Eden'.

South of the capital, across the Tagus Estuary, is the isthmus known as the Lisbon Coast. This is an area which is not yet fully developed for the international tourist trade and which has a variety of small, pleasant coastal resorts to offer the sun-seeking visitor. A new bridge across the estuary, the Ponte 25 de Abril, has made the peninsula much more accessible and has substantially boosted both the number of visitors and the level of development along the coast. From Lisbon, it is now just a short drive across the estuary and through the luxuriant pine groves of the interior to the southern coastal resorts of the peninsula – in particular Setúbal and Sintra.

COMMUNICATIONS

Communications in this region are often better than elsewhere in Portugal due to the proximity of the capital. The main railway lines from Lisbon are the Sintra, Cascais and Setúbal lines which provide regular services to the major towns and resorts. Bus services are also of reasonably good quality, with fairly regular and reliable timetables.

The roads are in general excellent, with motorways linking the capital with Setúbal, Estoril and Cascais, and good main roads connecting with the rest of the region's resorts. Some of the smaller beaches are reached by more minor roads – but these are always of an adequate standard.

CLIMATE

The region's climate is one of hot summers and mild winters with low rainfall all year round. August temperatures average 72°F (22°C) and higher. This falls to 52°F (12°C) in January.

The wettest months are December, January and February, but even during this time the rainfall is rarely very heavy.

Water temperatures are reasonable for swimming, but remember that this is the Atlantic coast so that the sea is never especially warm.

SPECIALITIES

Being a coastal region, fish is a popular traditional dish, with excellent selections of varied seafood on offer. The Portuguese national dish of *bacalhau* – dried, salted cod – should be available. Apparently, there are different recipes for each day of the year. Egg custard is a universally popular sweet and there are a number of other egg and sugar based sweets.

Red wine is produced in Colares – a light, dry and smooth vintage. The region is also well known for the Setúbal Muscatel wines.

WHERE TO GO FOR WHAT

The Estoril and Lisbon Coasts provide a suitable holiday destination for most kinds of tourists and travellers.

The sun worshipper is well served with good beaches along both coasts and an equable climate.

The socialite will also find enough night-life to make for an enjoyable vacation – particularly of interest here are the clubs of ESTORIL and CASCAIS.

For the sightseer, the region offers some excellent places of historical and architectural interest – especially at BOCA DO INFERNO, near Cascais, in SINTRA, with the Paláçio Nacional de Pena, and in MAFRA, with its vast monastery-palace complex.

For those in search of healthy holidays, a number of sports are on

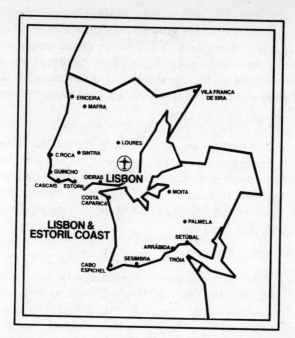

offer, including tennis and golf, but especially swimming, and other water sports such as fishing, sailing and scuba diving. SESIMBRA and PRAIA DO MONTE ESTORIL are two good locations for such pursuits.

The Estoril Coast

Following the main road westwards from Lisbon, one first comes to the little village of **CARCAVELOS**, with its excellent sandy beach. A large, modern four-storey hotel, the **Praia Mar** (Tel: 2473131), offers good facilities, including a night-club and bar, and stands almost on the beach. Alternative accommodation might be found in the **Albergaria Narcico** (Tel: 2470151). This inn has only seventeen rooms and *is* actually on the beach.

From Carcavelos, it is just five miles (8km) to the much larger town of **ESTORIL**, an expensive resort full of expensive people staying in expensive hotels. Nevertheless, it is not totally inaccessible to the less affluent visitor, and is worth visiting.

Since it became a fashionable resort for the international set in the late 19th century, Estoril has grown from a small fishing village to a town of 16,000 or more people. There are few outstanding sights and most visitors come to soak up the ambience of elegant wealth. In recent years Estoril has become slightly too expensive and its famous casino slightly shabbier, but this is still Portugal's smartest resort.

A central feature of the town is the **casino** – centrally situated on the Praça a Garett, with not only gambling but dancing, floor shows, and a cinema. Housed in a glass building with a pleasant inner courtyard, the pursuits on offer include roulette, baccarat, chemin de fer, blackjack and, of course, one-armed bandits. Open from 3pm to 3am.

There are some excellent beaches in Estoril, the best of which is the **Praia do Monte Estoril**, as well as opportunities for sailing, fishing, and other water sports. One important point should be made here. Much of the coast around Lisbon has been badly polluted by international shipping. Thus, if you do decide to swim in the ocean, you would be well advised to keep your head above water.

Golfers are catered for, too, with an eighteen-hole course at MONTE ESTORIL.

Another feature of the town is its radioactive springs – which reach a temperature of 91°F (33°C) and are recommended for the treatment of rheumatism and diseases of the joints.

This very elegant resort has, of course, some excellent hotels. The **Palacio** is the top establishment, with many former royal guests, and royal prices to match. The hotel also boasts an excellent à la carte restaurant, **The Four Seasons**. A cheaper alternative, though still a high class hotel, is the four-star **Hotel Cibra**, on Estrada Marginal, next to the Palacio (Tel: 2681811). It has eighty-five rooms in a modern, seven-storey glass building. The dining room offers good food and excellent views.

Moving into the lower price range, try the **Hotel da Inglaterra** on

Ave de Portugal. A pleasant family establishment, it offers thirty-eight rooms, a bar and swimming pool.

If you are not eating in your hotel, one of the attractive alternatives Estoril offers is the **English Bar**, also on Estrada Marginal (Tel: 2681254). The mock Elizabethan façade belies the excellent Portuguese food served here, with turbot and clams a particular speciality of the house.

On the beach, try the **Tamaris** snack bar – a place to relax with a drink and enjoy the beach life.

As well as the casino mentioned above, there are other night-time entertainments in the town. **Á Choupana** is a club on the Estrada Marginal with good though not cheap food, and dancing from 10pm until 3.30am (Tel: 2683099).

A younger scene can be found at the **Forte Velho** disco on the Estrada Marginal in São João do Estoril. Housed in a converted fortress on the edge of a cliff, the disco opens from 10pm and closes at three the next morning. You can take a break from the dancing and enjoy a drink on the parapet overlooking the sea below.

The Grand Salon Restaurant, with good international cuisine, also has a floorshow with showgirls on Las Vegas lines, and a small cinema open daily for both matinée and evening performances.

Just four miles from Estoril is **CASCAIS**. Once a small fishing village, Cascais now has a population of 11,000 and has developed into one of the most popular of Portuguese resorts outside the Algarve and is expanding at such a rate that it may not be long before it joins itself to Estoril to form one large resort town. Cascais stands on the western side of an attractive bay in which the local fishing boats bob with the tide. It is more of a tourist resort than the slightly aloof Estoril, but nevertheless has much to offer the more discerning traveller and is in no way a mass tourism ghetto.

For the sunseeker, there are three beaches. The largest is **Praia da Ribeira**, off Avenida de Dom Carlos I, and fronting the bay. Immediately adjacent is the slightly smaller **Praia da Rainha**, and further north-east, off Rua Frederico Arouca, is the excellent little beach of **Praia da Duquesa**.

In addition to the beaches, the visitor to Cascais will find a number of interesting sights to see. Standing above the south-west edge of the bay is the **Citadel**, testimony to the fact that this town was once the summer residence of the kings of Portugal. The Citadel is now the summer residence of the President of the Portuguese Republic. Nearby is the church of **Nossa Senhora da Assunção**, with some fine *azulejo* decoration.

In the south-west of the town, on the Estrada da Boca do Inferno, you will find the palace of the **Condes de Castro Guimarães**, with a small museum containing antique furniture, 18th-century paintings and other local artefacts. Close by is the large and pleasant **Parque do Marechal Caramona** with a small lake and a zoo. North of the park is the town stadium.

Also to be seen in the town are the regular fish auctions or *lotas*, on the main square: a babble of colourful buyers and sellers. The local fishermen here will tell you that one of their ancestors discovered America before Columbus. Afonso Sanches is alleged to have made the discovery of the New World in 1482 and to have returned to Portugal where Columbus 'stole' both the knowledge of the discovery and, after making the same trip himself, the credit!

A popular excursion with visitors to Cascais is that to the **Boca do Inferno**, a chasm carved out of the cliffs by the power of the ocean waves. The water roars and churns impressively in the 'Mouth of Hell', and the visit is well worth making.

Probably the best hotel in Cascais is the **Albatroz**, at 100 Rua Frederico Arova. It was originally the summer home of the Duke of Loulé and is built in an elegant, neo-classical style on a rocky ledge above the ocean. It is certainly a luxurious and elegant place to stay – former guests include Prince Rainier of Monaco, Cary Grant and Anthony Eden – but it is also luxuriously priced (Tel: 282821).

More reasonably priced accommodation can be found at the three-star **Hotel Baía** on Avenida Marginal (Tel: 281033) on the bay above the Praia da Ribeira. A modern four-storey building, it is comfortable and friendly. The roof terrace offers excellent views of the bay.

There is also an adequate choice of budget priced guest-houses and apartment hotels, if your finances are more restricted.

Dining out in Cascais should not be a problem as there are a large number of excellent – and busy – restaurants. In keeping with its accommodation, the **Hotel Albatroz** has an elegant and expensive restaurant serving excellent international cuisine in luxurious sur-roundings. More reasonable is **O Pipas**, at 1B Rua das Flores. A hospitable bistro, it serves good food at prices easier on the pocket. In the evening, visit the popular **John Bull Pub** on Largo Luis de Camões. Decorated in traditional English style, it serves reasonable beer and also has a good, economical restaurant.

Later, one might like to sample some of Cascais' night-life: there are a number of discos and clubs in the town. **Van Gogo** is at 9 Travessa Alfarrobeira. Formerly a fisherman's cottage, it has been converted into an upmarket disco with a young clientele, black glass interior and a high entrance charge. Less select – although still equipped with a careful doorman – is the **Palm Beach**, on Praia da Conçeicão (Tel: 280851). It stands on a hillside above the bay and has a good atmosphere with, again, a young clientele.

From Cascais, it is just three and a half miles (6km) to **Guincho**, a wide beach on the western Atlantic coast of Portugal and fringed by dunes. It does not have the problem of sea pollution faced at beaches nearer to Lisbon, but there are very strong currents and swimming can be dangerous.

From Guincho you can go on to **Cabo da Roca**, 'the most westerly point in Europe', 472 feet (144m) above the Atlantic waves. The lighthouse is open to visitors and the climb to the top is well worth making.

From Cascais, it is a short distance north to **COLARES**, a small holiday resort which is renowned for its wine-making. There is one adequate two-star hotel here (seventy-two rooms) and three guest-houses (all with bars).

Three-quarters of a mile (1km) on is the captivating town of **SINTRA** which Byron described as 'a glorious Eden'. Standing below the north slopes of the Serra de Sintra, the town is one of the oldest in the country. Its historic buildings stand in a setting of beautiful sub-tropical vegetation and flowers such as camellias, bougainvillea and mimosa scenting the air.

Sintra has a great deal to offer the sightseer – especially one with an interest in architecture, art and history. In the centre of the town is the Praça da Republica with a Gothic pillory column and, on the north-east side, the **Palacio Nacional de Sintra**, former seat of the royal House of Avis. A 14th-century edifice, the palace is built in Moorish and Gothic styles, its most prominent external features being its characteristic conical chimneys. Inside, one finds some excellent examples of Portuguese art, with some particularly fine *azulejo* tiles, as well as paintings amd tapestry. Architecturally, the Hall of Magpies, Hall of the Swans and the octagonal domed Hall of the Stags are especially interesting. You can enjoy a particulary fine view from the window of the bathroom of the last queen of Portugal.

Another of Sintra's principal tourist attractions is the **Moorish Castle** (8th century). Open from 8am to sunset, it is well worth visiting, and there is an excellent vista from the Royal Tower. The castle is, however, much overshadowed by another: the Palacio Nacional da Pena. Before visiting this, however, take a short trip up a side road from the Moorish Castle to the **Convento Santa Cruz dos Capuchos**. This convent, dating from 1560, is remarkable for the extensive use of cork in its construction. The guide will be delighted to show you around the monks' cells, now defunct and forlorn.

The Palacio Nacional de Pena stands at the very summit of a steep crag, 1,732 feet (528m) high. This amazing creation has a fairytale air. Built for Ferdinand of Saxe-Coburg in the 1840s, it is a grand piece of Wagnerian bravado. Conducted tours are available of the interior, complete with antique furniture, exquisite china and ancient weapons. Outside, there are magnificent views from the walls over the surrounding countryside to the ocean.

Surrounding the Palacio is the **Parque de Pena**, which has hundreds of varieties of trees and shrubs. From here, it is just a short distance to the highest point in the Serra de Sintra, **Cruz Alta** (1,772 feet/540m), which has more excellent views.

Other sites in Sintra include the church of **Santa Maria** and **São Martinho** and the luxuriant botanical gardens called **Monserrate**. These last were created by an Englishman, Francis Cook, in the 19th century, on a steep Sintra hillside. Hundreds of plant species adorn this beautiful garden, at the bottom of which you will find the **Palacio de Monserrate**.

Also in the town, housed in the former **Palacio Velenças** is the municipal museum with local Portuguese paintings and other arte-facts, but nothing of particular note.

The highest quality accommodation in Sintra is at the five-star **Hotel Palacio dos Seteais**, at 8 Avenida Bocage. Converted from another of Sintra's numerous palaces – the town was once the summer residence of the royal family – this is a luxurious establishment, standing in its own grounds. Inside, there are fine antique furniture and tapestries. There is also a library and music room. There are only eighteen very expensive rooms. However, dinner is excellent and open to non-residents.

More accessible to the average tourist is the **Tivoli Sintra** hotel on the Praça da Republica (Tel: 9233505). It has seventy-seven modern, comfortable rooms with traditional Portuguese décor. In addition, Sintra offers a number of good guest-houses, inns and budget hotels. Try, for example, the small **Estalagem da Roposa** on Rua Dr Alfredo Costa (Tel: 2930465).

A good restaurant at which to dine out is **Galeria Real**, with good cuisine in upmarket surroundings. This is located on Rua Tude de Sousa in São Pedro de Sintra (Tel: 9231661). Also worth sampling is **Quinta de Santo Antonio** at 2 Rua Cámara Pestana.

For advice on the sights of the town, try the very helpful tourist office on the Praça da Republica (Tel: 29311579).

Sintra could provide an excellent base for the tourist who wishes to visit more than one of the beach resorts along the coast. At any rate, it is worth carving a few days from your schedule to take in the town's remarkable sights.

The nearest beach resort is **PRAIA DAS MAÇÃS** about six miles (10km) from Sintra. A small beach resort with good swimming in the waters off this rugged coast, it has just one hotel (reasonable standard, nineteen rooms) and a guest house. In high season, a tramway connects with Sintra.

Further up the coast is ERICEIRA, a small fishing port with a pleasant beach and, again, good swimming.

A few miles inland from Ericeira is **MAFRA**, in general a rather uninspiring, pedestrian little town – with the exception of the remarkable monastery-palace.

The **Palacio-Nacional de Mafra** was built in the 18th century by King João V in fulfilment of an oath to the birth of an heir. A huge and magnificent baroque edifice, it took 50,000 men and £4,000,000 to create. Covering more than 290,000 square feet (40,000 square metres), it has almost 900 rooms, with 2500 windows and 5200 doors! The central feature of the building is the church, with its two towers, one of which can be climbed. The view is excellent and the ascent is worthwhile. In the vestibule of the church are fourteen large marble statues; marble is also used extensively in the interior decoration. Visitors to the complex are shown a selection of rooms and buildings, including the hospital and pharmacy – complete with the original fittings – the kitchen and the monks' cells. The royal apartments have a great deal of fine 18th-century antique furniture but can become rather tedious in their similarity and unrelieved sumptuousness. However, the library is very highly regarded by scholars and is most impressive, with 30,000 volumes, including the earliest edition of Homer in Greek and many other valuable manuscripts.

Elsewhere in the complex, there is a **Museum of Comparative Sculpture** with casts of fine sculpture from Portugal, France and Italy.

The Palacio is open daily from 10am until 5pm. For information call 52332.

There is little to see in Mafra once the Palacio has been visited, although the church of **Santa André**, in Gothic style, is of architectural note.

The only accommodation in the town is at the **Albergaria Castelão** on Avenida 25 Abril. It has nineteen adequate and comfortable guest rooms, a television and a reading room (Tel: 52320).

Continuing up the coast from Ericeira are the beaches of **PRAIA DE SANTA CRUZ, PRAIA DE PORTO NOVO** and **PRAIA DE AREIA BRANCA**. All are good sized beaches, with fine sand and good swimming in the Atlantic. Praia de

Santa Cruz, the most southerly of these three resorts, is very popular and friendly. Praia de Porto Novo boasts the additional attraction of a nine-hole golf course. Accommodation at all these resorts is somewhat limited and you would be well advised to check this in advance.

The Lisbon Coast

The Lisbon Coast is the name given to the narrow peninsula of land south of Lisbon between the broad estuary of the Tagus and that of the River Sado to the south. This area is not yet completely developed as a centre of mass tourism, but is undergoing very rapid change – partly as a result of the new suspension bridge across the Tagus estuary. The influx of both tourists and developers seems certain to lead to this region becoming far more tourist-orientated and commercialized than it was previously.

There is little tourism or travel development in the interior of the peninsula, with its wide pine groves, part of which is a 'natural park'. Indeed, all the main resorts in this region lie on the southern coast of the peninsula.

SETÚBAL is Portugal's fourth largest town, with a population of 60,000, standing in an area of orange groves, vineyards, and orchards. It is a centre for the production of Muscatel wine and for the sardine industry.

Few of the town's historic buildings survived the massive earthquake of 1755 and this has reduced the sights for today's visitor. Nevertheless, what is left of the old town does offer some points of interest. At the eastern end of the town is the church of **Santa Maria da Graça**, which dates from the 16th century and has some interesting pictures from the following century. Also of interest is the church of **São Julião** and the **Convent do Grilos** – the latter has some attractive *azulejos* and an impressive interior in rococo style.

To the north-west of the town, off the Avenida do 22 de Dezembro, is the **Igreja de Jesús** (Church of Jesus), dating from the 15th century. The municipal museum in the attached former convent buildings offer a fine selection of Portuguese, Catalan and Flemish art and some archaeological exhibits. Also worth a visit is the **Museum of Oceanography and Fisheries**, off the Avenida de Luisa Todi.

Outside the town, one can visit the **Forte de São Félipe**, dating from the 16th century and, three miles (5km) away, the **Torre de Outão**, a Roman Temple of Neptune.

The beach is not actually in Setúbal but is located at the end of the sandy 'spit' that stretches out into the bay from the opposite coast, at TRÓIA. This is reached by ferry or hovercraft and is now undergoing heavy development with the construction of a new tourist complex. Also at Tróia is a fine eighteen-hole golf course with some challenging natural water barriers.

The accommodation on offer in Setúbal includes the **Pousada de São Félipe** in a former *castelo*. Although expensive, it has the same high standards as all Portugal's *pousadas* (Tel: 23844). The three-star **Esperança Hotel** at 220 Avenida Luisa Todi is modern, clean and comfortable. It has seventy-six rooms, a night-club, bar and currency exchange facilities. The top floor dining room offers fairly good food and pleasant views. There are also a number of guest-houses of varying standards from four stars to none.

A good place to eat is **O Beca**, at 24 Largo da Misericórdia (Tel: 24617). The excellent food is served in a dining room decorated with old ovens and other local memorabilia and the prices are very reasonable.

Tróia features the new Torralta tourist complex with high rise blocks of hotel-apartments. Try the **Aparthotel Tróia** (Tel: 4422), which is comfortable, if simple, at a reasonable price.

A few miles inland from Setúbal is **PALMELA**, a small town in the foothills of the Arrabida mountains. The main point of interest is the impressive *castelo*, standing at a height of 1,200 feet. It was an important stronghold fortress during the Moorish era and has been substantially reinforced and enlarged since. In 1488 the Bishop of Évora was charged with conspiracy and imprisoned in a cistern in the castle.

Also to be found within the castle precincts is a ruined church – another victim of the 1755 earthquake – and the 14th-century keep, from which there is a good vista of the castle and the surrounding area. At the western end of the castle is the 15th-century **Convent of Santiago** with some fine *azulejos*, more examples of which can be seen in the nearby church of **São Pedro**.

The only accommodation in Palmela is also within the castle, in the

Pousada do Castelo de Palmela. There are fifty-eight rooms in keeping with the usual high standards of *pousadas* across Portugal (Tel: 2351226).

The other major resort on the Lisbon coast lies westwards from Setúbal. The small fishing village of **SESIMBRA** is a popular and sometimes overcrowded tourist resort offering swimming, fishing and good scuba diving. It is also a particular favourite of swordfish hunters.

The 17th-century *castelo* above the town has excellent views but is unremarkable with a simple church and a few unimpressive archaeological exhibits on display. The visitor may also want to visit the ancient **Fort São Teodosio**, close to the lighthouse.

Accommodation can be had at the **Hotel do Mar** on Rua dos Combatentes do Ultramar (Tel: 2233326). This four-star hotel has 120 rooms, all with their own terrace. A modern resort hotel, the facilities on offer include a bar, night-club and swimming pool, as well as two tennis courts and an aviary full of tropical birds. Alternatively, there is one other two-star hotel, as well as two small guest-houses from which to choose.

If you are eating out, try the **Chez Nous** restaurant at 11–13 Largo do Muníçipio (Tel: 223014). This pleasant little restaurant offers some very good seafood.

The Algarve

HISTORY

With over a hundred miles of stunning beaches, picturesque coastal villages and modern resort facilities, the Algarve has rapidly become one of Europe's fastest growing and most popular holiday destinations. Stretching from the Cabo de São Vicente, the southwestern tip of continental Europe, right across to the little town of Vila Real de Santo Antonio by the Spanish border, the Algarve is roughly

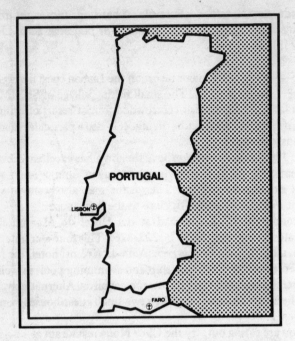

separated from the rest of Portugal by a range of mountains which have helped the region to maintain and develop a noticeable cultural and social independence. As it is, the Algarve sees a substantially higher number of tourists each year than the rest of the country put together and tourism has long since taken over from fishing as the region's main industry.

Portugal's famous southern region has scarcely any real historical past and, as a result, little in the way of impressive monuments and buildings to offer the hardened sightseer. The Algarve was the last region to force out the invading Moors and it took until the 13th century – fully a hundred years later than the rest of the country – before the Moorish political and military domination was totally ended. Even today some 600 Arabic words remain in the Portuguese language, including the name 'al-Gharb' (Algarve) itself which means, literally, 'garden', because of the striking fruit blossoms which have grown during the winter months for centuries.

A few hundred years later, during the first half of the 15th century,

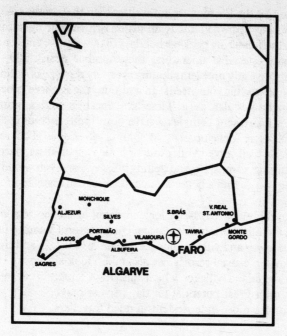

the region briefly became the focus of the world for international exploration and discovery. Prince Henry the Navigator, younger son of King João I of Portugal, established and maintained his famous School of Navigation at Sagres, the rocky southeastern tip of the country. Dreaming dreams of discovery, of which it was said 'no mortal ever dared dream before', both Columbus and Vasco da Gama were later to pay tribute to the pious pioneer whose voyages led the way for all European travels of discovery in the later Middle Ages.

But not even the Algarve, 150 miles away from Lisbon, managed to escape the devastating earthquake which wiped out most of the capital in 1755. Whole communities were killed and most of the region's old churches and homes destroyed in less than a minute of violent tremor. The region's own capital Faro was ruined for the second time in a generation having only just recovered from an earlier earthquake which had struck in 1722.

The tourist boom in modern-day Algarve only really began in the 1960s, and even since then has been more tempered and rigidly controlled by the Portuguese authorities than that on the coastline of neighbouring Spain. Virtually all major British tour operators offer hotel and self-catering package holidays to the Algarve and, combined with many specialist operators, they number nearly 200, so you shouldn't have any problems finding precisely the type of holiday (and price range) to suit your needs. In addition, the Algarve is becoming increasingly popular as a Timeshare location and a number of luxurious apartment complexes have been built, including a sprawling 2,000-acre development at Quinta do Lobo. The region is particularly well served with outdoor holiday specialists, particularly those offering water sport and golfing holidays, and you would need to go a long way to find a better stretch of European mainland for any of these.

In the following pages we look in detail at all the region's main resorts, including Albufeira, Lagos, Quarteira and Vilamoura, and at the main towns and villages along the Algarve Coast. In addition to the better known coastal resorts, we also take a look at some of the more interesting inland villages which, although largely undeveloped as resorts, offer great potential for day trips or maybe even a weekend excursion for more independent-minded travellers.

COMMUNICATIONS

The Algarve is by far the best connected region of Portugal, both in terms of travelling around once there and in getting to and from the area in the first place. The region shares an international border with Spain where the main frontier crossing, a fifteen-minute ferry crossing to meet road and rail links, is at VILA REAL DE SANTO ANTONIO. As with all Common Market land borders, the formalities of crossing into Spain (or vice versa) should not present any problems to British visitors with valid passports and normal common sense about what can and what cannot be taken across an international border.

The region has one airport, fortunately a large international one, just outside Faro. All scheduled and charter flights to the Algarve land and take-off from Faro and accordingly package holiday connections to and from hotels are good. Standby and APEX fares from Britain are always available to Faro and represent good value compared with standard fares.

A railway line runs eastwards from Lagos across to Vila Real and beyond into Spain. The main towns all along the way have stations in or nearby, but some of the resorts can be a good distance from the nearest station. Albufeira station, for example, is nearer the small town of Ferreiras and a good quarter hour away by bus, so if you intend to travel by train at all during your stay check well in advance just how far your hotel is from the nearest station. A main line connects the Algarve with Lisbon and, overall, train fares in Portugal are low.

Cheap long-distance buses link all the main centres in Portugal. **Rodoviaria Nacional**, as well as a few smaller private firms, run express coaches linking the Algarve towns with each other and with Lisbon. Local travel agencies, or your tour operator representative, should be able to provide information about timetables and reservations. Local and regional timetables look quite baffling but are normally kept up to date and are fairly rigidly followed by the bus drivers. Most of the R.N. buses which operate in the region are modern and comfortable, except for a few old boneshakers which visit the more remote inland villages and which suffer from a combination of age and abominable backroads!

Algarve taxis can be found at specific taxi ranks – at least one in every town or resort – and can be quite scarce at the height of the summer season. As a general rule, none have meters but follow instead a standard fare table based on mileage which you can ask to see if it is not already displayed inside the car. Tipping is not compulsory, but the average tip tends to be about 10 per cent of the fare.

If you choose instead to hire a car then you will find no shortage of hire firms in any of the main towns and larger resorts. Main roads throughout Portugal, but especially in the Algarve, are often congested in summer. Minor roads are seldom in good condition and are usually quite narrow. Advance booking with an international car-hire firm, such as Avis or Hertz, or else through your tour operator, is normally the cheapest and safest (from an insurance point of view if you have an accident) means of finding a car.

TOURIST INFORMATION

There are more than a dozen tourist information offices in the

Algarve, each with at least one member of staff who will speak English and all will be able to provide you with glossy colour brochures about the region. The main tourist office for the region is in Faro at Rua Ataide de Oliveira 100 (Tel: 24067-26068), open 9am until 10pm Monday to Thursday and 9am until 8pm Friday to Sunday. Tourist information is also available at Faro airport where you will also be able to pick up, for a few escudos, a copy of either *The Algarve News* or the *Algarve Magazine*. Both are published monthly in English and are the most comprehensive and up-to-date guide to what's going on in the region.

CLIMATE

The weather is mild and temperate all year round in the Algarve, with neither extremes of temperature featuring. The region has a long holiday season from April to October when it is warm and sunny. Winters also tend to be very mild but can occasionally be chilly in the evenings and substantial rainfall lasting for many days at a time is not uncommon. Strong Atlantic winds are bearable during the warmer summer months but can be a nuisance, blowing sand around, if you visit the Algarve in the autumn.

The winter air temperature seldom drops below the mid 50s°F (around 12–14°C) in the coolest months, from late December until late March. Once into April the temperature climbs into the low 60s°F (16–18°C) reaching the 70s°F (22–26°C) by June, July and August. Peak summer temperatures are often well into the 80s°F (27–32°C), with seldom so much as a hint of rain from one week to the next.

The weather inland tends to be slightly warmer but that may be preferable if you want to get away from the beaches for a while. It goes without saying that lengthy hot periods in summer may seem stifling to some people, particularly if spent on noisy and crowded beaches. But this is, after all, what the Algarve is famous for and you won't be disappointed if it is sunshine you want!

SPECIALITIES

Without a doubt, fresh fish and locally grown fruit are the main culinary specialities to be found throughout the Algarve. Many small

– and very much alive – fishing villages still flourish along the Algarve Coast. Shellfish is the main catch, almost always as fresh as the morning's tide, but no longer the inexpensive luxury it was a decade ago. Prawns, crabs and other fish are normally on (refrigerated) display in restaurants and shellfish particularly tends to be sold by weight rather than per portion so you might need to decide in advance just how hungry you really are! Look out for *gaspacho* for a starter – the Algarve version of the famous Spanish cold soup recipe with cucumber, tomatoes and peppers.

One of the Algarve's most amazing dishes is *Amêijoas na cataplana* – and you ought not to leave the region without attempting this quite unique blend of cockles, sausage, ham, paprika and assorted vegetables at least once. A close second must be *caldeirada de peixe*, the Algarve version of a rich fish stew which has to be eaten with knife and fork. One other delicacy deserves special mention. *Carne de porco com amêijoas* is claimed to be of Algarve origin and consists of baby cockles blended with chunks of pork. Well worth sampling.

Portugal is renowned for its wines and you won't be disappointed with the range available throughout the Algarve. Local specialities are limited, however, and the two you are likely to come across are *Lagoa* (red, white or rosé available) and *Tavira*. Both have an alcoholic strength between 12 and 14 per cent which is noticeable after a few glasses if you bear in mind that most wines drunk in Britain are between 9 and 11 per cent alcohol!

WHERE TO GO FOR WHAT

The sun worshipper will not be disappointed at practically any of the coastal Algarve resorts. The main beach area is a long sandy stretch of coastline heading eastwards from the excellent all-round resort at Albufeira. Equally stunning are the beach areas around Lagos, Praia Dona Ana, Vilamoura, Quarteíra and Armação de Pera. Many of the beaches have appealing natural qualities, primarily low red cliffs and rock formations. Some of the finest are at the resorts of Falesia, Albufeira, Carvoeiro and Dona Ana.

Sun and sand are the main reasons for going on holiday to the Algarve and although many resorts offer a lot more to see and do, a few do have quite disappointing beaches. If a good, clean, safe beach is essential to you when making up your mind which resort to choose, then you really ought to avoid Salema, Ferragudo and Baleeira. A number of beaches are exposed or without any facilities, including those at Bordeira and the eastern end of Alvor Três Irmãos.

Just about any of the large resorts will be ideally suited for family holidays, offering safe bathing with childminding facilities available in the evening. An increasing number of hotels offer early meal times for families with young children or courtesy baby-sitting services to allow parents to enjoy some of the resort's night-life. Albufeira, Monte Gordo and Oura da Agua in particular have a number of such hotels, and they will be highlighted in this chapter.

The socialite will appreciate the lively night-life of Albufeira and the more up-market Vilamoura further along the coast.

Sightseers ought to visit Faro or Sagres, or else consider exploring a few of the lesser known inland towns like Silves or Monchique.

The recluse should head anywhere but the Algarve Coast! Inland resorts can be surprisingly quiet but the coastal resorts will be anything but unless you can visit Portugal outside the main summer season.

Healthy holiday-makers keen on water sports, tennis, golf and walks will be well catered for at most of the larger coastal resorts and sports facilities at many resorts have developed into top professional status. Golf facilities around Loule Velho, Trafal and Meia Praia are excellent and beautifully groomed championship courses, together with an international tennis centre, have been developed at Vale do Lobo.

Faro and Resorts East

Stretching west from the attractive frontier town of Vila Real de Santo Antonio by the Spanish border, to the region's capital, Faro, this strip of coastline has been less extensively developed for tourism than the neighbouring region to the west of Faro. Travelling west from the border, the numerous small towns you will pass have managed to retain much of their traditional charm despite the growth in popularity of one or two large resorts nearby, namely Tavira and Monte Gordo. Continuing towards Faro you will encounter a series of offshore sandy islets known collectively as the *Ilhas* where the water is warmer and the volume of tourists considerably less than further west. Nowhere along the Algarve Coast can truly claim to be unexplored, but this impressive eastern stretch is about as close to being unspoilt as you'll find in the region.

Very much a showcase of 18th-century Portuguese town planning, **VILA REAL DE SANTO ANTONIO** sits right by the Spanish border and from here it is possible to cross over into nearby AYAMONTE in Spain. The great Guadiana River separates Vila Real from its Iberian neighbour and a car and passenger ferry service operates between the two border towns at least every half hour, in either direction, during the summer months. Vila Real itself was founded in 1774 by the Marquis de Pombal, who was largely responsible for the reconstruction of Lisbon after the devastating earthquake in 1755. In less than six months the bulk of the building had been completed. Most of the town's stonework is prefabricated and was originally carted all the way from Lisbon – some 300 miles away!

Modern-day Vila Real is a pleasant provincial town, as yet undeveloped as a tourist resort but with a lot of through-traffic in the summer months. The tourist office is located in the Rua da Princesa, on the waterfront. Vila Real is focused around a picturesque central square, the **Praca de Pombal**, so named after its famous architect. The square is paved with black and white mosaic tiles and surrounded on all four sides by two- and three-storey buildings. In the centre stands a narrow obelisk dedicated in very glowing terms to the former King José, on the throne at the time of the town's construction. Orange blossoms fill the square and help emphasize the striking sunray effect which is given by the tiles radiating outwards from the central obelisk.

The rest of the town has been built along rigid military lines – parallel streets and right angled corners everywhere. A particularly long esplanade, the Avenida da Republica, lines the Portuguese side of the river and makes a pleasant afternoon or evening walk. You can see across into Spain and horse-drawn carriage rides are available during the summer months past the shipyard and lighthouse at the edge of the coast. Carriage rides are also available to the ancient castle at Castro Marim, the original headquarters of the Order of Christ in the 14th century. Vila Real also has a small museum of printing, the **Manuel Cabanas Museum**, located just off the town square, which is open most days.

Wherever you wander in this peaceful, largely traffic-free little town you will not fail to notice the cosmopolitan flavour. Curious holiday-makers from the south-west Spanish coast, or Spaniards themselves make this popular day trip, and mingle with visitors from further west along the Algarve. Spaniards particularly seem to enjoy sightseeing in Vila Real where many basic foodstuffs and commodities are cheaper than at home. Portuguese escudos and Spanish pesetas are interchangeable in virtually all shops.

Vila Real is also the home of a great **fish market**, set up originally by Pombal himself in the 1770s. Tuna fishing goes on all along the Algarve Coast throughout the summer months, but the peak season lasts from April to July when huge shoals make their way to their spawning banks a few hundred miles west of Gibraltar. Naturally enough, locally caught fish is one of the culinary specialities available in Vila Real.

One of the most popular restaurants in town is **Edmundo's**, along the Avenida da Republica, which offers some magnificent views across the river and neighbouring Spain in addition to some truly fine food. Fried sole is one of their specialities, but they also serve succulent meat dishes including lamb cutlets and veal fillets. Slightly less expensive are **Gomes**, on Rua Aveiro 5 and **Bonança** at Rua Duarte Pacheco 34, also **El Conde** or **O Monumental**. around the central square.

The chance to take a day excursion across into Spain is something which shouldn't be missed. The 15-minute ferry ride costs less than 30p each way, and Ayamonte is an attractive little town, roughly the same size as Vila Real. Bus and rail connections are excellent – and it's possible to visit Huelva or even Seville in under three and half hours.

Just two and a half miles west of Vila Real lies one of only two major holiday resorts to the east of Faro. **MONTE GORDO** has been popular with literally dozens of major tour operators for the past ten years and that popularity has been reflected by the growing number of foreign visitors who choose to make it their choice of holiday destination each year.

Originally no more than a simple fishing village, Monte Gordo has expanded rapidly into a thriving and well-equipped tourist resort. The village itself is quite dull, with little to offer beyond basic facilities – bank, post office, souvenir and grocery shops and so on – and a lot of building work in progress. Shopping facilities in the village and at the resort proper are limited. But the resort has easily one of the finest beaches anywhere along this eastern Algarve Coast – if you're prepared to share it with several hundred fellow sun worshippers. Literally miles of fine white sands gently arch round the coast and the clear blue Mediterranean waters shelve gently to allow perfectly safe family bathing. The beach setting is backed by magnificent pine-forests rich with olive and citrus groves, but the overall effect is sadly rather lifeless. It can become particularly crowded in front of the town where all the hotels and bars are.

The immediate area has little to offer the sightseer. Day trips to Faro, just thirty-five miles along the coast, or over the border into Spain, are generally available through tour operators who visit Monte Gordo. An especially popular excursion is a full day trip across into the historic city of SEVILLE in Spain. A regular bus service runs to Faro from the village, but this usually takes at least an hour and a half and becomes both crowded and uncomfortably warm at the height of summer. There is a fair stretch of coastline around Monte Gordo worth exploring, as well as a few less well known inland sights nearby including Castro Marim, so hiring a car for a day or so would be an option worth considering.

Sporting facilities are available to those looking for an active time. The larger hotels all offer some sort of water sport activities – windsurfing or water-skiing – from the beach in addition to a few land sports. The hotels **Alcazar** and **Vasco da Gama**, both used by several large tour operators, offer mini-golf and tennis facilities as well as water sports.

Night-life in Monte Gordo has quite a cosmopolitan flavour to it in view of the number of foreign visitors the resort sees each year. On the whole, night-life centres around the large casino which sits down on the beach in a fairly unappealing location. In addition to gaming tables, there is generally some form of dancing available and a nightly floor show. Most of the hotels have discos each night and the local bars are always busy, if you enjoy that type of atmosphere. A few hotels, including the **Vasco da Gama**, **Dos Navagadores** and the **Alcazar** feature live music, depending on the time of year and the type of residents whose tastes they are catering for at any given time.

On the whole, eating and accommodation in Monte Gordo are the best features of the resort. A few tavernas and restaurants in the village serve good, traditional food and one of the best is **Copacabana** along the Avenida Infante Dom Enrique. Open seven days a week, this Oriental-looking place has indoor and outdoor seating, as well as good sea views. They offer mostly fish and meat dishes and serve them all to pretty near perfection. Try their steak Diane, fondue of veal, or even their grilled suckling pig.

The large hotels, without exception, also offer good quality international cuisine and almost all have spacious, air-conditioned dining rooms. The hotel **Albergaria** tends to cater particularly for the British tourist market and is renowned for its soups and local fish dishes. The hotel has an efficient waiter service and also offers a special children's menu. The Alcazar and Vasco da Gama both serve four courses for dinner, each with three impressive choices, and a poolside snack service at little extra cost. The food, and general service, offered by the hotel **Das Caravelas** was of poor value and quality compared with that normally available at Algarve hotels.

For a small resort, Monte Gordo is well served by respectable hotels. With the exception of the bleak Das Caravelas, all those used by British operators in this area represent good value for money and shouldn't disappoint you. The resort's finest is the four-star Hotel **Alcazar**, on Rua de Ceuta (Tel: 421-84), with a glorious palm-fringed façade and large, sheltered swimming pool and bar. Each of the ninety-five bedrooms has a soundproofed terrace – which helps you to avoid the nightly basement disco if you decide to turn in early.

Hotel **Vasco da Gama**, Avenida Infante Dom Henriques (Tel: 443-21), has a magnificent beach location for those who want the minimum distance between hotel and long hours soaking up the Algarve sunshine. Six floors high, all the rooms in this bright, modern hotel are well furnished and there is a smart children's pool and play area. This hotel is particularly popular with British holiday-makers and English is spoken by most staff.

Other particularly good hotels in Monte Gordo are the **Albergaria** in the village itself, which offers high quality basic accommodation mainly to young singles and couples in the 25–40 age group; the **Casablanca Inn** is clean and comfortable if you can forget the exterior (and interior) tacky décor which doesn't quite resemble the famous film of the same name; and the hotel **Dos Navagadores**, which offers ten storeys of cluttered though comfortable accommodation, but do take care on the poolside tiles and stair carpets which are showing signs of wear.

All along the Algarve Coast, small fishing villages have been developed into modest resorts, primarily offering short-term summer apartment accommodation on a self-catering basis with the very occasional option of staying in a modest hotel or pension. The first such resort beyond Monte Gordo is **ALTURA**, a small and very typical Algarve village with little to see or do beyond enjoying the wide, sandy beach just outside the village. Altura is rather isolated and, since there are only a couple of hotels here, accommodation and night-life are limited. Wings visited Altura recently and were not exaggerating when they termed it 'one of the less developed and more relaxed resorts'. Day trips to Tavira, Faro or into Spain are your main activity options from Altura during the day, unless you feel like tennis on one of only a couple of courts available.

The resort's main hotel is the three-star **Hotel Altura**, an unattractive 12-storey building with a reasonable restaurant and large swimming pool. Facilities for children are particularly good, however, with a wide play area available, cots and high chairs for meal times, early meal arrangements for young children if necessary, and a daily baby-sitting service if parents wish to leave the hotel for a day trip or evening in town. Windsurfing and cycle hire are available.

Limited apartment accommodation can be found further along the coast at PRAIA VERDE and ALAGOAS, but bear in mind that these tiny fishing villages have little to offer the visitor beyond a reasonable beach. Praia Verde has a very long stretch of sand which is backed by a large campsite, and the water shelves gently, making it suitable for children under no more than normal supervision.

Just past Alagoas lies the small village of MANTA ROTA. With nothing to speak of in the way of accommodation or tourist attractions, Manta Rota does boast one of the Algarve's finest restaurants and longest beaches. The **Stable**, Praia da Manta Rota (Tel: 952-46) hides at the end of a massive stretch of sand which merges neatly with the flat hinterland surrounding it. You really ought to search out this place if you fancy an excellent meal out while staying in this area. Every conceivable local speciality is cooked to perfection in this restaurant with ancient beamed ceilings. Portuguese beef steak, Algarve cockles, lobster and crab all caught and served as fresh as the day's sunshine!

In addition to these modest resorts, the east coast is dotted with a few more little villages which have managed to remain totally unaffected by the tourist boom. **CACELA** has no hotels or pensions, merely a few private rooms if you are lucky enough to get there early in the morning to search one out. The village atmosphere in one of these places is about as typically Portuguese as you'll find along the coast and they are an ideal choice of location to go and switch off for an afternoon since most tourists seem to leave them well alone.

Cacela has another fine long beach with huge dunes crowding round to form a small lagoon that is suitable for good bathing. The place is rather exposed compared with further along the coast, however, and there are no facilities like tavernas or cafés nearby. Bear in mind, too, that most of these tiny villages, including Cacela, are literally no more than a couple of old houses cluttered together, so don't go there expecting to find anything else – like shops, night-life or somewhere to cash a traveller's cheque!

One of the newest resort developments along this stretch of coastline is at **CABANAS**, located at the end of a long, narrow peninsula near to Tavira on the map, although the brochure map illustration appears to place the resort firmly on the mainland! Cabanas has emerged as a 'new, quality development' close to the fishing village of Cabanas itself.

Accommodation in Cabanas is limited to 146 apartments, spread over four buildings located quite close together, but none with more than four floors. All the apartments are fully self-contained, with private bathroom and kitchenette facilities and a daily maid service included. The nearest beach is just under half a mile away but you really need to cross the small estuary (there is a local fishermen's water taxi service available when they feel like it) to get the best sunbathing. At low tide it is possible to walk across to the mainland, but most times you will have to cross by boat. There are also good pool facilities, and sports facilities in Cabanas include tennis, basketball and volleyball, as well as a decent size playground area for children.

Night-life depends entirely on the type and number of people based in the resort at any one time. Nothing much is formally organized for residents at night, although there is a reasonable disco, **La Borda**, on the seafront. In short, Cabanas is an appealing spot for a holiday but it isn't really ideal for any particular type of holiday-maker. You are miles away from any proper night-life or decent shopping facilities, which involve a day trip to Tavira or Faro, or across into Spain. Even to find a decent day's sunbathing you have the hassle of crossing the estuary by the quaint, but tiresome, 'water taxi'. Cabanas is peaceful and sunny but, realistically, has little else going for it.

The largest resort east of Faro, and reckoned to be one of the most attractive and picturesque towns in the Algarve, is **TAVIRA**. With a population of just over 10,000, Tavira lies fourteen miles from the Spanish border near the mouth of the River Gilão. Once a thriving fishing port, its harbour is now totally silted up and the town is separated from the sea by a long stretch of sand known as the *Ilha de Tavira*. Beginning west of Cacela, the *ilha* runs all the way past Tavira down almost as far as the village of Fuzeta and is slowly developing into a modest resort in its own right.

Tavira remains an important tunny fishing centre and each year, particularly in the months of April to July, you can still witness the fascinating spectacle of the local fishermen going about their business in the traditional manner. For this is the time of year for the *copejo* – 'the great killing' – when all the fish are fat and healthy in order to make their annual migration eastwards in search of the warmer waters that make up their spawning ground. Those that survive long enough to return in August are too lean to be profitably caught. The *copejo* takes place when great barriers of nets are strung across the shoals' course in order to let hundreds of fishermen trap and spear their lucrative prey. The sea is often said to turn scarlet as this bizarre killing takes place. But rest assured that the annual ritual does not affect Tavira's near perfect bathing areas in any way!

Tavira is a busy and popular **shopping centre**, and also has quite a lot to offer the sightseer who may be feeling a little disappointed at the lack of obvious traces of the Algarve's past as he travels round the region. Some of the liveliest activity in town centres around the fruit and vegetable market by the long river esplanade. Starting early in the morning, the market is a fascinating sight to watch since you'll quickly discover that it is virtually impossible to buy so much as a bag of oranges without at least the token haggle. Stand back for a few minutes and watch a few Tavira housewives 'introduce' you to one of the Mediterranean's oldest artforms!

The town is divided in two by the River Gilão which flows right through its centre, and the most striking point of interest is the **seven-arch bridge** which was originally built by the Romans almost 2,000 years ago. Heavily repaired in the 17th century, the bridge survived remarkably undamaged by the earthquake a century later.

Occasionally referred to as 'the Venice of the Algarve', Tavira is striking not because the streets are flowing canals, but because of its initial appearance as a fairy-tale 'all white' Iberian town. Virtually every building has a vivid whitewash exterior. This phenomenon is particularly striking if you take a wander up to the old town from **Placa de la Republica**, the main square, in the town centre. Tavira's tourist office is located just off the square. You will soon reach the old ruined castle and the view over the rooftops is really quite breathtaking.

Nearby you can visit **Santa Maria do Castelo**, St Mary's Church, which was totally rebuilt after the earthquake on the site of an ancient mosque. The church has particular significance to the history of Tavira since inside you will see a large tomb containing the remains of **Paio Peres Correia**. It was Paio who originally recaptured Tavira from the Moors in the mid-13th century and was later to die in the town in 1275. A bold inscription recalls the memory of seven knights, all members of the Order of St James on crusade to the Holy Land in the 13th century, who were murdered by the Moors. The seven had been murdered whilst out hunting and, in so doing, the Moors had defied an important truce. In retribution for this, Paio Peres Correia took his revenge by attacking, and eventually recapturing, the town for the Portuguese. He has been revered as a hero ever since.

The town has another thirty-six churches, including the well known Renaissance period *Misercordia* in the old town which was constructed during the 1540s. Once back down in the lower town on the other side of the river, you'll be able to visit the **Carmo** and **São Paulo**, which both date from the 18th century. A few miles out into the country, heading towards Santo Estevão, there is an excellent museum, the **Monte da Guerreira**. One of the few valuable collections outside Lisbon, this museum is primarily a private collection of antique pottery, woodwork and paintings based in the owner's home. Open most days during the daylight hours, there is no admission fee and the trek to find it really is worthwhile.

On the whole, the beaches in and around Tavira are reasonable and certainly safe enough for family bathing. The best are located on the sandbar *Ilha*, reached by motorboat at the mouth of the river, or else near the fishing village of Fuzeta at the other end. Some hotels and holiday complexes, including the Club Pendras Del Rei complex, can be as much as a mile away from the nearest beach. Most brochures will highlight the fact that 'bicycles for hire' are available as if it were a neat little bonus when often they may be a necessity. If easy access to the beach is particularly important to you, more so if you have young children or are disabled, then take careful note of the distance from hotel to seafront. 'Beautiful beach one mile away from hotel' is quite a distance to walk, there and back, in the lazy Algarve sunshine. A few complexes like Club Pendras Del Rei have a rather novel private train service available for the exclusive purpose of transferring guests to and from the hotel and the beach.

All the beaches within easy reach of Tavira are really no more than attractive stretches of white sand which seem to go on into infinity. Although this doesn't prevent them becoming quite crowded during the peak summer season, it does ensure that everyone at least gets a few square feet of sand to lie down on when they arrive! The most popular beach spot is about two miles out of town near the village of SANTA LUZIA. The only ancient Greek inscription, dating back to the first century AD, ever to be found in Portugal once turned up in this otherwise unremarkable little village.

For such a popular resort, Tavira is not too well endowed with either large hotels or good places to eat out in the evening. Most of the bars and restaurants are clustered around the tree filled gardens which line the riverside. Two of the better eating places are **Ponto de Encontro**, in the Praca De Antonio Padinha, and the **Restaurante Imperial** along Rua José Pires Padinho just off the main square. The latter serves particularly fine regional food, including pork and clams and a wide variety of local wines, and is surprisingly inexpensive for a quality Algarve restaurant. More expensive but equally good value is **The English Rose** restaurant, with an utterly unpronounceable address at number 14 Avenida Don Matheus Teixeira d'Azevedo. Their three course lunches are particularly good value and the English owners have managed to perfect an ideal balance between native Portuguese and continental cuisine which appeals to locals and foreign visitors alike. Chicken with clams is one of many local specialities which are worth trying and so, too, are the egg-and-almond sweetmeats for which Tavira is justly famous. A smart bar adjoins the English Rose's dining area if you fancy no more than a drink in comfortable surroundings.

Tavira is primarily a self-catering resort and accommodation centres around one or two fairly large tourist complexes on the outskirts or even a few miles out of town. PEDRAS DEL REI is the largest, with over 600 units and most facilities – large swimming pool, restaurant, bars, supermarket and so on – on site. The complex is smart, modern and very popular with British tour operators, although it is five miles out of Tavira. Virtually all accommodation consists of clean, one (double) bedroomed villas with individual balconies, or small terraces if your bedroom is located on the ground floor. Facilities for families with active children are excellent – there is a separate club and play area for children and minding services are available if parents want to go out and enjoy a quiet evening together in town. Smaller tourist complexes have been built at QUINTA DAS OLIVEIRAS, a good distance out of town, and at PEDRAS DA RAINHA (Tel: 221-76), which offers excellent self-catering facilities similar to those available at its sister resort Pedras del Rei.

The main hotel in the immediate area is the sprawling eighty-bedroomed **Eurotel** about a mile and a half out of town. Eurotel is expensive, but provides an excellent array of services in return for standard room prices in excess of £30 per person, per night.

For the sports minded, you will find facilities for most water sports, in addition to tennis, golf, mini-golf and even horseriding, all within easy reach of your hotel, which is actually located deep within the grounds of a large country club. You are just over a mile from a wide beach area but Eurotel does have its own magnificent – multi-sided – swimming pool which tends to become the focus of the whole place. A small supermarket and collection of brightly coloured bars, most serving food as well as drink, would make it possible to spend a reasonable holiday in this one complex without ever having to stray into town or beyond. The atmosphere can quickly become sterile, though, unless you want nothing more than sun, swimming and the social companionship of predominantly British holiday-makers enjoying much the same type of holiday as yourself.

For the independent traveller reaching Tavira, accommodation is really difficult to find. You should seek out lists of private rooms normally available during the summer months from the tourist office and then just work your way through. A smart pension is located just a few doors up the street from the tourist office, **Pensão Mirante** at 83 Rua da Liberdade. There is another one in Rua Almirante Candido dos Reis and a third option above the Restaurante Imperial which we mentioned earlier. There are a number of rooms available along the town's main street, Rua da Liberdade. Check out the **Castela Rooms** (Tel: 23942).

The resort of ILHA DE TAVIRA itself lies about a mile and a half out of the town at the eastern end of the huge sandbank. The place has a fairly haphazard feel to it; most of the bars and cafés look very temporary and certainly flourish only during the summer months. The beaches are surprisingly varied, offering on the one hand sheltered and safe family bathing on the side of the *ilha* facing inland, and a much wilder sea on the side facing outward which has developed into an unofficial – but generally accepted – nudist haven. Buses run approximately hourly from Tavira's town square throughout the year, until the end of October when they stop altogether for two months. The bus connects with the small ferry which makes the short journey across to the *ilha* almost constantly between 7.30am and about 9pm from January to October.

Heading west again towards Faro will take you past the fishing village of BAVRIL, a modest place with nothing special to merit a stop. The beach here is fairly unappealing and you'd do slightly better to continue a mile or two further until you reach the next village, FUZETA. Although not yet a resort in its own right, Fuzeta lies at the far end of the next *ilha* past Tavira, ILHA DA ARMONA. The village's own beach runs into Armona's and both have been formed primarily from the movement in shore sand and a number of low off-shore sandbanks. The beaches tend to be less crowded in summer than near neighbours at Tavira or Olhão but, on the other hand, are quite low and exposed. Fuzeta itself boasts one or two modest cafés but, as yet, no proper restaurants or hotels.

The next town of any size is **OLHÃO**, about six miles east of Faro and within striking distance of two of the finest beaches in this eastern region. Olhão is the Algarve's second largest town with a population of just over 15,000 people. It grew up, and remains, a busy and prosperous fishing port. The town was founded as recently as 1700 by fishermen from Aveiro who despaired that nothing was ever going to be done to repair their own port, which had just been badly silted up as a result of a serious storm. These enterprising fishermen began work by building a chapel, **Nossa Senhora dos Aflitos** – Our Lady of Afflictions – which can still be seen today. It was widely believed at the time that the funds to embark on such an ambitious building came more from the profits of illicit contraband trade with the Spanish port of Cadiz than from fishing! During the Peninsular War, which lasted from 1808 until 1814, Olhão was one of the first towns to raise arms against the French. After the French had been soundly beaten, it was two local fishermen who had the task of setting out for Brazil, where the Portuguese royal family had taken refuge, to tell them that the war had at last been resolved.

The town was one of the few Algarve settlements fairly well known outside Portugal prior to the onset of the tourist boom from the 1960s. Artists from all over Europe have come and gone since the turn of the century to wonder at the unique casbah-like little town. Sadly, a lot of that appeal has disappeared and, in its place, many of the evils of any growing modern town – traffic jams, noise, run down back streets and so on – have emerged. Even so, Olhão today remains best known for its neo-Cubist street patterns. Nearly all the houses in the town have been built in white cubes, each no more than two or three storeys high with exterior stairs leading up to small well-kept terraces. The patterns are reminiscent of North Africa where the construction is common, and indeed Olhão of old did have strong trading links with Morocco. You'll get the best view of this amazing spectacle from **St Michael's Mount**, or else from the tower of *igreja matriz*, the parish church.

Other points of interest in the town include **Cabeca Hill**, with its ancient grottos filled with glistening stalagmites and stalactites, and the **fish market** by the waterfront. Look out for the *lota*, the fast moving daily fish auction in operation by the harbour. The fish market here is reckoned to be the best anywhere in the Algarve and, as a result, a host of unsightly canning factories have sprung up all around the outskirts of town. Nevertheless, the harbour area retains a certain atmosphere and there are a good number of open-air bars and restaurants which present a great opportunity to take the weight off your feet for half an hour or so – and just sit back and watch the world generally go by!

Finding your way around town in general shouldn't be too difficult, so long as you can retain your bearings to and from the huge main boulevard Avenida da Republica which leads straight through the centre of town. The main railway and bus stations lie in the centre of town, just off the Avenida da Republica, within a few minutes' walk of each other. The town's post office and main cinema are near here, too, but you'll need to walk round a good bit further to find Olhão's busy little tourist office. It is located in Largo da Lagoa and has the usual stock of information and leaflets available in addition to at least one English-speaking member of staff.

Finding somewhere good to eat in Olhão is only marginally more difficult than finding somewhere to stay. No tour operators specifically visit the town of Olhão, although most Algarve brochures will recommend the town as a possible option for a day trip. There are virtually no top-class restaurants or hotels in town, which is perhaps surprising considering its relative size in such a popular region of Portugal. There are a number of small cafés and taverna-type places scattered all over town and most tend to offer good but simple local dishes. Fish features prominently on nearly every menu in town. Look out for the restaurant **Escondidinho** in the centre of town, or **Ilidio's** on the Boulevard dos Pescadores, which are probably the best fish places in Olhão. The best hotel in town is the **Hotel Caique**, located along the Rua General Humberto Delgado near to both bus and train stations. Even this modest thirty-seven bedroom place merits no more than a couple of stars in anybody's book and quickly fills in summer. The independent traveller should try to avoid the town at all costs since there are scarcely any private rooms available, let alone any decent hotel accommodation. The only two other hotels in town are a two-star pension, **Pensão Helena** near the tourist office, and the one-star pension **Torres** on Rua Doctor Paulo Nogueira.

Two of the most attractive and idyllic beach locations in the Algarve lie just outside Olhão. ARMONA and CULATRA are both long, relatively peaceful, stretches of white sand, offering the minimum of facilities – a couple of modest bars – during the summer season. The drawback is they are fairly inaccessible, but nonetheless these beaches are particularly popular with young people who feel the ten-minute motorboat journey across to either is worthwhile. A few of the more remote and secluded stretches have become generally accepted as nudist beaches, a state of dress (or lack of it) which is really obligatory if you plan to visit one.

The Algarve's largest town and capital is **FARO**, approximately a third of the way along the coast from Spain. With its large international airport about four miles out of town, Faro is likely to be the first place you'll set foot in when you arrive in the region since all package holidays to the Algarve arrive and take-off from here. The town is, in fact, the southernmost point in Portugal and takes its name from the lighthouse (*faro*) originally built by the Moorish invaders more than a thousand years ago.

Even though Faro today has a long history behind it, there are surprisingly few really old buildings in the town. The town's earliest origins are said to date back to neolithic times but the original settlement owes its origins to the Romans. Recent archaeological excavations have revealed Faro to have been the site of the Roman town of Ossonoba, once influential enough to mint its own currency. Subsequent generations of Moors helped build up an already substantial southern Iberian settlement into a thriving market town.

Once the Moors were driven out by King Afonso III in 1266 and the town became permanently Portuguese, Faro went on to become a distinguished centre of book printing. A proud reputation grew up around this industry from 1487 onwards, when a large Jewish community established an influential press in the town; this was the first time that books had been printed in Portugal. The Jews were to make a significant contribution to the history of Faro in later centuries and an 1820 synagogue and an 1833 cemetery are reckoned to be the earliest post-Inquisition Jewish religious monuments anywhere in the Iberian peninsula.

Three major disasters, one man-made and two natural, hit Faro in the space of 150 years between the 16th and 18th centuries. In 1596, the favourite of Elizabeth I of England, the Earl of Essex, burnt down the entire town in order to castigate the Spanish who had temporarily occupied it. The Bishop of Faro's library was pillaged by Essex and the books he stole were subsequently to become the nucleus of Oxford University's famous Bodleian Library. A major earthquake seriously damaged much of the reconstructed city in 1722, but the whole place was again flattened by the earthquake in 1755 which devastated most of the country.

Faro's Bishop at the time of the second earthquake, Francisco Gomes de Avelar (1739–1816) was largely responsible for the reconstruction of the town in the latter half of the 18th century. De Avelar was responsible for the **Arco da Vila**, an attractive gateway to the city which you can still see in the old part of the town. One of the first sights you'll notice is **Gomes Square**, and the Gomes obelisk which the townspeople erected in recognition of the Bishop's good work in reconstructing their town after the earthquake.

The Algarve sightseer would do well to make Faro a must for even a day's visit since nowhere else in the region will you get the opportunity to see as many traces of the area's past in one place. An interesting collection of nautical artefacts can be seen in Faro's tiny **maritime museum**, built on the site of the former harbour master's office along the seafront; lanterns, model ships and paintings of every conceivable variety of local fish are on display and the museum is open most days during the summer months. Faro also has a substantial **ethnological museum** devoted to the crafts, customs and traditional industries of the Algarve. Open daily between 10am and 12.30pm, and again from 2.30pm until 6pm, the museum contains a reconstructed village street and numerous typical rooms from traditional Algarve homes dating back many generations. Many examples of traditional Algarve wickerwork are on display, together with the very water cart which traveller Ignacio Miguel, from Olhão, used daily until his death in 1974. The ethnological museum can be found just off the Rua de Santo Antonio in the centre of town.

Much more impressive is the **archaeological museum** proper, open daily, on Rua do Castelo, which has been built into the shell of the 16th-century Church of the Assumption convent. In addition to housing the region's finest cloister and largest chimney, the museum contains a fine collection of Roman and pre-Roman artefacts. The most spectacular exhibit is a completely reconstructed Roman mosaic, measuring more than thirty feet long, which was unearthed from under a nearby house in Faro during the construction of a sewer! The mosaic is located in a room of its own and displays a magnificent bearded sea god in its centre. Sadly the lower half of the god's face was damaged by the bulldozer which uncovered the mosaic about ten years ago.

Other rooms contain collections of prehistoric tools and weapons, mostly found locally, in addition to a host of statues unearthed by excavations at Estói a little way inland from Faro. A large hall in the museum contains part of a large art collection which was left to the town by Ferreida de Almeida, a distinguished local diplomat. A sizeable proportion of his paintings relate to the First World War, and no less than a dozen of his portraits are of himself.

Strolling through the old town of Faro is a pleasant way to spend an afternoon or evening and you ought to take a walk through the cobbled **Largo da Sé** (cathedral square) round from the archaeological museum. Just about the only part of town which remains cool as the summer temperature soars into the mid-80s°F (low 30s°C) is the old **cathedral**. A huge mosque, built by the Moors a thousand years ago, originally stood on the site of this magnificent structure which was started immediately after the invaders were forced out in the 13th century. Only the portico and tower remain of the original Gothic structure, but the remainder is a rather appealing hotchpotch of baroque and Renaissance architectural designs heavily remodelled after the 1755 earthquake. Some fine cherub carvings and rich giltwork have been preserved inside the cathedral's huge square structure and both the attractive gold and red baroque organ and the large Chippendale chair by the altar were gifts to the people of Faro from the former Portuguese colony of Macau.

The old **bishop's palace** can still be seen near the cathedral, but no visit to Faro would be complete without a look at some of the town's better known church buildings. The finest is the **Carmelite Church** – 'Igreja de Nossa Senhora do Monte do Carmo do Faro' to give it its full Portuguese name – which is often remarked upon as the most beautiful church in the Algarve. You'll find this marvellous baroque-style building at Largo do Carmo, near the town's main post office, and it is open seven days a week. Its two large towers are visible from quite a distance, rising up over a wide façade and looking down gracefully upon the rest of the sprawling town. The giltwork inside is truly spectacular, but you should also look out for the artistic 18th-century wood carvings inside.

For something completely different, but definitely *not* if you are at all faint-hearted, visit the **Chapel of Bones** to the rear of the Carmelite Church. Without a doubt Faro's most intriguing point of interest, the Capela d'Ossos was built only in the last century and is lined entirely with the skulls and bones of human skeletons. If you are lucky, the jovial 75-year-old English-speaking guide will tell you that an over-enthusiastic 19th-century bishop used over 1,200 human skulls, from deceased monks buried in the old Carmo cemetery, in the construction of the chapel. It seems that human skulls were both cheaper and preferable as construction material than good old-fashioned bricks and stonework and it was a fine way of preserving the memory of the long-dead holy men. There is a macabre fascination with this place, reckoned to be the largest such bone chapel in Portugal, but it isn't worth lingering *too* long pondering what happened to those 1,200 monks . . .

There is a picturesque public garden, **Jardim Manuel Bivar**, along the seafront near the main dock, and one other building worth visiting during your visit to Faro is the old **Church of St Francis**. In the centre of town just off Largo de São Francisco and a stone's throw from the archaeological museum, St Francis' is dedicated to the life and work of the patron saint of the same name. Large panels of tiles, glazed white and blue, record the saint's pious mission on earth many centuries ago.

Although most travel agents will offer, or at least recommend, a day trip to the regional capital, few tour operators offer accommodation in the town, despite the fact that there is a good range of respectable hotels normally available. Most operators will recommend an optional excursion to Faro's nearest beach, a massive stretch of coast past the airport at **PRAIA DE FARO**. Harbour ferries make the crossing continually throughout the daylight hours during the summer, but the service is not available during the winter months. The Praia de Faro islet is slightly over thirty miles from the town centre and regular bus services also make the journey along a busy but well-kept single-lane causeway.

The beach at Praia de Faro is massive and the islet helps form a sheltered picture postcard lagoon between it and the mainland. The far side is rather exposed and there are places where the water shelves alarmingly, so this wouldn't be the best place to consider taking small children unless you could watch them closely. Fishing and water-skiing facilities are normally available and there are all the usual deckchairs and sunloungers for hire as well. It is a popular spot, which accordingly becomes very crowded during the summer season with foreign visitors and locals alike all wanting to get away from the town for a day. It is worth considering other beaches slightly further along the coast in either direction before pitching on this one.

Unlike most of the resorts and towns along the Algarve coast, you will not be spoiled for choice for eating out in the evenings in Faro. One of the most popular places with British tourists is **Lady Susan**, on Rua 1 de Dezembro (Tel: 288-57). Owned by an English couple, this small but elegant establishment positively swings during the summer season. Local fish is the restaurant's speciality – particularly Algarve-style shellfish, including dressed crab and lobster and sole in white wine sauce – but they also serve a fine peppersteak and an appetizing array of flambé dishes. The place closes at weekends, which is a bit of a nuisance, but stays open until 10.30pm each weekday. Booking ahead is advisable because of Lady Susan's popularity, but this is, at least, a relatively simple task because of the English-speaking proprietors!

A real gem of a place is **Belle Epoque** (Tel: 227-46) on Avenida de República, opposite the Hotel Eva. This smart, middle-range restaurant has a very extensive menu and one of the most welcoming atmospheres of any place in Faro. Try the pork *alentejana* or the house speciality, steak belle epoque, for a memorable culinary treat.

Highly recommended by most guidebooks, including this one, is the **Restaurante Cidade Velha** on Rua Domingos Guerreio (Tel: 271-45). A moderately expensive place, you'll find this culinary paradise hidden away behind the town's imposing cathedral in a building more than two and a half centuries old – quite an achievement in Portugal given all the earthquakes. Cidade Velha offers one of the most varied menus of any restaurant in Faro, including a mouthwatering selection of fine local fish dishes, together with most red meats and poultry cooked in the most delicious sauces. Their fillet of pork, for example, is generally served with dates and walnuts delicately blended together.

Probably Faro's most splendid – and certainly one of the most expensive – restaurants is **Chez Duval**, located along Largo Pe da Cruz (Tel: 295-10). Taking up most of the ground floor of one of Faro's most elegant old buildings, Chez Duval is open seven days a week but serves only evening dinners at weekends. The traditional Portuguese décor is striking and the food even more so, although if you do not fancy attempting their adventurously prepared fish dishes at over £12 a head then you'd be best advised to look elsewhere.

Other good eating places in Faro include **Alfagher**, on Rua Tentente Valadim, which serves traditional dishes on a wide terrace under the stars; **Adega Rocha** on the Rua de Misericórdia for really fine local food; or **Laroque** for good local dishes served by the beachside. If you fancy sampling some of the Faro night-life, then the busiest and most popular disco in town seems to be **Sheherazade** in the Hotel Eva on the main Avenida da Republica. It remains open seven nights a week until 2am and is particularly popular with British visitors. Another popular night-spot is the disco **Kontiki**, just by the Hotel Faro by the harbour gardens.

The **Hotel Eva** (Tel: 240-54) is Faro's best hotel, with its bright night-club and chic rooftop swimming pool offering glorious views over the rest of town. Other good hotels include the four-star **Estalagem Aeromar** (Tel: 231-89), which is the best beachside hotel down at Praia da Faro, and the **Hotel Faro** in the town's main square overlooking the yacht basin. The latter is particularly popular with yacht lovers because of its unique harbour position, dominating the small yacht area like an ancient medieval castle. Two lower class hotels, **Residencia Correia** on Rua Infante Da Henrique, and **Pensão Dina** on Rua Teofilo de Braga often have a few rooms left even at the busiest weeks of the season.

Accommodation for the independent traveller can quickly become something of a nightmare since there really are very few rooms available to casual visitors in the peak summer season. The tourist office, open daily, at Rua Ataíde de Oliveira 100 ought to be able to find you somewhere for a nominal booking fee but it really would save a lot of hassle if you could book accommodation as far in advance as possible. One of your best hopes will be to try the **Pensão Residencial Marim** (Tel: 240–63) on the Rua Gonçalo Barreto. The American owner, Papken Oustayan, tries to meet most of the incoming British flights and is a proper gold mine of local information. The Marim is a tidy three-star place with affordable room prices.

Resorts West of Faro

Without a doubt, the main interest of British tour operators in the Algarve is concentrated on the stretch of coast west of Faro right along to Sagres, and for another twenty or thirty miles north again towards Lisbon. Virtually every small village is a bustling resort, popular with the tens of thousands of British holiday-makers who have chosen to come to this region year in year out since the mid-1970s. Glorious pine-forests sweep down towards the Algarve's famous white sands, but the coast is no longer the uninterrupted expanse of beach you would find east of Faro. The shoreline rises steeply in many places to create some spectacular cliff formations, almost always hiding some idyllic sun-trapped cove or grotto below. This main stretch of Algarve coast truly does offer something for everyone, as the brochures claim, whether you want swinging night-life, budget family holidays, sporting facilities to suit even the best professional or simply the chance to enjoy some of the finest beaches anywhere in Western Europe.

As you leave Faro, you'll pass through the ugly, sprawling suburb of Monte Negro shortly before reaching the first resort proper of **QUINTA DO LAGO**. This expensive new resort complex sits hidden away in almost 2,000 acres of prime pine-forest land. Calling itself 'the lowest-density leisure-living area in Europe', the resort consists entirely of top-class private holiday villas and apartments surrounded by some really excellent sporting and leisure facilities. Key attractions are a large riding centre, reckoned to be the best equipped in Portugal, and a 27-hole golf course now recognized as one of the top five anywhere in Europe.

Quinta do Lago's high-tech night-spot, the **Patio Club** disco, is one of the trendiest and most exclusive in the Algarve and is within easy reach of the luxurious **Terracos da Ria Formosa** residential apartments. The **Casa Velha** restaurant (Tel: 942-72) here is excellent; fine food in very simple but comfortable surroundings. The fish dishes are all in-house specialities, particularly the sole Casa Velha and the unusual – but recommended – option of smoked swordfish. You can reasonably expect to pay at least £20 per head, including wine, for a smart meal at the Casa Velha, which will be complemented most evenings by traditional guitar music in the background. Quinta do Lago also boasts a large swimming pool and a reasonable strip of coast to itself.

The next-door village of ANCÃO remains relatively unaffected by the tourist boom going on all around it, retaining a certain quaintness which is being slowly eaten away by the volume of curious visitors passing through from Quinta do Lago and nearby **VALE DO LOBO**. Vale do Lobo means, literally, Valley of the Wolf but rest assured that this shouldn't be taken seriously. Another contemporary development, Vale do Lobo has been built totally from scratch over the past decade as a tourist resort. Although designed to resemble a typical Portuguese village, with its whitewashed walls and winding lanes, the disguise doesn't really work and the rather painful brochure references to the whole place as a 'holiday village' could not be more accurate since there is no one else here but tourists and people to look after them. That said, Vale do Lobo does offer some really good facilities for those looking for a decent beach location combined with quality accommodation, although on the whole the site is more expensive to stay at because of higher food and drink prices compared with larger resorts further along the coast which have been developed from existing villages. Restaurant **Big Ben**, halfway down the bumpy road from Ancão to Vale do Lobo, serves some fine grills, despite its rather tacky name, if you fancy a break.

Vale do Lobo offers probably the best golfing facilities anywhere in the Algarve. The centrepiece of it all is a magnificent 27-hole clifftop golf course, designed by the former British professional Henry Cotton and elegantly secluded from the rest of the world by shrubs and landscaped greenery. An exclusive clubhouse and bar/restaurant is popular with most weary golfers. The spectacular seventh hole, overlooking the sea, is one of the most photographed individual golf holes in the world. Fig orchards, cork trees and a sprawling valley of maturing pines really do make this one of the most relaxing spots to play a few rounds, although the idyllic location will almost certainly result in your sacrificing a few balls over the cliff.

Accommodation, night-life and eating in Vale do Lobo tend to be centred around one of two places: the luxury 161 unit Vale do Lobo tourist complex, with its three swimming pools and all the usual facilities to scarcely make it worth your while leaving the site; or else the five-star luxury **Hotel Dona Filipa**. The Dona Filipa is a truly top-class hotel, run by Trusthouse Forte, with a reputation for luxury, comfort and good service. Most of the 129 air-conditioned rooms have their own balcony and all have their own bathroom suites. The interior is well-furnished with marble fireplaces, antique prints and has a surprisingly authentic Portuguese feel. In addition to a fine à la carte restaurant (for which a formal jacket and tie are required), the hotel also runs its own hairdresser, boutique, card room and large swimming pool. The main golf course is only five minutes walk away and should you ever tire of golf there are no less than twelve tennis courts available for residents' use at the nearby Roger Taylor Tennis Centre. Water sports are also available during the peak season.

Local folk artistes occasionally play live music in one of the resort's many bars during the summer and one or two discos are organized in the evening, including a particularly lively one most nights on the beach. The beach itself is particularly long and is entered through the main resort complex. Picturesque low red cliffs make a splendid backdrop and the beach facilities – sun loungers, bars and so on – are excellent. Vale do Lobo's beach is popular, though, so you can expect to share the sand and sea with a reasonable crowd most days. Overall, this place is a smart resort for even the most fussy but, being realistic, Vale do Lobo's appeal is wasted on non-golf fanatics.

A few self-catering apartments are available just a little way along the coast at TRAFAL, and there is another modest golf course nearby. Five minutes more along the busy main road takes you to **QUARTEIRA**, a booming resort town popular with literally dozens of British tour operators. Formerly a small Moorish fishing village made famous by the tales of travelling artists, Quarteira has been somewhat swamped by the level of tourist activity which has brought about the disorganized accumulation of large, modern hotel buildings you'll see here today. On the whole, the resort facilities are excellent but the place has been allowed to expand and develop at a quite alarming rate; so much so that there is very little in Quarteira other than large hotel and apartment complexes.

 Quarteira's finest attraction is its huge long beach – almost a mile of golden sand that just goes on and on and on. The main beach area is backed directly by a collection of large hotels which spill right down to the edge of the sand; the distance from beach to hotel in most cases is minimal, but this idyllic scene becomes distinctly noisy at busy periods. Bordered by umbrella pines, the beach shelves gently into the sea, thereby making it more than suitable for children, and the facilities are particularly good if you appreciate the availability of deckchairs, sun umbrellas, windbreak screens and that sort of thing. Small boats and pedalos are available for hourly hire and will seldom cost you more than a pound a time. Quarteira's beach is broken up by some amazing natural rock formations that will help you take some fairly original beach photos if nothing else. They are often good to shelter behind if you prefer to avoid the full glare of the afternoon sun, but it tends to be necessary to 'book' your spot early in the day, with a towel or picnic basket, before the crowds have similar ideas!

This is by no means the Algarve's most picturesque resort, not least because of the enormous amount of noisy and obvious building work constantly in progress, but Quarteira is praised for the fine selection of bars and restaurants along the seafront. One of the best is **Restaurante Atlântico**, on Avenida Infante de Sagres (Tel: 351-42), which serves fine local food, but is particularly known for its king prawns cooked in a special house style. **Restaurante O Pescador** (Tel: 347-55), on the other side of the large car park near the fish market, is open seven days until 10pm and serves a good peppersteak. For a flavour of distant England, check out **Bonnie's Wine Bar** by the seafront. This amazing place is the nearest you'll get to an English pub anywhere in town and is decorated with dozens of pennants and banners from British football teams which visitors have left or sent over. Bonnie's closes round about midnight most evenings.

Perhaps surprisingly for so well known a resort, Quarteira doesn't have that many hotels. What there are, including a whole range of holiday apartment blocks, seem to stretch on for miles along the fringes of the beach. The resort's best hotel is the **Dom José II** on the seafront (Tel: 343-10). Used by a number of British operators, including Enterprise, Dom José is reckoned to offer considerably better service than its official three-star rating suggests. All 134 rooms are smartly furnished with private bathrooms and balcony. Popular with British tourists, the hotel has its own disco, club room and small gift shop and offers an international three-course dinner menu. The swimming pool is rather small, mind you, for such a busy hotel and the number of sun beds tends to be quite limited.

Other reasonable hotels in Quarteira are the **Atis**, overlooking the front (Tel: 343-33), although another huge hotel is being built right in front of it, something you won't see in the brochures, and the **Hotel Quarteira Sol** (Tel: 654-20). The Quarteira Sol is a medium-size four-star building standing eight floors high. It is a few minutes' walk from the beach, but most of the rear rooms offer genuine seaviews – as opposed to sea glimpses – and the restaurant has a very good international four course dinner menu. **A Canoa** is a reasonable restaurant, just by the seafront.

Quarteira's westerly neighbour, by only a mile or so, is **VILA-MOURA**, which is reckoned now to be Europe's biggest ever private tourist undertaking spanning almost 4,000 acres. The resort has been constructed totally from scratch, right down to the last pillar box and snack bar and as a result has a very organized feel to it. After Albufeira, Vilamoura is the Algarve's second-largest resort and there are hardly any British tour operators to the region who do not now offer holidays to this part of the coast.

Nearly every tour operator's brochure which includes Vilamoura describes the resort with phrases like 'fast developing', 'still-growing', and 'expanding holiday development'. A recent description could scarcely have been more accurate when it said that 'the history of this settlement is yet to be written'. There were plans at one stage to build a whole new city, larger than Faro, on the site of the present resort but it was felt unlikely that there would be enough employment to maintain the new settlement outside the tourist season. As it is, though, the place is literally wall-to-wall hotels offering comfortable, though often impersonal, service and accommodation to tens of thousands of visitors each summer. It is, nevertheless, well laid out and all the main roads in the resort are treelined.

Perhaps surprising for such a new resort city, Vilamoura has Roman origins and you can still see the remains of **Cêrro da Vila** after which the resort was named just across from the luxury marina. Originally built by the Romans 2,000 years ago, the site was taken over first by the Visigoths, then by the Moors, before finally falling into disuse about five or six centuries ago. Vilamoura's only real point of interest is a small museum near the site which houses all the finds from recent archaeological excavations; everything from Roman lamps to Visigothic holiday money is on display.

Vilamoura's popularity today stems from three positive attractions: a magnificent beach, sport and leisure facilities of every kind, and some of the best night-life in the Algarve. In addition, of course, you have a wide range of accommodation options open to you; British operators run holidays to top-class luxury hotels and modest self-catering apartments as well as everything in between, so you may be faced with a rather bewildering choice once you settle on Vilamoura as your resort.

The beach itself is another typically enormous expanse of golden Portuguese sand stretching east and west from the marina and arching gently down from its backdrop of lush pine trees into the clear blue Atlantic water. Beach facilities are surprisingly limited for so popular a destination but most of the hotels are scarcely a stone's throw away from the seafront. Needless to say, the beach becomes extremely busy during the summer months but it is sufficiently long to absorb the many hundreds of residents and day trippers who come here daily.

In addition to the region's best facilities for conventional water sports – water-skiing, swimming, windsurfing, scuba-diving, deep-sea fishing and so on – Vilamoura has an excellent luxury marina with space for 615 boats. Although the Romans had the marina idea first, with an artificial harbour constructed very near the present-day site, you can easily spend a whole afternoon idly watching the comings and goings – and perhaps wondering why every other person strolling around the marina seems to own one of the luxurious crafts! A few yachts are available for hire from here, either for an afternoon or a few days, if you happen to have a few thousand escudos to spare.

Vilamoura is considered one of the best Algarve resorts for other sports, too, and you'll find horseriding, tennis and bicycle hire facilities readily available whichever operator you choose to travel with. All the larger hotels have their own facilities; the **Dom Pedro**, for instance, has three hard tennis courts and ample space for volleyball, badminton, table tennis and gymnastics. In addition, there is a thriving shooting club and two superb eighteen-hole championship golf courses – with a further couple planned over the next few years.

Night-life is rather confined to the hotels and villa complexes, where there are bars in abundance, but all the major hotels offer a variety of disco or live music entertainment. **Skippers** disco is particularly popular; another of the resort's top attractions is a sophisticated **casino** close to the Vilamoura Golf Club. The casino offers a traditional gambling saloon, with all the usual games including blackjack, baccarat and, of course, roulette. In addition, there is a posh amusement arcade slot machine saloon and at least two live floor shows nightly in the large club room upstairs. The casino makes a small admission charge to the main gambling saloon, but remains open until 3am every night of the year. Tourists must bring their passports to present on admission and be over twenty-one years of age.

A good pub is **The Runner Bar**, just behind the cinema, which is open daily 11 a.m. to 1 a.m. The English proprietors, Frank and

Margaret Knight, do their best to make British visitors feel 'at home'.

The **Viking Vilamoura** entertainment complex contains the resort's smartest night-club and an expensive top-class restaurant. Twice nightly entertainment in a sort of music hall atmosphere is on offer, but the range of shows is staggering. Be prepared for anything from a strip-show to an operatic excerpt! The restaurant is equally splendid with a long menu weighted very much in favour of local seafood. Expect to pay at least £20 per person for a really good meal. Equally classy for a good meal out is the **O Vapor**, located in a large – permanently moored – boat by the side of the marina.

Accommodation used by British operators to Vilamoura is concentrated on primarily two hotels, together with self-catering holiday and Timeshare apartments. The hotel **Dom Pedro** (Tel: 354-50) is a large four-star hotel five minutes from the beach and right in the heart of the resort centre. A surprisingly quiet hotel, despite its ten storeys and curious triangular lifts, all 261 bedrooms have private bathrooms with seaview balconies. The staff are polite, friendly and English-speaking, and all the public areas are bright and roomy. In addition to a sauna, masseur and unisex hairdresser, there is a large swimming pool and a free baby-sitting service (until midnight) available to residents. The international dinner menu is extensive and the food highly recommended. The hotel also offers an extensive sports programme and is a truly first class establishment all round.

The **Hotel Atlantis** (Tel: 325-35) comes equally highly recommended. Officially rated five-star de luxe by the Portuguese authorities, Thomson award it 4 Ts and aptly describe it as 'a high-class hotel . . . especially suited to keen golfers'. In addition to a similar class of service offered by the Dom Pedro, the fully air-conditioned Atlantis has a large children's play area and an appealing Moorish design. All age groups are welcomed at both hotels with the significant exception of young singles. The **Hotel Golf** (Tel: 352-75) is a secluded three-star establishment located at the edge of the golf course. Smaller than the other two, it offers a more relaxed atmosphere and would suit those looking for a more 'away-from-it-all' Algarve holiday. The hotel lays on courtesy transport to and from both the casino and marina for residents.

The standard of self-catering apartments available is surprisingly similar. On the whole, most are roomy, clean and comfortable; there really is too much competition for their operators to offer anything worse. Most are located at least a mile or so away from the beach area but shuttle buses normally operate. All apartments include basic household utensils and residents have access to one or two public facilities – including a television room, swimming pool area, disco, on-site shops and bars and so on.

A lot of this type of accommodation has grown up around FALÉSIA DE VILAMOURA a mile or two out of the main resort centre. Falésia de Vilamoura is a relatively little known stretch of coastline, just west of the tiny fishing hamlet of FALÉSIA. A few large hotels are certainly planned but, as yet, there is no other accommodation beyond the sprawling apartments already built. Beach facilities are not available other than a few seasonal bars and tavernas. The beach here is typically long, but you'll find it rather a steep hike down from the main road. Once down on the sand, though, the waterfront scene is as picturesque as it is crowded, with attractive red sandstone cliffs forming an unbroken backdrop.

A few less well known beaches lie between Falésia and the Algarve's resort flagship Albufeira, about eight or nine miles further west. **OLHOS D'AGUA** is one of the more interesting, if rather sleepy, fishing village resorts and would be a good choice of holiday location if you wanted a relaxing beach holiday within striking distance of the busy activity centre of Albufeira. Accommodation is mainly in self-catering apartments on the outskirts of the village and all offer similar high standards of facilities. The **Bela Vista**, **Brisamar** and **Olhos d'Agua** apartments are all located fairly close to one another within a few minutes' walk of the beach and a couple of well-stocked supermarkets. Skytours are one of the principal British operators to this resort and offer holidays to all three apartment complexes.

The village itself has a few respectable restaurants, including the **Atlantico** just at the edge of the village which you ought to make the effort to find if you enjoy good shellfish. You'll also find a busy bar/restaurant, **La Cigale**, along at one end of the beach which frequently plays live music in the evenings. The beach itself isn't terribly long, by Algarve standards, and its 300-yard length quickly fills in summer. Appealing rock formations appear out of the sand – highly photogenic but too dangerous a temptation to let young children climb unsupervised because of sharp edges. More importantly, the beach doesn't have any safety warning flags, one of the better features of virtually every other public beach in the region.

There are good beaches further along at MARIA LUISA and PRAIA DA OURA but it is worth bearing in mind that there is precious little else. Access to the 500-yard stretch at Maria Luisa is best reached through the modest **Hotel Balai** which overlooks the small natural bay. The red cliffs continue along the coast this far from nearby Olhos d'Agua, but are becoming distinctly crumbled so you'd be well advised not to let the children start climbing on them. The water here shelves quite steeply, too, so it would be a bad idea to come here with a family. More popular is Praia da Oura although, by this stage, the large hotel complexes have started and you are practically into Albufeira itself. Oura's beach is popular, but rather unspecial and scruffy whilst offering all the usual beach facilities.

The Algarve's largest and most popular resort is **ALBUFEIRA**, with its prime cliff-top location some twenty-four miles west of Faro. The town's population of over 8,000 quickly doubles during the summer months and the resort is easily Portugal's most popular holiday spot with British tourists. As a result over 150 British tour operators, including all the major ones and dozens of smaller specialists, offer holidays to Albufeira.

The town of Albufeira was known centuries before the tourist invasion began in the late 1960s. The cliff-top location and maze-like street layout had a crucial military significance in the 13th century when the Moorish invaders were being gradually driven out all over Portugal. For generations Albufeira was a Moorish stronghold, resisting all pressure from the advancing Christian armies to capitulate, until Afonso III succeeded in 1250. Just a few hints of the former Moorish character remain among the narrow streets of whitewashed houses and shops that cascade gently down the hillside towards the seafront.

Despite its relatively colourful past, however, there is little evidence surviving for the curious sightseer to explore. In Albufeira, as in just about every other town and village in Portugal, almost all of the buildings which predated the devastating earthquake of 1755 were wiped out on that single November morning. Details of current events in Albufeira, festivals, dances and so on should be available through your hotel or tour operator representative or else from the tourist office which you'll find at Rua 5 de Outubro (Tel: 521-44 or 554-28).

In the centre of town, in Largo Jacinto d'Ayet, a large modern statue honours Albufeira's most famous former son Vicente de Carvalho. A former Augustinian friar, de Carvalho was arrested in Japan during a period of brutal Christian repression in the 1630s. He was subsequently burned at the stake at Nagasaki but later beatified – the first step towards canonization – in his native Portugal during the 19th century.

Nearby is the attractive town hall which looks rather like a typically whitewashed and chimneyed Algarve church because of the large belfry and, incidentally, is one of Albufeira's coolest buildings during the summer months. The resort's most noticeable point of interest is the wide tunnel which connects the town to the crescent-shaped beach. The tunnel was blasted out of the hillside in 1953 and can be reached through Albufeira's main shopping street near the town's main square.

Albufeira is the Algarve's principal shopping centre with a wide selection of food, clothes, souvenir and traditional handicraft shops. A large **open-air market** also runs throughout the summer months starting near the main plaza and gradually winding down through countless narrow backstreets. Sunday is traditionally the best day for the market when the variety of goods on offer reaches its height. Quality local produce, including fruit, vegetables, live chickens, rabbits and ducks, mouthwatering herbs and cheeses, and local handicrafts are always on offer. One of the best bargains to look out for is traditional hand-sewn Algarve embroidery, but don't be shy to haggle if the tourist-inflated price of any item puts you off at first glance.

Albufeira is particularly well situated for day excursions to any of the other resorts along the coast lying, as it does, almost exactly in the middle of the region. You ought to ask at the tourist office about organized day trips inland, across into Spain or east to Portimão, Lagos or Sagres. There are a number of car hire offices in town and the local bus service connects Albufeira regularly with the rest of the coast if you prefer to arrange your own excursions. In addition, day trips to neighbouring caves are possible from the town's bustling fishing quarter, although these tend to be *ad hoc* private excursions arranged through local fishermen. Barter and agree your price first.

The resort's principal attraction, and the reason why thousands of visitors return here year in year out, is the wide sandy beach. Backed by the familiar red cliffs upon which the town has been built, the beach is clean and safe for family bathing and only a few minutes' stroll down through the tunnel from the town centre. Facilities are excellent if you wish to hire deckchairs, sunshades or whatever and most water sports, including windsurfing and water-skiing, are available. This is the Algarve of the brochure and postcard, but the whole scene shrinks substantially at high tide which means space is even more at a premium on an already crowded beach. The far end has a clutter of almost permanently moored small fishing boats (which you won't see on many brochure photographs) and they tend to take up even more precious space!

As well as a popular beach, with several more (including São Rafael and Oura) only a short distance out of town, Albufeira is the liveliest Algarve resort for night-life. Recent years have seen a shift in the volume of young holiday-makers away from Albufeira to resorts around Lagos, or east of Faro, because of the increased costs of staying in town. Nevertheless, a number of good bars, discos and restaurants are among the busiest and most popular in the region. The most popular discos are **Silver Screen** in the centre of town, which occasionally features less well known British bands live, and **Castell** in Rua São Goncalo de Lagos.

Eating out in Albufeira offers excellent possibilities. In addition to high-class à la carte menus at all the major hotels, there are a number of good restaurants and bars in the centre of the resort, particularly around the central square. Look out for **Restaurant Oasis**, open daily 8 a.m. to midnight, for local fish. A popular English-run restaurant, offering reasonably priced food, is the **Beach Basket** (Tel: 521-37) near the Sol E Mar Hotel. Quality home-cooking is the aim of Surrey-born owner David Shean and a mouthwatering variety of local fish and meat dishes are available. The intimate restaurant has a fine sun terrace, which overlooks the beach and is ideal for those romantic candlelit dinners . . .

Just up from the main square is **Restaurante Alfredo** (Tel: 520-59), serving banquet sized dinners in a deliberately run-down, but very atmospheric, setting. Open seven days a week during the summer, reservations are essential to avoid disappointment. **Fernando's** (Tel: 521-16) on the Avenida 25 Abril is another great fish specialist and a very popular eating place, too, despite its rather modest appearance. **O Tunel** (Tel. 541–8), close to the beach, serves good lunch time snacks, but if you fancy a truly first-class grill dinner then the place to head for is **Antonio's**, about three-quarters of a mile west of town on the Guia road. The old rustic style meals are complemented by some fine views over the town. **Mr Toby's**, at the end of the main market street leading off the square, is as typically English a restaurant as you'll find. With a bright interior and constant live music, the English owners do their best to serve up 'the best of British'. They have a newly-opened Chicken Terrace upstairs, which is worth the extra cover charge.

One other place worth looking out for in Albufeira is **Sir Harry's Pub**. In the town's market square, this place is fast becoming an institution in its own right. Described once as the 'most popular international rendezvous point', Sir Harry's certainly deserves its popular reputation amongst British visitors. The original proprietor was an English exile, Sir Harry (ex-RAF) Warner, who actually arrived in the Algarve before the tourist boom really started. This busy, comfortable British pub lookalike is now in Portuguese hands and is open every day throughout the year and serves reasonable bar snacks in addition to liquid sustenance.

In view of Albufeira's international popularity, there is a wide variety of accommodation available in town – with the exception of rooms in peak season for low-budget independent travellers who have been rather squeezed out in favour of the more lucrative package holiday-makers. There are, in total, about fifty different hotels, pensions, plus holiday and Timeshare apartment complexes currently operating in or around the immediate Albufeira area. Young Timeshare salesmen are a particular pest in Albufeira – dismiss their (frequent) advances firmly but politely. The finest hotel is the five-star luxury class **Hotel Da Balaia** (Tel: 526-81) set in its own grounds a couple of miles east of the cliff-top town itself. The 186 rooms are split into two large blocks, and all have balconies, bathroom suites and air-conditioning. The hotel offers the best facilities in Albufeira, including two heated swimming pools, private gardens, English-speaking staff, children's supervised play areas and, above all, the opportunity for a genuinely quiet and relaxing holiday. Sports facilities are extensive and both disco and live music entertainment are provided nightly.

The most popular de luxe hotel used by British operators is the large **Montechoro** (Tel: 526-51) situated 2½ miles from Albufeira. The Montechoro offers the best in four-star luxury and was designated 'Hotel of the Year' by the Portuguese Tourist Authority in 1986. In addition, Thomson Holidays have awarded the Montechoro two of their prestigious Gold Awards in their Winter Sun and Best TTTTT Summer Hotel categories. The fully air-conditioned hotel stands ten storeys high, offering some glorious views in all directions, and has no less than five bars to entertain even the most discerning tourist. In addition to the 'usual' quality facilities (sauna, swimming pool, hairdresser and so on), the Montechoro is situated close to the popular **Michael's** night-club and has a gymnasium and eight tennis courts with coaching available if required. The hotel even lays on its own organized programme of sports and evening entertainment if you should so choose. An elegant grill room provides à la carte service and a jacket and tie is required for dinner. Without a doubt, one of the Algarve's finest hotels for all-round value.

Another popular four-star hotel is the stylish **Sol E Mar** (Tel: 521-21). Its main attraction is a prime beach location, probably the best of any hotel in town since the old town centre and market are just around the corner. The seaviews are excellent if you get a room at the rear of the hotel, but limited otherwise. Sol E Mar has its own hairdresser and gift shop, plus a reasonable à la carte menu, but also operates a unique voucher system which allows residents to eat in one or two outside restaurants in town also owned by the hotel.

The medium-sized, three-star **Rocamar** hotel (Tel: 526-96) is located in a relatively quiet area of town about five minutes from the beach. The views from here are particularly appealing and this is one of the most leisurely central hotels in Albufeira with the option of good local music nightly. The **Boavista** (Tel: 521-75) on the hillside in town, and **Vila Recife** (Tel: 520-47) are smaller hotels offering more of a homely atmosphere with substantially fewer 'frills'. If possible, try to avoid the two-star **Hotel Baltum** which Enterprise uses. It looks smart enough in brochure photographs, but offers no more than the most basic two-star facilities. Its one obvious advantage is a central town location, but this has the effect of making the whole place extremely noisy and means quite a trek down to the beach.

Albufeira also has number of tourist apartment complexes offering no more than 'board only' accommodation, but which are popular with many British tour operators for families. Although substantially cheaper than full or half-board hotel accommodation, an important consideration with holiday and Timeshare apartments is the two or three miles which often lie between them and the nearby resort facilities. **Elma Apartments**, three miles out of Albufeira, is typical of most complexes with a number of self-contained shops and bar facilities helping to reduce the necessity of travelling into the town. The **Montechoro** complex (Tel: 533-87) has fifty-four spacious apartments on seven floors and an attractive feature of the **Solazur** apartments available here is the free courtesy bus which transfers residents daily to the beach or into town (assuming you choose to go, of course). The three-star **Hotel Topazio**, five minutes from the beach, offers both hotel and apartment accommodation and so eliminates the need for courtesy transfers to and from the beach.

In addition to the main resort beach mentioned earlier in this section, Albufeira has a number of less well known beaches easily accessible within a few miles west of town. All have safe paths leading down from the roadside and, on the whole, these satellite beaches tend to be smaller but less crowded during the summer months. BALEEIRA is nearest, although this small fishermen's cove is relatively unknown to foreign visitors. Favoured by many locals, this beach is one of the more attractive to look at but tends to be covered with rather a lot of seaweed after each tide. A number of small fishing boats take up more precious beach space and there are few facilities available. Don't bring children here because of the seaweed and lack of facilities, but this isn't a bad beach if you want to bring a picnic to sit on the rocks and get away from the town for a while. Otherwise, stick to further down the coast.

Nearby SÃO RAFAEL is considerably better known, and about twice the size of near neighbour Baleeira. Unfortunately it has the same problems with seaweed after tides, but odd-looking sandstone rock formations help give the place a decidedly secluded atmosphere. On the whole, a better beach than Baleeira but not suitable for children because there are no safety warning flags and facilities are limited to a makeshift beach café. In addition, the water shelves quite steeply.

CASTELO is another of the area's secluded coves, no more than 150 yards long but increasingly popular each summer. It is a very picturesque spot, despite the short walk down from the road, and is normally quiet even during the peak season. The beach is reasonably safe for children because of its gently shelving water and relatively small size, but there are no safety warnings here, or at neighbouring GALE. Small beach cafés have sprung up at both beaches, and Gale itself is a massive stretch of sand, backed by flat hinterland and rolling dunes, and also reasonably quiet.

The next major resort is **ARMAÇÃO DE PÊRA**, just to the west of Gale beach. Ancient fishing cottages lie at the heart of this fledgling resort which looks exactly what it is – a collection of new apartment block hotels which initially overshadowed, but are now helping revive, a struggling little fishing community. The village's true origins are lost, although it is known that the Phoenicians used the place as a trading post and stopping-off point *en route* to Cape St Vincent.

A unique natural attraction known to the Phoenicians, and certainly to countless hundreds of curious tourists each summer, are the enormous **sea grottos** at nearby Furnas. Excursions by boat are organized most days through the tourist office (Tel: 321-45), which you'll find open every day during the summer in the Avenida Marginal. These spectacular caves are entered through huge stone arches and their cathedral-like vaults are a sight truly worth seeing. Little else has survived for the sightseer to visit beyond an attractive little 18th-century **fort**. Complete with Nossa Senhora da Rocha (Our Lady of the Rock), a Romanesque chapel dedicated to the memory of Saint Anthony, the fort sits on a hundred-foot long stone promontory jutting out towards the ocean like the bow of a ship.

The village of Armação de Pêra rolls gently down towards a huge arched bay, curving round towards the resort's famous Golden Beach; the longest single stretch of uninterrupted beach anywhere in Portugal. It will take you the better half of a morning to just stroll from one end to the other and the vast stretch of golden sand just about manages to soak up the thousands of visitors who annually flock to this spot. Most of the beach is an unspectacular expanse of sand, backed by the village and high-rise hotels at the western end. These slowly give way to some gorgeous natural cliff and cove formations, which you can reach by well used paths, as you wander further west still.

Beach facilities at Armação de Pêra are good, reflecting the high volume of tourists who use them, and this would be a particularly sensible choice of resort to bring young children. The water is relatively shallow and the potential play area for children to run about enormous! A small part of the beach is still a thriving fishermen's area, making quite an interesting spectacle to watch as the fishermen gently merge with hundreds of sun-soaking tourists. A busy fish auction takes place early each morning but, on the whole, the fishermen's presence remains relatively unobtrusive if you are prepared to allow them to go about their business without troubling them for photographs or asking for 'complimentary' trips in their boat!

Night-life and opportunities for eating out in Armação de Pêra are very limited outside the constraints of your chosen hotel. The village's best restaurant is **A Santalo** (Tel: 323-32), on Largo 25 Abril. Meaning literally 'the Crab', A Santalo has been thriving since the days when Armação was no more than a tiny fishing village playing host to only the occasional travelling artist and reclusive curiosity-seeker. Offering an enormous menu, A Santalo specializes in seafood, including crab, funnily enough, and remains open each night until midnight. Its prime village location offers marvellous views in all directions. The open fire adds to the atmosphere as well as helping relieve the not uncommon late evening chill in the Algarve.

Panorama Sol Grill (Tel: 324-24) is a mile or two out of the village, on the main road west which takes you past the large Hotel Viking. Here you'll find fish and most meat dishes served in true baronial style! The place is quite expensive and normally you'll be asked to select your own cut of meat from the available butcher's array. This is no more than a formality, unless you happen to choose one of the live lobsters from the large aquarium – then the difference in size can be quite significant when you get your bill. Panorama Sol Grill is completely closed from November to February and every Wednesday from February until June.

Two relatively inexpensive restaurants worth recommending in the village are **A Grelha**, on the Rua do Alentejo; and **Pipa's** on the Rua Gaivotas which has some first-class seafood starters available. Armação de Pêra's primary hotel, the five-star **Hotel Viking** (Tel: 323-36), has a disappointing restaurant offering an international three-course dinner menu with no choice normally available for residents. They do, however, offer an impressive buffet lunch and the option of poolside snacks.

The Hotel Viking has 185 spacious and well furnished bedrooms spread over seven floors. An interesting feature is the fact that all rooms have a small refrigerator in addition to a private bathroom suite and good views over the sea or the nearby hills. The hotel is only a few minutes from the beach, but rather isolated from the village resort proper. Windsurfing and water sports are on offer from the beach and there is a disco nightly with live music occasionally. In addition to a replica 19th-century café set in the courtyard, the hotel has a large swimming pool with an outdoor bar nearby and its own tennis courts.

Hotel do Garbe (Tel: 551-87) in the Avenida Marginal is practically a self-contained resort in its own right. The modern four-star building offers virtually every conventional amenity, including occasional live music, hairdresser and giftshop, in addition to access to a superb sandy beach and attractively furnished public rooms on all levels. An impressive feature of this welcoming hotel is the four course international (à la carte) dinner menu.

Luxury apartment accommodation is available at **Vilalara** (Tel: 323-33), although be warned that past visitors have included film stars, politicians, diplomats and royalty who have appreciated the relative seclusion of this fine mini-resort one mile west of the village. Armação de Pêra is also expanding as one of several Timeshare resorts along this stretch of coast, which is encouraging since there is a sameness about all the hotels in Armação that becomes striking if you visit one or two of them. None cater willingly for young singles and all are in the three-to-five star category offering similar standards of sterile comfort.

A couple of picturesque coves, SENHORA DA ROCHA and PRAIA DO CARVALHO, lie to the west of Armação de Pêra and tend to be less crowded if you're staying either at Armação or in nearby Carvoeiro. Praia do Carvalho is slowly being taken for granted as part of the general beach-set in the immediate vicinity of Carvoeiro, but Senhora da Rocha remains the less well known and more appealing of the two. A small cove, scarcely more than a hundred yards in length, Senhora da Rocha is backed by cliffs and a small pension which, as yet, is not visited by any British tour operator. Limited beach facilities are available here and boat excursions are possible to nearby caves, but the water shelves quite sharply so would be unsuitable for children.

CARVOEIRO is a small but relatively better known resort which is slowly emerging from another of the Algarve's whitewashed fishing villages. The resort has not yet been over-developed; indeed, there is only one large hotel and a number of apartment complexes just outside the village. Socialites and sightseers will have little to occupy them in Carvoeiro, but the resort does have a few really good restaurants and one of the most attractive beaches west of Faro, although it is very small and can quickly become congested in summer.

The main attraction is the village square from where it is possible to watch the fishing fleet leave in traditional Algarve style. An ancient fishing boat has been turned into a bar just at the side of the square, but the beach is really the centrepiece around which the village has grown. Scarcely larger than a postage stamp in relation to the vast beaches on either side of it, Carvoeiro's 150 yards or so of coastline are set in a small cove with all the usual beach facilities, including a café, beach furniture available for hire and so on. Another more modest stretch of beach can be found at nearby VALE DA LAPA. There are no facilities, and transport there is a problem, if you're not prepared to hire a car for a day or so.

The surrounding cliffs at Carvoeiro make the water quite calm but it does tend to shelve quite steeply, so caution is advised if you bring children here. This potentially idyllic spot becomes quite congested during the summer months and this is not helped any by the collection of fishing boats which are permanently beached along the sand. The clifftop scenery becomes more interesting east of the main beach area and the views over the sea and surrounding cliffs increasingly spectacular.

Not far from the beach you will reach the **Algar Seco**, meaning literally 'dry gully', but really a peculiar collection of massive red sandstone formations which gently emerge from the sea. The site is quite overwhelming and is pictured on most of the brochures and postcards for the area. You can climb down well over a hundred steps, through elegant stone arches, to reach the base of the site and take some truly memorable photographs. If you prefer to have a closer look, day excursions by boat are organized during the summer period from the tourist office (Tel: 573-28), which you'll find in the village along Largo da Praia.

Carvoeiro really has nothing to offer in the way of shopping and night-life beyond the most basic facilities – including a post office and bank – and a few local bars. Portimão is only five miles away, to the west, and your nearest town of any size is Lagoa about three miles to the north. The best place to eat is **O Castelo** (Tel: 572-18), on the Rua do Casino. This place is a converted house with a large outdoor terrace offering some marvellous views over the nearby coast. It's relatively inexpensive and has a surprisingly up-market menu with a wide selection of non-fish dishes, including duck à l'orange and pepper-steak, along with a few local fish specialities. The restaurant is open only for dinners throughout the year, between 7 and 10pm, apart from Sundays.

You'll find the **Long Bar** (Tel: 575-17) right in the centre of the resort, and this is about the nearest to a London pub you'll come across in this part of the Algarve! Dominated by an enormous bar (hence the pub's name) modest lunches or dinner can be served with accompanying British beers if you so choose. Nearby **Smiler's Bar** is owned by a British couple and offers a similar type of 'home' hospitality – and is reckoned to be the busiest bar in Carvoeiro.

The only proper international hotel so far built in the resort is the modest **Hotel Dom Sancho** (Tel: 573-50) in Carvoeiro's main square. The hotel has no swimming pool but is only a couple of minutes' walk from the beach area. It is officially classed as a 'modern four-star hostel residencia' type building offering substantially fewer frills than a four-star hotel. All forty-seven rooms are air-conditioned with private bathrooms, although a few at the back have dull views of the hotel courtyard. On the whole, the hotel furnishings are clean and modest, although the outside furniture is quite tatty. The staff speak

English and the large dining-room offers a wide international menu in addition to local specialities. A flat roof area is ideal for sun-bathing, but distinctly unsafe for children because of the lack of safety railings.

Carvoeiro is expanding much more as a self-catering apartment, and Timeshare, destination, than as a conventional package resort. A total of nearly two dozen British tour operators offer primarily self-catering holidays to this part of the coast. One or two visit the **Rocha Village** complex, but the comfortable **Vale de Centianes** and **Quinta de Paradiso** complexes are the most popular with British operators. On the whole, Carvoeiro has potential as a holiday destination if you are looking primarily for sun and seclusion without wanting to pay the earth to visit the one or two really exclusive resorts east of Faro.

A number of holiday villas, operated by the Surrey-based Holiday Villas Ltd, are located a little way down the western coast at FERRAGUDO. This unattractive spot sits at the river mouth looking across to the larger resort town of Portimão, and here you'll find a small windsurfing school and a few reasonably lively local bars. The **Caldeirão** is one of the best known and a popular live jazz venue. Ferragudo itself is a rather dull old village built on top of itself in a pyramid fashion with an old church at the summit. There is a long stretch of beach, set in a pleasant enough location with a low cliff backdrop but in recent years the sand has occasionally been affected by pollution from passing trawlers and so Ferragudo must rank as one of the least attractive beach resorts west of Faro.

Much more appealing is the large resort **PRAIA DA ROCHA**, two miles from Portimão on the other side of the river from Ferragudo. Although known as a fishing village for generations before the earthquake in 1755, Praia da Rocha had the unique distinction of becoming the Algarve's first proper beach resort over half a century ago. It was in 1934 that the first two pioneering Algarve hotels opened their doors to British tourists; a steady trickle of holiday-makers came over the next thirty years, before the advent of mass charter tourism, to this resort which seemed practically as far off as Australia seems today.

  Praia da Rocha literally means 'beach of the rock'; so named after the huge natural rock formations which you can see nearby. These have been said to resemble bears, a huge triumphal arch and even twin brothers! Some of the more surrealistic formations have inspired generations of visiting artists and one of the largest is uncannily structured like an enormous seaside cathedral. Although still clearly a developing summer and winter resort, with at least half a dozen large hotels under obvious construction, Praia da Rocha already has a lot to offer undemanding visitors.

The resort's only historical attraction is **Fortaleza de Santa Catarina** (St Catherine's fortress), a ruin which sits above the beach and the mouth of the river. Originally built in the 16th century on the order of King João III to protect Portimão's sandbar, the fortress was falling into disuse by the time of the 1755 earthquake and accordingly was never properly reconstructed. It still looks pretty fearsome from the outside, but inside the appearance is totally different as it has been turned into a popular street café, complete with modest lunch menu and patio chairs. From your seat in the old parade ground you can overlook nearby Ferragudo and the rest of the bay. The long broad pier on which the fortress stands is perfect for a relaxing stroll and is as near to solitude as you're likely to find in this busy resort.

Before heading down towards the beach you'll pass the tourist office (Tel: 222-90) on Rua Tomas Cabreira. Both the beach promenade and nearby road are very busy and particular care is necessary with young children when crossing. Praia da Rocha's magnificent expanse of golden beach helps make the place an ideal choice for an all-round relaxing family holiday. A number of resorts lay claim to having the Algarve's finest beach, but this one must surely be among the frontrunners if not the pick of the bunch.

Within a few minutes' walk from the resort village you reach the beach which is attractively framed by low cliffs and smaller rock formations which gently rise out of the sand. A number of walkways stretch from the far end of the beach down towards the water – in order to give your feet some comfort from the scorching summer sands!

The water has a modest shelf making it safe for children, and although the narrower western end of the beach can become quite crowded during the summer, the beach is sufficiently long to allow people to spread well out. Pedaloes and small boats are available for hire, together with all the other usual beach facilities, and there are one or two seasonal cafés around the busier end of the sand.

Praia da Rocha has little to offer in the way of night-life beyond the range of live music and disco entertainment provided by the major hotels. The resort is fortunate, however, in having an interesting range of restaurants within easy walking distance of most hotels. One of the more unusual is the **Safari** (Tel: 235-40). You'll find it in a superb location, overlooking the beach on the Rua Antonio Feu, and what makes it special is the distinctly African feel to your meal which you won't find elsewhere in the Algarve. Although owned and operated by native Portuguese, most of the menu is inspired from traditional recipes from Angola, once one of Portugal's major colonies. Savoury fish soup is the recommended starter and most of the main courses have the word 'Safari' in their title, a reference to the restaurant's own unique blend of sauces and herbs which you'll go a long way to beat!

Restaurant **Rene** (Tel: 232-17) on the Estrada da Vau is a high-class restaurant offering a reasonable menu of food cooked in a more traditional French and Italian style than native Portuguese. **Tres Irmãos** (Tel: 242-11) is another restaurant with an excellent beach view location and is justly renowned for good quality Portuguese cooking in a homely atmosphere. The **O Bicho** restaurant in the centre of town has probably the best budget value reputation in Praia da Rocha and serves locally caught fish.

The **Titanic** (Tel: 223-71), however, on Rua Engenheiro Francisco Bivar can be recommended most highly and justifiably claims to be the smartest restaurant in town, with its gilt furnishings and crystal chandeliers adding a touch of 'Old Time' class to your meal. Virtually every popular international dish is on offer but, naturally, traditional Algarve dishes cooked to perfection are a speciality. The fully air-conditioned Titanic is open seven days for lunch, and until 11pm each evening for dinner.

Praia da Rocha has a wide range of accommodation alternatives available to suit the pockets of most package holiday-makers and independent travellers alike. Easily the resort's finest, and undoubtedly one of the Algarve's gems, is the large five-star **Hotel Algarve** (Tel: 240-01) located on the stylish Avenida Tomàs Cabreira. Although you can expect to pay five-star prices to stay in this plush place, you will be rewarded with some of the finest service and pampering available anywhere west of Monte Carlo. Although a modern building, the rooms and corridors are furnished in a luxurious manner that wouldn't look out of place in any 19th-century palace. The top-class suites, decorated in a variety of 18th- and 19th-century fashions, are magnificent. Outdoors you can enjoy the hotel's large gardens, a huge swimming pool and a tidy sun terrace. After your four course à la carte dinner you have the option of a disco or live music nightly once the children are safely in the hands of the hotel's childminding service.

Coming back to reality, the resort has one or two other hotels used by British tour operators which are all either three- or four-star graded. Easily the most nostalgic is the **Bela Vista** (Tel: 240-55) located right by the beachside and currently visited by only one British company. The Bela Vista was the Algarve's first ever hotel and the former stately old mansion-house has managed to retain much of the style and décor which helped make Praia da Rocha a popular winter resort in the 1930s. The hotel has a distinctly old fashioned feel to it, and the 27 bedrooms each offer individual furnishings and period creaky floorboards! Evening entertainment is restricted to Portuguese television or piano music, so retired people may find the unusually relaxing pace for an Algarve hotel particularly appealing.

The **Hotel Jupiter** (Tel: 220-41) stands nine floors high at the junction of two busy roads. A modern four-star building, the Jupiter is the most popular package hotel in Praia da Rocha, other than the Hotel Algarve, with more than half a dozen British operators including it in their summer programme. Overall, the standard four-star facilities available are good, including a reasonable international dinner menu served in the large, if gloomy, dining-room. It's worth considering that the hotel escapes little of the noise outside. Children are well catered for by way of special menus and early meal times if requested.

Praia da Rocha has a number of pensions and private houses with rooms available which the independent traveller should be able to find easily through the tourist office. **Residencial Sol** (Tel: 240-71) on the Avenida Tomàs Cabreira has thirty-two simply furnished but comfortable rooms available. The nearby **Estalagem San Jose** (Tel: 240-37) has a further fifty rooms, although remains closed from mid-November until the start of April.

Opened in 1983, the **Hotel Rochavau** (Tel: 261-11) is a three-star hotel about twenty minutes' walk away from Praia da Rocha at nearby PRAIA DA VAU. This clean hotel is becoming more popular with British visitors and offers a high standard of service for its three stars. Built on four storeys, the hotel has a smallish swimming pool and friendly English-speaking staff. There is no restaurant other than for breakfast, nor any night-life unless you are prepared to make your own or go into Praia da Rocha.

Vau has a few hundred yards of reasonable beach which usually becomes quite busy with the Praia da Rocha overflow. Situated below a low cliffed cove, the beach is backed by a large, and noisy, car park although there are a few more modest – but less crowded – sandy coves a little way round the western coast.

One of the Algarve's larger towns is the major fishing port of **PORTIMÃO** a mile or so further on from Praia da Rocha. With a population of over 10,000, Portimão is a bustling alternative to the better known beach resorts on either side of it. Although a large number of tourists find their way into the town for a day's shopping, only a handful of British operators offer accommodation specifically in Portimão and as a result it can be easily overlooked as a possible resort destination.

The town's early history is virtually unknown, other than the fact that a thriving fishing village was at least acknowledged on the site of the present resort over a thousand years ago. It is reckoned that Portimão might have been one of the great cities of the ancient world, but little evidence has survived from before the 8th century when it is known that the Moors took the town from the Visigoths and changed the name to Porcimunt, the origin of today's Portimão. A few historians have argued that the city was founded by the Carthaginian general Hamilcar Barca, and was named Portus Annibalis in honour of his son Hannibal who became better known because of his elephant companions.

Portimão is easily the poorest Algarve town of any size for sights to see: there is no castle, ancient viaduct or cathedral and what few historic buildings there once were disappeared when the entire town was wiped out by the earthquake in 1755. The buildings lost included a significant 14th-century Gothic church and, although this was immediately rebuilt, the 18th-century copy which you can visit today is said to be a pale shadow of its predecessor except for a single Gothic portal which was retained. A few painted tiles survive from the 17th century and you can still see a number of walnut carvings in the chancel. There is also a large cross brought over by pilgrims from Convento da Esperanca.

A number of impressive late 18th- and 19th-century houses remain in the town's old quarter and several palace-like mansions were built with the profits of the first fish factories, opened during the last century. These mansions are located in and around the town's numerous parks and squares, and are still occupied, but make an interesting walk round. Portimão's most attractive park is the **Largo 1 de Dezembro**, just opposite the tourist office (Tel: 220-65/236-95). Important events in the country's history are portrayed in a series of blue and white glazed tiles set into the benches.

Possibly Portimão's greatest attraction is the comings and goings of the busy fish industry in and around the **harbour** area. A number of enterprising fishermen may offer you the chance to witness this non-stop activity from their boats and if you are prepared to part with a respectable 'consideration' for the privilege, it is a spectacle you won't forget quickly. You can rapidly pass a full day doing little else than watching the loading and unloading of the boats – and you won't get a better spot on the Algarve to do just this. There's nothing quite like watching others work to remind you that you're on holiday!

The town is well served with good restaurants and although every last one seems to serve seafood as a speciality the best in town is **Lucio's** (Tel: 242-92) at 10 Tenente Morais Soräes near the bridge. Served in simple style, in a relatively small dining area, this is where the best of the daily catch – and most of the locals – finish up. Fresh fish prices change daily, so if you visit more than once don't be surprised if your favourite delicacy has gone up or down a few hundred escudos. **The Old Tavern** (Tel: 233-25) in Rua Judice Fialho is a poultry specialist, particularly chicken and turkey, and also one of the oldest surviving Algarve restaurants. Serving good value meals in simple surroundings that look quite stark, the Old Tavern is open later than most Algarve restaurants daily throughout the summer, except Sundays, until 1am.

Another favourite haunt with locals, usually a good sign for discerning tourists, is the **O Bichu** restaurant (Tel: 229-77) along

Largo Gil Eanes. *Cataplana* is O Bichu's recommended speciality, the amazing Algarve concoction of pork, clams and a hundred and one assorted vegetables and sauces! Helpings tend to be generous so you can expect good value whatever you choose from the inexpensive menu. Both **Alfredo's** and **Porto de Abrigo**, on Rua de Pe da Cruz, are reasonably expensive but well worth visiting for attractive and well-presented local seafood.

Portimão has one or two small apartment complexes on the outside of town, plus one or two good hotels. Of those, only the three-star hotel **Globo** (Tel: 221-51) is visited by British tour operators. Located in the heart of the old town, at 26 Rua 5 de Outubro, this well furnished and comfortable building was totally rebuilt from the shell of an outdated inn twenty-one years ago. Each of the 80 bedrooms has a private bathroom and stylish balcony, and the numerous public rooms are plushly finished with crystal lightshades, ebony panels and so on.

The **Bemposta Holiday Village** is a mile from Portimão and provides exceptional value for money and good facilities for a relaxing family holiday. This self-contained village of villas and studios, set in well landscaped gardens, has many extras which make it stand out from the other holiday complexes in this area: a good children's play area; free transport to beach and town; laundry; children's and adults' pools; and for the mums and dads there's a good restaurant and bar; plus tennis courts and a TV and video room, in case you hit a rainy day. All in all, a well run, well priced complex, ideal for young families.

The twin resorts of **PRAIA DE ALVOR** and **PRAIA DOS TRÊS IRMÃOS** lie just a little way along the coast from Portimão and although normally listed under the name of one or the other in travel brochures they share the same stretch of coast and effectively the same facilities. Praia dos Três Irmãos (Beach of the Three Brothers) lies side-by-side with the smaller stretch of coast adjoining the attractive little village of Alvor. Originally founded by Hannibal two centuries before the birth of Christ, the area, which was once a favourite hunting region of King João II (who ruled 1481–95), has had quite a tragic past since the late 12th century when it was destroyed totally by the Moorish invaders. Over the next few centuries it was lovingly rebuilt, only to be flattened for a second time in the earthquake of 1755.

The village of **ALVOR** is a rather curious accumulation of narrow streets and whitewashed houses all linked together in a maze-like pattern typical of the Algarve. A large number of foreign visitors rent complete houses in town during the summer months and, for the vast majority who prefer a shorter stay in a little more comfort, there are a host of tour operators offering holidays to the plush **Hotel Penina Golf** or surrounding self-catering apartments.

One or two points of interest in Alvor include the 16th-century Manueline **parish church** which contains not only a beautiful period portal, but the nationally-known *Senhor dos Navegantes*. This huge image of the Crucifixion was washed ashore centuries ago from an unknown destination and treasured by local fishermen who carried it proudly up the hill to the church. The view down across the estuary lake from the church is also well worth the trek even supposing the more material attractions don't appeal to you. The town's imposing **Chapel of São João** offers less intrinsic beauty but even more spectacular views across the whole bay to Lagos and beyond.

Oddly enough, the nine golden miles of combined Praia dos Três Irmãos and Alvor beaches are not the longest single stretch in Portugal. It just looks that way. It would be difficult to criticize much of those nine sandy miles since you are hardly likely to see more than a small part of them but, at the same time, it is accurate to say that by far the best beach areas are those which are most busy during the summer months, and those which are located within easiest reach of the main resort accommodation.

You may well be lucky to find a quiet little spot to yourself, but bear in mind that virtually all the facilities have been developed along at the beach's western end and that much of the rest can feel suddenly isolated if you stray too far from the body of the crowd. The water has a reasonably gentle shelf all around the bay, but the eastern end is the naturally more attractive and is pleasantly sheltered by old eroded sandstone cliffs which gracefully meet the beach a good distance off the sea. The huge bay turns gradually eastwards in a gentle arc and becomes noticeably flatter and scruffier around its middle section; westwards from here and the crowds really begin to gather.

Neither resort offers much in the way of night-life although the top-class **Barcade Alvor** restaurant (Tel: 202-11/2), located just on the beach, has a swinging night-club and is part of the large **Torralta** apartment complex nearby. Half a dozen British operators use these apartments which are unusually well served by small supermarkets, tennis courts, a disco, a heated swimming pool and a new-looking casino. All the apartments are located near the championship Penina golf course as well so in addition to beach-located water sports, most healthy activities are catered for.

Another truly first class restaurant is the **Maisonette Grill** (Tel: 242-01) adjoining the Hotel Alvor Praia. This place has won many awards over the last decade and can reasonably claim to be one of the Algarve's, if not Portugal's, finest restaurants. Naturally you can expect to pay for the privilege of eating here, but for a really superb meal in one of Portugal's renowned restaurants it is well worth it. If you can avoid feeling intimidated by the plush luxury which surrounds you, a mouthwatering menu of local and international à la carte specialities awaits you.

The **Hotel Alvor Praia** (Tel: 242-01) itself is the most popular hotel in Alvor with British tour operators and, like the Maisonette Grill, deserves one of the highest recommendations of any Algarve hotel because of its excellent facilities, prime location and overall good service above and beyond the five-star rating awarded by the Portuguese tourist authority. A large building, the fully self-contained Alvor Praia has 241 spacious bedrooms and facilities for residents that include a Finnish sauna and Olympic-size swimming pool. Fishing excursions can be arranged through the hotel reception and visitors are entitled to discount fees on the resort's 27-hole championship golf course, designed by Henry Cotton.

The **Penina Golf Hotel** (Tel: 220-51) offers a more exclusive type of five-star luxury, within easy reach of the golf courses. In addition to beauty parlour and sauna, the Penina Golf includes a landing strip for private aircraft among its numerous other attractions! The four-star **Hotel Dom João II** (Tel: 201-35) has over 200 rooms in a superb location overlooking the beach.

Praia dos Três Irmãos' largest hotel is the 325-room **Delfim** (Tel: 271-71). Standing on a picturesque hillside overlooking the beach, the Delfim is a totally modern building which dominates the landward view from the beach. Although a striking building from the outside, it can feel distinctly impersonal after a few days because of its sheer size. Although you can expect good service, everything from breakfast to the ground-floor shopping area seems to be done on such a large scale. Nevertheless, another reasonable base if you are prepared to get out and about to see more of the surrounding area than just the immediate beach and swimming pool.

Meia Praia and **Batata** are a couple of less well known beaches lying between Praia dos Três Irmãos and Alvor, and Lagos ten miles further west. Batata is easily the more deserted and less appealing of the two and runs into Meia Praia before reaching the fringes of Lagos itself. The River Alvor reaches the sea at one end of Meia Praia and the remainder of the beach is a long, exposed bay backed by a screen of low dunes. About 2km outside Lagos is the Algarve Microlight Centre. If you fancy an experience of a lifetime, why not call in and go up with an instructor in a 2-seater. For advance information, contact Gerry Breen, Algarve Microlight Centre, Aparto 254, 8603 Lagos Codex.

The Algarve's westernmost town of any size is **LAGOS** which has a distinguished historical pedigree going back until the time of the Celts. Legend has it that Bohodes, a chieftain from the city of Carthage, was responsible for founding the city on the edge of the stretch of sea which the African city dominated. The Carthaginians planted many of the vineyards and olive groves which remain to this day, and which interested the Romans several centuries later.

After the Romans left, the Visigoths sacked the city in the 5th century before Lagos became part of the Byzantine Empire for a couple of centuries. The Moors arrived in the 8th century and built the town's medieval towers and enormous tiered walls during the time of Abdemaran III, although these were later to fall to Sancho I in 1189 during the Crusading Wars. The town's true fame came in the 15th century when the Portuguese fleet sailed from here to conquer Ceuta in 1415. Around the same time Prince Henry the Navigator was living in Lagos, eventually dying here in 1460, and it was during his lifetime that the discovery of Madeira was first announced on the European mainland at Lagos.

Lagos has a number of surviving points of interest which the sightseer ought to make for, including the few scattered remains of the **medieval walls** which you can still explore at various points throughout the town. Lagos suffered heavily in 1755 and lost rather more than most Algarve towns because of a devastating series of thirty-foot high waves which finished off what little had survived the effects of the earthquake. What remains of the old town's walls will give you some idea just how large Lagos was at its commercial peak.

An ancient **chapel** dedicated to Nossa Senhora da Conceição stands in the upper town and bears witness to the constant rebuilding which took place over the troubled past centuries. The first chapel was built in 1325, although nothing now remains from that period, but a 15th-century chancel and 16th-century side chapel can be seen. The Doric columns are among the best preserved in the Algarve and a number of fine images and tiled stones can be viewed inside near the vestry. Further down town again, on the Rua Silva Lopes, the 18th-century **Igreja de Santo António** (Church of Saint Anthony) contains some of Portugal's finest gilt carvings, which themselves date back to the 17th century. The church also contains the tomb of Irishman Hugh Beaty who commanded the town's regiment of the Portuguese army in the later years of the 18th century.

Next door to the church is the **Museu Regional de Lagos** containing a fascinating, if distinctly disjointed, collection of artefacts relating to the town's chequered past. The first large room is dedicated entirely to local archaeology and includes both Neolithic remains and Roman mosaics found at Boca do Rio, near Budons. Different rooms are variously devoted to Algarve folk art, copper, lace, tapestry, cork work and so on, and 'later' historical artefacts going back as far as the 16th century. In addition to a small numismatic (coin) section, the museum still displays the original charter of Lagos, granted in 1504, which rests beside the original key to the city. Although of obvious local interest, the charter is reckoned to be one of Portugal's most important historical documents presently on display outside Lisbon because so few survive from before 1755.

A **customs house** on the Praça Infante Dom Henriques represents an interesting link with Portugal's former glory since it was on this site that the home of Henry the Navigator once stood. But like so many of the links with the country's fascinating history, it was wiped out in a single morning by the earthquake in 1755. An imposing **statue** of Henry stands watch over the small (unmarked) arcade in front of the customs house which today bustles only with tourists but was once the site of Portugal's first slave market. Countless slaves were captured along the nearby North African coast and sold here to the highest bidders. The remains of an **aqueduct** built between 1490 and 1521 stand in the centre of town, but more specific information about what there is to see and do at any one time in Lagos can be obtained from the tourist office (Tel: 630-31) on Largo Marquês de Pombal. They will also give details on horseriding and birdwatching trips in the area.

The town does not have its own beach, but the nearest one is the small stretch of coast at PINHÃO. Barely 150 yards long, this attractive little cove becomes quickly crowded during the summer months and most visitors seem content to travel a few miles along the coast, in either direction, to the larger beaches at Praia Dona Ana or Meia Praia. Pinhão has no obvious tide warning signs either, so holiday-makers with children ought to consider other beaches.

Lagos seems to be bursting with small cafés and tavernas wherever you go and the 'Pedestrians Only' area around Rua Direita and Rua Cândido dos Reis has become almost a continual street café during the busy summer months. An ideal spot to take the weight off your feet for a while and relax in the surroundings of some attractive old houses without being bothered by traffic. If you are looking for a more substantial evening meal, then the town centre has literally dozens of thriving restaurants from which you can choose. Two of the best in town are **Poso do Infante** (Tel: 628-62) on Rua Alfonso d'Almeida and the sophisticated **Alpendre** (Tel: 627-05) along Rua Antonio Barbosa Viana. Poso do Infante has a slightly less formal atmosphere but offers one of the best traditional menus in Lagos, including sole with banana. This oddity is often recommended and if you hear it mentioned often enough then you'll find it difficult to leave the Algarve without discovering its acquired flavour. The Alpendre, however, will smother you in sophisticated luxury. *Gourmet* maga-zine once called it the Algarve's 'most luxurious' restaurant and it does indeed have a breathtaking, if expensive, menu. You won't be disappointed by the quality of the food even if the speed and manner of service could be improved for such a highly praised establishment. A reservation is essential.

The **Dom Sabastião** (Tel: 627-95) on Rua 25 de Abril is a traditionally run Portuguese restaurant in the centre of town. It offers some of the best local dishes in town, including most seafood, but can become very busy in the summer months. It is open every day during the summer until 10pm. **O Trovador** (Tel: 631-52) is another specialist in fine local specialities and sits behind the large Hotel de Lagos on Largo do Convento da Senhora de Gloria. This place is one of Lagos' most popular out-of-season restaurants since it remains open throughout the year apart from Thursdays.

By far the resort's most popular hotel with British tour operators is the four-star **Hotel de Lagos** (Tel: 620-11) built in an unusual castle design along the Rua Nova da Aldeia. The split-level hotel sits amid three acres of its own grounds high above the town and all 300 bedrooms offer splendid views no matter in what direction you are looking. Meia Praia is your nearest beach and a courtesy bus shuttles backwards and forwards on the ten minute journey all day. A tidy sun terrace surrounds the medium sized swimming pool and the hotel has a spacious, comfortable interior, promising a generally relaxing atmosphere. The staff speak good English and children are particularly well catered for: early meals, high chairs, special menus and babyminding facilities are available and there is even a special children's swimming pool within sight of the larger main pool.

Three more modest three-star hotels in Lagos feature in British operators' brochures. The best is the thirty-seven room **Riomar** (Tel: 630-91) on Rua Candido dos Reis in the centre of town. A bright, clean hotel owned by an English couple, this is by no means the largest hotel in Lagos, but the Riomar is a popular and informally cosy establishment which seems to satisfy the British tourists who come here year after year. Breakfast only is available, but there are several good restaurants nearby. No in-house entertainment other than television and the bar.

Both the other two hotels, **São Cristovão** (Tel: 630-51) on Rossio de São João and **Meia Praia** (Tel: 620-01/2) near the beach, are disappointing. The São Cristovão has been built in a fairly dismal location by the main road fully a mile from the beach (without courtesy transport) and is a further fifteen minutes out of town. It does offer a lively bar and a rooftop solarium but the dining room menu is miserable – the average choice is between an omelette or 'dish of the day'. The options for either shopping or night-life are also very limited. The Meia Praia has an isolated location three miles from town in an unattractive suburb and has a decidedly shabby appearance. An average size swimming pool sits in the middle of a cramped and sometimes crowded sun terrace area. The hotel is clean and comfortable inside, but night-life and shopping in the immediate area are minimal and this is by no means one of the Algarve's better hotels.

Barely a mile west of Lagos at PRAIA DONA ANA lies probably the most photographed and naturally beautiful beach in the Algarve. A small island firmly landlocks a rich blue lagoon and, although only a few hundred yards wide, this busy little cove is surrounded by some truly spectacular rock formations and beaches. Centuries of wind and weather have carved these elegant sandstone sculptures in a multitude of rich colours which can be seen at their best from the top of the largest cliff. Well-worn steps lead the way safely to the top in order to make this possible.

A number of other beaches have been formed within easy reach of Praia Dona Ana's main cove but none are quite as spectacular. Most are signposted and all a good steep walk away from your resort hotel. A few such beaches are awkward to get to and only really reached if you are prepared to scramble down cliffsides or swim round from another point on the coast. This, obviously, makes them quite isolated and if you do decide to visit one, always remember how you plan to get back again. It is also worth bearing in mind that many of these beaches disappear altogether at high tide.

PONTA DA PIEDADE is the extreme point of the coast jutting out from Lagos and from the lighthouse here you will get a fantastic viewpoint from which to admire the Algarve sunset. During the summer boat trips are available from the point, and from Praia Dona Ana, to take you right round this remarkable stretch of coastline. Only the one rather basic seasonal café has appeared round about the main beach at Praia Dona Ana and, beyond this, there are no other facilities for eating or entertainment away from the hotels.

Praia Dona Ana's only hotel is the modern four-star **Golfinho** (Tel: 630-01) built near to the main cove. Curiously, the room prices vary quite starkly according to the view across the cove or otherwise. Offering average four-star accommodation with few extra touches, the Golfinho has a good beach location but is, nevertheless, just far enough out of Lagos to make you feel isolated if you tire of sun, sand or even the hotel's impressive bowling alley. The only other accommodation close to the beach is the **Via Dona Ana** apartments, which are quiet and comfortable, but little used by British tour operators. Thomson Holidays, however, awarded them one of their prestigious Gold Awards in 1986 in their 'Villas and Apartments' category.

The coastline rises from Ponta da Piedade and carries on round for a couple of miles until you reach the small town of **LUZ**, and its curving beach **PRAIA DA LUZ**. This stretch is known as Porto de Mós and the best way to reach it is through the car park half way along its two mile length, where the only beach facilities are located. Praia da Luz is one of the few places in the western Algarve which has a watersports centre, with scuba diving, water skiing, sailing, surfing and windsurfing.

The old fishing village of Luz has been rather swamped by the tourist invasion of the past decade, although the name usually printed in holiday brochures, and where most of the hotel and apartment developments have been constructed, is Praia da Luz on the outskirts of the village. It is by no means the perfect Algarve resort because of the substantial intrusion the fishing industry still makes into the day-to-day life of the village. Luz was first settled by the Romans who built and later abandoned great brine tanks here. The Moors were known to have fished for whales in the early 13th century from Luz and, by the 18th century, a modest **fortress** was erected to guard against pirates from North Africa and beyond, the remains of which you can still see today high on a hill beside the village. The only other attraction in Luz is the small **church** whose enormous tower is distinctly out of proportion with the rest of it. The church tower was destroyed during an aerial bombing attack in 1941, but was lovingly rebuilt by local people whose religious devotion remains as strong now as it has been for many centuries.

A steep cliff wall dominates Praia da Luz, separating it from Porto de Mós, and offering visitors some magnificent views over the resort and beyond to Lagos. The best vantage point to see this broad view is at ATALIA, though it is quite a climb which is not really recommended unless you are used to steep slopes. Some of the Portuguese Tourist Board's own literature reckons that if you do make it to the summit you may find that the feeling of freedom is in direct proportion to the effort you have made to get there!

This stretch of coast becomes gradually more exposed to the effects of severe Atlantic winds and tides as you head towards Sagres point, and one of the more obvious results are cool day-time breezes and sandier beaches. At Praia da Luz, 500 yards or so of one of the sandiest beaches west of Faro arches round in front of the village, but you may find that small fishing boats, both in the water and moored on the beach, restrict space somewhat. Beach facilities available here are reasonable but this is by no means one of the Algarve's best beaches.

Praia da Luz offers primarily apartment accommodation through British tour operators. The village has no hotels or pensions beyond one or two private rooms so independent travellers ought to stay well away from this resort. In addition to a number of small apartment complexes, visited by a total of about twelve British operators, the main accommodation is provided by the massive **Clube Luz Bay** (Tel: 630-45) offering almost 800 beds with tidy self-catering facilities. A special children's play area has been set aside and some basic shops complement good sports facilities, which include tennis courts, a golf course and a large swimming pool.

A mile or two further along the coast from Praia da Luz lies the village of **BURGAU**, and you can best reach it by following the signposted turning from the main coast road leading on to Sagres. Burgau is a typical fishing village and also earns the name *burrie*, meaning periwinkle, by the Algarve people. It has managed to retain much of its strong character, despite the vastly increased number of visitors it has received over the last few years, and the quaintness of its narrow backstreets and thriving fishing market help testify to this.

Burgau is reckoned to be a likely target spot for tourist development within the next decade but, for the time being, it remains only a minor resort. There are only one or two hotels in the village so far, and only a handful of British tour operators offer holidays to the self-catering apartments built within easy reach of the long beach. The beach itself is about a third of a mile long, and increasingly popular with visitors to nearby Praia da Luz as well as with visitors to Burgau itself. It is an attractive spot, pleasantly sheltered by low cliffs and a reasonably safe location for children to play and bathe although facilities are rather limited. A number of fishing boats are permanently moored on the beach and around the nearby slipway.

A rather desolate stretch of coast continues to wend its way westwards beyond Burgau and on past **SALEMA**. Until relatively recently, Salema was a successful fishing village like so many of its neighbours further along the coast. Half-hidden at the foot of a few hills, the village didn't have a great deal going for it until someone built a few houses to let in the summer. A few more followed and now Salema is on the verge of becoming a major package resort.

The village still has very little to offer beyond enjoyable Algarve nostalgia and a reasonable beach. Be warned that Salema is a particularly bad spot for prospective nudists to strip off since the local police here are extremely strict about upholding the letter of the law (which technically forbids nudism anywhere in Portugal). Half a mile of exposed sand and sea, with no safety warnings, is backed by low cliffs and a few developing holiday apartment blocks. Between those, and a smart but small four-star hotel, the **Infante do Mor**, only three British operators include this peaceful spot in their brochures. It would be a good choice for comfortable isolation on the Algarve if you feel the crowds and hassles of the better known sunspots might be too much for you.

Modest beaches occur at BOCA DEL RIO, BARRANCO and FIGUEIRA on the way, but these tend to have neither facilities nor crowds so don't expect another Praia Dona Ana or Albufeira if you decide to venture down from the main road to any one of them. One of the longest and most attractive stretches of golden sand in this area is at MARTINHAL, shortly before Sagres. Generally quiet, there are no proper facilities at Martinhal yet, but like Burgau this spot is likely to be developed for the foreign tourist market within a few years.

From here the coast tucks round into the little cove of **BALEEIRA**, in the middle of which sits the undeveloped village of the same name. Baleeira today prospers as Sagres' fishing port but there is nothing of interest other than the daily fish auction and a few rows of whitewashed fishermen's houses. The village has a reputation for hospitality towards foreign visitors, most likely stemming from the fact that they receive so few each year, and this will be useful if you plan to stay here overnight. There is no accommodation available at all unless you can negotiate a private room with one of the locals.

The last resort of any size along the southern Algarve coast is **SAGRES** at the extreme western tip. This rocky escarpment protrudes out into the Atlantic from the rest of the Portuguese mainland and is in fact the most southwesterly point in Europe. This is not difficult to believe if you take ten minutes to stand and watch the huge Atlantic breakers which lash against the town's rocky promontory all year round.

Few visitors to the Algarve make the relatively short trip along the coast to Sagres, but if you are among the few who do, then you will find a bleak, rather different type of town than anywhere further east. In ancient times it was believed a temple to honour Hercules had been built near here, although if that was the case nothing now remains. A cult following also grew up around the legend of Saint Vincent, the Dean of Valencia who was executed because of his Christian faith during the reign of the Roman Emperor Diocletian in the year 304 AD. Saint Vincent's remains were cast ashore near Sagres by a storm centuries later and pilgrims in Moorish-dominated Portugal defied the authority of their invaders to build a temple in his honour. Countless loyal ravens are said to have stood watch over this tomb until such times when St Vincent's own followers could reclaim the saint's remains and have them safely interred in Lisbon cathedral. To this day, Saint Vincent is the patron saint of Portugal's capital and the raven its symbol. Only a lighthouse still stands at **Cabo São Vincente**, the desolate western point from Sagres where the temple was said to have been built and where Prince Henry the Navigator finally died in 1460.

Sagres will always be associated with the voyages of Henry the Navigator since it was here that the medieval explorer lived for forty years and built up his famous School of Navigation. Until the 15th century this place was the edge of the known world. Sailors dared travel no further lest they fell off the end of the world and in ancient times sailors would gather in Sagres to watch the sun descend and sizzle into the sea each night ready for a new one to rise next morning. Henry shattered those notions by gathering together the brightest seafaring minds of his time. Sailors, map makers, geographers, astrologers, navigators and shipbuilders all came here and became fanatically devoted to their royal master. Soon his wooden caravels set forth on journeys beyond where any known voyage had gone before, so pushing back the boundaries of knowledge about the shape of the world and helping dispel notions that it was really flat.

As ever, what little evidence there was of Henry's existence in Sagres was almost entirely swept away in the earthquake three centuries after his death. A few Gothic-style houses are known to date from his time but none had any direct association with Henry. Also, the church of **Nossa Senhora da Graça** has a 15th-century image of Santa Catarina inside which is known to date from the same period as the Navigator. The town's youth hostel and tourist office (Tel: 641-25) have been built inside the rather formidable remains of the old School of Navigation, although no relics from the 15th century have survived. The tourist office have a half-hour film depicting tales from Henry's life which you can see (in English) at least once a day. Henry's own villa is said to have adjoined this fortress-like building but there is no surviving evidence to identify where precisely the Navigator's home was. Just about the only major structure that can be positively associated with Henry is the 130-foot wide **compass** and **sundial** inside the fortification which he is reckoned to have used in pursuit of his naval studies in Sagres. A small **chapel** survives inside, too, which is Sagres' only other point of interest other than the magnificent promontory, which is said to have inspired many of Henry's ideas.

Sagres offers almost nothing in the way of night-life or good restaurants and cannot really be recommended if you are looking for either a relaxing beach resort or somewhere offering a typical flavour of the Algarve. The nearest town with a reasonable range of shops and restaurants, plus one or two popular discos, is Lagos twenty-five miles away so it is worth thinking carefully before committing yourself to Sagres' desolate appeal.

Practically the only restaurant anywhere near Sagres lies a mile or so outside the town. **Cabo São Vincente** (Tel: 641-24) is located relatively near to the lighthouse and offers mostly fish dishes in a pleasantly isolated location past the bay of BELICHE. For the independent traveller, most likely to be making his or her way to or from Lisbon, the Cabo São Vincente normally has a few rooms available but these do fill up early during the summer months.

Accommodation in Sagres itself is very limited; indeed, there is only one medium-sized three-star hotel just outside the village which is visited by most of the British tour operators to this part of the coast. The **Da Baleeira** (Tel: 642-12) is five minutes away from a good stretch of beach but, otherwise, is very isolated. All 114 bedrooms have private bathrooms and balconies, although not all rooms offer sea views. The hotel certainly provides a relaxing and 'away-from-it-all' atmosphere because of its location and both the bedrooms and public areas are smartly furnished in modern designs. Night-life is limited exclusively to the hotel's à la carte dinner menu, Portuguese television or the live music which is occasionally organized.

Heading northwards from Sagres, the coast becomes noticeably bleaker and less attractive as a potential bathing spot. Sharp cliffs rise over 150 feet once you round the point and the sight of the wild Atlantic battering the rocks below you is occasionally very spectacular. There are a number of reasonable beach areas, but these are now quite a significant distance from any of the major resorts and scarcely worth the effort of hiring a car or using public transport to reach them.

Almost without warning, the cliff line breaks for a few hundred yards at the little beach cove of TELHEIRO. The coast becomes quite steep again, going up as far as the imposing natural rock formation known as the Tower of Aspa at PONTA RUIVA. The tower has been carved out of the red sandstone as a result of thousands of years of wind and weather and now stands over 500 feet above sea level. This is the highest point above sea level anywhere on the Algarve coast and, perhaps surprisingly, one of the highest coastal points in the whole country.

Beach facilities improve for a few hundred yards at PRAIA DA CORDAMA, the nearest beach to the town of VILA DO BISPO, which we look at in the Inland section of this chapter, and again at AGUIA PRAIA and the tiny coves of MIROUÇO and MOURANITOS a little way further up the coast. One of the best sandy stretches is at PRAIA DO AMADO, a popular spot for sailing, just before the point at Bordeira.

BORDEIRA itself is a little way inland and the only modest resort along this southwestern coast. The village itself is tiny with no more than a couple of basic shops and a few houses to greet visitors. Just one British operator offers self-catering apartment holidays to Bordeira and the nearest beach is a deserted 500-yard stretch of golden sand sandwiched between two much longer lengths of cliff line. The beach is only reached by clambering down a steep rocky path and, once there, facilities of any description are non-existent. An isolated spot best suited to reclusive sunbathers without any children.

A few more relatively isolated beaches feature along the coast beyond Bordeira. The best stretches are at VALE DE FIGUEIRA, PENEDO, MONTE CLÉRIGO, and the latter is the nearest beach to the inland village of ALJEZUR which is looked at in more detail in the Inland section. Beyond here the terrain becomes dramatically more barren as the Algarve region gently merges into the southern Plains.

Inland Algarve

To many people, including most British tour operators, the Algarve region stops at the coastal resorts covered in detail in the earlier part of this chapter. What many visitors forget, or simply don't realize, is that the region stretches inland to secluded and less well known resorts, hidden within some of Portugal's most dramatic natural scenery.

Taking our starting point at the Spanish border, as we did with the coastal Algarve, this Inland section will lead you through some of the more appealing towns and villages in this long stretch of countryside. Above all else, perhaps you will discover that Inland Algarve offers seclusion and surprises away from other tourists whilst, at the same time, never being too far from those famous southern beaches which most visitors come to Portugal for.

The district of **CASTRO MARIM** reaches inland from the River Guadiana which has been a natural frontier for over 2,000 years. The town of Castro Marim was an important trading centre for the Greeks and Carthaginians, from North Africa, long before the Roman invasion. In 27 BC, the Romans declared the river a border between the provinces of Lusitania and Baetica (Portugal and Spain respectively) and this explains the strategic importance of the town's magnificent old **castle** which can still be visited today.

Sitting on top of the highest of the several small hills which overlook the valley, Castro Marim was the headquarters of the Crusading Knights of Christ before they moved to Tomar in 1334. The castle has been built and extended many times, although recent archaeological discoveries in the surrounding area have revealed that the Phoenicians had an important site here long before even the Moors arrived in the 8th century. Most of the present day castle was built by the Knights of Christ in the early 14th century, but a few traces of the Moors' 12th-century extensions still remain.

Huge **town walls**, reinforced by King João IV (1640–56), screened the city up until the time of the earthquake in 1755 and many traces of them can still be seen around the town today. You can also visit the reconstructed 14th-century **Igreja de Santiago** (Church of St James) situated near the castle. The church has been rebuilt over the last few decades, having lain in ruins since being destroyed in 1755. Its huge dome rises above the rooftops of the town and inside its broad ceiling is decorated with Holy crosses that were said to have been constructed by a Knight commander of the town's Holy Order.

Castro Marim's other attraction is the Algarve's only large **nature reserve**. Controlled by the National Park Service, the reserve was established in order to protect the region's bird life, rare shellfish and lesser known animal species, together with over 100 scarce plant specimens. A number of traditionally migratory birds remain here all year round; like many sun-seeking permanent visitors, they have little reason to leave the area.

Most of the town's visitors come on day trips from the nearby resorts of Monte Gordo or Tavira and, accordingly, Castro Marim offers no hotel accommodation or good places to eat out. If you're lucky, you can find a private room in town and there are a number of reasonable tavernas and bars in Castro Marim but, like so many of these inland towns and villages, there is nowhere to recommend for the independent traveller who is intent on staying away from the coast.

The fen country of Castro Marim borders the winding road which runs northwards, roughly parallel to the Spanish border. The occasional boat passing along the river is about the liveliest thing to look out for as you pass through the villages of AZINHAL and ODELEITE on the way up to ALCOUTIM. Odeleite is best known for its wicker baskets, on display all over the village and available in every shape and size. There is a popular fishing spot at the wide river point of GUERREIROS DO RIO. Old artisan fishing nets are cast across the water by practised locals and gently hauled in again full of small fish some time later.

Once you reach Alcoutim, the most northerly village generally accepted as part of the Algarve, you may well believe that life has finally come to a firm halt. Whether or not that is the case, the pace of life in the village is much slower than along the coast. The old **castle** once stood guard over the streets of simple whitewashed houses and the **church** is one of the most appealing in this eastern part of the region. A Renaissance portal complements the bas-relief baptistry which is said to date from the second half of the 16th century. The village offers perfect tranquillity for an afternoon away from the beaches, although it may be a little too far inland to be practical for a short day trip.

Occasionally boat trips can be negotiated with local fishermen at any point down the river and this is a novel way of seeing this part of the region. Take care to negotiate a return trip before you leave your starting point! Tiny villages are scattered all across the north-east corner of the region, many of which are not even marked on tourist maps, and linked to the outside world by single-track dirt roads. This is the least populated Algarve region and the least attractive as well since it is made up of no more than one huge great plateau. There are no forests for miles, only patches of olive trees and open farming with ancient manual ploughs.

The main village is **MARTIM LONGO**, a cluster of houses linked by two churches at either end of the main street; the parish church dedicated to Senhora da Conçeião and the chapel of São Sebastião. The village sees a number of festivities each year, notably on Corpus Christi day, and these attract locals from neighbouring villages and tourists alike. Of the other villages, only Giões is worth visiting with its beautiful old church containing images with much religious significance dating back several centuries.

PRIVATE.
Keep Out

The road southwards to Cachopo takes you past a number of picturesque, if isolated, villages which all offer splendid vantage points if you are interested in the region's natural history. The terrain becomes more mountainous and you can detect a chilliness in the inland air throughout the year as you climb higher. You may enjoy a stroll through the villages of MEALHA, if you are travelling from the north, or AGUA DOS FUSOS or PORTELA if you are travelling from the coast, if you want the opportunity to experience the atmosphere of a typically quaint traditional Algarve village.

CACHOPO itself offers more of the same tranquillity, with its tiny church of **Santo Estêvão** in the centre of the village. The church has a solid, if outsized, tower and sits in a small square which is a popular meeting point for the people of its village. Fairs are held here throughout the year and tourist offices in any of the coastal resorts ought to be able to give you some indication when these are held since they vary from year to year.

A desolate, largely mountainous, area known as Serra do Caldeirão sweeps westwards from here and the whole area becomes even less populous than before. It is an awkward part of the region to cross since much of it is wild and uninhabited, and still said to be home to many wild boar. The mountain summit occurs at PELADOS, some 1,800 feet above sea level, but the nearest village is VALE DE ROSA. This is an inviting place to stop for an hour or so, but only really practical as an excursion if you can hire a car for a day or so. From Vale de Rosa the landscape becomes truly magnificent. You can see for miles across the valley and the rooftops. Cool mountain streams break the silence and monotony of the hot summer sunshine and the whole scene is as spectacular as it is isolated.

Several villages lie between this mountainous area and the popular stretch of coast between Tavira and Faro. **MONCARAPACHO** is a modest village a little way inland from Olhão which contains some fine examples of typical Algarve architecture. The **church** is striking as you enter the village, with its beautiful Renaissance portal dating back to the 16th century. Figures representing the Passion of Christ surround the door arch and images of Saint Paul and Saint Peter stand proudly above the cornice. Three naves stand inside behind the Renaissance chapel and evidence of Gothic architecture can still be seen on the high altar.

The village's **parish church** has an attractive side portico, and also worth visiting is the **Chapel of Santo Cristo** which contains many ivory images said to have been the cause of several miracles in earlier generations. Nearby a small **museum** containing exhibits of a mostly local nature is open most days.

A short distance further on from Moncarapacho is SÃO MIGUEL, a small village built on a hill over 1,300 feet above the coast. It commands glorious views in all directions, but the view southeastwards over Faro is the finest. On a clear day it is reckoned that you can see as far west as Vila Real or even Ayamonte over in Spain. Down below you almond and fig trees are planted for miles around and the landscape is broken only by a large radio transmitter aerial.

Some six miles north-east of Faro, is the village of **ESTÓI** which is fast becoming a popular excursion from the regional capital. Still largely undeveloped despite the number of visitors who come here each summer, Estói lies on a hillside and contains an attractive **church** which, unusually, dates back to well before the 1755 earthquake. Estói's main feature, though, is a remarkable palace which is well worth seeing. Built in the last years of the 18th century and remodelled about a hundred years later, the **Paláçio do Visconde de Estói** was decorated by the best artists of the day and stands a majestic three storeys high.

Although the building itself is not open to the public, the sprawling gardens are, and the walkways here are lined with busts of German emperors, Greek gods and Portuguese monarchs. The terraces are decorated with Roman mosaics and fountains cascade into elegant pools and ornamental rockeries. There is no entrance fee, but the porter who lets you in (when you ring the bell at the main gate) ought to be tipped.

Half a mile west of Estói lies **MILREU**, arguably the Algarve's first ever resort since it was a popular holiday destination with the Romans who knew it as Ossónoba. Once a thriving town, only ruins now remain for visitors to see and, as you wander round, you will be able to make out where the temple, spa and even a casino once stood. The remains of a number of houses have been uncovered but very little of this rather sad place has been excavated.

Continuing the road upwards again, you will pass through SANTA

CATERINA, an unspecial village built around a main road junction. Much more interesting is **SÃO BRÁS DE ALPORTEL** a few miles further west. This growing resort town has a long history and was the birthplace of the Portuguese poet and Governor of Silves, Ibne Ammar. Its earliest records date back to the 16th century when it was no more than a remote mountain village, but a thriving cork industry grew up and the village quickly expanded. In 1596 British forces, after sacking Faro, were swiftly beaten back by the people of São Brás who became known as cudgel-wielders for decades afterwards. The town today has a number of old buildings which are worth visiting, and the most traditional part of São Brás, as a whole, lies a little way south of the road Loulé-Vila Real, between Rua Teófilo Braga and Rua Pires Rico. The narrow backstreets lead down to a large **church** with a prominent temple dedicated to Senhora dos Passos. Numerous other paintings, carvings and artifacts inside date back to the 18th century. As you head back towards the town centre, the buildings become taller and more numerous and cramped together. A large **market** operates most days in the centre near the wide public gardens.

Night-life and eating out in town are restricted to a few local cafés and tavernas, unless you are prepared to go to nearby **SANTA BÁRBARA DE NEXE**, or even as far south as Faro itself. São Brás is unusual for a town of its size for having no large hotels. Indeed, the Portuguese Tourist Board acknowledges only one or two reasonable pensions in the town. **Pensão Santo António** (Tel: 421-75) on Poços dos Ferreiros is a tidy three-star place, but contains only ten rooms so advance booking is essential. Meon Villa Holidays, based in Hampshire, is the only British operator providing the option of holidays specifically to São Brás and they offer only self-catering apartment accommodation.

A few miles west, along the main road, lies the prosperous market town of **LOULÉ**. The craftsmen of Loulé are reckoned to be direct descendants of a Moslem community which sought refuge here after the Christian reconquest of the region in the mid-13th century. The town's most striking feature today is its chimneys. Chimneys are very much an art form in Portugal and nowhere better in the Algarve will you be reminded of this fact than in Loulé where they dominate the sky line for miles around.

Little remains of the town's medieval **castle** in the centre of town, although it is now possible to visit one or two of its towers and enjoy the magnificent views as a result of recent restoration work. The **Sanctuary of Mãe Soberana** is near here, amidst a cluster of older buildings, and a small **museum** has been built near the castle grounds. One of the more interesting features of the museum is the pre-Conquest well just outside the main door. A large number of older stones are also on display inside which originally came from the castle surrounds.

The neighbouring streets will take you through the oldest parts of town although, sadly, virtually none of these fine buildings pre-date the 1755 earthquake. One fine exception is the **parish church**, erected by King Dinis (1279–1325) in the later years of the 13th century; this contains three large naves and a huge Renaissance arch. Look out for the 17th-century painted tiles and the beautiful religious paintings completed in the latter half of the 18th century. A large public park, **Jardim dos Amuados**, sits opposite the parish church on land that was formerly part of the churchyard.

Another church worth visiting is the church of the **Misericórdia**, on Avenida Marçal Pacheco. Resembling a huge cake, this 16th-century building was originally built to look after the wounded in Afonso V's Tangier campaign. The building still looks after the sick today in its capacity as Loulé's health centre.

A large **market** is held each morning near the health centre, where traditional handicrafts are one of the main attractions for visitors to the town. The town hall lies on the Plaça da República, a broad avenue which slopes down from the main market area. You'll also see near here a number of old buildings, including the **school**, with balustrades and wrought-iron work dating back to the last century.

Loulé is only just beginning to become popular as a tourist resort, with only a couple of British operators offering self-catering holiday accommodation in the town. There are no reasonable hotels and only a few two-star pensions with less than a hundred bedrooms between them. **Pensão-restaurante Avenida** (Tel: 627-35) along Avenida José da Costa Mealha is reasonable and is one of the few places in town offering good local food. It is open daily except Sundays until 10pm and occasionally features live entertainment. **Pensão Ibérica** (Tel: 620-27) on Avenida Marçal Pacheco is the largest in town, with accommodation for three dozen people available.

A few miles south of Loulé lies the secluded hamlet of **SANTA BÁRBARA DE NEXE** which is becoming one of Inland Algarve's most popular resort destinations. Santa Bárbara is no more than a modest hamlet, but it can boast a four-star hotel. Only two British tour operators use the Hotel La Réserve, but a few more offer self-catering apartment holidays to modest villa complexes scattered around the outskirts of the village.

Santa Bárbara prides itself on maintaining its Gothic **parish church**, one of the oldest intact buildings in the Algarve dating back to the 15th century. The church contains some elegant Manueline ornaments and is known particularly for its fine display of 17th-century tiles along the aisles, in the vestry and in the triumphal arch where angels crown the region's patroness.

The **Hotel La Réserve** (Tel: 914-74) sits in six acres of its own country estate and this reclusive paradise is the only hotel in Portugal recommended as a member of 'Relais and Châteaux'. A total of twenty suites are available, at very high prices, for wealthy visitors who seek the ultimate in seclusion without feeling too isolated. English is spoken by most staff, and all twenty suites offer glorious sea views with private terrace balconies, television, radio, direct-dial international telephones and kitchenette areas. Two swimming pools are available for residents.

Adjoining the hotel is a restaurant of the same name, which offers similarly high standards and the finest in international cuisine, with an emphasis on French. Without a doubt one of Portugal's finest dining places, the £20 plus per head (including wine) will be thoroughly well spent. Local duckling served with new potatoes and huge local prawns in succulent rich sauces are among the numerous specialities available.

The village of SALIR lies some way to the north-west of Loulé. Winding streets are built on the hillside to the west of the village's crumbling castle. The castle is no more than a tower and two walls, increasingly hidden by the spreading roots of carob trees which are used by the locals as screens to protect beans and peas from the wind. Salir remains totally undeveloped, and the natural scenery in the surrounding area is very beautiful.

The main road westwards takes you through ALTE, a small village built round a picturesque little church with some remarkable tiles dating back to the 16th century. A hike to the top of any one of the four surrounding hills offers some of the best views of this central Algarve region. Between here and the coast, only the villages of Paderne and Boliqueime will interrupt your countryside journey.

PADERNE's origins before the time of the Moors are uncertain, although the village's name is believed to have been derived from the Latin word *paterno*. The ruins of a Moorish **castle** can still be seen although there are scarcely more than patches of wall and a tower remaining. A large stream runs through the immediate area which is surrounded by orange blossom and holm oak before you reach the sloping village itself.

A **church** lies half-way up the hillside on which Paderne has been built, and reveals a number of Manueline features in its chancel and façade which date it to the 16th century. Look out for the attractive bas-relief triumphal arch and a few images inside which are said to have been recovered from the castle chapel in the aftermath of the earthquake in 1755.

Nearby Boliqueime stretches down a steep hill shortly before the coast. It has nothing particularly worth seeing; even its simple white church is rather plain. But both Paderne and Boliqueime are easily accessible from the coastal resorts of Albufeira and Vilamoura so would be reasonable day trips away from the beaches if you wanted to see a little of inland Portugal.

Further inland again, the main road westwards continues on to **SÃO BARTOLOMEU DE MESSINES**. The village has an annual fair during the summer and, although not visited by any British tour operator, has some attractive self-catering apartments. **Apartamentos Turisticos Larga Vista** (Tel: 453-87) have a number of apartments available during the summer months. Facilities in the village are extremely limited if good restaurants and night-life are important to you, but for a relaxing, tranquil setting in the Inland Algarve region this is one of the best locations.

The road descends south-west from São Bartolomeu towards the town of **SILVES** and the River Arade runs past the quiet little town whose earliest traces date back over 2,000 years to the 4th century BC. The Romans arrived soon afterwards, to find a thriving market town already known as Cilpes, and built roads, bridges and industry in the surrounding area. But it was the Moors, who arrived in the Algarve in 711 AD, to whom Silves owes its oldest surviving monuments.

The town is spread evenly over the top of a huge, flat hill and easily the most prominent feature is the massive Moorish **fortress** right at the summit. Although built on the site of a Roman citadel, the fortress was heavily fortified by the Moors and one of its more immediately striking features (apart from its sheer size) are the two reservoirs which were built for the building's exclusive use.

The castle survived the 1755 earthquake well, though not entirely unscathed since evidence of 'modern' reconstruction can be clearly seen. It is still possible, however, to explore most of the surviving walls and towers and appreciate the commanding views which successive generations of warriors from the Romans onwards have enjoyed. You will see a sixty-foot deep Moslem **well**, thought to date from Almohades times in the later 12th century, and believed to be unique outside the Middle East.

Silves' **cathedral** (*sé*) was originally built in the 13th century on the site of a large Moorish mosque. Originally the home of the Algarve bishopric before it was transferred to Faro, Silves' cathedral is a huge three-nave temple which still retains the tomb of King João II and a number of important medieval wood carvings. The carvings in the chapel of Santíssimo date from the 18th century, but the high altar is said to pre-date that significantly.

Elsewhere in the town you can still see an old **bridge** with six arches, built in the 15th century and probably on the site of a Roman bridge of similar design. The **Chapel of the Misericórdia** was also built around the 15th century, although only its commanding portal remains intact in the present day building from before the earthquake.

Most of the town's other buildings were erected in the 19th century, including the hospital and council hall, but it is reasonable to suggest that to understand the history of Silves is to understand the history of the Algarve itself. Like so many towns and villages, Silves was prospering before being almost totally wiped out in 1755. A long, slow process of recovery continues to this day and the increase in the number of tourists has made a vital contribution to the town's development. Bonvista Travel Services Ltd, based in Chelmsford, are the only British tour operator to visit Silves – self-catering apartments on the outskirts of town – but this will doubtless change before too long. Discover Silves soon, if you can.

From Silves, it is only a few miles south to **LAGOA**, a popular day trip from the nearby coastal resorts of Armação de Pêra and Carvoeira. Lagoa has been an administrative centre for a number of decades and really has little to offer visitors other than a change of pace from the beaches. The town surrounds the **Praça da República**, which has a number of beautiful buildings surrounding it. The parish church dates only from the last century, but has some ornate gold décor outside.

Beyond Lagoa, the road continues along the coast towards Portimão or else begins to wind sharply northwards towards Monchique. On the way you will pass through **CALDAS DE MONCHIQUE**, one of the Algarve's best-known spa resorts famous since Roman days. The Moors used to visit here, and even King João II turned to it in 1495 in the hope of finding a cure for his dropsy. It failed. Five enormous natural springs pump out around 4 million gallons of water every day, and if you suffer from stomach ailments or rheumatism then the healing waters are said to be particularly helpful.

The area around here is surrounded by low mountains rising well over 2,000 feet into the warm Algarve air. **MONCHIQUE** itself is a quaint market town and a centre for local handicrafts, with scarcely a single street that doesn't twist and curve its way up the side of the hill on which the town has been built. The town has certain similarities to many smaller towns in the Highlands of Scotland and the surrounding countryside helps complete this image.

To see this area at its best, you really need to hire a car and either drive along these quiet, winding country roads or else set off on foot from Monchique for a day or even an afternoon's hike. The town itself is slowly developing as an inland resort and has one or two points of interest for visitors other than ready access to the Highlands of Portugal.

The **parish church** is the oldest monument in Monchique and you will probably spot it from quite a distance before you reach the town. A large building, the church has five huge stone columns and an attractive Manueline portal by the door. Smaller portals from the same period skirt the building all round. The chancel inside is elegantly framed by a semicircular arch of angels, standing guard over an Emperor's crown. Only the chapel of the Santíssimo inside survives from before the 1755 earthquake and the ornate decoration suggests it may once have been a chapel of the souls.

Further up the hillside, on the Rua do Porto Fundo, you can see the church of the **Misericórdia**. The building, which was recently restored, dates back to the late 18th century and includes some fine period carvings. The small, baroque-style **shrine of Senhor dos Passos** is also nearby and has two belfries enclosing a holy statue which is carried through the village every year during Lent.

You may notice that the surrounding countryside differs noticeably from elsewhere in the Algarve region. The colour of soil changes, as does the type of vegetation and even the climate since the rainfall is significantly higher around Monchique. The higher-than-usual rainfall combines with almost tropical summer temperatures to create a humidity unique in Portugal which makes the growing of yams, chestnuts, walnuts and even bananas quite common. The effects of unusual weather are worth bearing in mind if you are thinking about staying in Monchique for any length of time; the rainfall and humidity can spoil a visit to this part of the region if you have not anticipated it.

If this rather isolated Inland resort appeals to you, about half a dozen British tour operators offer a range of self-catering apartment, or pension, holidays. The best place to stay in town is the four-star estalagem **Abrigo da Montanha** (Tel: 921-31), although even out of season there are only a few rooms available for let. The **Bela Vista** pension, in the town's main square, is one of the best hopes for independent travellers. There are also a few reasonable eating places in the town, including the **Restaurante Chorette** on Rua Dr Samora Gil, but don't expect big resort comforts at any of these Inland towns or villages.

The village of CASAIS lies a few miles west and the only remarkable feature here seems to be the *lack* of whitewashed houses. White frames surround doors and windows, set against brightly coloured walls. MARMELETE is a slightly better known village another few miles west offering a similar traditional atmosphere far away from the Algarve's main tourist routes. The scenery around is quite something but car hire will be essential if you wish to enjoy it since bus services to these isolated villages are very intermittent.

Further south there are a number of villages scattered along the maze of tiny roads that criss-cross the region, but none are worth a special visit unless you really find yourself at a loose end and want to explore the Inland area for yourself. One possible exception is the village of **ALCALAR** within easy reach of the coastal resorts of Praia da Rocha, Portimão and Praia dos Três Irmãos and Alvor. You will need to look carefully to avoid missing it, but shortly before you enter the village there is an ancient **neolithic necropolis**. Not a lot remains of this prehistoric monument, other than a number of obvious holes in the ground (obvious, that is, once you know where to look) where Stone Age residents buried their dead. Recently excavated human remains and pottery artifacts have helped historians piece together the early history of the site and the best of these discoveries can be seen in the town museum in Lagos. It is reckoned that a number of the later graves were dug during the Iron Age and some could even be as recent as the time of Henry the Navigator in the 15th century; a curious site.

Not too far away from the old burial site, just off the main road leading towards Portimão, is the ruined church of **Senhora do Verde**. Almost hidden behind rich woodland, this once impressive building has been derelict for generations. The site was built in honour of the Virgin Mary and has an unusually strong religious significance since it was said that the Virgin herself once appeared on the bank of the stream which runs nearby.

A few more villages lie between Portimão and Lagos, and collectively these will make an interesting excursion if you feel like hiring a car and taking things at your own pace for a day. The beautifully named **MEXILHOEIRA GRANDE** is a typical Algarve farming village; these are about as common Inland as fishing villages are along the coast. The immediate countryside is irrigated by the nearby Bravura dam, set in a couple of square miles of barren farmland, and the village today is a curious combination of traditional Algarve architecture and less appealing modern buildings. The parish church has a side portico in a Manueline design, and was restored heavily at the end of the last century.

ODEÁXERE and SARAÇAL have little to offer, although you may be interested to know that Odeáxere is one of many surviving Moorish names for villages in this part of the region. The prefix *ode-* implies somewhere connected with water and you will see a small lagoon just outside the village. Right beside the lagoon is a wide, flat area which was used as a landing strip in the pioneering days of aviation when aeroplanes had to make a break in their journey between Casablanca and Lisbon. If you've ever seen the film *Casablanca* then you'll know how famous this journey was in wartime.

Further west, the Inland region becomes noticeably more bleak. Other than Sagres, there are no major coastal resorts beyond Praia da Luz and similarly few places of note in the corresponding areas away from the beaches. The main road continues west from Lagos through the villages of BÚDENS and RAPOSEIRA. Of the two, Búdens is worth making a detour to visit if only to see its 18th-century parish church with some marvellous period garments. A **shrine** to Saint Lawrence stands on the opposite side of the narrow street from the church. The saint was said to have been a fine matchmaker and it is still occasionally believed that courting couples can expect good fortune if they stand together under his image!

A narrow road branches off towards the mountains from Búdens, but is not recommended unless you are an experienced walker used to rough roads. You will reach Raposeira soon enough if you carry on along the main road, although the village only comes to life during the first few days of September when the **annual market** is held. Raposeira grew up from the trade of cattle and cereals farmed locally and the atmosphere during those hectic market days will be a particularly enjoyable contrast if you've left a large town or city to escape to rural Portugal for a couple of weeks.

Further along the road is VILA DO BISPO, a sprawling old village scattered across a wide hill. It has an attractive **parish church**, with its inside walls completely covered in decorative blue and white tiles. The main arch, and the pulpit, are good examples of rural baroque art dating from the later 18th century. The village is known locally as the Algarve Granary because of the people's ability to farm wild land round about it. Quality cereals, almonds, figs and cork suitable for exporting are all produced.

The main road northwards from Vila do Bispo will eventually take you to Lisbon and contains no real surprises until after the Algarve merges with the southern Plains beyond Odeceixe. The scenery is beautiful, particularly if you can detour down one of countless tiny dirt roads to appreciate the stunning clifftop coastline which you won't really be able to see anywhere along the main road. There are a few good beaches within easy reach from the road, and these are outlined in the earlier section of this chapter.

If making the long trek north by car, you may be lucky to find a quiet traverna in one of the small villages of CARRAPATEIRA or ALFAMBRAS. The largest village in this north-west Inland section is **ALJEZUR**, which stretches out over three hilltops; an old **castle** rests on top of one of them offering by far the best views over the surrounding area. The castle was seriously damaged by the earthquake in 1755 but the remains of a large water-tank are well worth seeing. This was the last stronghold in southern Portugal to be recaptured from the Moors in the 13th century. Modern day Aljezur was founded by a charter granted by King Manuel I in 1504 and is today spread across some of the most naturally beautiful countryside anywhere in the Algarve. The village has a peculiar layout, appearing to be split into old and new halves by fields of melon and sweet potato. Local history recalls that this unusual division was ordered by Bishop Francisco Gomes de Avelar in an attempt to protect the residents from a plague of mosquitoes.

The beaches near Aljezur are the best along the sharp western coast and MONTE CLÉRIGO, nearest the village, was the best known seaside resort in the centuries before the main developments began along the milder southern shores. The distinctive breeze near here is one of many reasons why the southern coast was chosen.

Madeira

HISTORY

Lying in the Atlantic, 535 nautical miles south-west of Lisbon, is the archipelago of Madeira, including Madeira itself, a smaller island twenty-three miles to the north-east called Porto Santo and a number of deserted islets.

The beautiful island of Madeira is popularly known as Flor do Oceano, or Flower of the Ocean. From the sea, seen by day, it is a wonderful sight, rising lush and green from the deep blue of the ocean, its characteristic outline shaped by high sea cliffs and terraces hewn from its inland peaks. By night, the island is equally distinctive; a thousand points of light glowing in the night.

The island was officially discovered by João Gonçalves Zarco, a protégé of Prince Henry the Navigator, in 1419. At that time it was uninhabited and covered in dense forest and vegetation. Prior to this, however, it was known to the Phoenicians – primarily for the purple dye produced there – and legend claims that it is part of the lost continent of Atlantis. After Zarco's discovery in the 15th century, Madeira prospered from the production of sugar and later wine. Today these two industries remain, plus it is also a major international tourist destination.

Madeira, like all of the archipelago, is of volcanic origin and is steep and hilly, rising at its highest point, Pico Ruivo, to a height of 6106 feet (1861 metres). Inland there are stunningly deep valleys and gorges, often cultivated by the use of terraces. The coasts are steep and rocky, with a few strips of coastal plain but no sandy beaches: one of the island's few disadvantages as a holiday destination.

The whole of Madeira is abundant with beautiful and luxuriant vegetation which thrives in the mild, sub-tropical climate and benefits from the extensive network of irrigation canals, or *levadas*, which criss-cross the island. In addition to European deciduous trees there are large numbers of sub-tropical species such as palms, fig trees, eucalyptus, mimosa and bamboo – as well as the unique Madeira Ebony, found only here.

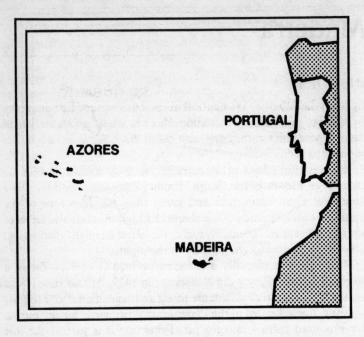

About one-third of the island is cultivated. Years of toil went into the creation of the thousands of hillside terraces which make up most of the agricultural land. The major crops are sugar cane, bananas and the vines from whose grapes the famous Madeira wine is produced. Other fruits are grown too – such as grapefruit, melons, sugar apples and passion fruits.

COMMUNICATIONS

The airport on Madeira is at the village of Santa Cruz, twelve and a half miles (19 km) from Funchal, the capital, and receives many direct flights from Europe as well as internal Portuguese transfers and connections.

The road network on the island is adequate, with an excellently engineered coastal road encircling the island, on an often spectacularly scenic route, connecting most places of importance. There are also a number of roads running right across the interior from north to

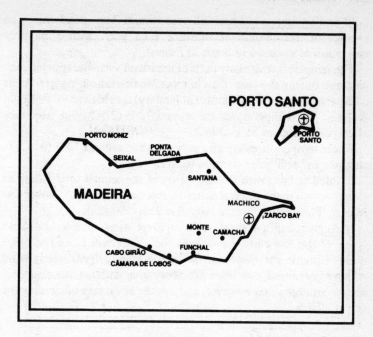

south (São Vincente to Ribeira Brava; Faiil to Funchal; Porto da Cruz to Funchal), as well as a number of roads linking villages in the interior with the coast.

There are fairly good bus and taxi services, the taxis having a black and green livery.

Other, more unusual, forms of transport on offer on the island include the famous toboggans from Monte and Terreiro da Luta to Funchal (see below); bullock drawn carts; and hammocks borne by two men – a form of transport criticized by some as archaic and demeaning for the bearers. All these forms of transport are primarily aimed at the tourist element, of course.

Very pleasant walks are often taken along the irrigation canals (*levadas*) that criss-cross the interior.

CLIMATE

 The climate is one of Madeira's major advantages as a holiday resort. Its southerly latitude makes for extremely mild and equable conditions all year round. The island enjoys an average of 2120 hours of sunshine each year, with a monthly maximum of around 250 hours in August.

The temperature in many parts of the island varies less during each day, and during the year, than in most Mediterranean resorts. At its coldest the average temperature (in January) is as high as 61°F (16°C). Average July temperatures are around 72°F (22°C), but later they often rise as high as 85°F (30°C).

Water temperatures are also very equable: around 70°F (21°C) in summer and still quite warm in winter.

Rainfall is low, with the most part of the annual total falling as cloudbursts – in the tropical pattern – especially between October and March. The annual average rainfall is 23in (590mm).

In August, a thin mist called the *capacete* often falls over the island – one of the few climate problems the visitor will face. The other minor climatic annoyance is the *leste*, a warm, dry, easterly wind which sometimes blows from Africa bringing with it a fine dust. It is not too troublesome, however, and has the advantage of clearing the sky of clouds.

SPECIALITIES

The most famous product of Madeira is the wine that bears its name. There are three main types of Madeira: Malmsey, Sercial and Boal. Malmsey is a sweet dessert wine and Sercial a very dry one – often drunk as an aperitif. Boal, and another type, Verdelho, fall between the two extremes.

Other specialities include the tropical fruits grown on the island – pawpaw, avocado, passion fruit and, especially, banana.

There is some excellent fresh fish available on Madeira and tuna fish steaks with fried maize (*bife de atum e milho frito*) is a popular dish. Black scabbard fish, beef cooked on a spit (*espetada*) and Madeira honey cake (*bolo de mel*) are other local delicacies.

Madeira is also well known for its embroidery and tapestry (*tela*). It is very expensive, however, so you need to shop around.

WHERE TO GO FOR WHAT

There is much on Madeira to suit most kinds of tourist or traveller.

The sightseer is supremely well catered for, as is the nature lover. Both will be treated to a feast of stunning natural scenery, particularly at Camara de Lobos, Cabo Girão (the world's second highest sea cliff), Santana and Curral das Freiras. There are also a good deal of man-made sights – churches, museums, architecture and the like – especially in Funchal.

The sun worshipper is also well catered for with 2,000 hours or more of sunshine each year and warm temperatures all year round.

The socialite will not perhaps find Madeira *the* most exciting holiday venue, but should not be bored, as Funchal's top hotels provide a number of night-clubs – as well as the casino. Nevertheless, much of the tourist emphasis in Madeira has been on the older age groups with less interest in 'night-life', although this is less so now than previously.

Madeira is a busy tourist resort, but despite this the recluse may be content in one of the quieter hotels in Funchal, relaxing peacefully by the pool. The island of Porto Santo, twenty-three miles north-east of Madeira, would probably ideally suit this sort of person as excursions and hotels here are available, but little tourist development has yet taken place.

Funchal

The life of Madeira centres on its capital, which is home to half the island's population. Attractively situated on the south coast of the island, Funchal is the only large port and sees considerable amounts of international shipping and cruise liners.

The town is a popular holiday destination and its steep, basalt cobbled streets provide a wealth of interest for all kinds of visitor.

The **cathedral** (*sé*) is in Manueline style and dates from the late 15th century, when it was the first cathedral in Portugal's colonies. The exterior is simple and not especially remarkable. Inside, however, the décor is more elaborate and of particular interest is the Moorish juniper wood ceiling with carving and ivory inlays. The cathedral is also noted for its lava archways and stained glass windows.

South of the cathedral, towards the seafront promenade of Avenida do Mar is the old **customs house** (Antiga Alfândega) dating from the

16th century. A little way westwards along the promenade is the **Palacio de São Lourenço**, a 16th-century fort now used as the Governor's Palace. Immediately in front, projecting out into the ocean, is the **Cais**, a long landing stage. Walk out to the end and enjoy an excellent view of the town.

Close by the Palace is the **Teatro** (theatre), standing on one side of the **Jardim de São Francisco**, a luxuriant park, with many tropical plants, including a number of palms.

It is not far from the park to the **Madeira Wine Association**'s building – an old convent at 28 Avenida Arriaga (Tel: 20121). The vast, vaulted store rooms are filled with hundreds of oak casks of Madeira wine. The walls are decorated with interesting murals showing the treading of the grapes. The Association is open to visitors and you can sample the many fine wines on offer.

From here, it is a short walk to the Praça do Infante and the nearby 15th-century **Chapel of Santa Catarina**. Beyond this little chapel is the **Parque de Santa Catarina**, in which stands the **Quinta da Vigia**, a fine old house which was once the home of an Austrian empress, but is now a casino. There is a marvellous view of Funchal from here.

From the northern side of the Jardim de São Francisco, the Rua da Carreira leads to the **Praça do Municipio**, the main square of the town with attractive black and white half-moon shaped paving stones. The **Town Hall** (*Camara Municipal*) is also in black and white, the whitewashed walls contrasting with black basalt stonework. In the square, too, is the 17th-century church of **São João Evangelista** and, on the south side, the former Bishop's Palace, now the **Museum of Sacred Art**, with 15th- and 16th-century Portuguese and Flemish pictures.

To the north-west of the city, on Calçado do Pico is the church of **Santa Clara**, which houses the tomb of the supposed discoverer of Madeira – João Zarco. Nearby is the **Quinta das Cruzes**, Zarco's former residence. It stands in a pleasant park with some beautiful orchids and is open daily (except Sundays) from 10am–noon and 2pm–6pm. Inside is a museum with fine antique English furniture, silver and china, and some unique chests constructed from the boxes used in the sugar trade in the 17th century. Further on up the Calçado do Pico is the 17th-century **Forte de São João do Pico**.

The church of **Nossa Senhora do Soccoro** is across town, towards the eastern end of the promenade. This is the base for an annual procession on 1 May, held in memory of the plague which beset the town in the mid-16th century. Nearby is the **market** (*mercado*), a colourful and busy place, with vendors offering a variety of fish and various fruits, including plums, cherries, avocados and freshly picked bananas.

Another interesting place to visit is the **City Museum and Aquarium**. The fascinating aquatic exhibits include moray eels, scorpion fish, turtles and sea cucumbers. The Aquarium is at 31 Rua da Mouraria (Tel: 29761).

Accommodation in the town is plentiful and covers the whole range of comfort, class and cost, from five-star international hotels – of which there are five – to small, cheap and comfortable guest-houses. The five-star **Reid's Hotel** is renowned worldwide, and justifiably so, as it is probably the best on the island. It stands in eleven acres of beautiful, luxuriant gardens, perched on the edge of the coast. There are 165 air-conditioned rooms, of which 150 face the ocean. All of the rooms reach or exceed the standards expected in a hotel of this class. The excellent facilities include three saltwater pools – one perched on a ledge and reached by elevator. There are also tennis courts and the hotel will happily arrange sea fishing, sailing and water-skiing for its more sporting guests. They will also arrange these activities for non-residents for a reasonable additional charge.

The quiet, elegant public rooms with their traditional décor are luxuriously comfortable, and several have excellent sea views. **Reid's Grill** is probably the best restaurant on the island. It offers a combination of excellent English, French and Portuguese cuisine – including many specialities – and such delicacies as Scottish salmon. Meals here are not cheap, though, and could be very costly depending on your selections from the menu. Expect to pay at least £14 per head for an averagely priced choice. Reid's Hotel, and the Grill, are at 139 Estrada Monumental (Tel: 23001).

The **Casino Park Hotel** is another luxurious five-star establishment, but, in contrast to the old-world dignity of Reid's, is of modern – though tasteful – design: by Oscar Niemeyer, architect of Brasilia. It has 400 air-conditioned rooms and a variety of pools, saunas, shops and conference facilities. There is also a health club and, as the name suggests, the **casino**. The popular night-club enjoys panoramic views.

Other top class hotels include the modern **Madeira Palácio**; the elegant **Savoy** with its **Galaxia night-club**; and the modern seventeen-storey **Sheraton** – the most expensive of the lot. The latter stands on a promontory over the bay, with excellent sea views.

None of these hotels is cheap, of course, but even if you cannot afford to stay in one, many of their excellent facilities are open to non-residents: although guests obviously have priority in most cases. There is also a good selection of middle range, middle priced hotels. One example is the **Hotel Santa Isabel**, Avenida do Infante (next to the Savoy). Small and welcoming, it provides very good facilities (Tel: 23111).

At the budget end of the market, there is also a good selection available. The **Quinta da Penha de França** at 2 Rua de Penha de França is a stylish old house, laden with antique furniture, silver and paintings. It has a fair sized pool, bar, currency exchange and lots of atmosphere (Tel: 29087). The **Hotel Madeira**, 21 Rua Ivens (Tel: 30071) enjoys an ideal, central position next to a park. Clean and hospitable, it has a rooftop pool, with panoramic views of the town and sea.

The absence of any beaches on Madeira means that a hotel with a pool is a big advantage, but if your accommodation does not have such a facility then there is the excellent **Lido Swimming Complex** on Rua do Gorgulho. The Olympic-size pool is open from 8am to 7pm.

For dining out with style, try the above mentioned Reid's Grill. In a more economical, but still high quality range is the **Restaurante Caravela**, at 15–17 Avenida do Mar (Tel: 28464). A modern building, it stands on the waterfront, and you can enjoy the view as you dine on the glazed terrace. It offers both local and international dishes and is open every day (lunch, noon–3pm, dinner, 6.30pm–10pm).

For a cheap but enjoyable meal of local food in a pleasant and unusual setting, try the **Bar-Restaurante A Gruta** on Estrada da

Partinha. The restaurant is in a cave set into the ancient defensive wall overlooking the harbour. Friendly and economical, an ample meal, with wine, will cost about £5.

A couple of good bars to sample in the evening are the **Prince Albert**, and the **Bar on the Rocks**. The Prince Albert, on Rua da Imperatri D. Amélia is in Victorian style, with memorabilia on display. The Bar on the Rocks, Rua Carvalho Araujo, is – as the name suggests – perched on the rocks in a stunning setting. A compelling place, there is piano music on offer here in the evening.

Around the Island

Although many visitors to Madeira spend all their time in Funchal – or even in their hotel – there is a great deal to see on the island and an organized excursion, or a do-it-yourself tour, is undoubtedly worthwhile. A number of tour operators, such as Countrywide Holidays of Manchester, offer specialist rambling holidays in Madeira – an excellent idea for those who want to see a large proportion of the island's numerous sights, with the help of an expert guide.

Six miles west of Funchal, through a landscape of lush greenery and banana groves, is **CÂMARA DE LOBOS** (Wolves' Gorge). A small, sheltered fishing port set among over-hanging sea cliffs, this was a favourite spot of Sir Winston Churchill. This, its beauty and its proximity to Funchal mean that it has become something of a tourist trap and consequently it is now losing some of its tranquil charm and simplicity.

The road north of here takes one on to the village of **ESTREITO DE CÂMARA DE LOBOS**. Famous for its wine, it lies in an important Madeira wine area. Men can be seen tending the vines on the narrow terraces that cling to the mountains' edges and low cloud drifts down from time to time, adding to the atmosphere of the place. Not far from here is **Cabo Girão**, claimed to be the world's second highest sea cliff.

The coast road continues on, through the village of Campanário to the fishing port at **RIBEIRA BRAVA**. Here, you can visit an attractive 16th-century **church** or the 17th-century **fort**. The road to the north of here takes one on to the **Pousada dos Vinháticos**, another of the excellent, government-run inns. Located at SERRA DE ÁGUA, this *pousada* is built in a traditional tavern style, with a pleasant terrace. It has twenty rooms, a bar and currency exchange facilities and is an excellent base for climbing in the surrounding countryside.

Continue along the coast road and you will reach **PONTA DO SOL** with the pleasant 15th-century church of **Nossa Senhora da Luz** with its attractive ceiling paintings. Admire the coastal scenery as you drive along.

The road on the right, travelling west out of Ponta do Sol, leads to the plateau of Paúl de Serra, a popular walking area. Farther along the coast is yet another little village, CALHETA, situated amid banana plantations. From here, you can turn off into a side road which leads north to the Rabaçal hut and a viewpoint from which you can look out at the **Risco Falls** – the highest of which plunges down 300 feet – and the **Vinte e Cinco Fortes gorge**.

The road climbs on from Calheta, through PRAZERES (excellent views) to PONTA DO PARGO, at the western tip of the island, where there is a lighthouse and a footpath to the 'fisherman's beach'. Travelling onwards, round on to the northern coast of Madeira, the road twists and turns its way down to PORTO MONIZ, another small fishing port. A short distance to the south-east there are rocky coastal pools suitable for bathing.

At this point on the coast, the road runs high above the sea, passing over ledges and through tunnels carved from the cliffs. It is a spectacular, scenic stretch of road, but not perhaps one for those who suffer from vertigo.

Passing through SEIXAL, a little place which produces some excellent wine, one travels eight miles (12 km) from Porto Moniz to reach the excellent **viewpoint** out to the mouth of the Ribeiro do Santo, from which it is not far to São Vincente.

SÃO VINCENTE lies in one of the wilder parts of the island. Partly destroyed in a landslide at the start of this century, it is a good place from which to climb the 5,000 feet high (1524 m) **Pico dos Tanquinhos**. From here, there is also another way up to the popular mountain walking area on the Paúl de Serra plateau, or you can take the north-south road back to Ribeira Brava on the south coast, via Serra de Água (see above).

After Ponta Delgada, another small village perched on a high promontory, the coast road loops inland briefly before continuing on through São Jorge – which has good coastal views – to **SANTANA**.

A beautiful, strange place with an air of unreality about it, like a lost citadel in a children's storybook, it is the main town of the island's most fertile district. Its cobbled streets are edged with houses with unusual pointed thatch roofs, set in an abundance of roses and other flowers. The surrounding scenery is complete with waterfalls and deep ravines.

Take a short detour, along a rather low grade road, and one reaches the mountain hut of Casa das Queimadas on the slopes of the island's highest peak – **Pico Ruivo**.

From Santana, the road continues through magnificent coastal scenery, past Faial, and the **Penha de Aguai** (Eagle Rock) crag to the **Pontela Pass**, whence you can take the north-east EN102 road back across the forested interior to Funchal.

En route to Funchal, is SANTO DE SERRA, with the island's only golf course. There are eighteen holes, a clubhouse with lounge and bar, and clubs and caddies for hire.

Also *en route*, just outside Funchal, is **CAMACHA**, a pleasant town of 6,000 people amid orchards, which preserves many old customs and traditions. Here, one finds a basket-making co-operative in what is one of the main centres for this industry on Madeira.

Alternatively (instead of turning off for Funchal), continue from Santana down to the Machico valley and the eastern coastal area called Baia de Zarco – after Madeira's discoverer.

Baia de Zarco

The road from the northern coast leads one first to the attractive fishing town of **MACHICO**, with its stony beach. Another popular tourist haunt, it is currently undergoing substantial development, with large numbers of villas and other accommodation appearing.

The town is named after an Englishman, Machin, who was supposedly shipwrecked here, along with his lover, before Zarco discovered the island. The couple had eloped from England in 1344 and, the story goes, the woman died soon after they were marooned. Her death was quickly followed by that of her grief-stricken lover.

Sights here include a small, 17th-century **fort** above the bay and a 15th-century **church**, which has a decorative painted ceiling. In the **Capela de São Roque**, devotees of Portugal's ubiquitous *azulejo* pictures will find some examples of this art.

There are two very good hotels in Machico. The five-star **Hotel Atlantis** is a vast complex with 590 rooms (290 with bath). There are comprehensive facilities, including a pool, bar and courtesy bus to and from Funchal (Tel: 962811). Alternatively, the four-star **Hotel Dom Pedro** (Tel: 962751) has a smaller range of still very good facilities in a modern style building of 429 rooms (218 with bath).

Largest of all, however, and cheaper, but in a lower class of accommodation altogether, is the **Aldeamento Turistico Matur**, with 702 rooms.

Also to be found in Machico is a yacht club, catering for some of Madeira's more affluent visitors.

The road east of Machico leads to the whaling station of CANICAL at the eastern tip of the island, and the nearby beach at PRAINHA, which is suitable for bathing.

To the south-west, it is four and a half miles (7 km) to **SANTA CRUZ**, which is situated amid sugar and banana plantations. There is an interesting 16th-century **church**, and **town hall**, plus the airport – from which it is twelve and a half miles (19 km) to Funchal.

Inland Madeira

 In addition to the coastal sights – and the detours inland – mentioned above, there are a number of other inland sights worth visiting.

A very popular excursion with visitors to the island is the trip to **MONTE**, five miles from Funchal. Here, you can have a look at the church of **Nossa Senhora do Monte** with the iron tomb of Emperor Charles, the last of the Hapsburgs, who died in 1922. The main attraction of coming to Monte, however, is leaving it – to return to Funchal on one of the famous toboggans. These wickerwork sleds career downwards under the force of gravity, with two men running alongside, steering the toboggan with ropes and acting as brakes. Steel yourself beforehand, but it is not as dangerous as it may feel, so sit back and enjoy the scenery as it flies past.

The toboggans also run down to Funchal from **TERREIRO DA LUTA**, a little further away and a little higher up. From here, you can also travel up to the pass on **Pico Poiso** at a height of 4630 feet (1412 m) and to the spectacular viewpoint at **Pico de Arireiro** (5940 feet/1810 m).

Another worthwhile trip inland is to the famous **CURRAL DAS FREIRAS** (Nuns' Valley).

The road runs north-west from Funchal, through pleasant hillsides and woods of deciduous and eucalyptus trees to **EIRA DE SERRATO**, a saddle on the slopes of the **Pico Serrato**, which affords magnificent panoramic views of the whole central mountain range. You can either take the road or the narrow bridle path down to the remote village of Curral das Freiras, hidden in the crater of an extinct volcano and surrounded by a sea of stone.

The village, one of the most fascinating and unusual of Madeira's sights, was founded by nuns from the Convent of Santa Clara in Funchal in the 16th century as a refuge from marauding pirates.

The Azores

HISTORY

Four hundred and seventy-five miles away from the mother country which claimed and colonized them in the 15th century, the Azores span 500 miles of the Atlantic Ocean. Once believed to be the remnants of the lost continent of Atlantis, they are volcanic islands whose origins – almost disappointingly – are recent in terms of geological time. Occasional volcanic activity adds a little more matter to them, although most of the volcanoes are now considered extinct,

the last eruption having occurred on the island of Faial in 1973. The islands' geological history is shown by their rugged scenery, thermal springs and fertile volcanic soils.

The Azores consist of three mini-archipelagoes; Santa Maria and São Miguel lie closest to Portugal, Flores and Corvo stretch out towards the New World, while the remaining group of islands lies somewhere in between.

They are believed to have been settled by the Carthaginians in the 4th century BC and first appeared on a map (drawn by Italians) in 1351. However, they were uninhabited when they were 'discovered' by Diogo de Silves, a captain of Henry the Navigator, in 1427 and claimed for Portugal. Settlements sprang up during the 15th century – Flemish as well as Portuguese, especially on the island of Faial, which was given to Isabella of Burgundy in 1466.

The islands became a vital staging post in the Age of Exploration and the quest for the New World, later gaining strategic importance during the wars of the Spanish Main. The sea off Flores was the site of

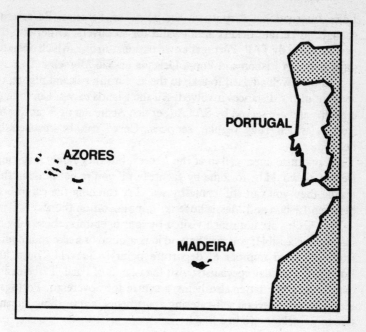

a renowned sea battle between England and Spain in 1591. Later still, Captain Cook revictualled there.

In the 19th century the islands were a centre of the now declined whaling industry. More recently, the islands' place on the transatlantic route has led many of their people to settle in the New World.

For now, they remain a haven of tranquillity, a principally agricultural archipelago gaining in importance as a tourist destination. The islands came to prominence when they were chosen as the honeymoon destination of the Duke and Duchess of York, in the summer of 1986.

COMMUNICATIONS

There is virtually no way round it. To get to one of the most isolated island groups in the Atlantic, you have to fly. What's more, if you want to get there without visiting Portugal itself, your best bet is probably a transatlantic flight from Boston, many of which stop off at

Lajes International Airport on the island of Terceira. Be careful, though, as certain tickets aren't valid for stopovers. Otherwise the best way is to fly TAP, Portugal's own national airline, which operates daily between Lisbon and Ponta Delgada on São Miguel.

You'd be well advised to take to the air for inter-island flights, on account of the distances involved. All the islands except Corvo have airstrips and are served by SATA (Servico Acoreano de Transportes Aeros), which runs regular services. Corvo can be reached by helicopter.

Many cruise liners call in at the Azores, but they rarely stay long. Best of all would be to come by yacht, but if you're not quite in that league then you can still come by sea. Try catching the cargo boat between Lisbon and Massachusetts, stopping off on the way.

The Azores are not much visited by tour operators, though by no means inaccessible; you may have to look around or make your choice from a limited number of departure points. Caravela Tours, the Portuguese holiday specialists, visit the islands of Faial, Terceira and São Miguel, the latter also being a centre for Sovereign. Portugala Holidays offer several self-catering apartments, a refreshing alternative to a week or two in a hotel.

CLIMATE

The highly maritime nature of the Azores is a controlling factor in the mild climate. Temperatures average around 58°F (14°C) in winter and a relatively low 75°F (24°C) in summer. The warmth and moisture of this regime are instrumental in creating the profusion of vegetation which characterizes all the islands.

SPECIALITIES

Local specialities are related to the traditional way of life, such as beautifully embroidered scarves and handkerchiefs or the lace which is made on Faial. The maritime history of the entire archipelago is reflected in the models of ships and the tiny whalebone items which can be bought.

Fertile pasture land abounds, and the Azores are justifiably famous for dairy produce, especially cheese. Vinegrowing is important, and a local wine, vino de cheira, is produced.

Santa Maria

Closest to the mother country at a mere 475 miles' distance, Santa Maria was the first of the Azores to be discovered by the Portuguese. Historians differ over the exact date, although it is generally accepted that the first Portuguese seamen under the captaincy of Diogo de Silves arrived somewhere between 1427 and 1432.

In 1427 the volcanic island was uninhabited, but settlement followed discovery and today – though only six miles wide and eleven long – it is densely populated, a network of green fields, vineyards and palm trees, and dotted with windmills. Many of the buildings date from the early part of its history. Despite its origins, Santa Maria is unique in the archipelago in having extensive limestone outcrops which provide local building material. The coastline has many small sandy beaches, such as that at SÃO LAURENÇO, beautifully secluded and without the trappings of the typical resort.

The main settlement on the island is the town of **VILA DO PORTO**, which supports a thriving ceramics business on the basis of the local red clays. It has a 19th-century **parish church** built on the remains of a 15th-century building, and the **Convento do São Francisco** dates from 1607. This was destroyed by pirates nine years later and was eventually rebuilt in the 18th century.

SÃO LAURENÇO, in the north-east of the island, has a beautiful beach and a 16th-century **parish church**, as well as a town hall in what was once a convent. Close by is the tiny village of SANTO ESPÍRITO, traditionally the site at which Mass was first said on the islands after their discovery; the church of **Nossa Senhora da Purificacão** stands on the spot. The village also has a small ethnographic museum.

Further along the north coast is **ANJOS**, another important site in the religious and exploratory history of the Azores. It contains the oldest chapel on the island and it was here, on the way back from the New World, that Columbus stopped to allow his men to fulfil a vow – that upon their safe return to land they would stop and pray at the first church they came to dedicated to the Virgin Mary. In the **chapel** is a triptych which belonged to one of the captains.

On the extreme west of the island is an airport constructed by the Americans in 1944, an indication of the Azores' strategic importance. Now scarcely used (there is an international airport on Terceira), the airport was built only after Britain had called upon neutral Portugal to honour a treaty dating from 1373.

Many of the traditions of the island, especially its folk music, are closely allied to those of the mother country. Its handicrafts, on sale in tiny gift shops, are decorative versions of everyday items such as tools and clothing, enlivened by intricate carving and embroidery. For the holiday-maker, the coastline provides plenty of locations for water sports, especially fishing, diving and water-skiing.

Not being one of the most heavily inundated parts of the Azores in terms of tourism, there is almost certain to be hotel space available in Santa Maria, especially in Vila do Porto (try the **Hotel do Aeroporto**, near the airport). However, the choice may be limited and it's well worth checking prices as well as availability before arriving. There are a couple of good and inexpensive restaurants in Vila do Porto.

São Miguel

São Miguel is the largest of the islands, 290 square miles in area and roughly rectangular in shape. Lying to the north of Santa Maria, it was the second of the nine islands to be discovered by the Portuguese. Known to its early settlers as 'Ilha Verde', or green island, a profusion of vegetation flourishes on the fertile volcanic soils. Its burgeoning, and prosperous, economy draws strength from an influx of tourists who come to see the variety of spectacular landforms resulting from volcanic activity. In addition to the tourists, São Miguel obtains money from agriculture, especially the growing of pineapples and tobacco. There are tea plantations at RIBEIRA GRANDE, on the north coast.

São Miguel is only narrowly second to Santa Maria in the timescale of discovery and settlement began in 1439 on the orders of Afonso V. **PONTA DELGADA** has been the capital of the island since 1546 and is also the seat of regional government in the Azores, sited on the west side of a bay on the south coast of the island. The promenade was constructed in 1860 by the building of a huge breakwater. It is to

Ponta Delgada that TAP operates its flights from Lisbon and scheduled arrivals take place daily. In the town itself, the convent of **Nossa Senhora da Esperança** contains an image given by Pope Paul III in 1530. Among the town's other churches, **São José** is remarkable for its collection of 18th-century tiles, while **São Sebastião** has a display of embroidered vestments.

Along the coast from Ponta Delgada, about twenty miles to the west, lies the town which preceded it as capital, **VILA FRANCA DO CAMPO**, noteworthy for the campanile of São Miguel. From the chapel of **Nossa Senhora da Paz** begins the annual pilgrimage of Os Romeíros. During Lent men go round the island on foot, praying at all the churches containing an altar to the Virgin Mary. An islet off the town, the ILHEÚ DE VILA FRANCA, forms a safe natural swimming pool. The coast road takes in a string of picturesque villages before arriving at the town of RIBEIRA GRANDE, its buildings largely of basalt, and with the 16th-century church of **Nossa Senhora do Estrelo**, which contains a rare Flemish triptych. An observation point gives beautiful views of the coast.

The richly vegetated interior of the island is a place of many volcanic sights. The town of FURNAS in the valley of the same name is a thermal spa; it contains the world's only natural pool of iron-enriched water and several geysers. **Terra Nostra** park in the interior is a botanical garden with exotic plants, swans and a thermal swimming pool. Here it is possible to sample a local form of cooking – *à la caldeira*. Food is wrapped in leaves and buried in the hot ground, where it cooks as if in an oven. Such meals can be arranged through some of the local hotels. Elsewhere in the interior is the **Lagoa do Fogo**, the crater of an extinct volcano with its inside walls covered in dense vegetation, and with the lake itself in the bottom.

Perhaps the most notable feature of the island is the LAGOA DE SETE CIDADES in the west of the island. A place of myth and legend (the name recalls Atlantis), this is in fact two lakes in the hollow of an extinct crater, forming an hourglass shape, the upper one blue and the lower startlingly green. The area is dotted with other lakes and offers beautiful views of the island.

Apart from the notable local cuisine, there are plenty of places to eat on the island, with especially good and inexpensive seafood restaurants at Ponta Delgada. Across the island is a wide selection of accommodation from the luxurious – such as the three-star **Hotel Canadiano** (Tel: 2 74 21) – to the basic, in the shape of several pensions. Apartments are also available.

São Miguel is an island known for its religious festivals, such as **Senhor Santo Cristo**, which takes place on the fifth Sunday after Easter. April–June is the season for the **Festival of the Holy Ghost**, which is especially colourful in the north coast village of RABO DE PEIXE. Appropriately, for an island so liberally stocked with spas, there is also the festival of **Senhor Dos Enfermhos** – Lord of the Sick.

As in the rest of the Azores, regional specialities are based upon utility. Basketry and simple handicrafts, rush mats and embroidered handkerchiefs; even delicate flowers made from fish scales can be bought.

Activities available to the tourist are widespread. Ponta Delgada boasts an eighteen-hole golf course, and there are plenty of chances for water sports, especially swimming, scuba diving and big game fishing.

Terceira

Terceira is the Portuguese word for 'third'. It is a highly appropriate name since the island was not only the third to be discovered, but is also the third largest in the archipelago at ten miles by twelve. Some fifty-four miles north-west of São Miguel, it is the most easterly of the central group.

Sometimes known as 'the lilac isle' on account of its glorious sunsets, Terceira, like most of the rest of the Azores, is very fertile. It has both green pastures and lava zones, the fields often divided by hedges of flowering hydrangeas, and wild flowers grow in profusion in the uncultivated areas. The volcanic interior, scattered with small geysers and lakes, consists of the mountains of the Serra do Cume and the Serra de Santa Barbara, one to the east and the second to the west.

Although discovered by the Portuguese, Terceira was actually settled by a Fleming, Jácome de Bruges. Throughout its history, the island has shared in the Azores' strategic importance and was visited by Vasco da Gama in 1493. Today it is the site of the international airport at LAJES, a fitting stopover point for many flights between the New World and the Old.

The chief town is **ANGRA DO HEROÍSMO** on the south coast. Initially known simply as Angra, it earnt the second part of its name as a result of the bravery shown by its inhabitants in the wars against Spain in the 16th century – although the title was not bestowed upon it until over 200 years later. A minor earthquake in 1980 caused much structural damage, but fortunately there is still much to see. Rising up to the hill slopes, the town is a bishopric and the **cathedral** has a good selection of ecclesiastical art. The town's dominant feature, however, is its castle, the 16th-century fortress of **São João Baptisto**. Built during the reign of Philip II of Spain, it has a beautiful main doorway and once served as a prison for Afonso IV. The town's churches include the **Convento de São Francisco**, home of the local museum, while in the **Misericordia** church Vasco da Gama buried his brother, Paul, who died on the historic visit to India. The **Town Hall**, with its sash windows, is a particularly Azorean piece of architecture.

Other places to visit include BISCOITOS, on the north coast, which has extensive vineyards, while a visit to the interior reveals many volcanic marvels. The village of CABRITA, virtually in the island's centre, is close to the grottoes of **Algar do Corvao**, containing warm water lakes. There is also the largest crater lake in the Azores, the **Caldeira de Guilherme Maniz**, measuring nine miles around its perimeter.

The international airport at LAJES has made Terceira an important island for tourism. The needs of the holiday-maker are well catered for, with plenty of hotel accommodation of varying luxury and price, both in the capital and in the coastal villages. Among them are the **Hotel da Angra**, in the capital, and the **Motel Nove Ilhas**, in Praia da Vitoria. Some have their own restaurants, often specializing in local dishes – naturally enough the emphasis is on seafood. Beaches are generally small, secluded and safe, while sailing boats can be hired and deep sea fishing trips arranged. There are bars, cinemas and night-clubs in Angra and there is a golf course.

Terceira also supports the religious **Festival of the Holy Spirit**. From Whitsun to the end of the summer, each settlement collects offerings which are eventually distributed among the needy in a festival which ends with riotous festivities and bull running in the main towns.

São Jorge

The long thin island of São Jorge lies in the middle of the central group. Its rocky sides rise steeply from the heavily-indented coast to the central ridge, its summit a startling 3,500 feet at **Pico da Esperança**, the Peak of Hope. Like the other islands, São Jorge is festooned with flowers and shrubs, especially the characteristic blue hydrangeas. Yet for all its topographic wildness, it is the agricultural centre of the archipelago. Lower slopes are clothed in vines and extensive pasture land on the plateau is the source of the renowned São Jorge cheese.

First settlement was at the village of TOPO, in the extreme south-east, but the capital is **VELAS**, about forty miles along the south coast. Here, in the picturesque town with its whitewashed buildings, can be found the **church** founded in 1460 under the terms of Henry the Navigator's will. Another church dates from the 17th century. The town is surrounded by cedar woods while the garden at **Quinta do Areeiro** is well worth visiting for its exotic plants and shrubs.

São Jorge is not an island geared to the needs of the tourist, and although it is a tranquil hideaway, it is by no means an easy place in which to holiday. It has no hotels, although Velas boasts a single guest-house and rooms are available in some of the villages. Restaurants are good but few on the ground, again mainly in Velas. The rugged coastline is not so well adapted for water sports as are many of the other islands.

Pico

The name Pico means peak and the island is appropriately named. Although only twenty-nine miles by nine, this obviously most volcanic of the Azores has Portugal's highest mountain, a towering, cloud wreathed 7,755 feet above the sea. Pico can be climbed – a track runs most of the way there – but it is a long trek requiring great care and it is sensible to get a local guide. The view from the top covers the entire group of islands.

The mountain is the obvious manifestation of the island's vulcan-
icity. Volcanic eruptions in the 18th century have left visible traces
and whole villages are built of the dark-coloured lava-based rocks
which abound. In a more subtle way, too, the volcano has affected the
island's economy – the highly fertile soils have made it the major wine
growing centre in the Azores. The former volcano itself is a nature
reserve, festooned with laurels, cedars and flowers.

Pico's history is inextricably linked with that of the seafarer (its
seamen are traditionally respected as the best in Portugal), and
recently it has lost a lot of its importance as the whaling industry has
declined. The island's capital, **LAJES DO PICO**, has a whaling
museum containing items of equipment and whalebone tools; it is
located in the **Casa dos Botes**. It also boasts fine old buildings and the
oldest church on the island, **São Pedro**. On the west coast, the village
of MADELENA is a good overnight stop before tackling the volcano, and
is near a cave, the **Furna do Frei Matias**. Near Lajes do Pico can be
found the **Furnha da Malha**, a natural tunnel a mile and a quarter
long.

The island boasts guest-houses such as the **Pensão Açor** in Lajes
and the **Pensão Residencial Pico** in Madelena, and both of the main
towns have restaurants. Although like São Jorge the coastline is too
rocky for much in the way of water sports, the rugged coastal scenery
provides ample visual compensation.

The whaling industry also provides the focus for a colourful
carnival, the **Festa dos Baleiros**, which takes place on the last Sunday
in August.

Graciosa

Despite being the smallest (eleven miles by four and a half) and most
isolated of the central Azores, as well as the flattest of the whole
archipelago – reaching 1,320 feet at Pico Timae – Graciosa retains a
particular charm. Known as 'Ilha Blanca' (the white island) on
account of the surging foam and the breakers which pound at the
rocky coast, it is patterned with wheat fields and vineyards and is
dotted with small windmills.

The capital is **SANTA CRUZ DA GRACIOSA**, a small town on

the north coast. It has a striking 16th-century **parish church** with three rose windows, and there is also an ethnographical museum focusing on local life, especially viticulture. Elsewhere on the island there are settlements around geothermal springs. At TERMAS DA CARAPACHO, on the south-east corner of the island, the springs are known for their medical properties and a bathhouse has been built.

Of all the attractions of the island, the most remarkable lies in the interior. The **Furnas do Enoxfre** is a caldeira – but the warm, sulphurous lake is 270 metres below ground, reached by a tunnel and a spiral staircase. Between eleven in the morning and two in the afternoon a little sunlight penetrates this peculiar feature, making those three hours the best time to view.

Because of its size, accommodation on Graciosa is limited: there is a guest-house at Santa Cruz, but little else besides. The island produces wine and wheat, and local pottery can be bought.

Faial

Only three miles from Pico lies the island of Faial. Its name means 'beech tree' and it is sometimes known as the 'blue island' – a comment on the hydrangeas which flourish there, both wild and trained into hedges. Although small (it measures nine miles by thirteen), it has gained disproportionate economic importance since it contains the largest port in the Azores, **HORTA**.

Horta is the island's capital, named after its founder. Like many others it was important during the Age of Discovery, but it retained its importance for sea travel and into the early days of flight. It was a naval base during both world wars and now serves as a popular haven for transatlantic yachtsmen, making the town the most relaxed and cosmopolitan settlement in the islands. It has a castle, the 16th-century **Fortress of Santa Cruz**, and two religious houses, **São Salvador** and **São Francisco**, both dating from the 17th century. There is also a museum of sacred art.

Two miles from the town is the **Quinta de São Laurenço**, a garden with a profusion of exotic plants, while the **Flemish Valley** is full of wild camellias. The highest point of the island, the crater lake of **Cabeco Gordo**, is a nature reserve.

The most recent volcanic activity in the Azores occurred at CAPELHINOS, in the north-west, in 1957. A volcanic eruption lasting for a year and a half eventually buried the village – the remains of some houses can still be seen, and there is a volcanic museum. The volcano itself was declared extinct in 1973.

As might be expected of so busy an island, there is plenty of accommodation, such as the four-star **Hotel Faial** (Tel: 2 21 81) in Horta itself. There are also restaurants to provide temptation for the long distance yachtsman, a disco and facilities for tennis and water sports, especially deep sea fishing. Island specialities are lace and embroidery. Carvings in wood and whalebone can also be purchased.

Flores

Flores, the island of flowers, is reputedly the prettiest of the islands. Though small, it has the distinction of being the westernmost point of Europe. It was the last to be discovered, being claimed in 1452 but not permanently colonized until 1528. It has many waterfalls and its seven lakes provide good fishing.

Flores enjoyed a brief moment in the limelight of world history when Sir Walter Raleigh used it as a base for his campaigns against Spain: it was from Flores that Sir Richard Grenville set out to take on a large enemy fleet in the epic battle which cost him his life. Nowadays, fishing is the island's economic mainstay and scenery its greatest resource.

The main settlement, **SANTA CRUZ DOS FLORES**, is no larger than a village, a fishing port with a small museum and several churches, while on the opposite side of the island, **FAJAZINHA** boasts an ornate 18th-century church, **Nossa Senhora dos Remédios**.

Accommodation is limited, although there is a hotel, **Estalagem das Flores**, in LAJES. The coast is ideal for water sports. Local specialities include handicrafts such as wicker and raffia work.

Corvo

Only ten miles square, Corvo has fewer than 400 inhabitants in one village, **VILA NOVA DO CORVO**, a place of red roofs and white walls in a rugged setting. It is supported by fishing and farming, and the main sight is the two volcanic lakes close to **Monte Gordo**. There is no guest accommodation.

Vocabulary

There's no need to try and get to grips with Portuguese just for your two weeks in the Algarve as almost everywhere in the tourist areas you will find English spoken.

English	Portuguese
Yes	Sim
No	Não
Please	Por favor
Thank you	Obrigado
Good morning	Bom dia
Good afternoon	Boa tarde
Good evening	Boa noite
Goodbye	Adeus
Excuse me	Desculpe
Where is/are?	Onde está/estão?
When?	Quando?
What?	O quê?
How?	Como?
Who?	Quem?

Why?	Porquê?
I understand/don't understand	Compreendo/Não compreendo
Do you speak English?	Fala inglês?
Can I have . . . ?	Pode dar-me?
I would like . . .	Queria . . .
. . . a room with a bath/shower a single/double room	. . . um quarto com um quarto de uma cama/banho/com chuveiro
What is the price per night/ week?	Qual é o preço por noite/por semana?
It is . . .	É . . .
It isn't . . .	Não é . . .
Is there/are there . . .?	Há . . . ?
There is/there are . . .	Há . . .
Good/bad	Bom/mau
Cheap/expensive	Barato/caro
Big/small	Grande/pequeno
Where can I get a taxi?	Onde posso encontrar um táxi?
Take me to this address, please	Leve-me a esta morada, por favor
Where's the nearest bank, please?	Onde fica o banco mais próximo, por favor?

Where can I change some travellers' cheques, please?	Pode cambiar-me um cheque de viagem, por favor?
Can you show me where I am on the map?	Pode mostrar-me no mapa onde me encontro?
I'm lost	Estou perdido
Can I have my bill, please?	Pode dar-me a conta, por favor?
Where's the ladies/gents toilet?	Onde é a casa de banho das senhoras/dos cavalheiros?
Can I use your telephone?	Posso telefonar?
Call an ambulance/police	Chame uma ambulância/ polícia
One	Um
Two	Dois
Three	Três
Four	Quatro
Five	Cinco
Six	Seis
Seven	Sete
Eight	Oito
Nine	Nove
Ten	Dez

Sunday	Domingo
Monday	Segunda-feira
Tuesday	Terça-feira
Wednesday	Quarta-feira
Thursday	Quinta-feira
Friday	Sexta-feira
Saturday	Sábado
Today	Hoje
Tomorrow	Amanhã
Yesterday	Ontem

INDEX

INDEX

Vila Nova de Cerveira, 165
Vila Nova de Gaia, 157, 159, 160
Vila Nova de Milfontes, 209, 222
Vila Nova de Ourem, 187
Vila Nova do Corvo (Azores), 348
Vila Praia de Ancora, 39, 164–5
Vila Real, 173–4, 195, 199
    black pottery, 173, 199
    Casa de Diogo Cão, 173, 199
    Fair of St Peter and St Paul, 173, 199
    Igreja São Pedro, 173, 199
    Sé de São Domingo, 173, 199
Vila Real de Santo Antonio, 135, 241,
        245, 248, 249–50
    bullring, 31
    ferry, 24, 244, 250
    fish market, 250
    Praca de Pombal, 249
    sailing, 35
    Spanish frontier crossing at, 244, 250
Vila Flor, 203
Vilamoura, 244, 247, 272–6
    casino, 274
    Cerro da Vila, 273
    family holidays, 41
    fishing, 35, 274
    golf, 33, 34, 36, 274, 275
    horseriding, 35, 36
    marina, 35, 274

    night-life, 31, 136, 248, 273, 274–5
    sporting complex, 36, 274
    Tennis Centre, 34, 36, 274
    windsurfing, 36, 274
Vimioso, 202
vinho verde, 134, 168, 195, 199
Vinte e Cinco Fortes gorge (Madeira),
    332
Viseu, 196–7
    Cathedral, 196
    Fiera de San Mateus, 197
    Paco dos Tres Escalves, 196
Vista Alegre, 177
Vizela spa, 37

water sports, 24, 32, 36, 231, 232, 248,
    251, 259, 274, 302, 347
Western Algarve Riding Centre,
    Burgau, 35
Wet and Wild water-slide park, 36
windsurfing, 24, 32, 36, 75, 274, 302
wine tours, 75, 108
wines:
    Azores, 339
    Madeira, 135, 324, 326, 328, 331
    port, 28, 134–5, 155, 158, 160, 193,
        195
    Portuguese, 24, 134–5, 155, 158, 193,
        195, 196, 199, 200, 230, 239, 247

    youth hostels, 118, 158–9, 189, 226,
        306

Katie Wood and George McDonald

The Round the World Air Guide

The long haul travel market is dramatically expanding and for little more than the price of a return flight to Australia you can now circumnavigate the globe. *The Round the World Air Guide* has been written specifically for the new breed of serious traveller and whether you are on a round the world ticket or using conventional long haul options, it will guide you to the best places and the best prices. It is the only book which covers all you need to know to plan and book your trip *and* acts as a practical guide to the world's fifty major destinations.

Full of essential information on:

* How to cut costs and get the most out of your ticket
* Stop off possibilities and side trips
* Airport facilities around the world
* Where to go and what to see
* Where to sleep and what to eat
* Dining out and nightlife

No frequent traveller can afford to take off without it!

Katie Wood and George McDonald

Europe by Train

Every year cheap European rail travel entices hundreds of thousands of people to sample for themselves the diversity and pleasures of the Continent.

Designed specifically for students and those on a tight budget, this is the only guide which looks at 26 countries from the Eurorailer's viewpoint. It is full of essential, practical information on:

* Train networks and station facilities
* The best routes
* Maximizing the benefits of rail passes
* What to see
* Where to sleep and eat
* Where the nightlife is

No traveller wanting to see Europe inexpensively can afford to leave home without this guide.

Katie Wood and George McDonald

Fontana Holiday Guides

No one can afford to take a chance with their holiday – yet people often do. Whether you want to sightsee or sunbathe, birdwatch all day or dance all night, the Fontana Holiday Guides tell you all you need to know to plan the best possible holiday for *you*: which resort, which tour operator, where to stay, how to travel, what to see and do.

Easy to read, objective, well researched and up to date, they are indispensable guides to getting fun – and value for money – out of your holiday.

Titles available:

Holiday Greece
Holiday Portugal
Holiday Turkey
Holiday Yugoslavia

Fontana Paperbacks:
Non-fiction

Fontana is a leading paperback publisher of non-fiction. Below are some recent titles.

- [ ] The Round the World Air Guide *Katie Wood & George McDonald* £9.95
- [ ] Europe by Train *Katie Wood & George McDonald* £4.95
- [ ] Hitch-Hiker's Guide to Europe *Ken Walsh* £3.95
- [ ] Eating Paris *Carl Gardner & Julie Sheppard* £2.95
- [ ] Staying Vegetarian *Lynne Alexander* £3.95
- [ ] Holiday Turkey *Katie Wood & George McDonald* £3.95
- [ ] Holiday Yugoslavia *Katie Wood & George McDonald* £3.95
- [ ] Holiday Portugal *Katie Wood & George McDonald* £3.95
- [ ] Holiday Greece *Katie Wood & George McDonald* £3.95
- [ ] Holiday Coastal Spain *Katie Wood & George McDonald* £3.95
- [ ] British Country Houses *Katie Wood* £5.95
- [ ] The Life and Death of St Kilda *Tom Steel* £5.95
- [ ] Back to Cape Horn *Rosie Swale* £3.95
- [ ] Fat Man on a Bicycle *Tom Vernon* £2.50

You can buy Fontana paperbacks at your local bookshop or newsagent. Or you can order them from Fontana Paperbacks, Cash Sales Department, Box 29, Douglas, Isle of Man. Please send a cheque, postal or money order (not currency) worth the purchase price plus 22p per book for postage (maximum postage required is £3).

NAME (Block letters) _____

ADDRESS _____

_____

_____